THE FRIENDLY GERMAN-ENG

THE FRIENDLY GERMAN-ENGLISH DICTIONARY

A Guide to German Language, Culture and Society
through *Faux Amis*, Literary Illustration
and Other Diversions

FRED BRIDGHAM

LIBRIS

First published 1996

Copyright © Fred Bridgham, 1996

Libris
10 Burghley Road
London NW5 1UE

A catalogue record for this book is available from the British Library

ISBN (hardback) 1 870352 65 3

   (paperback) 1 870352 67 X

Designed and produced by Kitzinger, London

Printed and bound by Biddles Ltd, Guildford

Contents

Introduction

There are words which look or sound the same in English and German but which may mean, or invariably do mean, something different. Thus, *bekommen* means to get, not to become. To say *ich komme eventuell* is not to promise that you will turn up. It is to say that you might perhaps come. A *Sportwagen* is a child's pushchair as well as a Porsche. *Turnen*, gymnastics, is what you do in a *Turnhalle*, not in a *Gymnasium*, which is a grammar school. Franz Schreker's opera *Der ferne Klang* (1912) might be translated as *The Distant Sound*, or even *The Lost Chord*. But since *Klang* is simply the general word for a sound or tone, *Der ferne Klang* does not suggest the 'clanging' dissonances soon to assault audiences' ears. *Mutation* means more than genetic mutation. It is what happens to the boys disqualified in P. G. Wodehouse's story 'The Purity of the Turf' from competing in the Choir Boys' Open Handicap, 'open to all those whose voices have not broken before the Second Sunday in Epiphany'.

Similarly, a *Krankenhaus* is an ordinary hospital. Cranks are *Spinner*, and the German equivalent of what Tom Lehrer once called the Massachusetts State Home for the Bewildered is an *Irrenanstalt*. Since *Kost* means food, *Reformkost* is what you buy in a *Reformhaus* – a house of correction only in so far as it sells the sort of food which is said to be good for you. For example, it is where you buy the oatmeal you use to make *Schleim*, gruel. *Reformkost* does not, therefore, mean currency reform, which is *Währungsreform*.

Another word for *Reformkost* is *Reformwaren*. Since *Waren* means wares or goods, a *Warenhaus* is a department store. In it you will find a *Reklamationen* counter. This is not where you reclaim any children you may have lost, or even collect goods you have paid for. It is where you make complaints, a rare but very occasionally a necessary activity even in the country of the *Wirtschaftswunder* (all forms of efficiency). What English calls a warehouse is a *Lager*. This is not a lager beer, which is *Pils*. It is where you keep things, and *Lagerung* is the process of cold conditioning during fermentation. It is where the English word 'lager' comes from.

Should you happen to have lost any children, as the parents of Hamelin town near Brunswick did, one obvious place to go to is the *Rathaus*. This is not where the rats spirited away by the Pied Piper had their abode. It is merely the town hall. The mayor of Hameln –

note the metathesis – should have paid up. Alternatively, he should have stuck to *Rattengift* (rat poison). He would have damaged the rats, just as the 'false friend' *Gift* produced a certain anxiety in the minds of the first recipients of what the Americans labelled 'Gift from the USA' when they sent food parcels after 1945.

Over a thousand further examples – from *Abort* (lavatory, latrine) to *Zylinder* (top-hat) – are collected in this book. Such faulty connections can be confusing (*irritierend* – itself a further example), or even embarrassing, a term rendered in German by *peinlich*. This no longer means painful in a literal sense, which is *schmerzhaft*. Likewise, a *Lustspiel* is not a sex game. It is the ordinary word for a comedy, an underdeveloped genre in German literature. When Kleist's *Der zerbrochene Krug* was produced under the title of *The Cracked Pot* at the West Yorkshire Playhouse in 1995, a programme note warned the audience that it was the only comedy in German literature, and added that, even then, it was a *Lustspiel* which was not normally very funny. The warning proved unnecessary, since the production turned out to be hilarious (*sehr lustig*). Just as *Lust* can mean anything from pleasure to enthusiasm, and has little to do with sex, so *Klaps* does not mean the clap or gonorrhoea. This is, in popular speech, *Tripper*, and medically *Gonorrhöe*.

But although there are many words which look the same in German and English yet have different meanings, neither English nor German has a generic term for them. One result of this was that Philip Thody and Howard Evans, with great reluctance on the part of the former, were obliged to use a French word in the title of their *Faux Amis and Key Words* (Athlone, 1985). They did, nevertheless, remove some ambiguities by pointing out that Frenchmen wear a *veste* over their *chemise* and, like the Germans, call a dinner-jacket a *smoking*. Even Italian has its *falsi amici*, and Spanish the Carmen Miranda-sounding *falsos amigos*. Thus English visitors to Rome soon learn to appreciate girls wearing a *succincto* – a mini-skirt, known to Germans as a *Minirock*. Likewise, it is misleading to tell a Spaniard that you are *constipado* (have a cold) when you have what the Germans call *Verstopfung* or constipation.

At the same time, there is no necessary link between the fact that the term *falsche Freunde* is not widely used in German and the relaxed attitude of Germans towards the presence in their language of English or American words. Unlike the Académie Française, they do not tilt at windmills by attempting to ban the German equivalent of what René Etiemble called *le franglais*. They are too sensible (*vernünftig*, not *sensibel*, which means sensitive), and quite happy to have their newspapers refer to the Chancellor as a *Bürger-King*, confident

that he does combine the better elements of kingship and the bourgeoisie, and in no way offended by the evocation of the successful
rival of McDonalds.

The aim of this book is nevertheless not merely a linguistic one. It
is also to bring out the difference between our two cultures, a contrast
embodied in the fact that *Kultur* is not merely culture, as the entry in
Section II shows. It is a word which summons up a much richer set of
associations than the narrower implications of culture, which is why
this book might be called *ein kleines Kulturlexikon* – or, indeed, quite
simply, a *Führer* or guide. Similarly, while 'folk' in England merely
suggests the people who live in the village or on the hill, *Volk* in
Germany is more redolent of a consciousness of racial identity evoked
by the slogan *Ein Volk, ein Reich, ein Führer*. There are, it is true,
occasions when an English word has a strong emotional content.
'This land is ours' is a claim based on a centuries-old right to possession. Yet the associations for Germans are wider and deeper. They
do indeed use the word to describe their own country as *das Land
ohne Revolution* and the country of Arthur Sullivan as *das Land ohne
Musik*, rather as Wales sees itself in contrast to its neighbours as 'the
land of song'. But a *Land* is a constituent state of the Federal
Republic, and furthermore is a region for which its inhabitants may
well feel more affection than for their *Vaterland*.

Just as the French are surprised by the English use of 'la crème de la
crème' to describe what they call *le gratin*, so the Germans give a
different set of associations to *ein Platz in der Sonne*. It no longer
evokes the nineteenth-century scramble for African colonies, but a
pleasant place to spend one's holiday in the sunlit south. Likewise,
Lebensraum calls to mind a deserted golf course or trout stream in
County Mayo. It is not what you obtain by invading Czechoslovakia.
Only the uninstructed may confuse the adjective *gemütlich* with what
the Germans themselves refer to as *das Gartenzwerghafte* or 'garden
gnome idyll'.They are wrong to do so. *Gemütlich* is a hurrah, not a
boo word. It is, after all, no mean achievement for a country whose
citizens enjoy *Wohlstand*, a high level of opulence, also to offer a
warm welcome to the traveller.

The Germans do not mind foreigners speaking their language
badly. In this, as in other ways, they differ from the French. But
they are even more appreciative of people who add an element of
competence to the basic politeness of speaking the language of the
country in which you happen to find yourself. One of my other aims
in this book is to increase the number of English speakers who raise a
deliberate rather than an involuntary smile from the native speakers
of German with whom they are talking on business or for pleasure.

INTRODUCTION

I have turned most often to *Die Zeit, Die Süddeutsche Zeitung* and *Der Spiegel* for topical illustration of the linguistic points under discussion, collecting examples from a year or two before reunification up to the present. 'Reunification' is a problematical word since it may suggest that some previous geographical or political entity has been reconstituted, which is not the case. I nevertheless use it to distinguish the coming together of the Federal Republic and the German Democratic Republic in 1990 from the German unification which most people associate with Bismarck and the founding of the Second Reich in 1871. The momentous events of what the Germans now call *die Wende,* or turning point, are reflected in the current state of the language, too. Following the opening up of the two parts of Germany to each other's lexical idiosyncracies, *Ossis* and *Wessis* continue to find unexpected opportunities for misunderstanding, and the interesting possibility of three-way confusion was suggested when a German friend and fluent English speaker drew my attention to a recent report on long overdue moves to change Germany's restrictive opening hours. 'The collapse of Europe's borders finally jerked the country's ossified service industry out of its complacency', it read, and my friend instinctively read this as a comment on how the *Ossis* had imported their notorious inefficiencies into the West. 'Ossification' will eventually have its place in the first German guide to English 'false friends'.

Acknowledgments

Since I have not attempted to give a comprehensive account of all the words discussed, readers in search of further meanings and nuances are referred to a good dictionary. Among bilingual dictionaries, Collins single-volume *German-English, English-German Dictionary* stands supreme, its examples splendidly idiomatic and invariably apt. Otherwise, the three volumes (A–R) of Trevor Jones's unfinished Oxford-Harrap *Standard German-English Dictionary* deserve honourable mention. For the Germans' own definitions of the words in their language, I have used Wahrig's *Deutsches Wörterbuch*, which is as comprehensive as most people will need. The six-volume Duden, *Das große Wörterbuch der deutschen Sprache*, is best used in conjunction with Duden's indispensable one-volume glossaries of foreign words, of etymologies, of stylistic points, and much else. But one has to go back to *Grimms Deutsches Wörterbuch* to find anything comparable in scale and achievement to the *Oxford English Dictionary*, and to *Meyers* redoubtable *Konversationslexikon* to keep one's conversation suitably encyclopedic.

As with the many illustrations of linguistic usage gratefully culled from *Die Zeit*, *Die Süddeutsche Zeitung* and *Der Spiegel*, I have given the sources of quotations from books directly as they occur, rather than in a bibliography.

I owe much to my students for their often unwitting demonstration that all is not as it seems in the treacherous crossings from one language to another;

more specifically, to the advice and expertise of Johanna Angus, Helen Chambers, Ingo Cornils, Nana and Niels Christiansen, Dagmar Döldissen, Heather al Gawad, Gisela Hargreaves, Bob Jackson, Douglas Jefferson, Günther Kloss†, Ken Knight, Iris Lamparter, Graham Loud, Adelheid Petruschke, Michael and Rendell Pietsch, Hugh Rorrison, Hjördis Roubiczek, Frank and Marie-Lyse Ruhemann, Maria Seissl, Billy and Helga Stewart, and Iain Boyd Whyte;

to David Rayvern Allen and James D. Coldham for information on the impact of cricket in Germany (see GULLY in Section VII);

to Michael Beddow for facilitating access to recondite computer aids, and to Andrew Rothwell and Richard Byrn for showing good-humoured patience with their word-processing pupil's recalcitrant Luddite leanings;

ACKNOWLEDGEMENTS

and to my editor and publisher, for his constant and enthusiastic encouragement.

It is an especial pleasure to acknowledge my indebtedness to four friends who read various drafts of the book with infinite patience, and who saved me from innumerable errors and fatuities. They are Raymond Hargreaves, Peter Hasler, Hermann Real and Philip Thody.

Yet I owe most to Ileana, my wife, to whom I dedicate this book.

How to use this book

Browsers – and users – will find themselves in one of ten Sections, each devoted to different aspects of German life and culture. Roman numerals at the top of the page indicate the Section for reference purposes (see below). The index (pp. 311ff) lists all Head-words and shows in which Section each is to be found.

The following conventional abbreviations have been adopted:

abbr. –	abbreviation
acr. –	acronym
adj. –	adjective
adv. –	adverb
conj. –	conjunction
interj. –	interjection
n.f. –	noun, feminine
n.m. –	noun, masculine
n.n. –	noun, neuter
n.p. –	noun, plural
pref. –	prefix
prep. –	preposition
pron. –	pronoun
v. –	verb
in cpds –	in compounds
US –	American English

With few exceptions the Head-words are German *faux amis* – words which look familiar to the English reader but whose meaning is significantly different. The exceptions are certain key words or expressions, either in English (e.g. *car insurance, fir tree, made in Germany, senior*) or in German (e.g. *Beamte, Berufsverbot, Dienst*), which serve to introduce important distinctions between our two cultures; and in addition, quite a few German compounds made up of recognizable components (e.g. *Feierabend, Frauenzimmer, fremdgehen, heimsuchen, Lungenbraten, Masskleidung, Mittelstand, Sitzfleisch*) where the meaning is nevertheless more (or at times less) than the sum of the parts.

With the exception of the occasional dual-entry (*Mass, Messe, Rat, Restauration*), or even triple-entry (*englisch, Referat*), words have been allocated to the Section in which they seem most at home –

Antibabypille to Section VI on Sex and the Family, for instance. Examples illustrating the use of a word have been chosen, all things else being equal, with an eye to the topics covered in that Section. This is especially the case when a word does not automatically suggest a specific context (an adjective such as *still*, say, or *seriös*). At all times the reader is directed towards other entries for points of related interest.

Cross-referencing works in two ways: either by explicit mention of another Head-word and the Section in which it is to be found (e.g. see FRAKTION in II); or simply by an asterisk (*) which means that the word asterisked is, or contains, a separate Head-word, in which case it will be necessary to consult the index to find in which Section it appears.

Since German words are often the building-blocks for compounds, the component parts of an asterisked word may be themselves Head-words (thus, *Not** and *Stand** as well as *Notstand** are listed in the Index). Or a word such as *Lastkraftwagen**, while not itself a Head-word, breaks down into three Head-words, *Last**, *Kraft** and *Wagen**. Or a word such as *Realkanzlei** has its own entry, but the asterisk alerts the reader to a separate entry under *Kanzlei** as well as other combinations with *Real-**listed in the index (*realisieren**, *Realitäten**, *Realpolitik**, *Realschule**). In the case of *Bergbau**, the Head-words are *Berg-** and *Bauer**.

Since English 'c' often becomes German 'k', a cross-reference to, say, *correct** will be found under *korrekt* (see also *konsequent*/consequently, *Kolleg*/college), but otherwise spelling is sufficiently similar to allow easy identification.

The German 'ß' has been used instead of 'ss' when the Germans themselves would use it, i.e. at all times except when 'ss' is used to denote the voiceless 's' sound between vowels if the preceding one is short, all diphthongs counting as long vowels. Exceptions are compound words and a few proper names: Richard Strauss (but Johann Strauß and Franz Josef Strauß); Theodor Heuss; Günter Grass. Nor is 'ß' used in upper case, so it will not be found, for example, in the Head-words in the text.

German nouns and their articles, when cited individually or in a phrase within the English text, rather than in a German clause or sentence, are always given in the nominative case – 'the difference between *Beamte* and *Angestellte*', or 'Hegel favoured *der vernünftige Beamtenstaat*' – where a native German speaker would expect an extra '*n*' in *Beamten* and *Angestellten*, signifying the dative plural, or *den vernünftigen Beamtenstaat*, to show that it is the object of the sentence. This practice has been adopted to help the reader identify the simple plural, or the proper gender, which might otherwise be obscured.

Translations, when not otherwise identified, are my own and aim to illustrate accurately, rather than elegantly, the meaning and usage of the word under discussion.

ADVOKAT n.m. a dated term for a lawyer (nowadays *ein Rechts-anwalt*, whether it refers to a solicitor or a barrister – the German legal system is discussed under STAATSANWALT below). Sometimes used pejoratively: *ein Winkeladvokat* is an incompetent, or unqualified, lawyer; one who works in a seedy part of town and is perhaps involved in shady dealings. Used figuratively: an advocate of liberty, for instance, is more likely to be called *ein Fürsprecher* or *Verfechter der Freiheit*.

AMIS n.p. not an allusion to French *amis*, but an abbreviation of *Amerikaner*. A survey carried out by the opinion pollsters of the Allensbach Institute in 1980 found that over half the population of the Federal Republic thought of the Americans as Germany's best friends (according to the US Census Bureau in 1990, one American in four – the largest ethnic group – is of German ancestry). Seventeen per cent said the French, only two per cent mentioned the British. In the post-war years, *die Amis* – the GIs stationed in central and southern Germany – also integrated more comfortably with the local population than the British *Tommies* in the north. After the Vietnam War and the 1968 student movement, however, and especially in the Reagan era, relations inevitably became soured by the growth of antinuclear feeling among young West Germans and the withering of Cold War attitudes.

Except for *der Iwan* (Russians) and *die Polacken* (Poles), there were no common wartime equivalents of Huns, Jerries, *boches*, frogs, wogs, Eyeties, etc. (but for the abusive language of the Nazi period, see Sternberger *et al* under UNMENSCH in II). Nowadays, foreigners, especially Turkish 'guest workers' (*türkische* Gastarbeiter*), are sometimes called *Kanaken* (originally South Sea islanders; also boorish, uneducated people), *Alis*, or even *Messerstecher* ('knifers'). Austrians may refer to the Italians as *die Welschen**, *Spaghettifresser, Makkaronis*, or (since early Italian immigrants were often pot-makers) *Katzelmacher* – as in Fassbinder's film of that name – and to German tourists who throw their weight around as *Piefkes* (Krauts*; in Berlin, however, *Piefkes* are ragamuffins). They may even taunt their Bavarian neighbours by calling them, of all people, *Saupreußen* ('Prussian swine' – see SCHWEIN in VIII), whereas to Bismarck, a true Prussian, the Bavarians were a cross between the sloppy Austrians and human beings.

APPELL n.m. a rhetorical appeal: *der Appell des Jungen Deutschland lautete 'Deutschland erwache!'* (the call of the Young Germany movement was 'Germany awake'). But when the Nazis adopted this particular slogan a century later to raise national consciousness once again, they appealed to people's baser instincts (*an die niederen Instinkte appellieren*) by adding *'Juda verrecke!'* ('Death to Jews').The person who lodges a legal appeal is known as *der Appellant,* but to appeal in this sense is more commonly *in die Berufung gehen, Revision* beantragen* or *einlegen.* Soldiers, *die zum Appell antreten,* fall in or line up for roll call. Similarly, hunters who say *der Hund hat Appell* mean the dog is obedient. But what draws you towards someone or something is *die Anziehungskraft,* now sometimes anglicized (especially *der Sex-Appeal*). Thus, T. J. Reed's punning description of the heroine's dilemma in Schiller's *Kabale und Liebe* (1784): 'Louisa dare not appeal to the Prince lest she appeal to him too much' (*Schiller,* 1991, p. 31) would not work in German: *Luise traut sich nicht, an den Prinzen zu appellieren, falls sie ihm zu sehr gefällt* (see FALL in II).

ARREST n.m. detention as well as arrest (though a policeman is more likely to say *Sie sind verhaftet!* than *Sie sind unter Arrest!*) To be under house arrest, *unter Hausarrest stehen.* A soldier confined to barracks for three days *muß drei Tage Arrest absitzen.* Similarly, *der Schüler bekam eine Stunde Arrest* means the schoolboy was kept in for an hour, given an hour's detention (nowadays more commonly: *bekam eine Strafstunde* or *mußte eine Stunde nachsitzen*).

Persönlicher Arrest is a somewhat dated term for the arrest of a debtor, while *dinglicher Arrest* is what English law calls distress or distraint (the seizure of a debtor's goods). Where a Scottish judge might still order the 'arrest' of a bank account or even a salary, Germans normally call this course of action *Sperrung* in the case of a bank account (*das Guthaben*) or *Pfändung* in the case of earnings (*die Lohnpfändung*). See also EXEKUTIEREN below.

ASSESSOR n.m. not someone who assesses taxes or the value of property, but a graduate civil servant who has completed his training period, while not yet appointed to a permanent position. Since all teachers are civil servants, a young untenured graduate teacher was until recently called *ein Studienassessor* (see below, REFERENDAR, and for the working of the Civil Service, BEAMTE).

The official who assesses what you owe the Revenue, however, is known as *ein Finanzbeamter* or *Steuerbeamter*,* while the function of *ein Steuerberater* is not to berate, but to advise you how to query the official calculations (see RAT below). *Ein Schätzer* is generally employed by an insurance company to assess the value of your house and its contents (see also EXPERTISE below), and *ein Schadensgutachter* to assess claims. A university assessor or examiner is *ein Prüfer*.

BARACKE n.f. not an army barracks, *eine Kaserne*, but as in French *baraque*, a hut or shack. *Eine Barackensiedlung* or *ein Barackenlager* is a transit camp made up of such huts, such as those erected after 1989 (as after 1945) *für Flüchtlinge und Aussiedler* (for refugees and emigrants, in practice mainly those from Eastern Europe); or else to house workers on short-term contracts, such as the *Gastarbeiter* on construction sites in Switzerland, who, unlike 'guest workers' in Germany (but like those once employed in the GDR), have no right of abode. The SPD headquarters in Bonn, dwarfed by the neighbouring tower-block of the CDU, is also familiarly known as *die Baracke*.

BEAMTE n.m. (from *das Amt*, office, post) someone who holds a tenured position *im Öffentlichen Dienst**, 'in public service' – a much broader category than the British Civil Service, for it includes teachers, doctors, lawyers, postmen, railway officials, as well as those in senior positions *in der Verwaltung*, in administration proper (*ein mittlerer Beamte* will have taken the *Abitur*, A-levels, as an entry requirement for the administrative grade). The distinction between *Beamte* (public employees in tenured, white-collar jobs) and *Angestellte* (salaried workers in the public and private sectors) is keenly felt.

The German *Beamtentradition* is still associated with Frederick the Great's eighteenth-century Prussia, and with the far-reaching administrative reforms subsequently carried out in the wake of the Napoleonic wars by, among others, Stein, Hardenberg, Scharnhorst and Humboldt. Indeed, it was as an antidote to such 'world-historical' individuals as Napoleon that Hegel favoured *der vernünftige Beamtenstaat unter dem Dach der Monarchie* (state run by civil servants according to the principle of reason and under the umbrella of the monarchy). But state control expanded under Frederick William IV of Prussia after Germany's first attempt at liberal democracy collapsed in 1849, while identification with the interests of the state (the term used is *staatstragend*) allowed *das Beamtentum* (bureaucracy) to remain in position, substantially unchanged, in Bismarck's authoritarian Second Reich*, and even in Hitler's totalitarian Third Reich, though it did not help to consolidate the democratic process in the intervening Weimar Republic. Nor did the process of *Entnazifizierung* (denazification) totally break the continuity of this tradition; most controversially, the judiciary suffered few consequences in the Federal Republic for having scrupulously implemented Hitler's laws.

Beamte today are appointed for life (*Ernennung auf Lebenszeit*) and are not required to contribute to their pension scheme (*Altersversorgung ohne Eigenbeitrag*); unlike unionized *Angestellte*, however, they do not have the right to strike, being still perceived as upholders of *Ruhe und Ordnung* (law and order), and expected to exercise *Mäßigung und Zurückhaltung* (moderation and restraint) in their political activities. On the other hand, unlike their colleagues in Britain and the United States, *Beamte* may stand for parliament at *Bund**, *Land** and *Kommune** level (see *passives Wahlrecht* under PASSIV in II). In fact, more than half the members of some *Landtage* (state parliaments) are *Beamte*, more often than not lawyers or teachers on secondment, and critics say this *Verbeamtung* (literally, 'conversion to civil servant status') of Germany's parliaments is disproportionate.

In a recent survey by the Allensbach Institute, *Beamte* were shown to have suffered a loss of prestige: they are associated most frequently with *Unkündbarkeit* (job tenure), *soziale Sicherheit* ('social security' in its literal sense) and a *Pension** (a generous pension; workers and *Angestellte* on retirement draw *eine Rente**), but also with *Trägheit* (indolence), *Faulheit** (sloth) and *Bequemlichkeit* (idleness).

There are drawbacks as well as advantages for aspiring *Beamte*. Conformity and loyalty, traditionally associated with the *Berufsbeamtentum* (the Civil Service in its narrower, British sense), are now expected of all public employees. In a key judgment of the *Bundesverfassungsgericht* (Constitutional* Court), reported in *Die Zeit* on 2 September 1988, one applicant for *eine beamtete Stelle* was rejected merely for having an attitude which suggested he lacked loyalty to the constitution* (*wegen Fehlens einer subjektiven Voraussetzung, nämlich der Verfassungstreue*). See BERUFSVERBOT and VERFASSUNGSPATRIOTISMUS in II.

BESIEGEN v. not to besiege (*belagern*) but to defeat. In July 1942, *die Deutschen belagerten Stalingrad*, the Germans besieged Stalingrad; by February 1943, however, Russian artillery and the Russian winter defeated the Germans, *besiegten die Deutschen*. The German Sixth Army under General Paulus, outflanked and besieged, was forbidden by Hitler to attempt a break-out, *aus der Belagerung auszubrechen*, but the propaganda benefit of what Hitler envisaged as a drama of deliverance of 300,000 men by General von Manstein's Eleventh Army was not forthcoming, and Paulus defied and enraged him by surrendering. See also BLITZ in II.

BLIND adj. blind, sightless, but curiously *blind schießen* means either to fire blanks (*blinde Patronen**; live ammunition is *scharf**), or else – and one trusts the Germans can tell the difference – to fire blindly or at random. When a shell fails to explode, it is called *ein Blindgänger*; so, too, is someone who fails to live up to expectation: a dud or a dead loss. Note also: *ein blinder Passagier*, stowaway; *der Blinddarm*, the 'blind intestine' or appendix; *der Blindband*, the dummy book a salesman shows a bookseller .

BOMBARDEMENT n.n. as in French, shelling but also bombing.

BOMBE n.f. an explosive device but also a great success – an ambiguity which Karl Kraus uses to good satirical effect at the end of Act I, Scene I of *Die letzten Tage der Menschheit* (1922) by juxtaposing Viennese reaction to the latest Viktor Leon operetta (*Bombenbesetzung*, all-star cast; *Bombenerfolg!* smash hit!) and news of the bombardment* of Belgrade (*Belgraad bombadiert!*). No connection, then, with 'to bomb' in the American sense of to fail (*durchfallen*, *scheitern*). *Eine Sex-Bombe* is a real cracker; so, too, were the *Bomben* regularly scored by the footballer Gerd Müller, known as *der Bomber der Nation*. Likewise, *er hat damit ein Bombengeschäft gemacht* means he did a roaring trade (not necessarily in explosives), while something that is *bombensicher* is either literally bombproof or figuratively as safe as the Bank of England (or else 'a dead cert'; also *es steht bombenfest**).

Eine Eisbombe is an elaborate ice-cream dessert or *bombe glacée*.

BRIEF n.m. a letter, not a lawyer's or civil servant's brief, which is *ein Auftrag*. If you want stamps, *Briefmarken*, go to the counter marked *Postwertzeichen* in any branch of the *Post*. In Austria, they are also available, along with newspapers and cigarettes, in your local *Tabaktrafik**.

Eine Brieftasche is a wallet; a briefcase, *eine Aktentasche* or *eine Aktenmappe**. Brief, in the sense of short, is *kurz* (*Kurze Begegnung*, *Brief Encounter*). For briefs/underpants, see SLIP in IX.

BUND n.m. (derived from *das Bund*, a bundle or bunch of things; hence *der* or *das Schlüsselbund*, key-ring or bunch of keys) a bond between like-minded people (see KOMMERS in IV). *Der Dritte im Bunde*, when two such friends are joined by a third, was originally the tyrant converted by the power of friendship in Schiller's heroic ballad *Die Bürgschaft* ('The Pledge' – see also FREIER in VI); now more often used ironically of the 'third man' in a conspiracy.

Or else a political alliance, such as that which brought together all 22 *Bundesfürsten* at the Congress of Vienna in 1814/15 and issued in the loose confederation of 39 sovereign German states (and power vacuum in central Europe for the next fifty years) known as *der Deutsche Bund*; or *der Dreibund*, the Triple Alliance formed between Germany, Austria-Hungary and Italy in 1882. Since 1949, *der Bund* refers to the Federal Government in Bonn, but exclusively in the sense of the central powers and responsibilities of Bonn as distinct from those of the *Länder** and the *Kommunen** (powers which are restricted in accordance with the principle of *Subsidiarismus* – see KOMPETENZ below – so that the word *Föderalismus*/federalism stands not, as in the United Kingdom, for centralization under Brussels, but for decentralization).

Also an abbreviation of *die Bundeswehr*, the army, as in *ich bin beim Bund*. National service is compulsory for males in the *Bundesrepublik*, though with community service (see ZIVILDIENST below) as an alternative to the army.

BUSSGELD n.m. not the fare (*das Fahrgeld*) which you pay the driver on entering a bus, but a fine or fixed penalty, especially for a traffic offence. When courts have discretion to decide what financial penalty to impose, this is done in multiples of one's *Tagessatz* or net daily earnings – a system of 'equal pain' for all rather than equal penalties, which, unlike the earnings-related 'unit fines' briefly tried out in Britain in 1993, works well in Germany. A common threat is *das sollst du mir büßen!* (you'll pay for that) – no connection with the southern German and Austrian *Bussi* or *Busserl*, a kiss.

However, most compounds of *Buße* retain the religious sense of atonement, rather than of mere deterrence. *Buß- und Bettag*, for instance, is a day for repentance and prayer (this public holiday is Lutheran in origin; predominantly Roman Catholic *Länder** also celebrate *Christi Himmelfahrt*, Ascension Day, ten days before Pentecost, and *Fronleichnam*, Corpus Christi, ten days after Pentecost, in both cases on a Thursday). But it was to make himself politically, rather than spiritually, acceptable that the Emperor Heinrich IV undertook *der Gang nach Kanossa* (see GANG in II), the most celebrated *Bußgang* (journey of penance) in German history and one which Henry II of England may have recalled a century later when he had himself flogged on the steps of Canterbury Cathedral in expiation for his role in the murder of Archbishop Thomas Becket.

CHARGE n.f. a literary term meaning 'rank', as in *die unteren Chargen der Parteihierarchie*, the lower ranks of the party hierarchy, or *die höheren Chargen*, the senior officers (in the army – though it is not technically a military term as such). But: 'You're on a charge, Private Müller': *Das gibt eine Disziplinarstrafe**, *Gefreiter Müller*.

Colloquially, to put a soldier on a charge is *einen Soldaten verknacken* – see under NICKEN, and for 'those in charge', under KOMMANDO below.

'Charge!': *zur Attacke!*; 'to sound the charge', *zum Angriff blasen*. In *Prinz Friedrich von Homburg* (1810), the orders are not to sound the call to charge until so instructed – *dann wird er die Fanfare blasen lassen* – but the amorous hero of Kleist's great play becomes so distracted during the *Paroleszene** (briefing scene) by the first evidence of reciprocated love that he can only imagine fanfares to this more intimate conquest.

In the theatre, *ein Charge* is a minor character part (see also STATIST in X), generally one so distinctive that the verb *chargieren* can also mean to ham or overact. In its other main context, *die Chargierten* are the office holders in student fraternities (*Verbindungen*), and here *chargieren* means to process in ceremonial dress (see KOMMENT in IV). A legal charge is *eine Anklage*; a financial charge, *eine Gebühr*.

CONSTITUTION normally translated as *die Verfassung*, but the constitution of the Federal Republic which came into effect on 23 May 1949 was called *das Grundgesetz*, or Basic Law, in order to symbolize the provisional nature of the division of Germany. (Partly for the same reason the very uncosmopolitan town of Bonn, soon to be disparagingly known as *das Bundesdorf**/*'Bonndesdorf'* or 'federal village', was chosen as capital.) *Das Bundesverfassungsgericht*, or Constitutional Court, the country's highest *Instanz**, has been called upon increasingly since reunification to pass judgement on sensitive issues (such as the law on abortion, *Paragraph** *218* – see ABORT in VI) thought by many to belong more properly to the government's *Kompetenzbereich**. But like the American Constitution, *das Grundgesetz* has also been an effective and popular Bill of Rights, while those who now proclaim a new form of nationalism reject 'mere' *Verfassungspatriotismus** (loyalty to the constitution, that is, to democratic values). See also SENAT below and BERUFSVERBOT in II.

Germans who speak of their *Konstitution* generally mean their physical condition.

DALLI adv. (originally Polish) not an injunction to dally (*herumtrödeln, bummeln*), but to hurry up, look smart, get a move on: *dalli, dalli!* Alternatively, *rühr dich mal!* come on, move; get going. The military command for 'at ease!' in Germany is *rührt Euch!* ('move') but the same *Kommando** in Austria reflects a subtly different expectation: *ruht!* ('rest'). In both cases, 'fall in!' is *antreten!* and 'attention!' *stillgestanden!*.

DEGRADIEREN v. to downgrade (a ticket) or demote (a soldier). *Der Wehrbeauftragte* (military ombudsman) and the civilian courts ensure that German soldiers are not 'degraded in the presence of the regiment*' either in the sense of being demoted (*degradiert*) or humiliated (*erniedrigt*) in public. The German language has on the whole been sharply attuned, and resistant, to American euphemisms such as 'degrade' ('with extreme prejudice'), favoured by General Al Haig and used in the sense of 'kill' or 'destroy'.

Note that *deklassieren* means to downgrade in a sociological sense (*herabsetzen*), but also to outclass (*weit übertreffen*), usually in a military, political or sporting context.

DELIKT n.n. no connection with delight or delectable, but an indictable offence (as in the English legal term 'delict' – cf. *in flagranti delicto*). These are graded according to the penalties prescribed in the *Strafgesetzbuch* (Criminal Code):

1. *Die Übertretung*, a minor infringement or misdemeanour, punishable by a short spell in custody (*in Haft*, but see also KITTCHEN below) or else by a fine (*eine Geldstrafe*).

2. *Das Vergehen*, a more serious offence which may involve a prison sentence (*Gefängnis* or *Freiheitsstrafe*) of up to five years.

3. *Das Verbrechen*, a serious crime such as murder (*Mord*) or manslaughter (*Totschlag*). There is no death penalty (*Todesstrafe*) in Germany or Austria (see EXEKUTIEREN below).

For *ein Kavaliersdelikt*, a mere peccadillo, see KAVALIER in VI.

DIENEN v. as in the motto of the Prince of Wales (*Ich dien* – properly, *Ich diene* – I serve). Frederick the Great also liked to think of himself as *der erste Diener seines Staates*, and encouraged his soldiers to serve with equal dedication (asking them on 18 June 1757 at the battle of Kolin: *Ihr Racker, wollt ihr ewig leben?* – 'You dogs, do you want to live forever?'). In a more libertarian tradition, the Marquis Posa memorably declaims in Act III, Scene 10 of *Don Carlos* (1787): *Ich kann nicht Fürstendiener sein* ('I cannot be the servant of princes'), thereby inspiring the French revolutionaries to make Schiller an honorary citizen. In pre-*Bundeswehr* days, *Haben Sie gedient?* would have elicited the same sort of response as 'What regiment were you in?' though the days when it was smart to have been a *Husar* (hussar) or an *Ulan* (uhlan, Prussian lancer) have long gone – see REGIMENT and RESERVE below.

Dienen is a key word for understanding traditional German militarism. Carl Zuckmayer's play *Der Hauptmann von Köpenick* (1930) makes fun of the German reverence for uniforms. An impecunious impostor discovers that the question *Haben Sie gedient?* opens all doors and enables him to take over the Köpenick *Rathaus**. The *Bürgermeister*, a mere *Leutnant der Reserve**, unhesitatingly obeys the 'captain's' orders: *Befehl ist Befehl* (orders are orders); *Kleider machen Leute* (clothes make the man – especially a uniform). *Eine Köpenickiade* still means a hoax involving impersonation.

The actual incident on which the play is based took place in 1906, when one Wilhelm Voigt made fun of Prussian *Kadavergehorsam* ('corpse-like' or blind obedience). Zuckmayer's play shows how little effort Hitler needed to exploit the habits of obedience characteristic of the Kaiser's Germany.

In today's *Bundeswehr*, the former supremacy of military values, associated with the idea of *dienen*, has been replaced by General Wolf Graf von Baudissin's concept of the *Staatsbürger in Uniform* (citizen in uniform) and the principle of *Innere Führung*. This latter – an ambiguous term – was interpreted, somewhat ambitiously, by a former Defence Minister, Gerhard Stoltenberg, in the *Süddeutsche Zeitung* on 2 July 1989 as *mitdenkender Gehorsam aus Einsicht*, 'obedience as a consequence of individual insight and understanding'. It suggests both self-discipline and democratic responsibility, moral leadership and civic education, and is clearly a deliberate reversal of Hitler's *Führerprinzip**. Since reunification, it is also the basis of *Konversion* – the process of integrating some, mainly lower, echelons of what was East Germany's *Nationale Volksarmee* into the *Bundeswehr*.

It was interesting to read the *Bundeswehrinspekteur** argue in *Die Zeit* on 5 October 1990 that despite the surplus of available soldiers, conscription should continue: *weil nur die Wehrpflicht die Streitkräfte im Volk verankert* (because only conscription anchors the armed forces in the people). *Wehrdienst* for those who are fit for military service – *für tauglich beim Militärdienst erklärt* – now lasts for nine months; in Austria, it is also called *Präsenzdienst* and is undertaken by those who have been '*assentiert*' (if not quite in the way suggested by the German-Czech journalist Egon Erwin Kisch: *Jedes assentierte Schwein** *bekommt** *gleich seine Legitimationskapsel** – *eine Blechnummer**, *die ins Ohrläppchen geklemmt wird* (Each poor sod, once he has been declared fit for service, gets a metal identification tag clipped on his earlobe – *Der rasende Reporter*, 1930, p. 181). Soldiers no longer goose-step (*im Stechschritt marschieren*) or click their heels (*zackig die Hacken zusammenschlagen*), and it is unfashionable to salute smartly; conscripts are posted as near as possible to their homes, often commuting at weekends or even daily ('*Heimschläfer*'*).

See also KOMMISS and BUND in this section and DIENST in III, and for community service as an alternative to military service, ZIVIL-DIENST below.

DOTIEREN v. either to remunerate, especially for services to the state, or to endow (from the French *doter*, though not in its usual sense of providing a dowry – see under GIFT in VIII), but not to dote on someone, which is *jemanden vergöttern* or *abgöttisch lieben.* Germany's most prestigious literary prize, *der Büchner-Preis*, is worth DM60,000, *ist mit DM60 000 dotiert* (for the difference in punctuation, see KOMMA in VII). The job of parliamentarian at *Land* level is much too remunerative, according to the *Süddeutsche Zeitung* on 3 September 1988: one would be hard pressed to find any other *Beruf, der sich selbst für so wenig Arbeit so hoch dotiert*, which pays itself so much for so little work. See also DIÄTEN in II.

EVIDENZBÜRO n.n. not an office which collects legal evidence (*das Beweismaterial, die Beweise*, or if circumstantial, *die Indizien*), but the Austrian term for a registry. In Germany this is *eine Registratur*, such as one finds in a government department or university, but the registry office in which you can get married is *ein Standesamt** in both countries. Austrian officials, *die eine Namensliste in Evidenz halten*, are not 'holding a list of names as evidence', but merely keeping it up to date – an extension of the occasional German use of *Evidenz* in such phrases as *die Evidenz einer Wahrheit*, meaning (like *évidence* in French) that something is self-evidently true.

EXEKUTIEREN v. both to put to death (the usual word is *hinrichten*), and to carry out a judgement, but note the specifically Austrian meaning: to impound or to confiscate. Hence, *er wurde wegen seiner Steuerschulden exekutiert* is not as drastic as it sounds, but means that the bailiffs, *die Exekutoren* (German: *Gerichtsvollzieher*), have seized his assets because of his tax debts (see also under ARREST above). Similarly, *die Exekutive* in Austrian usage refers to the forces of law and order, as well as to the executive in government.

EXPERTISE n.f. not expertise, which is *der Sachverstand* or *die Sachkenntnis*, but as in French, an expert's report or valuation for purposes of sale or insurance.

FINANZER n.m. not a financier (*ein Finanzier*), but a colloquial Austrian word for a customs official (normally, *ein Zollbeamter*).

FLINTE n.f. a flint-lock, nowadays a shotgun (*eine Schrotflinte*). A tobacconist will be surprised if you ask for a *Flinte*. What you need for your *Feuerzeug*, cigarette lighter, is *ein Feuerstein*. Consequently, *die Flinte ins Korn werfen* does not mean 'to set fire to a corn field', but to throw your gun away. As the innocent soldier-hero of Grimmelshausen's picaresque novel *Simplicius Simplicissimus* (1669) eventually discovers, this was often a wise policy in Germany during the Thirty Years' War, when *die Flinte* first appeared. Figuratively, it means to throw in the towel or give up the challenge. During an outspoken lecture in June 1990, Jurek Becker described how many fellow East German novelists withheld work from publication rather than submit to censorship and risk giving the impression: *jetzt hat er die Flinte ins Korn geworfen.*

FORCIEREN v. as in forcing the tempo: to step up, rather than to do under compulsion. *Der forcierte Gebrauch von Schußwaffen* is not the forced use of weapons (*im Notfall**, *unter Zwang*), but simply their increased deployment. *Forciert* can also mean mannered, over-deliberate.

FORMULAR n.n. a form to fill in, *ein Formular ausfüllen*, in triplicate, *dreifach*, quadruplicate, *vierfach*, etc. *Der Fragebogen* is now a more general, non-bureaucratic word, though it is also the title of Ernst von Salomon's gripping account of life under Weimar and the Nazis, published in 1951 and translated as *The Questionnaire*. A scientific formula is *eine Formel*, as is the formula which solves a political or diplomatic dispute; hence *formelhaft reden*, to talk in a set form of words or in stereotyped phrases. See also FORM in VIII.

FUNKTIONÄR n.m. formerly the East German equivalent of *Beamte** (civil servant), in which context it has now (like 'state functionary') incurred all the negative connotations of the regime itself. Otherwise a functionary in a political party, trade union, or sports club, though generally better rendered as 'official' (*die ehrenamtlichen Funktionäre*, for instance, are the honorary officials of a club).

GALERIE n.f. as in English gallery (an art gallery, *eine Kunstgalerie*, is run by a *Galerist*). But also a shopping arcade (especially the upper floor); and in the Alps, a tunnel open on the valley side. In Austria, it is in addition a jargon word for the criminal underworld, inhabited by *Galeristen* (see MILIEU below).

GÜLTIG adj. not guilty (though both words once meant paying for an offence, or in order to avoid one), but valid. On public transport, you generally have to validate (that is to say, somewhat paradoxically, cancel: *entwerten/ungültig machen*) your ticket yourself (and invariably so if you have a *Tageskarte*, a day ticket for all transport) by putting it in the franking machine (*der Entwerter*) inside trams and buses or on the platform of the *U-Bahn* or *S-Bahn*: *Karte erst nach Stempeln gültig*, ticket only valid when stamped. If you forget to do this and are caught, you are automatically *schuldig* (guilty), and liable to *eine sofortige Geldstrafe*, an on-the-spot fine. *Es gibt keine gültige*

Entschuldigung, there is no valid excuse. It was recently announced that the number of *Schwarzfahrer* (those caught *ohne gültigen Fahrschein* – see SCHWARZ below) on the *Bundesbahn* was around one million annually, with checks on between two and three per cent of the *1,1 Milliarde* (1.1 thousand million*) travellers.

Gültig is also the sense of *gelt?* or *gell?* (an abbreviation of *es gelte*, let it be valid). This is used in southern Germany and Austria instead of *nicht wahr?*, inviting consent to a question. Thus, in Fritz von Herzmanovsky-Orlando's whimsical (*skurril**) Austrian novel, *Gaulschreck* (1928, p. 45), one *Rat**Grosskopf proposes to a famous houseguest that they use the familiar 'du' form: '*Sag ma ananda Du! Gelt? Schani!' Das war Goethen doch zu viel* (roughly '"Let's call each other by our first names, O.K. Johnnie?" This was too much for Goethe').

HEARING n.n. a loan word, though not applied to a legal hearing, which is *eine Verhandlung* or *ein Termin** (to condemn someone without a hearing, *jemanden ohne Anhörung verurteilen*), but to a session of an open parliamentary or party-political enquiry. The other word here is *die Enquete*: a parliamentary commission of enquiry or select committee is *eine Enquetekommission*.

Applicants for a chair at a German university also have to undergo a *Hearing*, a question and answer session after their *Probevorlesung*, test lecture. When singers or actors audition, however, this is conveyed simply by adding *vor-* to the verb: *vorsingen, vorspielen*.

In the legal context, a preliminary hearing to decide if there is a case to be answered is carried out by the *Staatsanwalt**, and is called *eine Voruntersuchung*; it may involve *Zeugenvernehmung*, the hearing of witnesses.

INDIGNITÄT n.f. not indignity, but the situation of somebody who has forfeited his rights to inherit through one of various criminal acts against the testator. Whereas French law insists that property be divided equally among all legitimate and illegitimate children, German law allows people more or less the same kind of freedom as English law to dispose of their property after death. You can go so far as to disinherit your children if you feel morally indignant, *moralisch entrüstet*, because they are leading a dissolute life, *einen ehrlosen oder unsittlichen Lebenswandel wider den Willen des Erblassers* (thus *Paragraph** 2333* of the *Bürgerliches Gesetzbuch*).

A propos '*Erblasser*': even Germans can sometimes get mixed up over their compound words and confuse *ein* Erb*lasser* (somebody leaving property in a will) with someone who turns pale: er*blassen*. (Another example: *die Reinigung der* Stau*becken*, cleaning the reservoirs; *die Reinigung der* Staub*ecken*, cleaning dusty corners.)

INSPEKTEUR n.m. whereas *der Inspektor* is a rank in the *Beamtenlaufbahn** and has much the same range as the English word 'inspector' (but for 'detective inspector', see KOMMISSAR below), *der Inspekteur* is head of one of the three services (*Inspekteur des Heeres, Inspekteur der Marine, Inspekteur der Luftwaffe*), while *der Generalinspekteur der Bundeswehr* is the equivalent of Chief of the Defence Staff.

INSTANZ n.f. a legal term, meaning the appropriate court to deal with a case, rather than an 'instance' in the everyday sense of occurrence or example (*der Fall** or *das Beispiel*). *Eine Verhandlung in erster Instanz* is thus a hearing in the lowest court: it does not mean 'in the first instance', implying that worse is to follow.

In Germany, the *Instanzenweg* (the various stages of appeal or *Revision**) goes from *Amtsgericht* (corresponding to our local magistrates' court or county court) to *Landgericht* (higher district court) to the *Oberlandesgericht* of the *Land** (its high court and court of appeal). The *oberste* or *letzte Instanz* above this, with ultimate authority in civil and criminal cases, is the *Bundesgerichtshof** (Federal Supreme Court) in Karlsruhe (though Bavaria also has its own *Oberste Landesgericht* with final jurisdiction in certain areas). Various *Verwaltungsgerichte* deal with disputes between individuals and administrative bodies: the *oberste Instanz* in tax matters, for instance, is the *Bundesfinanzhof* in Munich, and in matters of social security, pensions and compensation for war victims, the *Bundessozialgericht* in Kassel. Finally, *das Bundesverfassungsgericht* in Karlsruhe is the *letzte Instanz*, with the widest remit, for all matters which impinge on the constitution* (see also SENAT below).

Instanz is also an administrative term, as foreigners soon discover: *man geht von einer Instanz zur nächsten*, one goes from one office or department to the next; or when a civil servant approaches his immediate superior, *er wendet sich an die nächsthöhere Instanz*. In Germany, things tend to be done *auf dem Instanzenweg*, through the proper official channels. For authority of a moral kind, see INSTANZ in V.

INTELLIGENZ n.f. not secret intelligence (*Informationen* or *geheime Nachrichten*) as collected by the *Bundesnachrichtendienst* (Federal Intelligence Service) in Munich; nor military intelligence/reconnaissance, which is known as *Aufklärung* (albeit not the open, universalist, anti-authoritarian 'Enlightenment' defined by Kant in his 1784 essay, *Was ist Aufklärung?*, though the word does cover many other kinds of elucidation or clarification, from political instruction to sex education).

Die Intelligenz is the intelligentsia (also *die Intelligenzija*) as well as the faculty which qualifies for membership. In spite of official parity of esteem in the GDR between *Kopfarbeiter und Handarbeiter* (cf. 'workers by hand and by brain' in the old version of the Labour Party's Clause 4; *Arbeiter der Stirn und der Faust* in Nazi terminology), members of certain professions, including actors, were entitled to a higher rate of pension* known as an *Intelligenzrente*. See also INTELLEKTUELLER in V.

JUSTIZ n.f. the administration of justice, that is to say the judiciary or the courts, not the abstract principle (*die Gerechtigkeit*). A miscarriage of justice is *ein Fehlurteil* (but in the case of capital punishment *Justizmord*, judicial murder). To bring to justice, *vor Gericht bringen.*

KAMMER n.f. 'chamber', as in *die Erste/Zweite Kammer*, the Upper/Lower Chamber of parliament, or *die Handelskammer*, Chamber of Commerce, or a professional association such as *die Ärztekammer*, the German Medical Council, or *die Anwaltskammer*, comparable to the Law Society or Bar Association. A lawyer's chambers, however, are known as *ein Anwaltsbüro* or *eine Kanzlei*.

The courtly association of *Kammer* – originally, like *Kabinett*, a prince's private chamber – remains in the honorifics bestowed in Austria on outstanding singers and actors: *Kammersänger* and *Kammerschauspieler*. But a *Kammerjäger* today hunts only vermin – he is a pest controller or exterminator (more formally known as *ein Raumentweser* or *Desinfektor*). In the domestic context, *die Kammer* is a box room or store room, *die Rumpelkammer* a junk room, and *die Schlafkammer* a common dialect word for a (small) bedroom, especially the attic variety (*Dachkammer*) depicted, for instance, in Carl Spitzweg's popular painting *Der arme Poet*. Soldiers also go to the *Kammer* (short for *Bekleidungskammer*) to be kitted out, and speak of the quartermaster familiarly as *der Kammerbulle*.

KANZLEI n.f., **KANZEL** n.f. the Federal Chancellery in Bonn is known as *das Bundeskanzleramt*, but a chancellery is more commonly *eine Kanzlei* (Hitler's *Reichskanzlei*, for instance) and the administration of each *Land* in the Federal Republic is housed in its own *Staatskanzlei*. (This term, meaning 'national chancellery', is also applied to foreign governments.) But the primary meaning of *Kanzlei* nowadays is a lawyer's chambers. In Kafka's novel *Das Schloß* (1920–24, published posthumously 1935), the labyrinthine bureaucracy of the Castle which the hero K. fails to penetrate owes much to the administrative *Kanzleien* of Austria-Hungary.

Kanzleisprache or *Kanzleistil* is thus officialese, gobbledygook, and official or bureaucratic instructions still often seem to have been written in *Beamtendeutsch** descended from the language of the chancery, *Kanzleisprache*, of Luther's day – an idiom far removed from the wonderfully fresh and vigorous vernacular he himself called *reines und klares Deutsch*, and into which he translated the Bible between 1517 and 1534. Similarly, when Schiller, in a letter to Goethe on 22 September 1797, criticized Kant's *Canzleystil*, he meant that his writings, though seldom imprecise, were often obscure – an example unfortunately followed by many subsequent German philosophers. By contrast, Kafka's German, like that of Schiller and Goethe, is of exemplary lucidity.

In Kafka's earlier novel, *Der Prozeß**, a further source of intimidating authority is *die Kanzel* (pulpit), as when, in the Cathedral scene, *Josef K. wurde scharf abgekanzelt*, Josef K. was sharply reprimanded. *Der Kanzelmißbrauch*, however, is 'the misuse of the pulpit' for political ends. Though this may animate life in rural Ireland and elsewhere in Europe, in Germany it has featured only sporadically in relations between Church and State since the time of Luther. One such instance was when the *Kanzelparagraph**, directed against political statements from the pulpit, was adopted by the *Reichstag* in November 1871 as the first piece of anti-clerical legislation in Bismarck's *Kulturkampf**.

KANZLER n.m. not the Chancellor of the Exchequer – Germany has *a Finanzminister* instead – but the head of government. Bismarck was the first *Reichskanzler* (1871–1890), Adenauer the first *Bundeskanzler* (1949–1963). *Ein Kanzlerkandidat* – usually referred to simply as *der Kandidat* – is not necessarily the leader of his or her party, but someone chosen, as in the US system, to lead it in an election campaign, the Contender. Here, *der Kanzlerbonus* can act in his (not yet her) favour – this fashionable term does not mean a financial bonus, but rather the respect traditionally paid in Germany to those in authority, and hence to the incumbent in office. A strong chancellor like Adenauer, who exploited the full powers of the *Kanzlerdemokratie*, enjoyed this respect more than some of his successors. Under Adenauer, the newly-founded CDU was said to be essentially *ein Kanzlerwahlverein*, an association for getting the Chancellor elected (an echo of the *Kurverein** *zu Rense* which elected the late medieval *Kaiser*). However, the *Süddeutsche Zeitung* was soon to be proved wrong when it observed on 2 September 1989: *einen Kanzlerbonus hat Kohl auch in der eigenen Truppe** *nicht* (Kohl does not even enjoy the prestige of office within his own ranks).

The *Kanzler* of a German university is not its chancellor (there is no such honorary, titular head, nor is there a ceremonial Degree Day apart from the *feierliche Promotion** to award PhDs), but its registrar or chief administrator. The vice-chancellor is called either *der Rektor** or *der Präsident.*

KASINO also **CASINO** n.n. a casino; an officers' mess; or the cafeteria in an office block.

KITTCHEN n.n. not kitchen (*die Küche*), but common slang for prison. *Er landete im Kittchen,* he landed in the clink; *er sitzt im Kittchen* (or simply *er sitzt*), he's doing time – which in 1995 applied to one in 980 of the population of England and Wales, but only one in 2,162 of the population of Germany. See also DELIKT above and NICKEN below.

KOMMANDO n.n. not an individual soldier specially trained for dangerous operations (*ein Angehöriger eines Kommandotrupps*), but either **1.** a military order, command. Hence, *ich führe hier das Kommando* simply means 'I'm in charge'; and when the commanding officer is out of action and one of the lower ranks assumes control: *Alles hört auf mein Kommando!* Military news broadcasts during the war always began: *Hier spricht das Oberkommando der Wehrmacht* – the *Oberkommando* or *Kommandozentrale* is supreme command/headquarters. Consequently, *Kommandohöhen* are the – usually raised – command posts on the battlefield from which the general and his staff would issue their orders; by extension, the *Kommandohöhen der Wirtschaft* which dominated the national economy in the GDR were heavy industry, agriculture, and the banks (the 'command economy': what the government said, they did). The verb *kommandieren* also means to be in charge of something, rather than to commandeer it (*requirieren**), while *abkommandieren* means to order soldiers to carry out a special task (or to second them to a different unit).

or **2.** the unit which performs such a task, for instance, a *Wachkommando* (or *Wachmannschaft**, the men on guard). More recently, the word has also come to signify a terrorist group, as in the phrase *ein Kommando der RAF** (*Rote Armee Fraktion**), as well as one of the small, *ad hoc* units of police or army combatting it, but equally any *Sonderkommando* ('special unit') delegated with a physical task. For those old enough to remember, *ein Sonderkommando* may still evoke those prisoners in Nazi concentration camps who were given extra rations in return for removing bodies from the gas ovens (see PROMINENZ in II). Those blessed with *die Gnade der späten Geburt* (Helmut Kohl's instantly memorable phrase meaning 'the blessing of being born late' – too late, that is, to feel responsible for Hitler), and certainly those born since the war, are more likely to think of a

Sonderkommando as, say, a gang of workers clearing the streets after heavy snow (see also KOLONNE above).

KOMMISS n.m. not to be confused with *Kommis*, once used of a shop assistant, clerk, accountant, buyer, or travelling salesman/commercial traveller/sales representative (French *commis-voyageur*, German *Handlungsreisender*; now, somewhat euphemistically, *Außendienstler*).

Kommiß, however, like *Bund**, is a familiar though older word for the army, as in: *ich bin beim Kommiß*. But the erstwhile *Kommißgeist* (life of drill and obedience) and clipped, insolent, peremptory *Kommißton** of the *Reserveleutnant** (*Weitermachen!* carry on!, *Schnauze!* silence!), once much admired and imitated as denoting authority, has disappeared from today's *Bundeswehr*, to be replaced by a new concept: *innere Führung* (see DIENEN above). Few will hanker after the dark, heavy, usually hard, wholemeal bread, known as *Kommißbrot*, on which Hitler's *Wehrmacht* was fed.

KOMMISSAR n.m. besides a government commissioner, such as the recently created post of *Staatskommissar für Aussiedlerfragen* (responsible for ethnic Germans wanting to return from their host country to Germany), and a commissar in the erstwhile Soviet Union, also a police superintendent (in Austria, *Kommissär*). In Herbert Reinecker's popular TV series from the 1960s and 70s, such as *Der Kommissar* and *Der Alte*, the *Kriminalkommissar* plays the role which we associate with a chief inspector – he is in charge of the *Mordkommission*, murder investigation/homicide squad – while the *Kriminalinspektor* is generally his assistant (Reinecker's more recent *Kriminalinspektor Derrick* is an exception). But the commissioner or chief of police is *der Polizeipräsident*, and headquarters *das Präsidium*. Note that in Germany *das Kommissariat* is the office or department of the superintendent*, while in Austria it simply means police station. A German police station is *ein Polizeirevier* or *eine Polizeiwache*.

The adjective *kommissarisch* means temporary, so that *der kommissarische Leiter einer Dienststelle* is merely someone covering for the man in charge of a station/office.

KOMMUNAL adj. not communal in the broader sense of shared with others, which is *gemeinsam* (see GEMEINSINN and GEMEINSCHAFT in II), but specifically pertaining to *die Kommune* (also known as *die Gemeinde*), the smallest unit of local government in Germany. Thus, *die Kommunalobligation* is not a communal obligation, but rather local government borrowing – a source of much friction *zwischen Bonn und den Kommunen*. A quite different sort of *Kommune* is a small community of people living together and sharing resources, though this is more commonly called *eine Wohngemeinschaft*, abbreviated by initiates to *unsere WG*.

KOMPETENZ n.f., **KOMPETENT** adj. either **1.** professional expertise, rather than the more general ability to do a job (*die Fähigkeit*), though it is a fine distinction, not altogether observed in the definition of the Peter Principle given in the *Süddeutsche Zeitung*'s obituary of its inventor on 18 January 1990: *alle Unfähigkeit habe die Tendenz, sich gegen die Kompetenz durchzusetzen* (all incompetence has a tendency to prevail over competence – see also FLASCHE in VI). or **2.** the legal right to exercise authority. A bureaucrat reluctant to exceed his powers will say *das übersteigt meine Kompetenz* or *da bin ich nicht kompetent*. *Kompetenzstreitigkeiten* are thus disputes as to who has the right to do what, and are common at all levels of administration, though not in industry, where *Mitbestimmung* (co-determination) ensures that demarcation disputes are virtually unknown (see MONTAN and TARIF in III). The splendid *Kompetenz-kompetenz* is the right of the federal state (*Bund**) to limit the rights of its constituent *Länder** through changes in the constitution*. On the other hand, the decentralizing effect of *Subsidiarismus* ensures that decisions are taken at the lowest appropriate level – the individual *Länder* enjoy *Kulturhoheit**, for instance, 'cultural autonomy' or independence in matters of education and culture. This German principle, in part derived from Roman Catholic social doctrine (*Subsidiarität* was the word coined in 1931 to render Pius XI's notion that high authority should take a subsidiary role in social matters), looks set to exert increasing influence on decision-making processes in the European Community as well, leaving to Brussels only those decisions individual states cannot decide for themselves.

While an English speaker might question whether the competent authorities are truly competent, the German term does not lend itself to this mode* of irony or ambiguity – witness the novelist Siegfried Lenz's remark, cited by the *Süddeutsche Zeitung* on 10 October 1988: *wo es um die Sache des Friedens geht, gibt es keine Inkompetenz* (in the pursuit of peace nobody is unqualified or without responsibility).

KONVENTIONALSTRAFE n.f. not conventional punishment (*die übliche Strafe*), but specifically the financial penalty for breach of contract.

KONVOLUT n.n. a bundle of papers, documents, brochures; or a letter file (*eine Sammelmappe**). Convoluted syntax is *gewunden*, a convoluted plot *verwickelt* or *verschlungen*.

KONZIPIENT n.m. in Austria, an articled clerk (German, *ein*

Jurist zur Ausbildung). In Germany, a dated word (from *konzipieren*) for someone who drafts a speech or project (*ein Konzept**). See also REFERENDAR below.

KRIMINALER n.m. not a criminal (*ein Krimineller, ein Verbrecher*), but the person whose job is to catch him (an abbreviation of *Kriminalbeamter** – see KOMMISSAR above). In Austria, *das Zuchthaus* (prison with hard labour – now, as in Germany, abolished) was once familiarly known as *das Kriminal.* A detective story, murder mystery, crime thriller, etc. is *ein Krimi.*

LAND n.n. Germans use the word for the countryside; for their country; but also for the *Länder* (federal states) which make up Germany. So *Land* – as in *Landesbank* – often signifies 'regional' as distinct from 'national'. On a more emotional level, however, its focus is not always that of the present *Länder*, since several of these were somewhat arbitrarily constituted when the Allies declared Prussia officially dead in 1947 and sought (successfully) to create a new federal balance. Swabians fondly refer to their newly-created and prosperous state of Baden-Württemberg as *ein Musterland* ('model state') and pronounce it *Muschterländle*, giving it a distinctly Swabian flavour. Identity is often understandably even more localized, as, say, in North-Rhine Westphalia, when at *Karneval** the phlegmatic Westphalians sing: *O Münsterland, o Münsterland, ist wieder außer Rand und Band**. The function of a *Landsmannschaft* is specifically to keep alive political, as well as emotional, memories of former German territories forfeited in 1945; best known is *die Sudetendeutsche Landsmannschaft*, the Association of Sudeten Germans displaced from their *Heimat**, which is now incorporated in the Czech Republic (people living on the northern slopes of the Sudeten mountains never referred to themselves as *Sudetendeutsche*, but as *Schlesier*, Silesians).

Each of the eleven western and five re-constituted eastern *Länder* has its own *Landtag* (state parliament; only Bavaria's is bicameral) and *Landesregierung* (state government), though in the city states (*Stadtstaaten* as distinct from the *Flächenstaaten*) the ruling body is called *der Senat**, presided over by the *Erster Bürgermeister* of Hamburg (parliament: *die Bürgerschaft*), the *Oberbürgermeister* of Bremen (parliament: *die Bürgerschaft*) and the *Regierender Bürgermeister* of Berlin (parliament: *das Abgeordnetenhaus*). The *Länder* have powers comparable to those of US states (policing and education were already enshrined as affairs of the federal states in 1871), and a *Ministerpräsident* ('*MP*') on whom the honorific *Landesvater* is sometimes bestowed, respectfully by political supporters, ironically by others, since the term itself harks back to the age of feudalism. *August der Starke* (Augustus the Strong, 1670–1733), Elector of Saxony and King of Poland, with 354 acknowledged bastards to his credit (if that is the word; see BANK in III), was clearly bent on being a *Landesvater* (and that is the word) in the fullest sense. As yet, *Landesmutter* has referred only to the 'first lady', though Austrians still think affectionately of Maria Theresa, who ruled Austria from 1740 to 1780, as their *Landesmutter*. When Gerhard Schröder (like Oskar Lafontaine and Björn Engholm, one of Willy Brandt's young protégés in the SPD) took over from Ernst Albrecht as Prime Minister of Lower Saxony, he made it clear that the new generation of '*Enkel*' (grandchildren) rejected any such paternalism: *Ihr Verständnis ist eher eines von Landesvater und Landesmutter. Unser Verständnis ist eher eines von einem aufgeklärten Manager und einer dazu passenden Frau* (You see yourselves as 'father and mother of the people'. We see ourselves as enlightened managers with wives to match – *Die Zeit*, 18 May 1990).

Students in Tübingen still jokingly distinguish between *Landeskinder* – those of their number who are 'home-grown' – and what they call *Reigschmeckte* – those who have been drawn there (*herein*) in order to taste (*schmecken*) the local wines. And when, in Schiller's *Kabale und Liebe* (1784), the Duke's freedom-loving English mistress, Lady Milford, is told: *gestern sind siebentausend Landskinder nach Amerika fort* ('yesterday 7,000 of our countrymen left for America'), the reference is to the practice of Schiller's despotic *Landesherr* (ruler), Duke Karl Eugen of Württemberg, of selling his subjects as mercenaries.

LEGITIMIEREN v. in Germany, you are asked more often than in Britain to prove you are who you say you are. *Können Sie sich legitimieren?* (more simply, *Ihr Ausweis, bitte!* – see also PASS below) is thus simply a request for your identification papers. *Die Legitimation* can mean the identification papers themselves (*Ich habe keine Legitimation bei mir*), as well as the authority or justification for doing something.

LEVITEN n.p. *jemandem die Leviten lesen* means to haul someone over the coals, to read someone the riot act – from the Law (*Leviticus*) which Moses commanded to be read out by 'the priests the sons of Levi' (*Deuteronomy*, 31:9).

MAGISTRAT n.m. not a magistrate (*ein Friedensrichter* or *Schiedsmann*), but the municipal authorities of Berlin, Frankfurt, and some other cities (elsewhere the elected *Stadtrat**, which controls the administrative *Stadtverwaltung*). In Switzerland, however, *ein Magistrat* is not a town council but a Federal Councillor.

MARINE n.f. the navy – short for *die Bundesmarine* which replaced *die Kriegsmarine*, or else *die Handelsmarine*, merchant navy – but not used in compounds such as marine life (*Meeresfauna und -flora*) or marine insurance (*Seeversicherung*).

MILIEU n.n. can mean, as in French, the criminal underworld or the red-light district (*das Amüsierviertel, die Strichgegend*). Or else simply environment, background (*aus welchem Milieu stammt er?*); or local colour, atmosphere – notably the tenements (*Mietshäuser*) and ragamuffins (*Bengels*) that the Berlin cartoonist Heinrich Zille depicted before the First World War as '*mein Miljöh*'.

MÖRDER n.m. not murder (*der Mord* or *die Ermordung*), but the murderer.

NATIONALISIEREN v. to naturalize (*einbürgern**) as well as to nationalize (*verstaatlichen*).

NICKEN v. to nod in agreement, or to nod off (*einnicken; er macht ein Nickerchen*, he's taking forty winks*), not to nick one's chin while shaving (*sich leicht am Kinn schneiden*) or to 'nick' someone else's property (*klauen*).

In equivalent German slang, a thief who is 'nicked' (*geschnappt*) may end up *verknackt, im Knast, im Kittchen** ('in the nick'); *ein Knacki* is any jailbird, not just one incarcerated as a safe-breaker (*Safeknacker*) or for breaking into cars (*Autos knacken*). See also KNACK- in VIII.

A propos nodding: Field Marshal Keitel, one of the *Führer*'s yesmen, was known as *Knick-Keitel*, a nick-name (*Spitzname*) derived from the phrase *einen Knicks machen*, to bob or curtsy.

NOTORISCH adj. often better rendered as chronic, constant, or simply well-known, than as notorious. Though *ein notorischer Lügner* is indeed 'a notorious liar', *ein notorischer Verbrecher* is an habitual criminal, one who is known to the court (*gerichtsnotorisch*) and consequently has a bad reputation (*berüchtigt*), rather than one who commits notorious crimes (*infame Verbrechen*).

NOVELLE n.f. besides the literary genre (see NOVELLE in X), an amendment or supplement to an existing law, or a new bill modifying it. Germans complain of German *Novellierungssucht* these days (the obsession with changing things), but *die Novellierung eines Gesetzes* (passing an amendment to a law) is far removed from the wholesale *Nivellierung der Gesetze* ('levelling' of the laws, forcing them into line with German law – the better known term is *Gleichschaltung*) which took place when Hitler annexed Austria.

OFFIZIÖS adj. not officious in the sense of excessively dutiful (*diensteifrig, dienstbeflissen*), or interfering (*sich ständig einmischend*), or pompous (*wichtigtuerisch*), but semi-official. The non-attributable briefings given to the parliamentary lobby in Westminster are thus *offiziös*, whereas statements made by the government *Sprecher* (spokesman) in Bonn are *offiziell*. Note also *ein Offizialdelikt** – an offence for which proceedings are brought by the *Staatsanwalt** directly and *ex officio*.

ORGAN n.n. either **1.** an organ of the body: often used of the voice, especially a penetrating one, *ein durchdringendes Organ*, or one used to good rhetorical effect, as for example by the defence counsel in one famous fictional trial: *Buck machte sein Organ milde und warm . . . [Buck] machte sein Organ männlich und stark** (Heinrich Mann, *Der Untertan*, 1911, p. 225).

or else **2.** an organ of the state. *Neues Deutschland* was the main journalistic *Organ* in the GDR, though when East Germans talked of *die Organe*, they meant the police and the security service (*der Staatssicherheitsdienst*, universally known as *die Stasi*).

The musical instrument is *die Orgel*.

PARADE n.f. either **1.** a military parade (hence *ein Paradebeispiel*, perfect/prime example; *das Paradestück seiner Sammlung*, the showpiece of his collection);

or **2.** a parry in fencing. *Der Hieb ist die beste Parade* means that attack – *Hiebfechten* is sabre fencing – is the best defence. This is the argument used by *der Spekulant* (speculator, i.e. war profiteer) in Act I, Scene 25 of Karl Kraus's *Die letzten Tage der Menschheit* (1922) to explain why the Germans had to bombard* Rheims Cathedral in 1915;

or **3.** a save in football: *hervorragende/glänzende Paraden*, brilliant saves. See also ROBINSONADE in X.

Paradieren means to parade, also in the figurative sense: *er paradiert gerne mit seinem Wissen*, he likes showing off/flaunting his knowledge; if someone cuts him (off) short, *man fährt ihm in die Parade*.

PARAGRAPH n.m. specifically a section or paragraph in a legal document (otherwise *der Absatz* or *der Abschnitt*, though the *Grundgesetz* – see CONSTITUTION above – is divided into *Artikel*). People identify certain controversial issues by the relevant section in the *Strafgesetzbuch* (Criminal Code). Accordingly, *er hat sich auf Paragraph 51 berufen* means that he pleaded insanity; *ein Hundertfünfundsiebziger* (*ein 175er*) – the paragraph is now abolished – was common parlance for a homosexual; and an ironic adaptation of Mozart's lullaby (K.350) reflects the severity with which *Paragraph 218*, which deals with abortion, was once applied during the Nazi era (and is still applied by judges in Catholic Bavaria): *Schlafe, mein Prinzchen, schlaf, dich schützt der Paragraph* ('Sleep, little prince, sleep, the law protects you'). Germans nowadays think of their country as *ein Rechtsstaat** (a state under the rule of law), which helps explain the *Paragraphendschungel* ('paragraph jungle', proliferation of red tape) and *Paragraphenreiter* ('paragraph riders', pedants, sticklers for the rules – mainly officials). See also STRAFEN below.

PASS n.m. specifically a passport. *Ein Passierschein* is a military pass, *eine Freikarte** a free pass or complimentary ticket, and *ein Ausweis* the general word for a pass, covering identification papers, permit, membership card, or library ticket.

PATRONE n.f. a cartridge (for a gun, film cassette, fountain-pen), or an explosive charge. See also MINE in IV and PATRON in VIII.

PIONIER n.m. besides a pioneer, a sapper or engineer in the army, also until 1990 a member of the politicized East German equivalent of, say, the Boys' Brigade (*Junge Pioniere*).

PRAGMATISIERUNG n.f. what looks like another euphemism for redundancy, such as *die Rationalisierung*, is in fact the Austrian term for job tenure. This is the privilege of those employed by the state (in Austria, as in Germany, a much broader category than the British Civil Service – see BEAMTE above). *Die Pragmatik* is a statute defining the grade structure of the civil service, or the grading of civil servants, especially school teachers. Thus: *Professor* darf man sich nennen, wenn man pragmatisiert wird*, on receiving tenure one can call oneself 'Professor'. Both *Pragmatisierung* and *Pragmatik* reflect the old sense of pragmatic as relating to a state decree.

In the nineteenth century, German historians such as Leopold von Ranke popularized *die pragmatische Geschichtsschreibung*; this was pragmatic in that it investigated causes and effects and drew practical lessons. The Germans themselves, however, have traditionally thought of the English as being pre-eminently *pragmatisch*, if perhaps less so in recent years – see EMPIRIE and IDEELL in V.

PROTOKOLL n.n. as well as a formal code of etiquette (which in Germany extends to all levels of public life), the normal word for the record of a meeting. *Wer führt das Protokoll?* who is keeping the minutes? The verb *protokollieren* is also used when the police take down a statement, or when a student writes notes.

PROZESS n.m. a trial, court case, or lawsuit, as well as a process. The unfortunate protagonist of Kafka's novel, *Der Prozeß* (1914/15, published posthumously in 1935), never discovers what he is on trial for. This is partly because in Continental courts a process of investigation (by the *Staatsanwalt**) precedes the trial, in which the whole past life of the accused is admissible evidence. Joseph K. fails to benefit from the 'process' of introspection central to a tradition stretching from St Augustine to Freud.

Jemandem den Prozeß machen, to take someone to court; *mit etwas/jemandem kurzen Prozeß machen*, to make short work of something/someone.

QUÄLEN v. not to quail (*zittern, vor Angst* beben*), but to torment or torture. Used figuratively, especially of a child, *ein Quälgeist* is a nuisance. In the old saying: *wer die Wahl hat, hat die Qual*, it's so hard to choose.

RANKE n.f. not a rank in the armed forces (*der Rang*, see also CHARGE above), but a tendril. Hence *Rankenwerk* – the intertwined foliage or arabesques characteristic of *Jugendstil* (art nouveau) ornamentation. *Ränke*, however, are intrigues, or the machinations of a *Ränkeschmied*. For rank and file, see BASIS in II.

RAT n.m. either **1.** advice/counsel; or **2.** council; or **3.** councillor. The original sense of *Rat* – 'something life-sustaining' – survives only in such compounds as *Vorrat* (supply, provisions), *Hausrat* (household goods), even *Heirat* (marriage, viewed as the acquisition of a house); conversely, *Unrat* is something worthless – filth or refuse. In *Professor* Unrat* (1905), Heinrich Mann caricatured a pillar of society in the *Kaiserreich**; significantly, when Josef von Sternberg made a film of the novel as *The Blue Angel* in 1930, with Emil Jannings and Marlene Dietrich, he omitted the final rebellion against society of Lola Lola's victim, and even had to change the name to Professor* Rath.

Der Stadtrat, town councillor, is also the word for the council itself, which meets in the *Rathaus* (Town Hall) before traditionally adjourning below to the *Ratskeller* – often the best restaurant in town. The one in Bremen is said to contain Germany's best-stocked wine cellar.

Within the civil service, the suffix *-rat* indicates both rank and title, as in *Regierungsrat* (roughly: Senior Executive Officer) or *Ministerialrat* (Assistant Secretary). Goethe's official title, as chief minister of the tiny principality of Weimar, was *Wirklicher Geheimer Rath* (Privy Counsellor), and his mother, by virtue of her husband's position in Frankfurt, was known as, and is still referred to as, *Frau Rath Goethe*. In Austria, an even more title-conscious country than Germany, the honorific *Hofrat* (comparable to Privy Councillor) is still bestowed; as is the title *Kommerzialrat* (German *Kommerzienrat*, 'commercial counsellor'), on distinguished financiers/industrialists. See also KAMMER above.

A rat, however, is *eine Ratte*. The town council of Hameln, it will be remembered, failed to reward its mysterious *Rattenfänger* as promised: *Der Rat will ihm dafür nicht geben, / Was ihm ward zugesagt soeben* (see Achim and Brentano, *Des Knaben Wunderhorn*, 1806/08). An example of exportable Austrian humour is Alfred Polgar's comment (though it is usually attributed to Karl Kraus) on the writers and intellectuals* fleeing from Germany to Austria in 1933/34: *die Ratten betreten das sinkende Schiff*, 'the rats are boarding the sinking ship'. (Chancellor Dollfuss, aptly known on account of his diminutive stature and authoritarian leanings as *Millimetternich*, had just eliminated parliament.) See also -RAT in IV.

RECHT n.n. the law in general (laws are *Gesetze*, subdivided into *Paragraphen**). The plural *die Rechte* (Latin *Jura*) is used to denote the academic discipline which originally comprised both canonical and secular law. Hence, *ein Doktor beider Rechte* would have studied both branches for his doctorate. But *ein Recht* is also an individual human right. Memories of the infringement of both kinds of *Recht* under Hitler's *Unrechtsregime* have led to a heightened respect for the *Rechtsstaat*, the constitutional state founded on the rule of law.

Significantly, the phrase *eine rechtsstaatliche Gesinnung* has come to mean a predisposition towards law and order. This is perhaps because *die Rechte* (singular) is also the political Right – hence *die Parteien der Rechten* (right-wing parties), *ein Rechter* (a right-winger), and the perception that politicians who turn a blind eye to right-wing extremism are *auf dem rechten Auge blind* (see ZIVILCOURAGE in II). By contrast, those on the left, *die Linken*, seldom omit the adjective used in article 28 of the constitution* – *der soziale Rechtsstaat*.

Lawyers neatly divide the world into *Rechtssubjekte** (people as legal entities) and *Rechtsobjekte** (everything else). *Ein Rechtskurs*, however, can mean either a law course or a right-wing bias – the two are not invariably connected since German universities were more radically politicized than those in Britain or the United States. See also BRAUN in II for the controversial continuity of *Rechtspflege* (the administration of justice) after the war.

The adjective from *das Recht* is *gerecht*, meaning just, fair, legitimate. (Nietzsche's Zarathustra slyly observes that when people say *ich bin gerecht*, it sounds just like *ich bin gerächt*, 'I have been avenged' – *Werke* II, p. 352.) But *recht* as an adjective means correct (*du hast recht/unrecht*, you are right/wrong – whereas *du bist falsch*, you are false, is a moral judgement), which in turn provides the word for a know-all, *ein Rechthaber*. This is also *ein Besserwisser*, or when ironically applied to one of the west Germans who are now teaching their eastern compatriots how democracy works, *ein Besserwessi*.

REFERAT n.n., **REFERENT** n.m. in local government, as in other large organizations such as broadcasting and the press, *ein Referat* is a department: for instance *das Kulturreferat**, run by the *Referatsleiter* or *Referent* (though this may also be a specialist adviser brought in from outside). Alternative terms are *das Dezernat* and *der Dezernent*, and in central government *das Ressort** and *der Ressortleiter*. Both the reference you need when applying for a job, and the referee who furnishes it, are *eine Referenz*. See also REFERAT in IV, and REKOMMANDIEREN below.

REFERENDAR n.m. a trainee in the higher civil service (see BEAMTE above): a graduate who has passed his first *Staatsexamen* and is doing in-service training before taking his second *Staatsexamen*; or else a student teacher (*Studienreferendar*), likewise between his first and second state examination; or an articled clerk (*Rechtsreferendar*).

REGIMENT n.n. besides its military meaning, the original sense of government, rule or regimen is more common in German than in English. Thus, the process by which theology and law gave way to philosophy as the foremost university faculty in the early eighteenth century is described by Wilhelm Schmidt-Biggemann as *ein Prozeß**, *der große Folgen für das Regiment haben sollte* (*Aufklärung in Deutschland*, 1979), that is, as having important consequences for the government of the country (rather than affecting graduate intake into the regiment). Nor is Erich Eyck's book *Das persönliche Regiment Wilhelms II* (1948) an account of the Kaiser's personal regiment, but of his personal rule (though 'the fault of William', A. J. P. Taylor contended in his review, 'was his failure to rule, not that he ruled wrongly' – *Europe: Grandeur and Decline*, 1967, p. 161). And Luther, in his address 'To the Christian Nobility of the German Nation' (*An den christlichen Adel deutscher Nation*) of 1520, was attacking the spiritual, not the military rule of Rome as contemptible and inspired by the devil: *das schändliche, teuflische Regiment der Römer*. (See also KONFESSION in V for Luther's support of the system known as *Landesherrliches Kirchenregiment*.) John Knox's monstrous regiment of women, however, is best translated as *abscheuliche Frauenherrschaft*.

As the British army contracts, some feel it should be countering rank 'inflation' by thinking in terms of larger units than the regiment, like the German army which has traditionally fostered loyalty to *die Division** of up to 20,000 men, and in which *der Oberst* (colonel) commands *eine Brigade* rather than *ein Regiment.*

REKOMMANDIEREN v. in Austria, where French linguistic influence is strongest, to register a letter or a parcel (in Germany: *einschreiben*). Kafka wrote, without much confidence, to Felice Bauer on 24 November 1912 that the Post Office could hardly lose all his twice-daily letters to her, *selbst wenn sie, da heute Sonntag ist, nicht rekommandiert werden können* (even if they cannot be registered as it's Sunday today). Another, somewhat formal, Austrian usage is *ich tät mich ihm bestens rekommandieren,* 'please present my compliments to him' (Elias Canetti, *Die Blendung*, 1965, p. 248). *Ein Rekommandationsschreiben* (more commonly, *ein Empfehlungsschreiben*) is a letter of recommendation or (open) testimonial.

REQUIRIEREN v. to requisition or commandeer, whereas to require is *brauchen, nötig haben.* See also KOMMANDO above and REQUISITEN in X.

RESERVE n.f. as in English, but it is worth remembering that the rank of *Leutnant der Reserve* once had a social cachet in German-speaking lands comparable to that of a British officer in a good regiment* (someone trained to shoot people in his work and animals in his spare time). As the novels of Theodor Fontane (1819–98) show, this was especially the case after unification in 1871, for which the Prussian General Staff was given much credit, when *Schneidigkeit* (energy, smartness, dash) and a spurious military notion of honour counted for more than civilian values (for the traditional respect for uniforms, see DIENEN above). By way of contrast, the entire male population of Switzerland still returns to military training for three weeks each year until the age of sixty.

Typisch englische Zurückhaltung is the more likely phrase for 'typical English reserve', though *reserviert* is also used in the sense of *zurückhaltend.*

RESSORT n.n. not a holiday resort (*ein Ferienort* or *Urlaubsort*; on the coast, *ein Seebad**; if it is a health resort, *ein Kurort**), but a government or administrative department such as *das Umweltressort* (Department of the Environment), *das Sportressort* (the Sports Desk in TV or radio), or even *das Klatschressort* (the gossip column in the raucous tabloid *Bild*).

Also used figuratively for a field of activity or area of responsibility – or lack thereof. In German, the sentiment which American satirist Tom Lehrer ascribed to the man who moved from developing Hitler's V2s (see BLITZ in II) to American moonshots – 'Once the rockets are up, who cares where they come down? That's not my department, says Wernher von Braun' – would be *das ist nicht mein Ressort.* See also REFERAT above.

REVISION n.f. either **1.** a judicial appeal (verb: *in die Revision gehen* – see APPELL and INSTANZ above); or **2.** a financial audit (verb: *prüfen*); or **3.** a final proofreading (verb: *Korrektur lesen*); or **4.** a revision of options, opinions, policies (*der Revisionismus*, revisionism), or text (verb: *revidieren, überarbeiten*). Revision for an exam, however, is *die Wiederholung* (repetition) *des Stoffs**.

REVISOR n.m. an auditor (it is the German title of Gogol's *Government Inspector**), or else a proof-reader (also *ein Korrektor**). See REVISION above.

ROBBEN v. not to rob (*bestehlen, berauben*; *der Überfall auf die Bank*, bank robbery), but to crawl on one's elbows – like a seal, *eine Robbe.*

RÜSTIG adj. not rusty (*rostig*), but (still) strong and active. *Ein rüstiger alter Herr* is a sprightly old gentleman – one who might follow the maxim *wer rastet, der rostet* ('who rests rusts', 'better wear out than rust away'). No longer associated with the idea of preparing for war (*rüsten*), or such derivatives as *der Rüstungswettlauf* (arms race), *die Rüstungsbeschränkung* (arms limitation), *die Rüstungskontrolle** (arms control, or the supervision of an arms limitation agreement), *abrüsten* (to disarm). Similarly, *sich entrüsten* no longer means to disarm, but to be incensed, scandalized (*moralische Entrüstung*, moral indignation).

SCHARF adj. sharp, but also live, as in the warning that live ammunition is being used: *Achtung, hier wird scharf geschossen!* (For firing with blanks, see BLIND above.) *Eine scharfe Waffe* is thus a loaded gun as well as 'a sharp weapon'. *Ein Scharfschütze* is a marksman.

By extension, *Sei vorsichtig, der Köter ist scharf!* means 'Watch out, that brute of a dog is fierce and likely to bite you.' *Scharf* also has the sense of strict: *ein scharfer Richter* is not necessarily a judge with a sharp mind, but one who hands out harsh sentences. What no longer exist in Germany, however, are *Scharfrichter*, executioners, so called on account of the sharp-edged instruments of their trade. See EXEKUTIEREN above, and additional meanings of SCHARF in VI and VIII.

SCHWADRONEUR n.m. no connection with a squadron of cavalry (*eine Schwadron*), or aeroplanes (*eine Staffel*), but a slightly dated term for a blusterer. *Er schwadroniert gern*, he is given to big talk, hot air.

SCHWARZ- in cpds. indicates illegality: *der Schwarzmarkt* (black market), *die Schwarzarbeit* (moonlighting). On the eve of reunification, in 1989, there were thought to be about a million *Schwarzarbeiter* (workers not entered in a *Handwerksrolle* or trade register), and those caught, according to *Die Zeit* on 13 July 1990, were subject to *Bußgelder* in Höhe von 25,5 Millionen Mark* (fines of DM25.5 million).

Schwarzfahren means to drive without a licence, or travel without a valid (*gültig**) ticket – a practice deemed *unfair* on notices in the trams and buses. *Schwarzhören* is either to go to university lectures without paying the fees, or to listen to a radio (presumably also *ein Schwarzsender** or pirate radio station) without a licence, while *ein Schwarzseher* is either a TV licence dodger, or else – especially *ein professioneller Schwarzseher* – a pessimist.

SENAT n.m. not the equivalent of the US Senate (the second chamber in Bonn is *der Bundesrat**, made up before reunification of three to five delegates from each of the *Länder**, now three to seven), but

either **1.** the administration of each of Germany's three city states (Hamburg, Bremen, Berlin), its members being *Senatoren*; the *Bausenator*, for instance, is head of planning and building control – a crucial responsibility in Berlin today. Historically, this system also obtained in other independent Hanseatic cities – one thinks of Senator Thomas Buddenbrook in the novel *Buddenbrooks* (1901), set in the *Hansestadt* Lübeck, Thomas Mann's own birthplace.

or **2.** a panel of judges. Thus, the *Familiensenat* of an *Oberlandesgericht* (see INSTANZ above) deals with problems of divorce and custody. Germany's Supreme Court, the *Bundesverfassungsgericht*, has two parallel panels of eight judges, so that judgements concerning the constitution* are made either *im ersten Senat* or *im zweiten Senat* (a rare and celebrated instance of *Patt** – stalemate – is recorded under AKTION in II). The seven male judges and one female judge recently called upon to give a ruling on abortion law (see PARAGRAPH above and ABORT in VI) were inevitably described as the *Schneewittchensenat* ('Snow White Senate').

SENIOR although *der Senior** can mean the senior partner in a firm as well as a senior citizen, the idea of seniority is more often conveyed by *höher*: *höheres Alter*, seniority in age; *höherer Rang*, in military rank; *höherer Dienstgrad**, in the civil service; *höhere Position*, in most other contexts.

Or else by *Ober-*, as in *Oberarzt* (senior physician) or *Oberstufen-*

schüler (senior pupil), though *Herr Ober* is the traditional way of addressing any waiter, not just the *Oberkellner* (head-waiter – but see WIRTSCHAFT in III). Frederick the Great, who regarded agriculture as 'the first of all the arts', served the state (see DIENEN above) as his own *oberster Landrat**, but as Thomas Mann tells us admiringly in *Friedrich und die große Koalition* (1915), he also insisted on being *sein eigner Oberbaurat, Oberbergrat, Oberhofmarschall und was noch alles* ('head of planning and building, mining, the Court, and much else besides' – rather like Pooh-Bah in *The Mikado*, who, though not Lord High Executioner, is Lord High Everything Else).

After the *Spiegel-Affäre* in 1962 (see under FALL in II), the Hamburg news magazine took to calling its erstwhile tormentor Franz Josef Strauß '*Oberbayer*' ('Upper Bavarian', but also 'Bavarian supremo' – a term currently used of the President of Bayern München football club); it was probably a Bavarian who dubbed first Frederick the Great, and then Bismarck, '*Oberpreuß*'.

SENIOREN n.p. senior citizens, old folk. A *Seniorenpaß* enables senior citizens to travel at a reduced rate, a *Seniorenteller* ('old people's dish') assumes you will want to eat less when you are over sixty (*in den Sechzigern*; not to be confused with *in den sechziger Jahren*, in the Sixties).

SOLD n.m. what a *Soldat* (soldier) or *Söldner* (mercenary) is paid. *Der Sünde Sold* (the wages of sin), we are told, *ist der Tod*. The 'sold' sign on used cars says *Verkauft*.

SOUVERÄN adj. sovereign, but note also such common figurative uses as *er beherrscht sein Gebiet souverän*, he has a masterly or commanding knowledge of his field; *er ging souverän darüber hinweg*, he calmly ignored it.

STAATSANWALT n.m. the 'state attorney' in Germany, like the French *juge d'instruction* but unlike the prosecuting counsel in England, attempts both to discover as much as he can about the case before the trial, and subsequently to present the 'truth' as objectively as possible in open court. As *der Richter* (judge) also questions the accused *zur Person* (on his personal circumstances and history), as well as *zur Sache* (on the facts of the case), the privately employed *Rechtsanwalt* appears to have a less prominent role than that of an English defence lawyer. Defendants are not required to plead guilty or innocent (*sich schuldig/nicht schuldig bekennen*) and *das Plädoyer* ('plea') refers instead to the concluding speech of both *Staatsanwalt* and *Rechtsanwalt*. In spite of such features, reminiscent of an inquisitorial rather than an accusatorial system, Germans seem to prefer their system to ours. The atmosphere in the courtroom is certainly less tense and less formal.

Der Generalstaatsanwalt is in charge of public prosecutions at state level, while *der Generalbundesanwalt* is the equivalent of our Attorney General. See also ADVOKAT and PROZESS above.

STAATSSEKRETÄR n.m. undersecretary: *Parlamentarischer Staatssekretär*, Parliamentary Undersecretary; *Ständiger Unterstaatssekretär*, Permanent Undersecretary. These are political appointments and correspondingly high-profile (non-tenured) posts, unlike those of *Ministerialdirektor**, Permanent Secretary, or *Ministerialdirigent* (also *Ministerialrat**), Assistant Secretary. Senior ministers remain *Minister* in Germany, perhaps because the ministers appointed after 1871 and known as *Staatssekretäre* (in fact, permanent officials, headed by the Chancellor) were unconditionally royal appointments, outside the control of the *Reichstag*. Today's *Bundeskanzleramt* (Cabinet Office) has, in descending order of importance, one *Bundesminister*, two *Staatsminister*, and one *Staatssekretär*.

STAB n.m. not a stab with a knife (*ein Stich*), but staff, as in *Stabschef* (chief of staff) or *Stabsoffizier* (staff officer). Also a staff/stave (*Stabreim* is the medieval alliterative verse form revived by Wagner), a conductor's baton, a pole-vaulter's pole, or the bar of a cage (as in Rilke's poem, *Der Panther*, with its well-known rhyme: *als ob es tausend Stäbe gäbe*). *Stäbchen* are chopsticks.

The 'stab-in-the-back theory', propagated by discontented officers after 1918 to explain the 'treachery' of the new republican government while the German army allegedly remained undefeated ('*im Felde* unbesiegt*'), is known as *die Dolchstoßlegende* (see DIKTAT and HELM in II).

STAND n.m. status or class. In the *Standesamt* (registry office) you change your *Familienstand* (status) from *ledig* (single) to *verheiratet* (married), while the idea of social standing is retained in *Standesbewußtsein* (status consciousness) or *Standesunterschied* (class difference). *Die Stände* were formerly the estates of the realm, though the *ständische Verfassung*, based on the three pillars of *Lehrstand, Wehrstand* and *Nährstand* (those who supply education, defence and food) which Joseph von Görres argued in 1814 that a future united Germany should readopt, was just another Romantic myth (see RESTAURATION in II). *Ein Standgericht* is not concerned with this type of standing; nor is it a 'standing' court (permanence is conveyed by *laufend, ständig* or *Dauer-*), but a summary or drumhead court martial which *im Notstand** (in a state of emergency) imposes *Standrecht* (military law). As in English, a newspaper stand or taxi stand is a *Stand* (though at a sporting fixture you sit or stand in the *Tribüne*); to take the stand when giving evidence, *man tritt in den Zeugenstand*; and *ein Ständchen* (serenade) should properly be sung while standing under your beloved's window. *Der Stand* can also refer to the score in a match (*der Spielstand*; *der Pausenstand* is the half-time score), the reading on a meter, or the level of the exchange rate, while *der Stand der Dinge* signifies how things stand in general.

STRAFEN v. to punish, not to 'strafe' (*im Tiefflug beschießen*: to shoot at the ground from the air) – a connotation derived from the 1914–18 German war slogan *Gott strafe England!* (May God punish England) which British troops confused with the method used to bring this about, first employed to such demoralizing effect in the German counter-attack at Cambrai in 1917 (see BLITZKRIEG in II).

But German focuses unequivocally on the notion of punishment in such combinations as *der Strafzettel* (parking ticket), *der Strafraum* (penalty area), *die Strafgebühr* (surcharge), *das Strafporto* (excess postage), *das Strafgericht Gottes* (divine judgement). When the lawyer Ernst von Pidde decided inopportunely in 1933 that Wagner's *Ring* was particularly culpable as *eine Abfolge orchestral aufgeputzter Strafbestände* (a sequence of criminal acts dressed up in orchestral form), he lost his job, but had time on his hands to pursue his *Aktion* Saubere Oper* (Campaign to Clean Up the Opera) with Prussian thoroughness. In his book, *Richard Wagners Ring des Nibelungen im Lichte des deutschen Strafrechts* ('in the light of the German Criminal Code'), he detailed every instance of *Mord* (murder – *Paragraph* 73*), *Blutschande* (incest – *Paragraph 173*), *Verschleppung* (abduction – *Paragraph 239*), *Diebstahl* (robbery – *Paragraph 242*), and *Tierquälerei* (cruelty to animals – *Paragraph 17*), concluding with the conflagration of Valhalla, a particularly bad case of *Brandstiftung* (arson – *Paragraph 308*; see BRAND in IX).

TASTEN v. the first clause of the Constitution* declares that the dignity of man is inalienable: *Die Würde des Menschen ist unantastbar*. This derives from the verb *tasten*, to touch, not to taste (see under KOST in VIII, PROBE in X). That which, figuratively, cannot be touched is thus *unantastbar*, while the sense of touch itself is *der Tastsinn* (taste is *der Geschmacksinn*), and *die Tasten* are the keys on a piano, typewriter or computer. The Untouchables in India are *die Unberührbaren*, though *unberührbar* might also be used of someone who appears to be emotionally frigid.

TESTIEREN v. not to test (*testen*; see also PROBE in VIII), but to make a will (*ein Testament*) – French *tester* has both meanings – or else to attest or certify.

TRESSEN n.f.p. not tresses of hair, which are *Locken*, but silver or gold braid or piping, especially on a military uniform. Thus, *die Tressen verlieren* means to lose one's stripes (see DEGRADIEREN above), not to have a hair-cut.

TRUPPE n.f. *die Truppe* often means the army as a whole, especially the men as distinct from the officers, whereas *ein Trupp* is a squad or troop. (In the GDR, however, *unsere Truppe* was used to convey a genuine sense of solidarity among friends and colleagues, like 'the boys' or 'our gang'.) *Unerlaubte Entfernung von der Truppe* is absence without leave, though in Heinrich Böll's story *Entfernung von der Truppe* (1964) the phrase applies both to a soldier's desertion in 1938 and to the author's own post-war *Entfernung* or *Entfremdung* (sense of alienation) from West German society: a sort of 'goodbye to all that' (colloquially, *ohne mich!*, count me out!).

WACHMANN n.m. in Germany, a general word for watchman (a military *Wachmannschaft* is the watch/the men on guard; *eine Wach- und Schließgesellschaft*, a private security firm), but in Austria, a policeman. The reverse is true of the analogous, if somewhat dated word *Wachtmeister* – a sergeant in the Austrian army (German *Feldwebel*), whereas one might still address a German police constable, albeit a trifle quaintly and although it is the lowest rank, as *Herr Wachtmeister*.

Such patriots as, in song, once kept *die Wacht am Rhein*, are now sometimes said to be stationed, in spirit, *auf Wache an der Oder-Neiße* (see HEIMAT in II).

Besides meaning 'to keep watch', *wachen* also means 'to be or lie awake' ('*Stille Nacht, heilige Nacht, alles schläft, einer wacht*'; to wake up is *aufwachen* or *erwachen* – '*Wach' auf, du Christ!*'; '*Erwache! Erwache! Heiliges Weib**!'), while the transitive verbs are *anschauen* or *beobachten* (to watch) and *wecken* or *aufwecken* (to waken; *Wer ist der Held, der mich erweckt?*).

WALL n.m. not a wall (an inside wall is *eine Wand*, an outside or free-standing wall – such as the Berlin Wall – *eine Mauer**), but an embankment or military rampart, such as *der Westwall*, which we know as the Siegfried Line. In many German towns, *Am Wall* or *Am Wallgraben* (moat) are pleasant walks with trees and grass on the site of earlier fortifications, though Hamburg's *Neuer Wall* is its Bond Street. See also WALLFAHRT in V.

ZIVIL adj. civilian (*in Zivil*, in civvies; *ein Zivilist* is any non-military person), but not civil in the sense of polite (*höflich*). The civil liberty (*das Freiheitsrecht*) most often cited is that guaranteed the citizen by Article 2 of the Constitution*: *das Recht auf die freie Entfaltung seiner Persönlichkeit*, the free development of one's personality. When this activity leads to civil disobedience (*ziviler Ungehorsam*), it is sometimes construed as *Zivilcourage*.

Note that a civil engineer is *ein Hoch- und Tiefbauingenieur*. For civil war and civil rights, see BÜRGER in II.

ZIVILDIENST n.m. not the Civil Service (see BEAMTE above), but community service (also called *Ersatzdienst*), chosen by one young German male in three – though the proportion is much higher among *Gymnasiasten** – as an alternative to *Wehrdienst**, military service (women are exempt). Therefore, *ich bin im Zivildienst** does not mean 'I am a civil servant', but that as part of my compulsory service to the community I have been sent to a hospital as an orderly, a gardener, or a receptionist, or to look after the elderly or handicapped, sometimes in their own homes, or even to a private environmental organization such as Greenpeace. Critics of the use of *Zivildienstler* (colloquially, *Zivis*) as untrained cheap labour make the point that they are not *marktneutral* as planned, but upset the fine balance of labour relations and youth training schemes.

When conscription was re-introduced in 1956, everyone had a constitutional right to refuse to serve in the armed forces, but still had to undergo a '*Gewissensprüfung*' – an interview to assess whether their pacifism was genuine or not. This unpopular 'conscience examination' was abolished in 1984, and '*Zivis*' now get almost automatic exemption after making a simple written declaration, though they still have to work for twelve months – three months longer than their colleagues *beim Bund**. There are very few who reject both *Militärdienst* and *Zivildienst – solche Totalverweigerer müssen dafür ins 'Kittchen'**.

HISTORY
and
POLITICS

II

GESCHICHTE
und
POLITIK

AKTION n.f. not the action of a play (*die Handlung*) or a legal action (*eine Klage*), but an individual action (also *eine Tat*) or – nowadays the first sense one thinks of – a communal action or campaign organized by an *ad hoc* group of citizens (*eine Bürgeraktion*). However, the *Nacht- und Nebelaktion* launched by Defence Minister Franz Josef Strauß against *Der Spiegel* in October 1962 was both semi-official (*offiziös**) and clandestine – a 'night-and-fog' operation (*Nacht und Nebel* was the German title of Alain Resnais's film about the Nazi death camps); the case subsequently brought by the Hamburg news magazine against Strauß was controversially rejected in 1966 when the first *Senat** of the Constitutional* Court was split equally (see PATT in VII and FALL below). Military actions, such as the *SS-Einsatzkommando** raids behind the Eastern front during the war, are also known as *Aktionen*, but 'killed in action' is simply *gefallen*.

As was memorably demonstrated by the people of Leipzig in October and November 1989, the initiative for a *Bürgeraktion* or *Bürgerinitiative** lies with the people. Citizens' action campaigns against nuclear weapons and power stations (*antinukleare Aktionen*; *Aktionen gegen Nuklearwaffen und Kernkraftwerke*) reflect widespread public participation and concern, as does *Aktion Sorgenkind* (Children in Need) on TV, though the *Aktion Saubere Leinwand* ('Clean Screen' Campaign) of the 1950s would probably have little support in today's permissive society. See also *Zivilcourage* under ZIVIL in I.

AKTIVIST n.m. an activist or militant, but in East Germany an honorific bestowed on those who, by achieving the annual economic target or *Planaufgabe* well before '*Plansilvester*', were able to celebrate New Year's Eve early (and where, accordingly, *eine Aktivistenbrigade* was the opposite of a group of subversives). Such Stakhanovites may now find a more pleasurable outlet for their activities in a culture which prizes *aktives Leben* (the active life), *Aktivurlaub* (action holidays), and even the prospect of becoming more *koitusaktiv* (sexually active).

But the word was also applied to those who wore white armbands with the slogan 'No Violence!' during the Leipzig *Montagsdemonstrationen* in 1989 (*die Aktivisten der Bürgerbewegung mit der weißen*

Armbinde: *Keine Gewalt!* – *Die Zeit*, 23 September 1994). Equally, when the East German activist Jens Reich talked of *Alternative* aus der Protestszene* being involved in the early demonstrations, he meant that they, too, conformed to these Gandhian principles and were not responsible for the strident, nationalistic banners which appeared in the chanting crowds only after 9 October 1989 (see BÜRGER-INITIATIVE below).

AKTUELL adj. not actual or real (*eigentlich, wirklich, tatsächlich*), but up-to-date, topical. When *Die Zeit* wrote of Konrad Adenauer on 7 October 1988, *daß die deutsche Einheit für ihn kein aktuelles Ziel war*, it meant that German unity was not in his view a goal which could currently be achieved in the 1950s and 60s. His actual objective, *sein eigentliches Ziel*, was therefore the integration of the Federal Republic within the Western alliance (see also DEMENTI below).

A current affairs programme is *eine aktuelle Sendung*; few can have been more current than *Aktuelle Kamera*, the TV programme in the erstwhile GDR which helped foment the events of November 1989. The most burning issue of the day and the latest fashion in clothes are equally *aktuell*.

ALTERNATIVEN n.p. a vogue word, increasingly hijacked by neo-Nazi thugs (but see also AKTIVIST above). In the 1980s, it embraced three established political parties (*Die Grünen**, *Alternative Liste*, and *Grün-Alternative Liste* or *GAL*), thus reflecting a more constructive approach than that once adopted by the *Außerparlamentarische Opposition* or *APO* (the extra-parliamentary opposition which arose in response to the *Große Koalition*, grand coalition, of 1966–69 and the subsequent reintroduction of an emergency powers act; see NOTSTAND below) – not to be confused with the East German *APO* or *Abteilungsparteiorganisation der SED* (party representation at the workplace). One fundamental objective, to which many subscribe who do not otherwise aspire to the *alternativer Lebensstil* of the contemporary '*Ökowelle*' or '*Ökofreaks*', is the replacement of nuclear power by *alternative Energien*.

AMPELKOALITION n.f. a coalition of the three parties whose colours are those of a set of traffic lights, *eine Ampel*: the socialist SPD (red), the liberal FDP (yellow) and *die Grünen** (green). Operative at *Land** level – in Brandenburg, for instance – in spite of the Bonn coalition between the conservative CDU/CSU (whose colour is not blue, but black – see SCHWARZ below) and the FDP.

ASOZIAL adj. refers to any social drop-out, but often used to suggest attitudes which are aggressively antisocial (see AUTONOME and CHAOT below), rather than merely asocial or unsociable (*ungesellig*). Those arbitrarily designated '*asoziale Elemente*' by the Nazis were something different again: namely, all opponents of the regime.

ASYLANT n.m. asylum seeker – a loaded term. *Paragraph* 16* of the constitution, which unequivocally guarantees right of asylum to all political refugees (*Politisch Verfolgte genießen Asylrecht*), was severely tested in the late 1980s when the trickle increased to a flood. In addition to emigrants from the GDR (*Übersiedler*), and from Poland, Romania, Hungary and the Soviet Union (*Aussiedler*), some of whose claims to be 'ethnic Germans' and thereby in a privileged position appeared tenuous, came *politische Flüchtlinge* or *Asylbewerber* from Balkan and Third World countries, for whom the word '*Asyl*' was an 'Open Sesame' on the German border.

Some sceptics have consequently come to think of the word *Asylant*, with its potentially negative *-ant* suffix, as a near synonym for *Querulant* (malcontent) or *Bummelant* (idler), and to speak of *Wirtschafts-Asylanten* or *Wirtschafts-Flüchtlinge* seeking economic rather than political asylum. Nevertheless, the amendment to *Paragraph* 16* passed on 1 July 1993 (and a matter of heated public debate ever since), whereby *Asylanten* must come directly from a country where their lives are demonstrably endangered, remains a model of enlightened humanitarianism when set against the spectre of bogus refugees raised by Britain and addressed in the Asylum and Immigration Appeals Act (1993). Defenders of Germany's traditional open-arms policy sometimes allude to the 6 million German *Asylanten* who have found refuge in the USA since the first Mennonites founded Germantown, Philadelphia, in 1683. See also under AUSLÄNDISCH below.

AUSLÄNDISCH adj. not what 'outlandish' has come to mean in English (*befremdlich, sonderbar, ausgefallen, extravagant**), but simply foreign (*ausländische Freunde*, friends from abroad); or, in adminis-trative jargon, alien. Until the end of the 1980s it referred in practice to Mediterranean *Gastarbeiter*. When the '*Anwerbestop*' in 1973 halted recruitment, though not the ensuing influx of relatives, the number of *Ausländer* rose to five million. But it was only with the additional million and a half *Asylanten** admitted since 1989, mainly from *Ostblockstaaten*, accompanied by a growing perception that '*das Boot ist voll*', that the word *Ausländer*, like *Asylant*, acquired pejorative connotations.

AUTONOME n.m. anarchistic *autonome Gruppen* emerged dur-ing the 1980s, projecting themselves as *eine Gegenkultur* (counter-culture) and turning peaceful '*Protestszene*' into turbulent '*Terror-szene*'. Armed, helmeted and masked (the government quickly imposed a *Vermummungsverbot bei Demonstrationen*, requiring dem-onstrators to leave their faces uncovered), they infiltrated idealistic *Bürgerinitiativen**, notably the first, largest and longest-running of them all – against Frankfurt Airport's *Startbahn West*. (The extension of the west runway, first planned in 1962 and completed only in 1984, threatened a large swathe of forest, striking a chord in the German psyche which developed into the Green movement.)

BANN n.m., **BANNEN** v. enchantment/to enchant, rather than – the original meaning – banishment/to banish. Thus, *die Deutschen gerieten in den Bannkreis Hitlers* ('entered the magic circle', were captivated); *er blieb wie gebannt stehen* (he stood spell-bound). We are told that Oskar, the hero of Günter Grass's novel *Die Blechtrommel* (*The Tin Drum*, 1959, p. 72), is drawn both to Rasputin, *der die Frauen bannte* ('who bewitched women'), and to Goethe, *der sich so gern von den Frauen bannen ließ* ('who so readily succumbed to female charms'). In the older feudal and religious sense: *Luther wurde in den Bann gelegt*, banished, outlawed (by Charles V, after appearing at the Diet of Worms in 1521); a heretic was doubtless meant to feel the full force of having *den Bannfluch gegen ihn geschleudert*, 'the curse of excommunication hurled against him'. By extension, *böse Geister werden gebannt* (evil spirits are exorcized); *die Gefahr ist vorläufig gebannt* (danger temporarily averted).

A legal ban is *ein Verbot*, such as the admirable *Fahrverbot für LKWs am Wochenende* (ban on lorries using German motorways at weekends). In spite of national stereotypes, not everything is *verboten* unless specifically permitted. Rupert Brooke might feel more at home today in Munich's *Englischer* Garten*, 'where *das Betreten*'s not *verboten*', than in the fragrant environs of The Old Vicarage, Grantchester.

BASIS n.f. in the political context, a vogue word meaning 'grass roots', appropriated from the Marxist *Basis und Überbau* (base and superstructure) but not in the Marxist sense of economic base, and not applied to the political left only. *Basisarbeit*, political ground-work, is carried out by *Basisgruppen*, action groups. Compare the contrasting history of VOLK below.

BERLINER n.m. In June 1963, President Kennedy proclaimed from the balcony of the Schöneberg *Rathaus**in West Berlin: 'All free men, wherever they may live, are citizens of Berlin. And therefore, as a free man, I take pride in the words *Ich bin ein Berliner*.' No one misunderstood, or has forgotten, this splendid declaration of solidarity, though he should have said *Ich bin Berliner. Ein Berliner* is a doughnut.

BERUFSVERBOT n.m. a key word for understanding both the West German state and the attitude of the radical left towards it, especially in the sixties and seventies.

The term suggests that a specific profession is banned. This is not the case. What is 'forbidden' are certain professions to certain people. In other words, the term refers to the practice (which goes back to Metternich in Austria and to Bismarck's *Sozialistengesetze*, laws against the Socialists, and was widely implemented by the Nazis, mainly on ethnic grounds) of excluding 'political extremists' from entering or exercising any of the professions which carry the status of *Beamte**. This practice, including all the bureaucratic procedures needed to support it, became controversial in the early seventies when student radicals put *der Marsch durch die Institutionen*, the (long) march through the institutions, on their agenda, aiming to change the system from within. The officially designated *Radikalenerlaß* (edict against radicals, 1972), universally known as the *Berufsverbot*, was aimed at preventing this. Students, postmen and engine drivers, university dons and school teachers, doctors and nurses in state hospitals, as well as civil servants (*Beamte**) in the British sense, suddenly found themselves threatened with dismissal or exclusion from public employment. The title of a case history documented by the writer Peter Schneider quietly emphasizes how easy it was to fall foul of this legislation: . . . *schon bist du ein Verfassungsfeind* (. . . *and suddenly you are an enemy of the constitution*, 1975).

While critics of the *Berufsverbot* complained of *Gesinnungsschnüffelei* (spying into people's political views), its advocates invoked the right of a democracy to protect itself against 'the enemy within'. They claimed that the Federal Republic, unlike the Weimar Republic, was *eine wehrhafte Demokratie*, a democracy capable of defending itself. The *Berufsverbot* was hotly debated during the chancellorships of Willy Brandt and Helmut Schmidt, but it slipped from public awareness after the swing to the right in 1982 (a *Wende** unaccompanied by any Tory-style 'countermarch through the institutions'). Since 1990, public attention has been focused on *Berufsverbote*, *Gesinnungsschnüffelei* and political discrimination as they were practised in the GDR. See also under DEUTSCH and VERFASSUNGS-PATRIOTISMUS below and ART in X.

BIEDERMEIER n.n. like Regency England, Biedermeier Germany reflected a transition from Romantic sensibility* to the new industrial and technical age. The word suggests something like

'Victorian values', as well as the style of furniture or decoration of the period from 1815 to 1848 (see RESTAURATION below).

An article in *Die Zeit* on 9 October 1987, entitled *Biedermeier, Bonn und die bürgerliche* Regierung Helmut Kohls*, observed that Chancellor Kohl shares his nick-name 'pear' (*Birne*) with the rotund French 'citizen king', Louis-Philippe (*poire*) – though a *Birne* is also the heavy weight used to demolish buildings, suggesting the clumsy, sledgehammer methods by which he clobbers all opposition – and that both men are thought of as being *bieder* or *biedermännisch*.

All these terms once meant worthy and honest, but now mean conventional, provincial and somewhat philistine. They are frequently applied to Switzerland ('*die biedere Schweiz*') – for instance, in Max Frisch's anarchistic version of the English morality play *Everyman* (in German, *Jedermann*), *Biedermann und die Brandstifter* (*Biedermann and the Fire-raisers*, radio play 1952, staged 1957). Critics in the east bloc saw this as a comment on the ease with which the Nazis had taken over Germany, those in the west also as an exploration of communist infiltration in Czechoslovakia prior to 1948.

BLITZ n.m. used absolutely, lightning, or a flash of light, while the London Blitz is known to Germans as *der Blitzangriff auf London*. See also BLACKOUT in X.

(What Churchill called the Battle of Britain, Germans called *der Adlerangriff*, 'Eagle's attack'. The VI and V2 rockets were '*Vergeltungswaffen*', retaliatory weapons, as in Hitler's threat: *es wird Bombe mit Bombe vergolten*, 'we'll retaliate bomb for bomb'. In an older and gentler tradition, *vergelten* also means 'to reward', and *vergelt's Gott*, still used in Bavarian and Austrian churches during collections, means 'God bless you'.)

Blitzkrieg is the tactic of a sudden, all-out attack, aiming for breakthrough, *der Durchbruch*, at the enemy's weakest point and the destruction of his equilibrium. (*Durchbruch* was to be a key word from the early years of the Nazis' '*Kampfzeit*' or struggle for power – others are *Schlacht, Einsatz, Einheit, Front* – all reflecting their militarization of the language.) Though it had been a crucial part of the Schlieffen Plan since at least 1905, it was the appearance of tanks on the British side which provided the element of surprise essential to *Blitzkrieg* and broke the Hindenburg Line at Cambrai in November 1917 (albeit the subsequent 'expanding torrent' which Liddell Hart – in *Strategy: The Indirect Approach*, 1967 – has shown to be equally essential, failed to materialize). The Second World War began with full-scale *Blitzkrieg* against Poland, but German defeat was ensured when the Russians under Zhukov indirectly attacked Paulus's Sixth

Army at Stalingrad to win their first *Blitzkrieg* victory. See also STRAFEN and BESIEGEN in I.

Eine Blitzaktion* is consequently a 'lightning action' such as a police raid, or even the constabulary's response to *ein(e) Blitzer(in)* or streaker (whose flash of inspiration will have begun, somewhat less overtly, as *ein Geistesblitz**). But *sie wurde geblitzt* means a flash photograph was taken of her driving too fast through a *Radarkontrolle** (see TACHOMETER and TEMPO in VII).

BRAUN adj. from the colour of the party uniform, connotes a Nazi past, as in a headline of *Die Zeit* on 6 November 1987: *Wie braun war Heidegger?* (How 'brown' was Heidegger?). When *'die braune Zeit'* began in 1933, others, *'die Beefsteak-Leute'*, chose the disguise *außen braun und innen rot* ('brown on the outside, red on the inside' – like steak, see ENGLISCH in VIII) in order to conceal their communist convictions under a 'brown' veneer. After the war, a *'Persilschein'* (denazification certificate) ensured that one's past had been at least laundered and that no brown stains remained. Of the 6,080,000 Germans who appeared before a *Spruchkammer* (denazification court), mainly in the American zone, 1,700 were convicted as *Hauptschuldige* (main offenders), 23,000 were designated *Belastete* (seriously incriminated), 150,400 as *Minderbelastete* (less incriminated), and 1,006,000 as *Mitläufer* ('fellow travellers', non-active party members), while those who were exonerated, *Entlastete*, numbered 3,939,000 (see also LAST in III).

In the case of lawyers, the government in November 1986 still defended the controversial continuity of personnel after 1945 as necessary for *die Wiederherstellung der Funktionsfähigkeit der Rechtspflege* (meaning the re-establishment of the rule of law): in practice, no single judge or *Staatsanwalt** was ever found guilty of administering less than justice between 1933 and 1945.

See SCHWARZ below for further colour symbolism, but for *eine kleine Braune*, KAFFEE in VIII.

BRAV adj. no longer means brave, but sometimes the contrary of brave: thus, as *Die Zeit* noted on 26 August 1988, at a time when the German government seemed peculiarly disorientated, *wirken noch die Bravsten kühn*, meaning that even the most stolidly unadventurous and uninspired appeared bold – a reference to the SPD, which had overtaken the CDU in the opinion polls for the first time since the *Wende** in 1982, but were themselves to be overtaken by the events of 1989. See also BRAV in VI.

BÜRGER n.m., **BÜRGERLICH** adj. the two, once congruous meanings – either **1.** citizen; civic; or **2.** burgher; middle-class, bourgeois – have diverged significantly since the eighteenth century. In the first sense, politically neutral, like *das Bürgerliche Gesetzbuch* (Civil Code), or the definition of soldiers of the *Bundeswehr* as *Staatsbürger in Uniform* (see DIENEN in I) – though, of course, this notion *is* political when compared with that of *der unpolitische Soldat* associated with General von Seeckt, commander of the Weimar Republic's armed forces (*die Reichswehr*) from 1920 to 1926 and chief proponent of an autonomous, unpolitical army.

In the second sense still, or once again, controversial. Hegel had been careful to distinguish between the State and *die bürgerliche Gesellschaft* (civil society), but this distinction was to be obscured in Germany, above all in Marxist terminology; *bürgerlich*, like *bourgeois* in England, became a derogatory or even contemptuous term. Berlin's Frenchified middle classes were perhaps a real *bourgeoisie*, but not so *das Bürgertum* (citizenry) of provincial, small-town Germany. The *Bürgerschreck*, or bogey of the middle classes, challenged bourgeois values: the writer Carl Sternheim ironically entitled his plays *Aus dem bürgerlichen Heldenleben* (*From the heroic life of the bourgeoisie*, 1908–1922); the poet Gottfried Benn resolved to be *lieber lächerlich als bürgerlich* (ludicrous, if need be, anything but bourgeois); even Thomas Mann, himself the epitome of the patrician burgher, found *Bürgerlichkeit* the most problematical of conditions.

Problematic for a different reason, *der Kleinbürger* (petit-bourgeois) has commonly been allocated a key role in theories of fascism. Though a sociological and descriptive term rather than a merely derogatory one, for Karl Marx it meant much the same as *Spießbürger*. This was originally someone who carried a *Spieß* (spear) instead of more advanced weaponry, and *ein Spießbürger* or *Spießer* has come to signify all that is parochial and narrow-minded. (*A propos* narrow-mindedness: the small town of *Krähwinkel*, the fictitious setting of August von Kotzebue's comedy *Die deutschen Kleinstädter* (1803) where Johann Nestroy subsequently located his satire on the 1848 revolution, *Freiheit in Krähwinkel* (1848), is the archetypal cultural backwater, though for Berliners this is also Bonn). *Schildbürger*, on the other hand, is a term of humorous condescension, derived from those in feudal times who were armed only with a *Schild* (shield) and applied subsequently to the inhabitants of Schilda in Saxony, the subjects of a famous sixteenth-century comic *Schwankbuch**; a *Schildbürgerstreich* is thus the sort of foolishly self-defeating action which the English automatically think of as Irish, the French as Belgian, the Germans as Frisian, etc. (see WITZ in V).

More recently: *Längst hat sich das Wort 'Bürger' vom Staat gelöst und ist in eine neue Liaison mit dem Partikularen, Anti-Zentralen* *eingegangen: Bürgerinitiativen*, Bürgerforen, Bürgerbegehren.* (The word *Bürger* has long since detached itself from the state and entered into a new liaison with particularistic and anti-central tendencies: citizens' action groups, open debates, public petitions.) Thus Hans Maier, erstwhile *Kultusminister* (Minister of Education) in conservative Bavaria, as reported in *Die Zeit* on 28 November 1986. He concludes: *Es darf nicht dahin kommen, daß der Staat mit den particuliers auf gleicher Stufe um die Verteilung der Macht kämpfen muß.* (We must not reach the point where the state has to struggle for its share of power on the same footing as individuals.) His reaction to the role of *Bürgerinitiativen, Bürgerforen* and *Bürgerbegehren* in bringing down the government of the GDR is not on record.

The SPD has made no attempt to project itself as *eine bürgerliche Partei*; this term refers unambiguously to the parties of the centre or centre-right, the CDU/CSU and the FDP (Liberals*); however, the CDU and the SPD both aim to be *Volksparteien* (see VOLK below; also BASIS, LAGER, KLIENTEL in this section).

Ruhe ist die erste Bürgerpflicht ('Calm is the citizen's first duty'): this memorable proclamation by the governor of Berlin in 1806 (which should be put into context with the sentence preceding it: *Der König hat eine Bataille verloren*, 'The King has lost a battle') is the title of a splendid novel by Willibald Alexis (1852) charting the long decline of Prussia after the Battle of Jena. It was also the reaction of both German governments to the uprising against the East German state in 1953, but it is not a clause of the constitution, nor, happily, a maxim which finds favour today.

A topical compound of *Bürger* is *Ausbürgerung* (deprival of citizenship, expatriation). This was the fate of the GDR song-writer Wolf Biermann, among others, in 1976, and one which contrasts ironically with the *Einbürgerung* (naturalization or resettlement) of RAF* terrorists from the Federal Republic, who, it was revealed in 1990, enjoyed the protection and patronage of the Communist authorities in building new lives in the GDR. On the other hand, those who courted expatriation during the Leipzig demonstrations in 1989 – for instance, by appearing on Western television – lost the sympathy of most of their fellow-protesters (see BÜRGERINITIATIVE below and AKTIVIST above).

See also BÜRGERLICH in VIII for the culinary connotations of *gutbürgerliche Küche*, as well as the origins of the hamburger.

BÜRGERINITIATIVE n.f. 'citizens' initiative' (also *Bürgeraktion**), often a protest group concerned with environmental, especially anti-nuclear issues. In East Germany, however, something quite different: since, ideologically, the GDR could recognize no conflict of interests between citizens and the state, *eine Bürger-initiative* there meant, not do-it-yourself politics, but 'voluntary' unpaid work, usually to improve housing and the environment (*'Aufbaustunden'*, for instance, spent turning the space between newly-erected housing blocks into a half-way acceptable 'land-scape').

This changed, as Jens Reich recalled in *Die Zeit* on 23 September 1994, with the growth of the pacifist *Schwerter zu Pflugscharen* move-ment (which took the politically correct 'swords into ploughshares' policy literally, but dialectically subverted its significance). It was followed, in 1988, by the first of the public demonstrations centred around Leipzig's *Nikolai-Kirche*, against environmental pollution (*Umweltverschmutzung*) and the banning of the Soviet magazine *Sputnik*; then, in March 1989, for permission to travel to the Federal Republic (*Ausreise in die BRD*); in May 1989, to protest against the rigging of local elections (*Fälschung der Kommunalwahlen*); and on Monday, 4 September, the first of the *Montagsdemonstrationen*, when 1,200 participants called for 'freedom to travel instead of mass exo-dus' (*Reisefreiheit statt Massenflucht*) and the removal of the security police (*Stasi 'raus!*). On 11 and 18 September, there were again over 1,000 demonstrators; on 25 September, 5,000; on 2 October, 10,000; on 9 October (the turning point, when Egon Krenz had to decide whether or not to take Honecker's advice and send in the tanks), 50,000; on 16 October 120,000; on 23 October, 150,000; on 6 Nov-ember, 400,000. The citizens of the GDR had demonstrated the original meaning of the word *Bürgerinitiative* and (with the Russians' indulgence) brought down the regime. See BÜRGER, ZIVIL-COURAGE, AKTIVIST, SCHRECKEN in this section.

CHAOT n.m. a term derived from *Chaos* and used by some, often politicians, to brand all demonstrators as probable *Verfassungsfeinde* (enemies of the constitution* – see BERUFSVERBOT, BÜRGER, BÜR-GERINITIATIVE above), by others to describe the more militantly anarchistic elements only (see AUTONOME above). In this political context, *chaotisch* has increasingly come to imply violence and crime. In student parlance, it also signifies somebody who is simply disor-ganized in his work or thought.

DEMENTI n.n. not dementia (*die Demenz, der Schwachsinn*), but as in French, the official denial of a rumour or published statement, as when politicians deny words attributed to them. Adenauer once told a journalist (the orthography is meant to convey his unmistak-able Rhenish): *Sie kriegen dat Interview, aber ich jebe et Ihnen fünnef-zich Prozent jelogen, dann verdienen Sie noch wat am Dementi* (I'll give you your interview, but I'll throw in fifty per cent lies, so you can make a bit more when I deny it – see Wolf Schneider, *Deutsch für Profis*, 1984).

In public, Adenauer would probably have denied (*dementiert*), or even have denounced as demented (*verrückt, schwachsinnig*), the contents of his secret note to Britain in December 1955, revealed in *Die Zeit* on 15 June 1990. In this, he gave as his reason for putting the integration of the Federal Republic in the West before German reunification: *daß er kein Vertrauen in das deutsche Volk habe* (that he had no faith in the German people). He perhaps agreed with Lord Ismay, NATO's first Secretary General, that NATO existed to keep the Americans in, the Russians out, and the Germans down. More probably he subscribed to the journalist and historian Sebastian Haffner's view of *Wiedervereinigungspolitik als Lebenslüge* (the politics of reunification as an 'existential* lie', a lie you need in order to get on with life), a formulation which even Willy Brandt (see OSTPOLITIK below) found appropriate only months before the event itself.

DEUTSCHLAND n.n., **DEUTSCH** adj. *Deutschland, Deutschland über alles, über alles in der Welt* means 'I put my country of Germany above all else in the world' – a sentiment comparable to the English 'I vow to thee, my country', or the American 'My country, 'tis of thee'. They are the opening lines of Hoffmann von Fallersleben's *Deutschlandlied*, written (on Helgoland, then still a British island) in a spirit of patriotic aspiration some thirty years before Germany achieved political unity. Understandably, subsequent victories over the Danes, the Austrians, and the French (the Franco-Prussian War of 1870/71 is known as *der Deutsch-Französische Krieg* – a slight anachronism) led to the belief that the new national anthem referred to a German desire to dominate everyone else as well. This was certainly not Bismarck's intention, but if we remember Ferdinand Freiligrath's famous formulation of 1844, *Deutschland ist Hamlet*, it might seem, in retrospect, that all exhortations to avenge its entombed liberty led inexorably, within Germany itself, only to the imposition of rule by Bismarck's Fortinbras (see Gordon Craig, *Germany 1866–1945*, 1981, p. vii).

The first two verses* of the *Deutschlandlied* are now tactfully omitted, and the third verse which speaks of *Einigkeit und Recht und Freiheit für das deutsche Vaterland* – sentiments as appropriate to the occupied, divided Germany of the 1950s and 60s as to the as yet ununified one of Hoffmann's time – was declared the official national anthem. Haydn's famous melody (itself an attempt to match the patriotic fervour of Arne's 'God save the King') is familiar to us as the hymn-tune 'Glorious things of thee are spoken, Zion, City of our

God', while the Austrians had previously sung it to the words *Gott erhalte Franz den Kaiser, unsern guten Kaiser Franz* ('God save Franz, our good old Kaiser, God save good old Kaiser Franz') – a version heard once again when Germany won the 1990 World Cup under Franz Beckenbauer, jocularly referred to as '*Kaiser*' Franz.

A *Deutschstunde* is a German lesson at school, but Siegfried Lenz's best-selling novel of that name (see ART in X) is a 'lesson about Germany' in a rather fuller sense. This is also what *Die Zeit* meant when on 20 April 1990 it described the tricky negotiations between Chancellor Kohl's representative, Rudolf Seiters, and his East German counterparts: *das war Seiters' erste Deutschstunde*.

At Mrs Thatcher's personal *Deutschstunde* at Chequers a month earlier (reported in the *Independent on Sunday* on 15 July 1990), experts invited to help her play the anti-German card on German reunification refused to do so, though not before listing among characteristics they thought of as essentially *deutsch*: 'their insensitivity to the feelings of others, their obsession with themselves, a strong inclination to self-pity, aggressiveness, assertiveness, bullying and egotism, a capacity for excess, to overdo things, and a tendency to over-estimate their own strengths and capabilities'. Even Nietzsche, himself pre-eminently *deutschfeindlich* (anti-German) in the face of genuine post-unification *Deutschtümelei* (hyper-Germanness) a century earlier, nevertheless thought his compatriots' fundamental *Ernst* (seriousness) and *Sachlichkeit* (objectivity) excellent qualifications for the mandarins of Europe they would one day become (*alle Art* von Mandarinen Europas heranzuzüchten* – *Zur Genealogie der Moral*, II, 3).

Der deutsche Michel is the plain honest German as caricatured (by the Germans themselves) in the nineteenth century with nightcap and candle, or with beer-mug and clay pipe. According to Heine, the 1848 revolutions passed him by, *Derweil der Michel geduldig und gut / Begann zu schlafen und schnarchen, / Und wieder erwachte unter der Hut* / Von vierunddreißig Monarchen* ('While Michael meekly fell asleep and snored, and woke still under the protection of thirty four monarchs' – *Michel nach dem März*). He is a world, and two world wars, apart from 'the Hun who is always at your throat or at your heels' (Churchill), and whose 'German greeting' (*der deutsche Gruß*) was the Hitler salute (see also ENGLISCH in V).

For the sense of *deutsch* still common in the eighteenth century, see ART in X. *Mit jemandem deutsch reden* today means to speak straight from the shoulder, just as *auf gut deutsch* is roughly parallel to 'in plain English'. On a musical note, the *Deutsch-Verzeichnis* of Schubert's works (1947) is named after its compiler, Otto Erich Deutsch.

DIÄTEN n.p. the plural of diet, but also parliamentary expenses. When these were controversially raised in 1988, neither the *Süddeutsche Zeitung* nor *Der Spiegel* could resist the pun: *Dicker durch Diäten*, Diets make you fatter (and richer – see DICK in VII). On the other hand, German schoolchildren find nothing amusing about the Diet of Worms of 1495–1521; to them, this is *der Reichstag zu Worms*, and worms are *Würmer*.

DIKTAT n.n. as when a secretary takes dictation (*nach Diktat schreiben*) or schoolchildren do a dictation (*ein Diktat schreiben*), but also a dictate. The harsh terms of the Treaty of Versailles meant that it was resented in the 1920s and 30s as a *Diktatfrieden* (dictated peace), and widely known as the *Versailler Diktat* (see STAB in I, HELM below, and POET in X).

DISKOTHEK n.f. in the former GDR, a political or cultural discussion as well as a dance: used to gain the minds and hearts of the young, under highly qualified and ideologically sound *Kulturfunktionäre für sozialistische Jugendunterhaltung*, otherwise known as *Diskosprecher* or *Disk-Jockeys* (an approach the Jesuits seem to have missed). In various forms, such as the *Rentnerdisko* (pensioners' social evening) or *Veteranendisko* (meeting of old party members), one of the main cultural institutions of the country.

DIVISION n.f. a military or mathematical division, but not a parliamentary one. This is officially known as *ein Hammelsprung*, which signifies rams jumping over a gate (a more virile metaphor than the counting of sheep), under the guidance of the *Haupt-Einpeitscher* (literally 'chief whipper-in' – a less well-known, journalistic word which raises a smile, probably a straight anglicism, though also perhaps an echo of Goebbels' attempts *als Einpeitscher der Nation* to work the country up into a frenzy); if there is a three-line whip: *bei der Abstimmung besteht Fraktionszwang**. The Germans do not appear to share the French view that whipping is *le vice anglais*; for them, the English* disease, once rickets, is now strikes (70 days lost per 1,000 employees between 1989 and 1993, compared with 18 in Germany).

DRÜBEN adv. 'over there' – once meant America as seen from Europe, but after the creation of two independent German states, increasingly used by West Germans of East Germans (*die drüben*), and vice versa.

Goethe's Faust had rejected any thought of an afterlife with the words: *nach drüben ist die Aussicht uns verrannt; Tor, wer dorthin die Augen blinzelnd richtet* ('that perspective is now closed to us; a fool who squints in that direction' – ll. 11,442–3). In an ironic and provocative adaptation – *nach drüben ist der Ausweg uns verrannt* – the East German song-writer, Wolf Biermann, suggested that what was closed to his compatriots was escape to the other life of the Federal Republic. (In a further ironic twist, verses like this led to his own unwilling expatriation – see BÜRGER above).

EGAL adj. a gallicism, conveying indifference or lack of preference, rather than equality: *das ist mir egal*, I don't mind one way or the other, I couldn't care less. French *égalité* becomes in German *Gleichheit*, and equality of opportunity *Chancengleichheit*, as guaranteed by Articles 2 and 12 of the Constitution*.

ENGLISCH adj. one splendid memorial to all things *englisch* as an erstwhile synonym for 'natural' and 'free' is Munich's *Englischer Garten*. A creation of the American Benjamin Thompson (who as Count Rumford later became Bavaria's Minister of War *and* in 1799 founded the Royal Institution of Great Britain), this royal gift to the people (and attempt to ward off revolution) was laid out in 1789 in the 'English' landscape style because formal French gardens were associated with the ruling classes. Long thought of as a German Elysium on account of nude bathing in the Eisbach, its *paradiesische Zustände* (now somewhat tarnished by drug trafficking around the Monopteros temple) might therefore be described as *englisch* (if decidedly un-English) in the sense of the word explained in section V.

The heavily symbolic setting of Goethe's novel *Die Wahlverwandtschaften* (*Elective Affinities*, 1809) is similarly a country estate containing a landscaped garden and lakes in the new English style, somewhat reminiscent of a further real-life example of the genre which now lies partly in Germany, partly in Poland. This was the life's work of Hermann, Fürst von Pückler-Muskau (1785–1871). Impoverished by schemes to divert the River Neisse through his estate, the anglophile prince divorced his beloved wife Lucie, came to England in search of an heiress, was caricatured by Dickens in *Pickwick Papers* as Count Smorltork, and is now remembered for having devised the *Fürst-Pückler-Eis**.

Germany in turn exploited the lingering vogue for things 'Gothick' by exporting the first plaster garden gnomes to England in 1815.

EVENTUELL adj. or adv. as in English 'eventuality' (*im Brandfall**, in the eventuality of fire), refers to the realm of possibility, never to future certainty. *Godot kommt eventuell* does not mean that he will come eventually (*endlich, schließlich, zum Schluß*), only that he might come. In negotiations, *eventuell* indicates a concession: *das können* *wir eventuell arrangieren*, we might just be able to arrange that. When in 1907 Kaiser Wilhelm unwisely described his Berlin–Baghdad Railway project and the expansion of German influence into the Persian Gulf as *vitale Interessen . . . dafür schlage ich mich eventuell!* (see Fritz Fischer, *Griff nach der Weltmacht*, 1967, p. 57), even he meant only that he *might* fight to defend interests thought to be vital as Germany attempted to join in the Great Game.

FALL n.m. literally, a fall, and figuratively, downfall (as in the proverb about pride: *Hochmut kommt vor dem Fall*); or else an instance or case (*ein Sterbefall* is not a lethal fall, but simply 'a death'); and when it becomes news, an affair. On 16 January 1984, *Der Spiegel* carried the story: *Der Fall Kiessling, Wörners Fall* – an inept investigation into the private life of NATO's deputy commander by the military security service (*Militärer Abschirmdienst*, or '*MAD*') did not lead to the dismissal of Defence Minister Manfred Wörner but, surprisingly, to his appointment as NATO's Secretary General. The same pun, a characteristic of '*Spiegeldeutsch*', again prefaced the 23 March 1987 issue: *Fall Mathiopoulos, Brandts Fall* correctly forecast Willy Brandt's forced resignation after twenty-three years as chairman of the SPD for proposing that the party adopt as *Parteisprecherin* (party spokesperson) a young woman who was neither German nor a member of the party. A more significant affair was *der Fall Guillaume* – the uncovering of one of Brandt's top aides as an East German agent – which led to the resignation of West Germany's first Socialist chancellor in 1974. *Trotz dieser Fälle* (in spite of these cases), it is Brandt's – literal – *Kniefall* at the memorial to the Warsaw ghetto, when he knelt in homage to a city razed to the ground by German troops, which people still remember.

Such ancient precedents as *der Sündenfall*, also known as *der Fall Adams* (the Fall), have an obvious sexual meaning – nicely caught by Kleist in the opening scene of his comedy, *Der zerbrochene Krug* (*The Broken Jug*, 1808; see also IRRITIEREN in VII). *Richter Adam*, a village magistrate and would-be seducer attempting to explain away his scratches, meets with the sceptical response: *der erste Adamsfall, den Ihr aus einem Bett hinaus getan*, 'Adam's fall! The first time you fell *out* of bed'. (Connoisseurs of the homophonic pun might also like to imagine the 'silent rise' envisaged in a discarded line of Rilke's: *Dies ist das schweigende Steigen der Phallen* – S. *Werke* 2,473.) Nevertheless, the word *Fall* does not immediately suggest a sexual affair or scandal. This is probably *eine Affäre* if public, though *eine Affäre* need not be sexual: *die Profumo-Affäre*, but also *die Dreyfus-Affäre, die Watergate-Affäre*, and – Germany's own *cause célèbre* – the *Spiegel-Affäre* in 1962, when the magazine published an article entitled *Landesverrat* ('Treason') against the then Minister of Defence, Franz Josef Strauß, and its editor Rudolf Augstein spent 103 days in prison under examination while Strauß (unsuccessfully) brought a case against him (see also AKTION above and SENIOR in I). The common (or garden) type of affair of a Lady Chatterley, finally, is *ein Verhältnis* – a word which should now be used with caution: see dictionary.

The past participle of the verb *fallen* is *gefallen* ('killed in action' is one specific sense), but *gefallen* is also a verb in its own right, meaning 'to please'. This allowed the satirist Karl Kraus to divide women into *Gefallene und solche, die nicht gefallen haben* ('fallen women, and those who weren't attractive enough').

FORMAT n.n. besides the format of books and/or papers (*im Format DIN A4 = Deutsche Industrie Norm*, size A4, roughly equivalent to foolscap), also a somewhat vaguer measure of personal achievement and/or class. In *Der Mann ohne Eigenschaften* (*The Man without Qualities*), a complete version of which was published only in 1952, Robert Musil memorably caricatured the cult of personality of the inter-war years, modelling the character Arnheim on Walther Rathenau – undoubtedly *ein Mann großen Formats* (p. 190) and Foreign Minister of the Weimar Republic. Rathenau was murdered by nationalist zealots in 1922 for negotiating an *entente* between Germany and the Soviet Union at Rapallo, and after boldly arguing for acceptance of the Allies' reparation demands by citing Beethoven's resolute *Muß es sein? Es muß sein!* (*Gesammelte Reden*, 1924, p. 203. 'Must it be? It must be!' – the inscription on the canon in Opus 135, but also Beethoven's response when some musicians queried a fee of 50 guilders for hire of his Opus 130.) See also *Dolchstoßlegende* under STAB in I, HELM and PROFIL below.

FRAKTION n.f. the parliamentary/US congressional party, or a coalition of parties, such as the *Unionsfraktion** (the MPs of the two main conservative parties, CDU and CSU, working *als Fraktionsgemeinschaft** – in co-operation or coalition). Hence, *eine fraktionelle Entscheidung* is not a decision which fractionally succeeds or fails (*eine knappe Entscheidung*), but a decision taken by the *Fraktion*, implemented *unter Fraktionszwang* (under the whip) by the *Fraktionsvorsitzender* (also known as the *Fraktionschef**, *Fraktionsführer** or *Geschäftsführer**, parliamentary party leader/US floor leader – a decisive job in Germany's loose, coalition politics).

Though also used, mainly outside parliament, of an unofficial grouping or faction, the parliamentary term – unlike Dr Johnson's sly definition of Whig as 'the name of a faction' – is not in itself derogatory, but only by association in such compounds as *Stahlhelm-*

Fraktion (see HELM below) or *Galgen- und Prügelstrafenfraktion* (though such a 'hang 'em and flog 'em lobby' would be unconstitutional in Germany). Parliamentary splinter groups are generally referred to as *Splittergruppen*.

A mathematical fraction is *ein Bruch*; the fraction of a second, *der Bruchteil einer Sekunde*.

FÜHRER n.m. Some 1,500 Nazi terms – from *Ahnenbruch* to *Zinsknechtschaft* – were dropped from the 1947 edition of *Duden*, but you can now use the word *Führer* in most contexts without reminding anyone of the war. *Ein Lokführer*, for instance, is an engine driver, but it is still perhaps the case that *Reiseführer*, tourist guide, or *Bergführer*, mountain guide, are more often abbreviated when they refer to the book than to the person. A Pole, learning German after long residence in England, was understandably hesitant when asked to describe his occupation: 'some sort of Führer'. '*Geschäftsführer?*' 'That's it.' A *Geschäftsführer* is a managing director, or else the manager of a store, secretary of an association, or party whip (see FRAKTION above).

The qualities of leadership developed in the *Führungsakademie der Bundeswehr* (army staff college) in Hamburg do not include charisma or rhetoric, and Hitler's *Führerprinzip* (one leads, the rest obey) has now been replaced by the notion of *Innere Führung* (see DIENEN in I). There is no German equivalent of 'follow my leader'.

GANG n.m. not a gang of criminals (*die Gang*, more commonly *die Bande*), but the noun from *gehen* (to go), hence the gang of 'gangway', or of Burns's 'till all the seas gang dry'. Accordingly, Schiller's ballad, *Der Gang nach dem Eisenhammer*, is not about a gang after an iron hammer, but *The Path to the Forge* (which awaits the would-be murderer rather than his intended victim). Nor is *ein starker Seegang* a gang of pirates (*Seeräuber*), but a heavy swell at sea (to which *der Seemannsgang*, the sailor's way of walking, is one answer).

Frundsberg warned Luther at Worms: *Mönchlein, Mönchlein, du gehst einen schweren Gang* ('you have chosen a difficult path, little monk'), but we know that the subsequent course of events, *der Gang der Dinge*, led in the opposite direction to Heinrich IV's humiliating *Gang nach Kanossa* (the castle in northern Italy where in 1077 Pope Gregory VII made him wait in the snow for three days before revoking his excommunication – see BUSSGELD in I, BANN above, and for the best contemporary account, the *Annals* of Lambert of Hersfeld). To lose face through some such humiliating surrender is still the sense of *den Gang nach Kanossa antreten* or *nach Kanossa gehen*. Bismarck, for example, told the *Reichstag* on 14 May 1872:

Nach Kanossa gehen wir nicht, and yet, ever the realist, was obliged to do just that when by 1887 he saw he could not win the *Kulturkampf** (see also REALPOLITIK below).

Oswald Spengler's 'sombre murky vision of the doom of our civilization' (H. Stuart Hughes), *Der Untergang des Abendlandes (The Decline/Going Under of the West)*, having been written before the war, made curious reading when it was published in 1919, seeming as it did to put victors and vanquished in the same moribund boat and welcoming a *Zeitgeist* still allegedly in need of raw, violent energy (see also INGENIEUR in IV). What the times in fact produced, as Karl Kraus pointed out in *Die dritte Walpurgisnacht* (1933), were *Untergangster des Abendlandes* – a pun which nicely contrasts the Nazis' underhand methods with their own self-estimation as *Übermenschen* (supermen) – see UNMENSCH below.

Note also *der Urnengang*, going to the polls, election (the sort of euphemism which Kraus spent his life attacking). *Die Gänge* are also the gears of an engine or the courses of a meal (see GANG in VIII).

GAU n.m. or n.n. originally a large geographical region, such as Breisgau or Allgäu; then appropriated by the Nazis as their main administrative unit, under a *Gauleiter*. Now also (in capital letters) an acronym of *größter anzunehmender Unfall* – a technical term widely used since the Chernobyl disaster in March 1986 to mean 'worst possible accident' (the media inevitably dubbed Chernobyl a '*Super-GAU*'). When some months later a fire at the Sandoz chemical plant in Basle badly contaminated the Rhine, the term *Rhein-GAU* was applied with bitter irony to the catastrophic consequences for the beautiful region of Rheingau. See also BRÜTER in III.

GEMEINSCHAFT n.f. community, rather than society – a distinction first encapsulated in the title of Friedrich Tönnies's book, *Gemeinschaft und Gesellschaft (Community and Society,* 1887). In the 1920s, nostalgia for the idea of an organic community with shared and unquestioned values was a siren song to many, especially the young, repelled by the chaotic novelty of party politics and aggressive materialism. Hitler promised to end *die Wirren der Gesellschaft* (the confusions of the Weimar Republic) by appealing to the *Schicksalsgemeinschaft* of the German-speaking peoples – the belief that they shared a common destiny. In November 1989, in very different circumstances, East Germany's last prime minister, Hans Modrow, unsuccessfully floated the elusive idea of a *Vertragsgemeinschaft*, literally a 'community regulated by treaty', as the slow path to reunification.

Germans love *Arbeitsgemeinschaften*, which are study-groups or working-parties. One such, the *Bundesarbeitsgemeinschaft Kritischer*

Polizisten (Federal Association of Critical Policemen), may sound like an invention of Professor Branestawm, but the *Süddeutsche Zeitung* carried a report on 7 May 1990 that this admirable body was concerned it might lose the confidence of the public if required to carry out *Bespitzelung für den Staatsschutz* (state-security snooping). In the school context, an *Arbeitsgemeinschaft* is an optional or extracurricular subject. Even the pursuit of some communal pleasure or shared hobby is often called an *Arbeitsgemeinschaft* – thereby demonstrating the importance of being earnest in Germany (see SERIÖS in VI).

GEMEINSINN n.m. not a transliteration of 'common sense', which is *der gesunde Menschenverstand*, but civic sense. German travellers to England in the late eighteenth and nineteenth centuries were struck by this quality in the English, and also called it *Gemeingeist**, public spirit.

Their admiration stemmed partly from the fact that, until the establishment of the Federal Republic in 1949, German society offered less scope for the people to participate in decision-making at every level of society. Today, in marked contrast, concern for *das, was dem Gemeinwohl dient* (what serves the public interest) is high and widespread, and *Zivilcourage** more evident than *das preußische Obrigkeitsdenken* (the mode* of thought associated with Prussian authoritarianism).

Germans occasionally misuse 'common sense', as when they say *es gibt keinen common sense bis heute* but actually mean 'there is as yet no agreed meaning' (properly: *keine Übereinstimmung*).

GIFT n.n. not a gift (*das Geschenk*), but poison. Though the root of the word ('to give') is still visible in a bride's *Mitgift* (dowry), *Gift* itself has retained only its euphemistic sense (of giving someone a drink=potion=poison). It was unfortunate that American aid packets dropped over Germany in 1945 bore the inscription 'Gift from the USA'. Conversely, the German word *giftfest** should not be confused with Christmas presents – it means 'immune to poison'. *Die Zeit* reported on 28 August 1987 that Peter Glotz, the party secretary of the SPD, had recommended *Die TAZ* (an abbreviation of *Tageszeitung*), then a newly founded left-wing Berlin newspaper, *als tägliches Gegengift zur FAZ* (as a daily antidote to the *Frankfurter Allgemeine*). There was no such antidote available to those citizens of Passau whose secrets were threatened when a schoolgirl working on a local history project happened upon the '*Giftschrank*' in the town hall – a locked cupboard containing potentially incriminating files from the Nazi years – and subsequently exposed the contents in her film *Das schreck-*

liche Mädchen (*Nasty Girl*). A *Giftschrank* is literally a poison cabinet, but until quite recently it also referred to the restricted-access library shelves where erotic/sexual/pornographic literature was kept away from innocent students. Leipzig university had an entire '*Giftturm*', so called because it contained pernicious Western reading matter for access to which one required what was popularly known as a *Gift-schein* (see SCHEIN in IV). Perhaps unsurprisingly, *blondes* Gift* is a 'blonde bombshell'.

GOTHA n.m. 'And dark the Sun and Moon, and the Almanach de Gotha' – the lament in T. S. Eliot's *Four Quartets* refers to the German equivalent of Debrett's *Peerage*. Yet titles are still quite frequently used in Germany, while in Austria they are officially banned – an irony, since it is a much more title-conscious country. Prussia had no equivalent of duke (*Herzog*), marquess (*Marquis*), or viscount (*Viscount*), but only *Prinz* (Prince), *Fürst* (non-royal Prince), *Graf* (Earl or Count), *Baron* or *Freiherr* (Baron), *Freifräulein* (Baroness), *Freifrau* (Baroness by marriage).

German aristocrats have tended to keep their prestige in what is ostensibly an egalitarian society. This is partly because they behaved reasonably well between 1933 and 1945, combining courage in battle with the distaste for Nazism which led Claus Graf von Stauffenberg and other Junkers (see GUT in III) to try to kill Hitler on 20 July 1944. It is also because they have traditionally – unlike most of their British counterparts – been patrons of the arts, *Kunstmäzene*. The prestige of the Wittelsbachs in Bavaria still partly stems from the readiness of Ludwig II to build fairy-tale castles in which to indulge his passion for Wagner – a passion which threatened to bankrupt his country at the time but has since proved extremely profitable.

GRETCHENFRAGE n.f. the crucial, 'sixty-four-thousand-dollar' question which Gretchen puts to Faust: *Wie hast du's mit der Religion?* ('What's your attitude to religion?' *Faust I*, l. 3415). His evasive answer is a much-cited Romantic credo: *Nenn's Glück! Herz! Liebe! Gott! / Ich habe keinen Namen / Dafür! Gefühl ist alles* ('Call it happiness, heart, love, God! I have no name for it. Feeling is all!' ll. 3454–6).

As with Hamlet's dilemma, the form of the question in Goethe's play – seemingly straightforward, even naive, but actually tricky – is commonly applied to difficult matters of conscience. And to political convictions, as in the *Süddeutsche Zeitung* on 4 July 1989: '*Wie hältst du's mit Amerika?' ist eine Frage, die hierzulande ideologische Gräben aufreißt, Ehen erschüttert und Freundschaften killt* ('What's your position on America?' is a question in this country which tears open ideological rifts, shatters marriages and kills friendships). But for US/ German relations, see also AMIS in I.

HEIMAT n.f. home or homeland, though generally more localized (Heinrich Heine's beloved Rhineland, for instance – see LAND in I) than the political *Vaterland* towards which Germans might harbour more ambiguous feelings (see VERFASSUNGSPATRIOTISMUS below). *Heimatliebe* comes close to Orwell's definition of patriotism, as distinct from nationalism, as 'devotion to a particular place and a particular way of life, which one believes to be the best in the world but has no wish to force upon other people' (*Notes on Nationalism*, 1945). But just as Gertrude Stein spoke for many of her compatriots when she declared 'America is my country, Paris is my home town', it is also true that the French capital frequently became a second *Heimat* for those compelled to leave their *Vaterland* for political reasons, yet whose native *Heimatliebe* was not in doubt: Heine, for instance (see INTELLEKTUELLER in V, ZENSUR in X), or Kurt Tucholsky, who was happy to sit in the *Parc Monceau* (1924) and *ruh von meinem Vaterlande aus* ('take a rest from my fatherland').

Before unification, the distinction was perhaps less pronounced. Schiller's famous image in *Das Lied von der Glocke* (1800) of *heilige Ordnung* ('sacred order') 'weaving the most precious of all ties, the desire for a country of one's own' – *Und das teuerste der Bande / wob, den Trieb zum Vaterlande!* – was essentially an anti-revolutionary expression of frustration that a unified German culture was not yet mirrored by political reality (see KULTUR and REICH below). And when the humiliation inflicted on Germany by Napoleon over the following decade made political unity seem more remote than ever, Mme de Staël, perhaps unwittingly, spoke no more than the truth when she exclaimed on hearing of Kleist's suicide: *N'a-t-il pas eu une patrie?* (see NOVELLE in X). Even the fervent nationalist Ernst Moritz Arndt, writing of *Des Deutschen Vaterland* on the eve of the Battle of Leipzig (1813), would roundly declare *Das ist des Deutschen Vaterland, / Wo Zorn vertilgt den welschen* Tand* ('where wrath eradicates foreign fripperies'), only to concede that Germany was in reality united by its culture and piety alone: *So weit die deutsche Zunge klingt / Und Gott im Himmel Lieder singt* ('as far as the German tongue rings out and sings songs to God in heaven').

One memorable example of such songs*, which the Romantic era produced in extraordinary profusion, is *In der Fremde* ('In foreign parts') by Joseph von Eichendorff (1788–1857) with its quintessential lament for the poet's lost *Heimat*: *Aus der Heimat hinter den Blitzen rot / da kommen die Wolken her, / aber Vater und Mutter sind lange tot, / es kennt mich dort keiner mehr* ('From my home beyond the lightning red, the clouds pour, but father and mother are long dead, I am known to none there any more'). The mood is evoked with equal poignancy in Edgar Reitz's film *Heimat* (1985), a marvellous re-creation of life over three generations in a Hunsrück village in Rhineland Pfalz echoing a long tradition of regional, provincial, even parochial *Heimatdichtung*. This was interrupted in the 1920s and 30s by strident *Blut und Boden* (blood and soil) nationalism, but with the sentimental *Heimatfilme* of the war years Goebbels also adapted the older tradition to subtle propagandistic effect. Even the Nazi slogan *Heim ins Reich* (demanding the return of territories with German-speaking populations) appealed to ancient folk-memories, kept alive after the war in *Landsmannschaften** formed by the more militant of those twelve million *Heimatvertriebene* who had been expelled from their homeland of *Schlesien* or *Ostpreußen* (and whose return '*heim ins Reich*' was consequently very different from that which Hitler had promised them).

A profoundly different vision of homeland, divested of any ele-ment of rural idyll, was offered by the Marxist philosopher Ernst Bloch in *Das Prinzip Hoffnung* (*The Principle of Hope*, first published in the west in 1959), its concluding words an invocation of something 'which will illuminate all our childhoods and in which no one has yet set foot' (*das allen in die Kindheit scheint und worin noch niemand war*): *Heimat*. This is not so different from the wistful climax of Wagner's *Wesendonck Lieder*: *unsre Heimat ist nicht hier* ('our true home is not of this world'). Both are examples of that other-worldly Romantic tradition which, Thomas Mann was convinced, *wird in unserem Herzen in gewissem Maße** immer Heimat bleiben (*Von deutscher Republik*, 1922).

When former *Bundespräsident* Gustav Heinemann was asked in the 1970s: *Lieben Sie Deutschland?*, he replied, laconically, *ich liebe meine Frau*. But West Germans did slowly learn to love what Heinemann called his *schwieriges Vaterland*, and a less enigmatic note was sounded by Martin Greiffenhagen in *Die Aktualität** Preußens (1981): *Der Mensch soll seine 'Heimat' nicht in einer politischen Partei suchen* (people should not seek their spiritual home in a political party), *sondern in einer Gruppe vertrauter Menschen* (but in groupings of like-minded friends) – essentially a plea for the growth of civil society and pragmatic politics, and against the *Gesinnungspolitik* of a Mrs Thatcher, or even a Jimmy Carter (in opposition to whose 'conviction politics' Helmut Schmidt and Franz Josef Strauß found themselves briefly united).

HELM n.m. not the helm of a ship (*das Steuer* or *das Ruder*), but a helmet. The steel helmet which replaced Prussia's distinctive *Pickel-*

haube (the spiked leather helmet designed by Schinkel – an unlikely but inescapable link with the British bobby) is *der Stahlhelm*.

It also gave its name to a paramilitary *Frontkämpferbund*: an association of soldiers who had fought at the front and which by 1928 claimed a membership of a million. This included women (some of whom christened their daughters *Stahlhelmine*) and those too young to have seen active service in the First World War, but all the keener for radical change along totalitarian lines rather than mere restoration of the monarchy. *Der Stahlhelm* cultivated *die Dolchstoßlegende* (see STAB in I), called for strong leadership and an end to parliamentary democracy, talked of the need for *Lebensraum* ('living space') for Germany, and an end to the *Überfremdung des deutschen Lebens* (foreign infiltration of German life) – all of which led predictably to the assimilation of the movement into the Nazi *SA* (*Sturmabteilung*).

Like many words from the Nazi era (see UNMENSCH below), *Stahlhelm* remains *ein brisantes Wort* (an explosive term). When, in 1987, Bernhard Friedmann proposed in his book *Einheit statt Raketen* (*Unity instead of Missiles*) that German reunification should be added to the agenda of the superpowers' nuclear disarmament talks – a linkage of '*Deutschlandpolitik*' with security policy still considered politically taboo – opponents spoke of the emergence of a *Stahlhelm-Fraktion** on the more nationalist wing of the conservative *Unionsparteien**.

KABINETT n.n. in a political context, the equivalent of a British 'cabinet' or US 'administration'. *Der Kabinettschef** nevertheless does not correspond to the French *chef de cabinet*, a minister's chief adviser (this is *der Ministerialdirektor**), but is the Chancellor himself. *Eine Kabinettsumbildung* is a cabinet reshuffle, though regular rotation of ministerial jobs is not part of Germany's *politische Kultur**.

In *Das Kabinett des Dr. Caligari* (1920), the word refers to the showcase in which the mad magician exhibits his somnambulist. Siegfried Kracauer's *From Caligari to Hitler* (1947) supports the view that the cruelty of German Expressionism foreshadowed the larger horrors of the Third Reich. See also KABINETT in VIII.

KLIENTEL n.f. besides the clientele of a shopkeeper, lawyer, or prostitute (see FREIER in VI), also those who vote for a political party (though this has few of the obvious advantages of Italian *clientelismo* – see VITAMIN B below). For the *typische Wählerklientel* of some political parties, see LIBERAL below.

KOLONIALWAREN n.p. literally 'colonial wares', though *ein Kolonialwarengeschäft* no longer specializes in spices from East Africa or cocoa beans from Samoa (the German overseas empire lasted only some thirty-five years, from 1884 to 1919); it is a slightly dated term for a grocery shop (like *ein Tante-Emma-Laden*, corner shop). Most people now buy their *Lebensmittel* (groceries) in the local *Lebensmittelgeschäft*, or in a *Supermarkt*.

KONZEPT n.n. not so much a single abstract notion (*ein Begriff*), more an overall conception or vision of a goal to be achieved, and how it might be achieved. *Das Konzept* of a united Europe, in contrast to the 'pragmatic' English approach, possibly owes something to what E. M. Forster called 'an interest in the universal which the average Teuton possesses and the average Englishman does not' – a gap which Forster attempts to bridge in *Howards End* (1910; motto: 'only connect'). *Das Konzept* is also a hallmark of the contemporary German theatre, a favourite *Konzept* of East German opera directors being to set Wagner's *Ring*, post-holocaust, in a sewer.

When the Christian Democrats returned to power in the *Wende** of 1982, they made a determined effort to regain the ideological high ground from the Left and replace its *Begriffe von 1968* (see KULTUR below for a similar internal confrontation in 1914); these concepts included *Ostpolitik**, *Mitbestimmung*, *Emanzipation*, *Anti-Baby-Pille** and *Solidarität* (in the new version, solidarity of the workers became solidarity of the family – an expropriation reminiscent of the 'citizens' charter' in Britain a decade later). As *Die Zeit* concluded on 3 June 1988: *die CDU mußte erkennen, daß sie dafür kein Konzept mehr hatte*, the CDU was forced to acknowledge that it had no longer any programme to deal with all this. A second meaning is therefore programme or plan: *das paßte ihm vorzüglich ins Konzept*, that suited his plan perfectly (or, in unconceptual English terms, that was grist to his mill); *die Kölner gingen konzeptlos vor* (the Cologne players had no strategy).

Finally, *ein Konzept* may be a draft or rough copy of a speech, article, etc. Thus, *er sprach anderthalb Stunden frei** *ohne Konzept* means he spoke for an hour and a half without notes, not that he had no conception (*keine Ahnung*) of his subject. The cut and thrust of a confrontational debating chamber is unfamiliar to German politicians, who all sit facing the speaker in the semi-circular *Bundestag* and show little enthusiasm for heckling speakers from the opposition parties in an attempt to put them off – *die Opposition aus dem Konzept zu bringen*. (*Du hast mich aus dem Konzept gebracht*, you've made me lose the thread of what I was saying).

KRAFT n.f. physical strength/power/force – Beethoven entitled the third movement of his Opus 132 *Neue Kraft fühlend* to celebrate his 'renewed vigour'. This original sense has evolved in English to mean craftsmanship (see HANDWERK in III, KUNST- in X) and, ultimately, craftiness (see CLEVER in IV). Nietzsche thought that this sort of linguistic shift reflected deeper truths about society, though the German words *Kraft* and *kräftig* have no such range of associations. In power politics, the word is *Macht*, as in Nietzsche's *Wille zur Macht* (will to power), or Hitler's so-called *Machtergreifung* (seizure of power), the Nazi slogan *Kraft durch Freude* (power through joy) being something of an exception. *Personenkraftwagen* (*PKW*) – which predates the Nazis' attempts at linguistic Germanization – is still the official designation of a car, and a lorry is still a *Lastkraftwagen**(*LKW* or *Laster*). All drivers must carry a *Kraftfahrzeugschein* (registration document), though not the vehicle's *Kraftfahrzeugbrief* (logbook).

KULTUR n.f. what Mrs Thatcher's advisers had in mind at their meeting at Chequers on 24 March 1990 (see DEUTSCH above): 'the Germans' conviction that their victory over France in 1870 stemmed from a deep moral and cultural superiority rather than – as in fact – a modest advance in military technology.'

Certainly, *Kultur* is not merely Swift's 'sweetness and light' or Arnold's 'the best that has been thought and said in the world'. When in 1890, the year of Bismarck's fall*, Friedrich von Bernhardi described *die großen germanischen Kulturaufgaben gegen Rußland* (see Fritz Fischer, *Krieg der Illusionen*, 1970, p. 78), the 'great cultural tasks facing Germany in Russia' which he envisaged – and subsequently spelt out in his best-selling, self-fulfilling prophecy, *Deutschland und der nächste Krieg* (*Germany and the Coming War*, 1912) – were rather different from those facing the Goethe Institut today. 'Culture is already beginning to be spelt with a K', G. K. Chesterton had observed in 1915 (*The Crimes of England*), while a contemporary cartoon showed a pickle-helmeted* Hun brandishing the club of German *Kultur*. Further support for the view that war was merely a continuation of cultural (especially musical) supremacy by other means seemed to come from Thomas Mann, who spent the First World War pointedly celebrating the 'defensive' campaigns of Germany's most famous soldier-composer, Frederick the Great, and arguing that the soulful depths of German *Kultur* were the very antithesis of western *Zivilisation* (one of the central *Ideen von 1914* which challenged those of 1789 – see also KONZEPT above). This was a distinction rejected by Freud, whose *Kulturkritik* was universal (*Das Unbehagen in der Kultur* of 1930 is known in English as *Civilization and its Discontents*). But others sceptical of *Kulturpropaganda* replied that *Kultur* was simply civilization as conceived by the Germans: cultural arrogance fused with militarism.

The question was whether Germany's *politische Kultur* had taken a 'special path', unlike that of the other Western nations (traditionally-minded German historians had defended the Second Reich in terms of a *deutscher Sonderweg* – a phrase which Leftist intellectuals turned polemically against them after 1968, only to apply it themselves to Hitler – see SOGENANNT below). It took Germany at least a century to recover from the effects of the Thirty Years' War (1618–1648) which reduced its population by one third and made it, in Helmuth Plessner's phrase, *eine verspätete Nation* (a latecomer among nation-states). In the eighteenth century, Lessing, Goethe and Schiller sought in *Kultur* a means of joining together all those who spoke the same language but who lived in some three hundred different states (in 1789, there were in fact precisely 1789 individual political units, ranging from Austria and Prussia to the tiny territories of *Reichsdörfer* and individual *Reichsritter*; after Napoleon and the Congress of Vienna, the number was 39) – 'the miraculous creation of a soul without a body', as Gustav Freytag later observed. In Bavaria and Austria, *Thron und Altar* were also a cohesive force, but the defeat of Austria at Königgrätz in 1866 spelt the end of any likelihood of a Catholic Greater Germany or '*Siebzigmillionenreich*'. In order to make good her position (the '*Ausgleich*' of 1867), the new *Doppelmonarchie Österreich-Ungarn* (the Dual Monarchy of Austria-Hungary) was obliged to shift attention south-eastwards along the Danube towards the Balkans, with dire consequences for the future peace of Europe. It was left to Bismarck to complete the process with the '*Kulturkampf*' of 1871–87 (during an electoral address in March 1873, the liberal Rudolf Virchow first referred to the struggle against the Catholic Church as a *Kampf für die Kultur*), essentially a defence of secular authority, especially in education, against the Principle of Papal Infallibility, the Dogma of the Immaculate Conception, the Syllabus of Errors and other pro-clamations with which Pius IX had responded to the evils of modernism. In the wake of this virulent struggle against 'ultramontane' influence – even though Bismarck quickly switched to targeting the socialists as the principal '*Reichsfeinde*', and in negotiations with the more conciliatory Leo XIII (see *Gang nach Kanossa* under GANG above) substantially modified the '*Mai-Gesetze*' of 1873 subordinating all Church life to state regulation – the Catholics lost faith in the state, and the liberals were exposed as fanatically doctrinaire (problems which returned to haunt the Weimar Republic).

When, shortly before he was murdered by nationalist zealots in 1922, Foreign Minister Walther Rathenau (see FORMAT above) declared that 'Germany should forego material ambitions in order to fulfil her world task of culture', he used the word *Bildung**, not

Kultur – 'a word which Germany ought to prohibit by law for thirty years to come' (*Die neue Gesellschaft/The New Society*, 1921). But it was not to this tainted, traditional *Kultur* that Goering was alluding when he allegedly said *Wenn ich Kultur höre . . . entsichere ich meinen Browning* (whenever I hear the word culture, I release the safety catch of my revolver – in fact a quotation from the first scene of the Nazi writer Hanns Johst's 1934 play, *Schlageter*). The reference is to those aspects of Weimar culture which the Nazis alleged were alien to the *Volk** and ruining the German soul. Goering shrewdly continued to pilfer paintings (see ART in X) produced by this '*Kulturbolschewismus*' – a new term applied to all forms of modernism in the arts, still echoed in the sense of outrage felt by one conservative Austrian newspaper in the 1950s when it was suggested that Bertolt Brecht be given Austrian nationality and appointed Director of the Salzburg *Festspiele*: *Kulturbolschewistische Atombombe auf Österreich abgeworfen* ('cultural-bolshevist atom bomb dropped on Austria'; see account in *profil**, 28 July 1986).

The impression that some things do not change in Austria is borne out by the reassuring inscription on the imperial porcelain of Vienna's public lavatories (see KLOSETT in IX): *in allen Kulturstaaten erhältlich*, meaning 'available in all civilized countries'. Professor Gustav Jäger's revolutionary woollen underwear, known as a *Jägerhemd* or *Reformkleidung** (the beneficial effects of which, expounded in his *Normalkleidung als Gesundheitsschutz* of 1880, found a lifelong advocate in George Bernard Shaw), was similarly advertised as being *patentiert in allen Kulturstaaten*. Even today, a toilet bag or washbag is still called *ein Kulturbeutel* (in Germany, *eine Kulturtasche*).

Oddly, though German is pre-eminently a *Kultursprache* (a language of the civilized world), it does not appear to distinguish between cultured and cultivated – both are rendered as *kultiviert*. Colloquially, someone who eats like a pig, or who cannot keep up a conversation, is said to be lacking in culture: *von Kultur keine Spur**.

For the current *Kulturhoheit* (cultural autonomy) of the German *Länder**, see KOMPETENZ in I.

LAGER n.n. inextricably associated with the concentration camps a generation ago (for instance, in the preface to the 1967 edition of Sternberger, Storz, and Süskind, *Aus dem Wörterbuch des Unmenschen**), but by the 1980s a fashionable political term. *Helmut Kohl denkt in Lagern* (*Die Zeit*, 2 February 1990) means that he has a 'laager' mentality (in its more defensive form, *eine Bunkermentalität*), that is, a notion of what constitutes *das bürgerliche* *Lager* (natural conservative voters) as entrenched as that of the South African Boers. This led to the dismissal, in 1989, of Heiner Geißler, General Secretary of the CDU, whose controversial *Lagertheorie* set out to determine whether the party should swing back to the middle ground, or further to the right of the European Christian Democratic mainstream, in order not to lose potential *Klientel** to the *Republikaner* (*die REPs**). For what the English think of as lager, see BIER in VIII.

LIBERAL adj. neither a home for lost causes nor, as some think, 'the party of beards and jumpers' (Norman Stone, *The Sunday Times*, 16 September 1990), the *Freie Demokratische Partei* (FDP) embodies two very different strands of liberalism. When the great pathologist and anthropologist Rudolf Virchow (1821–1902) led the Liberal opposition against Bismarck, German liberalism was still associated with individual freedom rather than with *laissez-faire* Manchester* liberalism or free-market economics. After 1871, the liberal bourgeoisie was to achieve economic and cultural freedom, but its continuing lack of political freedom seriously inhibited the development of Germany's *politische Kultur**.

Germany's best-known Liberal and for long her most popular politician, Hans-Dietrich Genscher, presided over a cautiously pragmatic foreign policy with the idealism of a Gladstone and the passionate commitment of a Lloyd George, but without the enthusiasm for economic intervention and planning of a Keynes or a Beveridge. The FDP is mainly the party of private enterprise and big business; or, as Lothar Späth put it (*Süddeutsche Zeitung*, 22 August 1987), not a broadly based *Volkspartei** like his own CDU, but *eine aggressive Unternehmerpartei* (a party of aggressive entrepreneurs) with a natural constituency of 'Yuppies', *leistungsorientierte Aufsteiger* (in fact, most Germans profess respect for *Leistung*: performance, achievement, results, output).

When Genscher (as reported on 21 November 1986 in *Die Zeit*, which calls itself *eine liberale Wochenzeitung*, a liberal weekly) warned his fellow Liberals that they would find *kein ruhiges Plätzchen im bürgerlichen** *Lager** (no natural slot in the conservative camp), he meant that conservative policies were *too* 'liberal' – in the English sense of the word. (If not quite in the American sense – quite different from European usage – in which Republicans attack Democrats as 'tax and spend liberals' or 'high-spending, big-government liberals'.) The Berlin Liberals, before deciding to continue their local coalition with the conservative CDU in 1988, warned against its *zunehmenden Hang zu Subventionen und staatlichen Wohltaten* (growing fondness for subsidies and state benefits), and insisted on implementing Liberal policy: *einen Abbau bürokratischer Hemmnisse zugunsten der Wirtschaft* (dismantling bureaucratic obstructions for the good of the economy) and *mehr Chancengleichheit ohne staatlich verordnete*

Gleichmacherei (more equality of opportunity without state-decreed egalitarianism – *Süddeutsche Zeitung*, 17 September 1988). No wonder it was not unusual to see Mrs Thatcher referred to in Germany as *eine Liberale* and in France as the embodiment of *libéralisme* in the sense of free enterprise and financial deregulation (the 1980s' version of the 'permissive society' – see KONZEPT above).

Somewhat paradoxically, given its increasingly precarious hold on the 5% of the vote necessary for parliamentary representation, the FDP has been out of (coalition) government only once, during the grand coalition of the two main parties between 1966 and 1969 (see PRO-PORZ and MANDAT below). Some say this is due to its unprincipled opportunism; party members themselves admit to a deepening *Profil-neurose** after their poor showing in the 1994 Federal elections (and since then even more disastrously at *Land** level, when they crashed out of state legislatures in twelve of the last fourteen elections). They might choose to jump ship again in mid-term as they did in 1982 (see WENDE below), or carve out a new position for themselves during a renewed spell in opposition if the Greens usurp their place as government 'kingmakers' (see under EVANGELISCH and SELBSTBEWUSST in V). Nevertheless, it is fitting that Liberals sit to the right of the conservative CDU and CSU in the *Bundestag*, and that the financial and economic ministries (as well as the foreign ministry) are their traditional preserve.

LISTE n.f. in the German electoral system, the voter has two votes, the first for a candidate, the second for a party list. This second vote (*Zweitstimme*) determines half of the members elected and also the overall proportions of party representation in each fixed-term parliament. The *Liste* drawn up by each party at *Land** level is headed by its best-known politicians, for whom a *Listenplatz* is thus a convenient safety net. (There are no by-elections, vacant seats are simply filled by members of the same party from its list.) A frequent voting tactic is 'splitting one's ticket': *panaschieren* (*panaschierte Blätter* being variegated leaves, *ein Panaschee* a multi-coloured ice or fruit purée). See also PROPORZ below.

MANDAT n.n. either **1.** the authorization or brief which a *Man-dant* (client) gives his lawyer or tax adviser. Or **2.** – as in English mandate – the somewhat elastic concept invented by the League of Nations after the First World War, which had put an end to Germany's belated attempts from 1884 onwards to catch up in the race for colonies (von Bülow made his famous demand for 'a place in the sun', *wir verlangen auch unseren Platz an der Sonne*, in the Reichstag on 6 December 1897).

But also **3**. the mandate a constituency gives its elected representative, that is, an individual parliamentary seat. Accordingly, *ein Mandatsverlust* does not mean that a government has lost its mandate to govern; it is simply a lost seat. *Helmut Schmidt hat 1987 sein Mandat niedergelegt*, Helmut Schmidt resigned his seat in 1987 – he had ceased to be Chancellor in 1982 (see WENDE below). One anomaly of the system of proportional representation is that, though the Liberals* have seldom been out of office in Germany's coalition governments, they have not won a single *Direktmandat* since 1957 (see LISTE and PROPORZ in this section).

MARK n.f. Originally a border country, as in the Welsh marches. *Die Mark Brandenburg* was in the continuous possession of the House of Hohenzollern from 1415 to 1918. Under the more familiar name of Prussia (*Preußen*), it became, in 1871, the dominant power of the newly united Germany of the Second Reich* under the leadership of Bismarck.

Prussian supremacy, which in military terms goes back to the Great Elector (*der Grosse Kurfürst*, Friedrich Wilhelm, who reigned from 1640 to 1688), if not to the Teutonic Knights (*der Deutsche Orden* or *die Deutschherren* of late medieval times), exemplifies the triumph of will-power over geography. The soil is so sandy and infertile that audiences immediately recognize the point of the question asked by the Elector in Kleist's *Prinz Friedrich von Homburg* (1810) on finding his sleep-walking general weaving, somewhat prematurely, a laurel crown: *Wo fand er den in meinem märk'schen Sand?* ('Where did he find laurel growing in my Prussian sand?') On 12 August 1988, *Die Zeit* observed that Potsdamer Platz, formerly the busiest square (with the first traffic lights) in Europe, had once again been reduced to *märkischer Sand* by the Berlin Wall. But the process has been reversed, Potsdamer Platz is now Berlin's biggest building site, adjacent to Hans Scharoun's Philharmonie (1956–63) and Staatsbibliothek Preußischer Kulturbesitz (1964, 1967–78) and Mies van der Rohe's Nationalgalerie (1962–68), and soon to see the realization of plans as ambitious as Schinkel's *Spree-Athen* ('Athens on the Spree') or Speer's futuristic metropolis.

In June 1948, the *Deutsche Mark* became the currency of the German Federal Republic, a reform (still known as *die Währungsreform*) which involved changing 10 old marks (*Reichsmark*) for one new *D-Mark*. When the Russians seized upon the reform as an excuse to close all land routes to West Berlin, the airlift (*Luftbrücke*) which kept the city supplied until the blockade was lifted in April 1949 was the first allied victory in the Cold War (*der kalte Krieg*). The creation of the deutschmark (a term not used by Germans themselves) was the starting-point for the post-war economic miracle (*das Wirtschafts-wunder*); from the early 1960s, when it stood at over DMII to the pound, it steadily strengthened to a rate of DM2.95 when Britain finally stopped 'shadowing the deutschmark' and joined the ERM in 1990, though even this rate proved dramatically unsustainable for the pound in September 1992. The deutschmark had already assimilated the East German currency after the *Währungsunion* on 1 July 1990, when in order to prevent further movements of population to the west (and, economic critics complained, for electoral advantage) every East German was permitted to exchange on average 4,000 eastern Marks into deutschmarks at a rate of one to one.

Comparison between the currencies of West and East Germany (where the official designation was *MDN – Mark der Deutschen Notenbank –* or simply *die Mark*) had inevitably led to the colloquial terms *Westmark* and *Ostmark.* These meant something quite different during the Nazi era, however. Territories which Hitler had 'repatriated' were renamed: after the *Anschluß* on 13 March 1938, Austria (*Österreich*, meaning 'Eastern Reich*') became *die Ostmark* (which it had been in the early Middle Ages), signifying the eastern territories of the Greater German Reich, while *das Saarland* (Saarland), *Elsaß* (Alsace) and *Lothringen* (Lorraine) became part of a notional *West-mark.*

Note that *das Mark* means marrow, often used figuratively in such expressions as *bis ins Mark*, to the core, or *es geht mir durch Mark und Bein* (humorously, *durch Mark und Pfennig*), it goes right through me, sets my teeth on edge.

MASS n.n. not a religious mass (see MESSE in V), or the mass in $e=mc^2$ (see MASSE in III), but either **1.** a tape-measure or rule; or **2.** a measurement; or **3.** moderation.

Matthew 7.2, 'and with what measure ye mete, it shall be measured to you again', becomes in Luther: *und mit welcherlei Maß ihr messet, wird euch gemessen werden*; accordingly, Shakespeare's *Measure for Measure* (his only biblical title) becomes *Maß für Maß*; in the plural, the long 'a' sound in *ihre Maße* (her vital statistics) means they are unlikely to be confused with *ihre Masse** (her bulk).

In the third sense, *Die Zeit* carried the following headline on 7 October 1988: *Kein Maß, kein Mittelmaß.* This punning epitaph on one of Germany's most colourful politicians, Franz Josef Strauß, might be rendered as 'no moderation but no mediocrity'. Another Bavarian, the architect of the *Wirtschaftswunder* Ludwig Erhard, got the balance right as Minister of Economics from 1949 to 1963, but as Chancellor in 1966 failed to implement his belt-tightening electoral slogan: *Maß halten!* ('keep within the bounds of moderation'). He

lost the confidence of the Liberals* in his coalition, the SPD demanded that he ask for a vote of confidence (*die Vertrauensfrage stellen*),
and he duly fell to the *Mißtrauensvotum* (the first time this provision
was enacted in the Federal Republic). Germany nevertheless continued to follow his advice.

Visitors to Munich's *Oktoberfest* may still feel that Bavarians'
consumption of beer is *ohne Maß und Ziel*, immoderate. This is in
part because the Bavarian beermug contains a full litre – the measure
is called, somewhat confusingly, *die Maß* (see MASS in VIII), providing ample opportunity for such puns as *er trinkt Bier in Maßen*. For
the difference between made-to-measure and off-the-peg clothes, see
MASSKLEIDUNG and KONFEKTION in IX.

MAUER n.f. Walter Ulbricht stated on 15 June 1961: *Niemand hat
die Absicht, eine Mauer zu errichten* (Nobody intends to erect a wall*).
As *Die Zeit* observed on 18 August 1989: *nach diesem prophylaktischen
Dementi* stieg die Zahl der Flüchtinge erst recht an* (it was only after
this precautionary denial that the number of refugees really took off).
In fact, plans existed in East Berlin *Tresoren* under the code-word
Chinesische Mauer II (Chinese Wall II) three years before construction began on 13 August 1961. *Mauer-Power**, along with many other
graffiti on the Berlin Wall, ended on 9 November 1989 when the
first East German '*Mauerspechte*' ('Wall-woodpeckers') took up their
hammers to demonstrate the power of the people.

MITTELEUROPA n.n. a concept popularized by Friedrich
Naumann's book of that name (translated in 1915 as *Central Europe*)
and enthusiastically taken up by the Kaiser, signifying a central
Europe under German domination, destined to break the Anglo-
Saxon *Kulturmonopol** and based on what *Reichskanzler* von Bülow
referred to during the Bosnian crisis of 1908/09 as *Nibelungentreue*
(suggesting blood-brotherhood between Germany and Austria,
modelled on the unshakeable loyalty celebrated in the medieval
German epic, *Das Nibelungenlied*, though nowadays more often used
ironically). *Mitteleuropa* was associated after the war, in a less
aggressive form, with Walther Rathenau (see FORMAT above), and is
of renewed relevance since 1989, though for those with long
memories the *Mitteleuropa* of the *Kaffeehaus**, like Middle England,
has disappeared for ever – or into the novels of Milan Kundera.

A sharp distinction needs to be drawn between *Mitteleuropa* and
Mitteldeutschland. The trouble with this term, which Konrad
Adenauer used in the 1950s and 60s to describe the GDR, and which
Helmut Kohl began to use again around 1990 (though by this time it
referred only to Thuringia and Sachsen-Anhalt, not to Saxony,

Brandenburg, or Pomerania), is that it still leaves a putative *Ost-deutschland* somewhere in Poland or the Soviet Union. Since reunification and the recognition of the Oder-Neiße line as Germany's eastern border (after some delay which did little to allay Polish apprehension), German claims on East Prussia or Silesia are confined to fringe exile groups – see HEIMAT above.

NOTSTAND n.m. not a music stand (*ein Notenpult*), but from *Not**(emergency) and *Stand**(situation), hence a state of emergency. Hitler used the Weimar Republic's *Notstandsgesetz* to eliminate parliament in 1933 (the parliamentary *Opposition* thereby finding itself transformed into *Widerstand*, resistance); consequently, the reintroduction of an emergency powers act to deal with terrorists in the 1970s was widely challenged.

NULL n.f. zero or nil, as well as null (*null und nichtig*, null and void). *Nullpunkt* (freezing point, figuratively 'rock bottom') or *die Stunde Null* were the terms most widely used to describe Germany's situation in 1945, somewhat contentiously, since they implied a complete break in historical and political continuity. Looking back, Heinrich Böll was to write: *ich neige dazu, den Nullpunkt auf 33 zu setzen* (I am inclined to see 1933 as the zero point – *Literatur-Magazin* 7, 1977, p. 53). But in 1945 there had been a perceived need, *das Wörterbuch des Unmenschen* abzustoßen, eine diskreditierte Sprache abzustoßen und – auch bei der Sprache wieder – bei Null anzufangen* (to get rid of the inhuman, discredited language and begin again, in language too, with tabula rasa). Theodor Adorno went even further, declaring it impossible to write lyric poetry after Auschwitz (*nach Auschwitz noch Lyrik zu schreiben*). But Böll's novels also show that people who had done quite well out of the Nazi system readily seized on the opportunities of democracy. President Richard von Weizsäcker put a more positive construction on such opportunism in a nicely judged speech marking the fortieth anniversary of the end of the war: *Es gab keine 'Stunde Null', aber wir hatten die Chance zu einem Neubeginn* (There was no 'Zero Hour', but we had the chance to begin afresh) – a chance given when the Americans rejected a proposal of the US Treasury Secretary Morgenthau in 1944 to reduce Germany to a purely agricultural economy, and instead chose to finance reconstruction in 1947 with the plan named after George Marshall, US Secretary of State.

In nuclear disarmament talks (*nukleare Abrüstungsgespräche*), the 'zero option' is *die Null-Lösung* (a term which does not waken memories of Hitler's *Endlösung* or Final Solution). There has been a recent proliferation of such '*Null-*' combinations, as the *Süddeutsche*

Zeitung observed on 29 April 1987: from *Nulltarif* (free admission, free travel, and so on) to the *Nulldiät* by which Chancellor Kohl regularly tries to lose weight (see SPECK in VIII). Even more barbed was the headline in *Die Zeit* shortly before the collapse of the GDR helped the Chancellor revive his flagging fortunes: *Die Null vor dem Komma** (the nought before the decimal point – figuratively, *eine Null* is a dead loss, a nonentity). Adolescents express their apathy to politics, for instance, by saying they have *Null-Bock auf Politik*, a formula so popular that the 'couldn't care less' generation is now known as the *Null-Bock-Generation*.

OSTPOLITIK n.f. though all German leaders, including Hitler, have of necessity had their own *Ostpolitik* ('Eastern policy' or 'policy towards the East'), in practice the term now refers to the normalization of relations with the Soviet Union and its satellite states after 1970.

The preamble to the 1949 Constitution* of the Federal Republic called on the German people 'to achieve in free self-determination the unity and freedom of Germany': *in freier Selbstbestimmung die Einheit und Freiheit Deutschlands zu vollenden*. (The word *Wiedervereinigung*, reunification, was avoided lest it suggest a claim on former German territories.) However, the determination shown by the Russians in putting down the workers' riots in East Berlin in 1953, repressing the Hungarian rebellion of 1956, and destroying the possibility of 'socialism with a human face' in Czechoslovakia in 1968, made West Germans realize it was unlikely that Germany would be united by confrontational methods. At the height of the Cold War, West Germany's relationship with the USSR had stagnated under Adenauer, Erhard and Kiesinger, whose emphasis lay on '*Westpolitik*' (the integration of the FRG into the Western alliance), so it was a breakthrough when Willy Brandt, the first Socialist Chancellor of the FRG, resolved in 1969: *Wir müssen uns auf die Ostpolitik konzentrieren*. This policy was initiated by Brandt's Warsaw Treaty of 1970 and bitterly resisted by the *Unionsparteien**. It replaced their conservative *Hallstein-Doktrin* (which had sought to undermine the East German regime by cutting off aid to any state which officially recognized its legitimacy) by recognizing *de facto*, if not *de jure*, the borders of the GDR and thus its existence as a separate state. Chief negotiator Egon Bahr coined the phrase *Wandel durch Annäherung* ('change through coming closer to each other', that is to say, convergence, rapprochement, as implemented through Brandt's *Politik der kleinen Schritte*).

Though trade credits and humanitarian deals continued after the *Wende**in 1982, many conservatives still opposed paying the price the

East Germans wanted to 'let their people go', and the very word *Ostpolitik* was removed from the 1986 edition of the semi-official (*offiziös**) guide *Tatsachen über Deutschland* (*Facts about Germany*). Arguably, *Ostpolitik* hastened the fall of the East German regime. Nevertheless, shortly before this happened, the newly appointed general secretary of the CDU, Volker Rühe, attacked it in a memorably offensive parody of Bahr as *Wandel durch Anbiederung* (bringing about change by currying favour, toadying to Honecker; see BIEDERMEIER above).

Whatever idealism remained in the Latin tag *ex oriente lux, ex occidente luxus* (from the East comes light, from the West luxury) has disappeared in the more recent version: *ex oriente nix* (from the East: zilch).

PAROLE n.f. a watchword, motto, or political slogan. *Deutschland, einig Vaterland* ('Germany, united fatherland') is a line from the communist poet Johannes R. Becher's text for the national anthem of the GDR. Thought inappropriately nationalistic, it was omitted from the sung version (as were the first two verses of *Deutschland*, Deutschland über alles* in the West) – but when chanted in Dresden by a crowd of 300,000 on 19 December 1989, this *Parole* convinced Helmut Kohl, on his first official visit to the GDR, that reunification was inevitable. See also AKTIVIST and BÜRGERINITIATIVE above.

To release on parole: *auf Bewährung entlassen*.

PASSIV adj. *das passive Wahlrecht* is eligibility to stand for political office (at 25); *das aktive Wahlrecht* is the right to vote (at 18).

POWER adj. poor, derived from and pronounced like French *pauvre*, not English power. The noun *Powerteh* is best known nowadays from the Prussian princess's famous observation to Bismarck: *die Armut kommt von der Powerteh*. This diagnosis was perhaps less fatuous than it sounds. *Die große Armuth in der Stadt kommt von der Powerteh her* ('the great poverty in the city comes from *pauvreté*') is how Inspector Broesig puts it in *Ut mine Stromtid* (1862–4; part 3, chapter 38) by the great *plattdeutsch* (Low German) novelist Fritz Reuter – a rousing condemnation of the total impoverishment or pauperisation of the urban proletariat in Berlin compared with the mere poverty of agricultural workers. And Wolf Biermann, writing in *Die Zeit* on 16 November 1990, had the same '*ausgepowert*' people in mind, *die mit ihrer sozialistischen Planwirtschaft gescheiterten Partei-Chaoten* kriegen die kapitalistische Kurve viel eleganter als die ausgepowerten Proleten* (those party thugs with their failed socialist command economy are taking the bend into capitalism much more smoothly than the impoverished proles).

Die Power, however, like *das Powerplay* of ice-hockey players, is (almost) English: *Gib dem Auto mal ein bißchen Power*, drive a bit faster; as a verb, *powern* colloquially refers to the unscrupulous exercise of power. For *Mauer-power**, see MAUER above.

PROFIL n.n. image, the cultivation of which is known as *Profilierung* (or *Imagepflege*, or even *Image-Kosmetik*); *ein profilierter Politiker* is one who has made his mark, *Profilneurose* the price of failure to do so. When *Die Zeit* reported on 13 May 1988: *die Profilneurose der FDP wird immer akuter*, it meant that the party was no longer sure what it stood for – a crisis of identity which became even more acute after the Liberals'* share of the vote fell from 11 to 6.9 per cent in October 1994.

One's *Qualifikationsprofil* is usually of more substance – the qualifications needed for a job. *Das Profil* is also the tread on a tyre. In Austria, *profil* is a news magazine comparable to *Time* or *Der Spiegel.*

PROMINENZ n.f. VIPS, prominent figures, as in *viel Prominenz war anwesend*, or *die versammelte Prominenz.* In *Se questo è un uomo* (1960), Primo Levi recalled that he, too, once belonged to the *Prominenz*: in Auschwitz. To survive one became 'an *Organisator*, *Kombinator*, *Prominent* (the savage eloquence of these words!)', attached to the gas chambers as part of a *Sonderkommando**, or to the latrines and showers as *Scheißminister* and *Bademeister** – *If this is a man*, 1969, pp. 94–96, 155). It has been memorably said of Levi that, though he survived, he did not 'survive survival', *er hat das Überleben nicht überlebt.*

PROPORZ n.m. Proportional representation. The German electoral system combines *Proporz* or *Proportionalwahl* with the first-past-the-post system of British single-member constituencies. Each voter has two votes: the first for the member of parliament (*der Abgeordnete*) representing the constituency, the second for the competing party lists (see LISTE above) at *Land** level. This second vote determines a party's proportion of the 672 seats in the *Bundestag*. Directly won seats (*Direktmandate**) – that is, half of the 672 – are deducted from the party's proportional entitlement. The other 336 seats are filled from each *Land*'s party lists.

A party has to win at least 5% of the vote to enter parliament – this proviso or *Sperrklausel* (blocking clause) is a pragmatic solution to the fragmentation of parties in the Weimar Republic – or else it must win a minimum of three *Direktmandate*. Initially, in 1949, the *Sperrklausel* meant 5% in each *Land*, but after alterations to the *Grundgesetz* in 1953 and 1956 it now applies nationwide. Exceptionally, in December 1990, the first election after reunification, voters and politicians in the East were granted a localized blocking clause, *um ihre Partei über die Fünf-Prozent-Hürde zu hieven* (to lift their party over the 5% threshold). This dispensation ensured representation for the initially unpopular erstwhile Communist Party, the SED, now renamed PDS. By 1994 the PDS no longer needed preferential treatment, for though they sank below the 5% threshold nationwide, they won four *Direktmandate* *.

Proporz exists in other areas, too: for instance, the representation of the Churches on public bodies such as the *Rundfunkrat* *.

PUNKTUELL adj. or adv. not punctual (*pünktlich*), but signifying a selective approach, dealing only (or in sequence) with selected points: *ein Thema punktuell behandeln*. Consequently, *punktuelle Verkehrskontrollen* are not traffic controls held at some specified time, but, on the contrary, random spot checks.

On 1 May 1990, the *Süddeutsche Zeitung* reported *Oberbürgermeister* * Georg Kronawitter's hope that Munich's newly elected red-green coalition would observe *eine punktuelle Zusammenarbeit mit der FDP*, meaning *ad hoc* cooperation with the Liberals in certain areas (see AMPELKOALITION above). With proportional representation (*Proporz* *) at all levels of government, the Germans sensibly* apply *punktuelle Maßnahmen* (*ad hoc*, pragmatic measures) when *strittige Punkte* occur – points on which the parties hold divergent views.

QUER- in cpds. not queer (see under PUFF in VI and FAGOTT in X for sexual connotations), but diagonal or crossways – at an angle to the norm in a literal sense. Figuratively, *ein Querdenker* (an independent, critical thinker; one who thinks 'against the grain') is a fashionable term for a party intellectual (as is *Vordenker*, a leading intellectual, theorist, strategist, policy-maker; see also *Vorturner* under TURNEN below) and was frequently applied to Kurt Biedenkopf and Heiner Geißler, former general secretaries of the CDU whom Helmut Kohl found too *querköpfig* (awkward) and replaced.

Eine Querflöte is a transverse flute, to distinguish it from *eine Blockflöte*, which is a recorder, but also a recent metaphor for the 'bloc' parties allied to East Germany's ruling SED, to whose tune they danced.

When asking the way: *die erste Querstrasse links* means the first turn on the left, but 'to be in Queer Street' is *pleite sein, blank sein*.

RAF acr. *Rote Armee Fraktion* * (Red Army Faction) – the main urban terrorist group in the 1970s and 80s. The *Bundesamt für Verfassungsschutz* (Office for the Protection of the Constitution – the equivalent of MI5) was then held by many, especially on the left, to be unduly repressive (see BERUFSVERBOT above); but when this Cologne-based agency launched an initiative in 1986 to facilitate '*Aussteiger*' (former terrorists who wished to 'climb out'/leave such organizations as the *RAF*), the new law enabling them to turn State's evidence, *das Kronzeugengesetz*, was initially thwarted by '*Law-and-order-Politiker*' and the *Bundeskriminalamt* (Federal Criminal Police Office).

REALPOLITIK n.f. now as in English, political realism divorced from morality. The term was popularized by Ludwig von Rochau's book, *Grundsätze der Realpolitik* (1853), a criticism of the failure, through excessive idealism, of the German liberals* to achieve their ends in 1848. The point was subsequently made by Bismarck on becoming Chancellor in September 1862, when he offered Wilhelm I a choice between *königliches Regiment* oder Parlamentsherrschaft*, 'rule by king or by parliament' ('I am first and foremost a royalist', a Prussian second, and only then a German', Bismarck declared in 1881, underlining his anachronistically entrenched loyalty to the House of Hohenzollern); and again in a speech a week later to the budget committee of the Prussian *Landtag*, outlining his pro-gramme for German unification under the King of Prussia. This would be achieved, he said, not by *Preußens Liberalismus* but by *Eisen und Blut*, 'iron and blood' (Keynes, prophetically outlining *The Economic Consequences of the Peace* in 1919, reminded his readers that 'the German Empire was more truly built on coal and iron than on blood and iron'). After 'dropping the pilot' in 1890 (the German title of the famous Punch cartoon would be *Der Lotse verläßt das Schiff*), the new Emperor, Wilhelm II, rapidly moved away from Bismarck's *Realpolitik*, especially neglecting his efforts to keep France and Russia apart and thus avoid a future war on two fronts (Bismarck's '*cauchemar des coalitions*').

The Federal Republic's *Ostpolitik* from the late 1960s onwards is often described as *realpolitisch* – based on a shrewd assessment of what the other side wants. Some even claim that the *Bundes-verfassungsgericht* has introduced *Realpolitik* into its constitutional* deliberations. When a more strongly negative term is needed, the Germans talk of *Machtpolitik* (Might is Right) – the sort of power politics which, Bismarck told the Reichstag in 1887, was 'not a policy based on national interest; it is seeking only prestige. We will not do that.' Unfortunately, his successors did.

REICH n.n. any dominion or realm, originally, and usually still, under some high authority – figurative (*das Reich der Träume*, the world of dreams) as well as territorial (*Königreich*, kingdom, as well as *Kaiserreich*, empire). The occasional German reference to Britain as *das Inselreich*, for instance, is not an ironic allusion to her lost empire, but simply to the 'island kingdom' (an image of Britain which matches her perceived lack of enthusiasm for Europe, of course). Unfortunately, the same cannot be said of the spectre conjured up by British allusions to a German 'Fourth Reich'.

Germany's imperial history began gloriously, if somewhat inadvertently, when Pope Zachary rewarded the Franconian* Charlemagne for his military aid by crowning him, to Charlemagne's surprise, 'Emperor of the Romans' on Christmas Day 800. But it was only in 1486 that what had hitherto been known as *diutisciu lant* (*die deutschen Lande*) acquired the rather fanciful and paradoxical title *das Heilige Römische Reich Deutscher Nation* (the Holy Roman Empire of the German Nation), which officially lasted until 1806. When we now say Reich, however, we think either of the newly-united Germany from 1871 to 1918 (the 'Second Reich'), or under Hitler from 1933 to 1945 (the 'Third Reich'). Though the intervening Weimar Republic was neither a kingdom nor, after Versailles, an empire, Duden's definition of *Reich* as *der deutsche Nationalstaat von 1871 bis 1945* suggests a continuity, if only in the use of the word. Long before the modern *Reich* existed, Goethe and Schiller, in an epigram entitled *Das Deutsche Reich* from the collected *Xenien* of 1796, pinpointed that fateful and recurrent gulf between, on the one hand, the geographical and cultural extent of the German lands, and on the other, political reality: *Deutschland? aber wo liegt es? Ich weiß das Land nicht zu finden. / Wo das gelehrte beginnt, hört das politische auf.* ('Germany? but where is it? I do not know where this country is to be found. Where learned Germany begins, political Germany ceases.')

The fact that the East Germans continued to call their railway the *Reichsbahn* suggests that they did not consider the word *Reich* politically 'contaminated'.

REP abbr. not a commercial representative (*ein Handelsvertreter*), but a member of the right-wing political party *die Republikaner*, support for which caused some alarm in the 1980s. Much of their thunder was stolen by the events of 1989, when Oskar Lafontaine characterized their declining impact as a *Repsodie in Schwarz**, 'Rhapsody in Black' (*Süddeutsche Zeitung*, 7 October 1989 – a pun which catches the exaggeratedly clipped vowel sounds some Germans still think of as 'correct' English). Not to be confused with those who came to be called *Vernunftrepublikaner* ('rational republicans') in the 1920s – well-educated Germans like the historian Friedrich Meinicke, who, though convinced that Germany was simply not ripe for parliamentary democracy (*Ausgewählter Briefwechsel*, 1962, p. 138), discarded 'the ballast of conservative ideas' and learnt to live with, if not to love, the Weimar Republic (Peter Gay, *Weimar Culture*, 1968, p. 24).

RESTAURATION n.f. the restoration – not of the English monarchy in 1660, but of the French after Napoleon's defeat, and the return to the *status ante quo* elsewhere. In Germany and Austria a time of ultraconservatism: *die Restauration der alt und fromm gewordenen Romantiker* (Jürgen Habermas, *Die Moderne*, 1990, p. 143), for instance, refers to the fact that so many of the enlightened thinkers of the Romantic generation later converted to Catholicism. Also known as *Biedermeier**, or else *Vormärz*, that is, as taking place before the European revolutions which began in March 1848. Heinrich Böll frequently referred to the years after the currency reform in 1948 as *eine Restaurationszeit* – by which he meant a restoration of many of what he saw as the wrong German values. See also NULL above and RESTAURATION in VIII.

RUCK n.m. a sudden jolt or movement, rather than the brawl permitted in rugby. In politics, *ein Ruck* is a swing or shift (*nach rechts* or *nach links*); this in turn might galvanize the government into action, jolt it out of its complacency: *der Regierung einen Ruck geben*. Thus, *ein Ruck* is often a forward motion, whereas the many combinations of *Rück-* signify backward, reverse, or behind. Note also: *Hau-ruck-Politiker* (from *hau ruck* meaning 'heave-ho', 'altogether now') – politicians who are none too subtle in their methods.

RUMOREN v. not to circulate rumours, *Gerüchte in Umlauf setzen*; or to be rumoured, *es geht das Gerücht* (it is rumoured from Bonn, *gerüchtweise verlautet aus Bonn*); but to make a noise, usually a dull, rumbling sound, like distant thunder: *es rumort in meinem Magen*, my stomach is rumbling; *er rumort noch in der Küche herum*, he can still be heard pottering about in the kitchen. Less common as a noun, though even louder, *ein Rumor* is a din or racket.

Figuratively, to cause a stir, go through one's mind, go round and round in one's head: *in seinem Kopf rumorte nur ein Gedanke*, a single thought preoccupied him. Or else, picking up on the threatening or foreboding nature of the sound, used of unrest among people. In Rüdiger Safranski's biography of Schopenhauer (1987), for instance, the section entitled *Es rumort zwischen Mutter und Sohn* tells of the pessimistic and misogynous philosopher's rumbling quarrels with his socialite mother, a writer of best-selling novels. *Es rumort im Volke* means there are mutterings among the people, 'the population is growing restive'. Thus, though the German Question had ostensibly been solved with *kleindeutsch* unification (excluding Austria), population growth from 38 million in 1871 to 64 million in 1914 ensured that the question of further expansion in fact rumbled on behind the scenes: *tatsächlich rumorte sie im historischen Untergrund weiter* (Imanuel Geiss, *Die deutsche Frage 1806–1990*, 1992, p. 48).

RUSS n.m. soot, or else 'Russky' (an abbreviation of *der Russe*, as in the jingoistic 1914 catch-phrase recorded by Karl Kraus in Act I, Scene I of *Die letzten Tage der Menschheit*, 1922: *a jeder Ruß – an Schuß! a jeder Franzos – an Stoß! a jeder Britt – an Tritt!*). But the headline in the *Süddeutsche Zeitung* on 28 January 1989, *DER RUSS MUSS RAUS*, did not mean 'Russians go home'; it merely introduced an article on cleaning chimneys.

SCHRECKEN n.m. what might produce a shriek (*ein Schreckensschrei*): either a fright/scare (also *der Schreck: mir sitzt/steckt der Schreck noch in allen Knochen/Gliedern*, my knees are still like jelly); or else horror/terror (*das Gleichgewicht des Schreckens* is the balance of terror).

With his translation of Psalm 73 v.19 (on the consolation felt by the pious at the fate of the ungodly) – *Sie gehen unter und nehmen ein Ende mit Schrecken!* – Luther introduced a phrase into the language which has had a particular resonance in our own day. Thus Kafka's Gregor Samsa, deluding himself at the beginning of section II of *Die Verwandlung* (1912; see also MIST in III, SCHULD in V) on the peace and prosperity he believes he has brought his family, is nevertheless granted a momentary insight into his terrible fate: *Wie aber, wenn jetzt alle Ruhe, aller Wohlstand, alle Zufriedenheit ein Ende mit Schrecken nehmen sollte?* Similarly, as *der große Stumpfsinn* (the great stupor) envelops the Magic Mountain, Hans Castorp senses the impending thunderclap of the First World War, *der der 'Sauregurkenzeit** *einen schrecklichen Jüngsten Tag bereiten werde . . . ein Ende mit Schrecken** (see HOSPITANT and INGENIEUR in IV, and with the balmy summer of 1914 in mind, SOMMERTHEATER below). It was in anticipation of even more sinister horrors that Thomas Mann ended his premonitory tale *Mario und der Zauberer* in 1930 by focusing on the sense of liberation felt when the humiliated waiter Mario shoots his hypnotist-cum-demagogue tormentor: *Ein Ende mit Schrecken, ein höchst fatales** *Ende. Und ein befreiendes Ende dennoch.*

Major Ferdinand von Schill had Germany's liberation in mind when, on 12 May 1809 in the market-place at Arneburg on the Elbe, during his single-handed war against the French, he expanded the phrase into the stirringly patriotic, anti-Bonapartist rallying cry:

Lieber ein Ende mit Schrecken als Schrecken ohne Ende. When Goebbels noted these same words in his diary on 27 March 1945, however, it was by way of explaining why the attrition of Allied bombing had extinguished all hope of German civilian resistance in the West. His compatriots clearly felt differently about the 'horrors' of capitulation to the *Amis**, but the maxim does at least explain his own suicide *en famille* a month later. British newspapers picked up the same formulation from interviews during East Germany's disintegration and the accelerated process of reunification which ensued, variously rendering it as 'Better a painful end than an endless worry' (*The Independent*, 17 March 1990) or 'An end with horror is always preferable to horror without end' (*The Times*, 17 August 1990). In the event, there was mercifully little horror (see BÜRGER-INITIATIVE above), though subsequently also less conviction that 'it's best to get unpleasant things over and done with' (see VER-FASSUNGSPATRIOTISMUS below).

SCHWARZ adj. black, symbolizing either Roman Catholic or conservative, usually both. *Zwischen Osnabrück und Münster, da wird es finster* is an allusion to the cities' ecclesiastical traditions (Bishop Graf Galen of Münster was something of a hero during the war), as is one witty declension of the adjective: *schwarz, Münster, Paderborn* (black, blacker, blackest – see KONFESSION in V). So, 'true blue, Cheltenham, Tunbridge Wells' would only be a partial equivalent since, outside *Brideshead Revisited*, the two strands are less often linked in England. The phrase *der schwarze Süden* now evokes primarily the political conservatism of the southern *Länder** of Baden-Württemberg and Bavaria – and, since reunification, of Saxony too (though it was once known as *das rote Sachsen* – see *Wendehals* under WENDE below). Further south still, *schwarz-gelb* (black-and-yellow) designated patriots whose allegiance was primarily to the Habsburg dynasty.

Blue is not the colour of German conservatism, then, though when Goethe remarked on Byron's death in 1824: *Ich bin niemals rot gewesen wie Lord Byron; mein Kolorit von Hause aus war immer anderer Art, etwa ein artiges Blau* (I was never red like Lord Byron; my colouring from the start was of a different kind: a pleasant shade of blue, perhaps), he may have been thinking of his patrician background and innate abhorrence of revolutionary excesses (in contrast to the red-blooded Byron). Oddly enough, in his own theory of colours (*Zur Farbenlehre*, 1810) it is red which symbolizes divine bliss as the intensified culmination (*Steigerung*) of the polar opposites, yellow and blue. But for most people, blue is the colour of German Romanticism – a movement from which Goethe increasingly distanced himself – and is associated with the infinite blue of sea and sky, or the elusive *blaue Blume* (the archetypal symbol of yearning in Novalis' novel *Heinrich von Ofterdingen* – see FATAL in V). Also SCHWARZ- in I and BLAU in VIII.

SKANDIEREN v. the scansion of verse, but perhaps more frequently used nowadays to mean the rhythmic chanting of political slogans (*Parolen**) at demonstrations or rallies.

SOGENANNT adj. attr. so-called. Newspapers controlled by Axel Springer, such as *Bild* and *Die Welt*, invariably referred either to *die sogenannte DDR*, or else to *die 'DDR'* (the so-called German Democratic Republic), thus demonstrating their hostility to the spirit of *Ostpolitik**.

With a much more contentious usage, *die sogenannte Judenvernichtung des Dritten Reiches* (the so-called annihilation of the Jews), Ernst Nolte recently sparked off an ill-tempered debate between historians of the Left and the Right, turning on the question whether Hitler was evil *sui generis* or merely reacting to a genuinely perceived Bolshevik threat (*'Gulag vor Auschwitz'*) – thereby, according to Jürgen Habermas, relativizing the evil of the Third Reich (Nolte, *Zwischen Geschichtslegende und Revisionismus?*, 1980; Habermas, *Eine Art Schadensabwicklung. Die apologetischen Tendenzen in der deutschen Geschichtsschreibung*, 1986; both in the documentation published by Piper Verlag in 1987 as *'Historikerstreit'*, esp. p. 33).

SOMMERTHEATER n.n. the 'silly season' in politics and journalism during July and August when parliament is closed (in Italy, *governo balneare*, seaside government). Also known as *das Sommerloch** or *die Sauregurkenzeit** (see SCHRECKEN above, and for summer festivals, FEST in VIII).

SPENDEN v. not to spend money (*Geld ausgeben*), but to make a donation. This distinction was somewhat obscured in the *Parteispendenaffäre*, when the Flick Organization enterprisingly, if illegally, tried to buy political influence through generous *Spenden*, not just to one, but to to all the main political parties. Rather than being publicly declared (as required by law in Germany) some of these contributions were 'laundered' in a *Spendenwaschanlage*, that is to say, made indirectly in order to avoid taxation – a dodge more familiar to English readers. Subsequently, the Greens unsuccessfully attempted to list their *Diäten** (parliamentary allowances) as *Spenden* to party funds in order to qualify for maximum *Wahlkampfkostenerstattung von der Staatskasse** (election campaign expenses from public funds). Even Graf Zeppelin, as *Die Zeit* informed its readers on 7 July 1989, had only been able to continue making his *Luftschiffe* after the crash of 1908 by recourse to a *Volksspende* (public contributions). *Ein Spender*, however, is not a (big) spender, but a machine or receptacle such as a *Honigspender* (honey dispenser). See also SPENDIEREN in VIII.

STURM n.m. storm or gale, but also assault or attack. Figurative and literal Nazi usage ranges from Julius Streicher's noxious anti-Jewish tabloid, *Der Stürmer*, to the rogue *Sturmabteilung* (*SA*) of Hitler's old *Duzfreund* Ernst Röhm, purged along with his brown-shirted *Sturmtruppen* (Storm Troopers) at Bad Wiessee on 30 June 1934, 'the Night of the Long Knives'.

Jürgen Klinsmann is also *ein Stürmer* – an attacker or striker. An unassailable military position is *sturmfrei**, and consequently a room where one can do as one pleases is known as *eine sturmfreie Bude*. For *Sturm und Drang*, see STRESS in VII.

SUBJEKT n.n. whereas Frederick the Great expected unquestioning obedience from his *Subjekte*, Hegel developed the view a generation later that only those who understood the state's policies were *Subjekte*. Marx adapted this notion of the autonomous *Subjekt* to his theory of class conflict, and many East Germans felt in October 1989 that they were at last *Subjekte*, shaping their own history. Alas, economic forces in the newly united Germany ensured they remained its *Objekte*.

They are, of course, *Bürger**, citizens (the more official word is *deutsche Staatsangehörige*) and not 'subjects' in the English sense. The word Germans associate with a 'devoted* subject', and use only ironically, is *der Untertan*, which is the title of Heinrich Mann's novel (1911) ridiculing a middle-class 'Man of Straw' (the novel's English title – see ROMAN in X) and his smug, misplaced subservience to the Kaiser. West Germans may have grown genuinely loyal to the constitution (see VERFASSUNGSPATRIOTISMUS below), but those in the east had become accustomed to being put down in the battle against authority, or of ducking under, and thus acquired *eine Untertanenmentalität*; as Jochen Gauck, the parson-politician in charge of the dissolution of the *Stasi* network, pointed out to *Die Zeit* on 27 July 1990: *Der DDR-Bürger hat ein Manko an Ich-Stärke und Selbstbewußtsein**. *Untertanenmentalität prägt seine Seele bis in die Gesichtszüge hinein*. (The citizen of the GDR lacks self-confidence and a firm sense of self. Servility leaves its mark on his soul, on his very features.) By contrast, only a Mozart would think to rhyme *dero gehorsamster unterthänigster diener* ('Your most obedient and humble servant') with *mein arsch ist kein Wiener* (in a charmingly lewd letter to his favourite cousin or '*Bäsle*' on 10 May 1779 – see BASE in VI). In the eyes of his first employer, Archbishop Hieronymus Colloredo, Mozart was *ein Subjekt* in its other, pejorative, modern sense – a dubious character, a shady customer, not to say *ein verkommenes Subjekt*, debauched. Note also *Rechtssubjekt* under RECHT in I, and the special East German sense of *Objekt* in IX.

TRABANT n.m. figuratively, *Trabanten* is a rather old-fashioned word for the children in one's charge. The 'vivacious lady book-keeper, open for new experience' who advertised in the *Heiraten* (Marriage) column of *Die Zeit* on 15 September 1989: *Buchhalterin, 36, plus 2 Trabanten, Raum 6, lebenslustig, offen für Neues*, was not offering two Trabant cars as an enticement, but two 'kiddie-winks' – the automotive equivalent being '*unser Trabbi*' (less fondly: *Asphaltblase, Pappe*, Plasteschüssel*, Plastepanzer*), whose two-stroke lawnmower engine infringed every known *Paragraph** of West German emission control laws. *Raum 6* refers to postal code 6 – since reunification 60 – namely Frankfurt (the postal districts move in an anti-clockwise direction from Berlin which is 10, and Hamburg 20, to Munich 80, Nürnberg 90, and Dresden 01). Finally, it is also likely that the lady had recently arrived from the GDR – a *Trabantenstaat* or satellite state of the USSR.

This is an emotive word. In a speech after launching the Tirpitz at Wilhelmshaven on 1 April 1939, Hitler turned his attention to the Poles, to whom he had recently offered condominium over Slovakia. At this point, as Karl-Heinz Janssen notes in *Die Zeit* on 25 August 1989, *fällt ihm nur noch das verächtliche Wort 'Trabantenstaat' ein* (the only word he can find for Poland is the contemptuous one: *Trabantenstaat*).

TRANSPARENT n.n. a banner with a political slogan (*eine Parole**), as well as a transparency (*Transparentpapier* is used *zum Pausen**, for tracing). Transparency as a quality is *die Transparenz*, and the call for *mehr Transparenz* refers to more openness in government, decision-making, etc. On the other hand, suspect motives or transparent lies are described as *durchschaubar*. The normal adjective is *durchsichtig* (*eine durchsichtige Bluse*, see-through blouse) rather than *transparent*.

TURNEN v. *wenden* or *drehen* means to turn, *sich wenden* or *sich umdrehen* to turn around, but *turnen* is even more specific: to do gymnastics (also to climb skilfully over obstacles, or – of a child – to romp). Hence, *die Turnhalle*, gymnasium; *Turnschuhe*, gym shoes, sneakers; *die Turnhose*, PT shorts. The *Vorturner*, gymnastic coach, can also occur in the political sphere: in the 1970s, for instance, the leader of the SPD in the *Bundestag*, Herbert Wehner, was often referred to as the *Vorturner der SPD-Fraktion** (see also *Vordenker* and *Querdenker* under QUER above).

In 1811, while Prussians were still prevented from taking arms against Napoleon, *'Turnvater'* Jahn (Ludwig Jahn, the 'Grand Old Man of Gymnastics') first channelled the patriotic energies of young Berlin *Gymnasiasten**and university students into gymnastic displays. *Turnvereine* (gymnastic clubs) subsequently joined the *Burschenschaften* (student fraternities) in opposition to internal repression and censorship (the Carlsbad decrees of 1819), culminating in the famous festival of gymnastics and singing at the 'Romantic' ruined castle of Hambach in 1832 (the *Hambacher Fest** was Germany's response to the revolutions in France and Belgium), and in the 1840s becoming increasingly *völkisch**.

ÜBERHANG n.m. beware of 'overhang' in the combination *Überhangsrecht**: your neighbour's right to cut off branches of your tree hanging into his garden (though never on a Sunday: most Germans agree with Hegel that conformity is the ultimate freedom). An *Überhangsmandat** is merely a figurative 'overhang' – a directly elected parliamentary seat over and above the proportion allocated to a party – an occasional anomaly in the German voting system which explains why there may sometimes be more than the 672 MPs elected in 1994 (see LISTE and PROPORZ above).

Though German is famously fond of compound nouns, often made by adding a verb to an adverb, it has few such mirror-image compounds as outbreak/breakout, layout/outlay or upturn/turn-up, and fewer still with identical meanings such as onlooker/looker-on, outlook/lookout or uptake/take-up. Accordingly, a German hangover is not an *Überhang* but *ein Katzenjammer* ('caterwaul') or *ein Kater* ('tomcat') – for remedies, see MUSKELKATER in VIII.

ÜBERSEHEN v. not what an overseer does (*ein Aufseher beaufsichtigt* or *überwacht*, oversees, supervises), but either **1**. to command a view of a landscape, etc. (more commonly, *überschauen*), or have an overall view of a subject (*eine Übersicht* or *ein Überblick* – the US 'overview' is probably a germanicism); or else **2**. to overlook in its opposite sense of failing to see something (an accidental oversight is not *eine Übersicht*, but *ein Versehen*). As in English, this may also be deliberate – the Emperor Sigismund, for instance, agreed with Nelson: *wer nicht übersehen und überhören** kann, taugt nicht zum Regieren* (whoever does not know how to turn a blind eye or a deaf ear is not fit to rule).

No longer much used as a separable verb meaning 'to see something overmuch' (*davon habe ich genug gesehen*), to get tired of seeing it, though one does still use it reflexively in this sense: *den Film habe ich mir übersehen.* 'He couldn't see enough of her', however, becomes *er konnte sich an ihr nicht satt sehen.*

UNION n.f. in politics, refers to the two *Unionsparteien* (those with the word *Union* in their names) – the conservative *Christlich-Demokratische Union* and its Bavarian sister-party, the *Christlich-Soziale Union*, with *Die Junge Union* the equivalent of the Young Conservatives. Just as the CDU was dominated, first by Konrad Adenauer (see '*Kanzlerwahlverein*' under KANZLER in I), then by Helmut Kohl, the CSU was long the fiefdom of Franz Josef Strauß (see FALL and MASS above, SENIOR in I), who in the late 1970s unsuccessfully attempted to establish it nationwide. When this threat recurred before the 1990 election, Helmut Kohl warned his old rival's successor: *Wenn die CSU in der DDR kandidiert, dann wird die CDU in Bayern kandidieren* (If the CSU puts up candidates in the GDR, the CDU will put up candidates in Bavaria). To have two separate parties is regarded by many as a political ruse to give them more weight than they would have taken together.

UNMENSCH n.m. not an 'un-person' in Orwell's sense. This would be *eine Unperson*, whereas it is those who rule in totalitarian regimes, not their victims (see OPFER in V), who are the *Unmenschen* (brutes, monsters) – though not, of course, in their own view or language. The prostitution of language under the Nazis is comprehensively recorded by Sternberger, Storz, and Süskind under the title *Aus dem Wörterbuch des Unmenschen* (first published 1945). The fact that this particular association has lapsed with time was illustrated by a recent brush with a Bavarian official over an *Aufenthaltserlaubnis* (residence permit) which ended with the conciliatory phrase: *ich bin kein Unmensch* ('I'm not an ogre'); harassed officials, one was told, *haben Unmenschliches geleistet*, worked wonders, achieved the impossible (dealing with ever-growing floods of refugees). The term predates the Nazis: the official was not suffering from political amnesia but simply drawing on a long linguistic tradition.

He might equally have said *Übermenschliches*: both adjectives can mean 'superhuman', though more commonly they mean different things, and the nouns invariably so. Nietzsche, for instance, described Napoleon as *diese Synthesis von Unmensch und Übermensch* (*Zur Genealogie der Moral*, 1,16), but for Nietzsche the real opposite of the Superman is the herd, and it was the Germans of the Second

Reich he had in mind, though he did not call them *Untermenschen.* This still offensive term came into use only during the 'supermania' of the Third Reich.

Finally, *der Mensch* itself: a word which does not automatically convey the Yiddish sense of a humane* person or fully paid-up member of the human race contained in the advice given to Jack Lemmon as a supposed philanderer in Billy Wilder's film *The Apartment*: 'Be a mensch, Baxter'. It comes close, though, when Sarastro assures his fellow priests that Tamino is not merely a Prince – *Noch mehr, er ist Mensch.* Yet this famous line should not be taken as evidence of any democratic sentiment in *Die Zauberflöte,* but rather of the innate nobility with which Tamino, unlike the *Naturmensch* Papageno, is endowed. In addition, as Nicholas Till has shown (*Mozart and the Enlightenment,* 1992, pp. 270–319), '*Mensch*' was part of the esoteric Rosicrucian symbolism which drew Mozart into membership of the aristocratic masonic lodge, *Zur neugekrönten Hoffnung* (whereas Haydn joined *Zur wahren Eintracht,* the standard-bearer of the secular enlightenment in Vienna). For *das Mensch* ('cow', 'slut'), see MENSCH in VI.

VERFASSUNGSPATRIOTISMUS n.m. not a false friend, but an important, if slightly elusive, concept, given that Britain has no written constitution. It is little wonder that many post-war Germans, having been utterly betrayed by their erstwhile leaders and living in a divided country, transferred their allegiance to the *Grundgesetz* – one of the most liberal constitutions ever adopted and implemented by a nation – and came to see the *freiheitlich-demokratische Grundordnung* it prescribed as a proper focus for their patriotic feelings. Where Heine in 1844 had diagnosed *Vaterlandsliebe* (patriotism) as a sickness, *eine Krankheit im Grunde,* he had also anticipated something akin to *Verfassungspatriotismus* with a vision of German thought and its theory of liberty winning hearts and minds throughout the world (while countering expansionist tendencies), thereby providing a basis for civil society everywhere: *das ist mein Patriotismus.*

Individual articles in the constitution periodically become a topic for debate in the Federal Republic. Very schematically, where the Establishment claims it is upholding and protecting the constitution, others see such 'protection' as a way of distorting and subverting it, and have taken its defence upon themselves. The resultant strategies (where even the terrorists of the *RAF** paid lip service to the constitution) have been diverse and complex (see BERUFSVERBOT above). Jürgen Habermas has argued that the main post-war achievement of the Federal Republic has been its total assimilation of Western political thought as enshrined in the constitution, precisely because it has supplanted *die Ideologie der Mitte* – the belief that Germany occupies, culturally and politically as well as geographically, a central position between East and West (a view which Thomas Mann expounded at great length during the First World War and which revisionist historians seemed set to revive – see KULTUR and SO- GENANNT above and the documentation published by Piper Verlag in 1987 as '*Historikerstreit*', p. 75). Unlike such manifestations of *Hurrapatriotismus* as 'for king and country' or 'my country, right or wrong', *Verfassungspatriotismus* suggests unjingoistic respect for the universal ideas embedded in the constitution, including the private pursuit of happiness (the Enlightenment values on which, according to Habermas, the German bourgeoisie had turned its back for two centuries). When those who resisted instant reuni- fication were attacked in the popular press as *vaterlandslose Gesellen* ('unpatriotic wretches' – Bismarck's term for the Socialists), Günter Grass responded in *Die Zeit* on 5 October 1990: *So habe ich mich bis heute als Verfassungspatriot begriffen. In seiner Machtfülle wird der neue Staat einen solchen Patrioten kaum vermissen.* (I always thought of myself up to now as one whose loyalty is to the constitution. The new all-powerful state will hardly miss a patriot like me.) But other, younger writers, such as the playwright Botho Strauss, have begun to align themselves with the more traditional brand of patriotism.

'*Währungspatriotismus*', while not yet in the dictionary, describes a very different form of loyalty, founded on equally solid values, though values of a different kind. It was clearly felt by a German friend who experienced difficulties in developing a sense of national identity in the early sixties: *meine Heimat* ist der Geltungsbereich der D-Mark West* (I am at home wherever the D-Mark is operative) – a sentiment reflected in the question the magazine* *Stern* recently put to a leading conservative politician: *Herr Schäuble, muß nicht auch die Union* dem Währungspatriotismus der Deutschen Rechnung tragen, die ihre D-Mark behalten wollen?* – should not the CDU and CSU take into account the 'loyalty to the currency' of those Germans who want to retain their D-Mark (no. 41, 1992, p. 45). The German government's enthusiasm for a single European currency must seem all the more striking to English readers who in the same thirty-year period have seen their pound shrink to less than one fifth of its former value vis-à- vis the D-Mark (see MARK above).

VITAMIN B n.n. '*B*' for *Beziehungen* (connections). *Um diese Stelle zu bekommen, brauchst du Vitamin B* is a jocular expression suggesting that you will need to pull strings to get the job, but the healthily open nature of German society ensures that there is nothing comparable to the Italian system of *clientelismo*. Surviving remnants of the old-boy network that ruled East Germany are widely known as *eine Seilschaft* (roped party), a mountain climbers' term which, since reunification, lends credence to Dr Johnson's dictum that those who do not hang together will surely hang separately (but see EXEKUT-IEREN in I). For the old-boy networks which have grown up around student fraternities, see KORPORATION in IV.

VOGELFREI adj. not free as a bird, but, in the Middle Ages, free for the birds – as potential *Vogelfutter* ('bird food', carrion), outlawed.

VOLK n.n. certain combinations, such as *Volksgerichtshof* (the Nazi Roland Freisler's notorious 'People's Court') or *Volksschädlinge* (the law of November 1938 branding Jews 'parasites on the *Volk*', which excluded them from most economic activities and imposed a huge collective fine), were coined by the Nazis and are now, of course, taboo. Some still echo their Nazi past, such as *Volksgemeinschaft* ('national/tribal community'), *Volksgenossen* ('fellow Germans'), even the adjective *völkisch*. Others less so, such as the nationalist *Volksstaat* (nation state) – supposedly the result of harmonizing abstract laws with a 'sovereign' *Volksgeist** (the 'spirit of the people', out of which, according to Herder in the late eighteenth century, language, laws, and customs develop organically).

East Germany, which disclaimed all responsibility for the Third Reich, had no hesitation in calling its parliament the *Volkskammer*, its policemen *Volkspolizisten* or '*Vopos*', and its army the *Nationale Volksarmee* (*NVA*), as befitted a true *Volksrepublik* (people's republic); nor in defining *das gesunde Volksempfinden* ('healthy public feeling') – what every decent citizen should feel. Disagreement on this point on 17 June 1953 prompted the Secretary of the GDR Writers' Union to distribute leaflets which proclaimed *daß das Volk das Vertrauen der Regierung verscherzt habe* (that the people had lost the confidence of the government). Brecht, who had declined to support the revolt, suggested a solution in his poem *Die Lösung* (published shortly after in the journal *Sinn und Form* as one of the *Bukower Elegien*): *Wäre es da / Nicht doch einfacher, die Regierung / Löste das Volk auf und / Wählte ein anderes?* ('Would it not be easier for the government simply to dissolve the people and choose another one?')

When the actual voice of the people (*das Volksbegehren*) was first heard in the GDR, it declared: *WIR sind das Volk* ('*We* are the people'). The swift transition from this defiant call for democratic socialism within East Germany to a more strident *Parole**demanding reunification of the two Germanies: *Wir sind EIN Volk* ('We are *one* people') caused some apprehension among those who advocated regionalism and European integration in place of the nation state. See AKTIVIST and BÜRGERINITIATIVE above.

See also *Volkstrauertag* under KARNEVAL in VIII, *Volkshochschule* under HOCHSCHULE in IV.

WELSCH adj. not Welsh (*walisisch*; a Welshman is *ein Waliser*) but either **1.** as applied uncensoriously to *Welschschweizer*, French-speaking inhabitants of *Welschland* (French-speaking Switzerland; more commonly, *die französische Schweiz*); or **2.** a derogatory term for Italians, Spaniards and the French (see AMIS in I). This goes back to Walther von der Vogelweide, who accused the Pope of wishing that *ir tiuschez silber vert in mînen welschen schrîn* ('that their German silver gets into my Roman coffers'). There is no doubt which nation Wagner had in mind at the end of *Die Meistersinger von Nürnberg* (1868), when Hans Sachs forcefully rejects the 'foreign (French) fripperies polluting German lands' – *und welschen Dunst mit welschem Tand | sie pflanzen uns in deutsches Land* – in favour of good solid German virtues (see MEISTER in III), a familiar appeal to *Kultur**as the authentic force for German unification. Stefan George, whose 'cultural' credentials are hardly less impressive, nevertheless found *er kann nicht schwärmen | von heimischer Tugend und welscher Tücke* ('he cannot enthuse over indigenous virtue and alien vice' – *Der Krieg*, written during the Great War, published in *Das Neue Reich*, 1928). But Eduard Engel's popular *Entwelschung: Verdeutschungswörterbuch*, first published in 1917 and dedicated to the cleansing of the German language, showed what way the wind was blowing.

Note also *Kauderwelsch*, double-dutch, and *Rotwelsch*, the argot of the underworld. 'To welsh/welch' on something: *sich vor etwas drücken*; on someone: *jemanden sitzen lassen*.

WENDE n.f. a change or turning point – in politics, the term was applied initially to the decision of Hans-Dietrich Genscher's liberal* FDP in 1982 to withdraw support from the socialist SDP of Helmut Schmidt in favour of the conservative CDU/CSU, thereby making Helmut Kohl (who proclaimed *eine geistig*-moralische Wende*) Chancellor without an election being held. Now mainly used of the events of 1989; for the former citizens of the GDR this was, of course, the only *Wende* (while in 1991 the word *Wendehals*, turncoat, was chosen by *Die Zeit* as the 'Wort des Jahres').

WINDEN v. used reflexively, to writhe in pain or squirm with embarrassment, as when Theo Sommer warned of the post-*Wende**

danger: *daß die neue Führung sich windet, anstatt den Lauf der Dinge wirklich zu wenden*, 'that the new leadership might wriggle and squirm, rather than really try to change things' (*Die Zeit*, 27 October 1989). In which connection the adjective *windig* (windy – Salzburg, like Chicago, is *eine windige Stadt*) has an apt additional sense when used of a person or thing: dubious, untrustworthy (*ein windiger Kunde*, a shifty customer).

WINDISCH adj. a pejorative Austrian term for the Wends or Slovenes (see WELSCH above); also the origin of the *Windhund* (greyhound) which just happens to run *so schnell wie der Wind*. Figuratively, a *Windhund* is someone who is out to make a fast buck.

ZIVILCOURAGE n.f. the courage to stand up for one's beliefs – in contrast to military obedience, or exhibiting civvy street's equivalent of dashing courage, on which the military thought they had a monopoly. Generally a virtue of the underdog, though – surprisingly – it was coined in 1864 by Bismarck, the very embodiment of the *Obrigkeitsstaat* or authoritarian state, and is also the not altogether apt German title of John F. Kennedy's *Profiles in Courage*. Subsequently associated with defiance of Nazism, as when Dietrich Bonhoeffer, himself a shining exception to his observation, writes from prison: *wir haben in diesen Jahren viel Tapferkeit und Aufopferung, aber fast nirgends Civilcourage gefunden, auch bei uns selbst nicht* (there has been much bravery and sacrifice, but hardly anywhere, even among ourselves, the courage to stand up and be counted – *Widerstand in Ergebung: Briefe und Aufzeichnungen aus der Haft*, pub. 1951); and more recently, with defiance of authority in general, or of the prevailing current of opinion. When refugee hostels in Rostock, Cottbus and Eisenhüttenstadt were attacked in the summer of 1992 (see ASYLANT above) without any mainstream German politician putting in a personal appearance to demonstrate solidarity with the victims, the Commissioner for Foreigners' Affairs in Berlin concluded: *öffentlich eine solche Zivilcourage zu zeigen, ist für die Deutschen schwer* (to show 'civil courage' like that in public is difficult for the Germans – see *auf dem rechten Auge blind* under RECHT in I). But *Die Zeit* was being ironical when it observed on 12 August 1988: *Wer sich 1968 in der Studentenorganisation der Union* organisierte, der hatte echt Zivilcourage* (whoever joined the conservative students' organization in 1968 really did have the courage of their convictions).

ECONOMICS,
INDUSTRY,
AGRICULTURE

III

WIRTSCHAFT,
INDUSTRIE,
LANDWIRTSCHAFT

ACKER n.m. simply a field under cultivation (with numerous compounds, mainly the names of flowers and birds). Although it used to be a unit for measuring area (like acre), a modern German farmer will give the size of his farm in *Hektar* (one hectare, a hundred metres by a hundred metres, is about the size of Trafalgar Square). Less officially, he may tell you how many *Morgen Land* he works (a unit varying in size from region to region, originally how much a man could plough in a morning), but the *Morgenland* is the Orient whence the Three Kings (*die heiligen Drei Könige* or *die drei Weisen*) came.

Note: *Bleib/Geh mir vom Acker!* is not the anxious cry of a possessive landowner denying you the right of way under the German equivalent of the Criminal Justice Act, but a desperate plea not to be bothered. Somebody who has *keine Ahnung von Ackerbau und Viehzucht* doesn't know his arse from his elbow. Literally, *Ackerbau* is field farming or agriculture, often combined with *Viehzucht*, cattle farming, and the verb *ackern*, to slog away, is still a byword for hard work. See also FELD below.

AKKORD n.m. a musical chord, or else a legal settlement, especially one between management and workforce on the piece rate for a job. Thus, *auf* or *im Akkord arbeiten* means to do piecework, to be paid by results, not necessarily to work harmoniously with others (though this went without saying in the Nazi *Planwirtschaft* or planned economy, when teams of factory workers *im Gemeinschaftsakkord* aimed at ever higher production targets). To be in accord with someone is *mit jemandem übereinstimmen* or *in Einklang stehen*. In the political sense, an accord is *ein Abkommen*, as in *das Abkommen von Helsinki*. 'Of its own accord', *von selbst* or *aus freien Stücken*.

AKQUISITION n.f. the job of *ein Akquisiteur*, as he is technically known, is either to sell advertising space (*Inserate akquirieren*) or to promote sales (*er macht Akquisition für Thermopane*, for instance, though most German windows are already double-glazed). More commonly, acquisition is *der Erwerb* (a scheme whereby tax relief is obtained on investment in property is known as *das Erwerbermodell**); the thing acquired is *eine Anschaffung*, if acquired by dubious means, *eine Aneignung*.

ALP n.f. *die Alp* (like *die Alm*) is an alp or alpine pasture, but *der Alp/ Alb* is a mischievous elf* or goblin believed to cause nightmares (*Alpträume*).

ANGER n.m. still used of a village green, *der Dorfanger*, otherwise a somewhat dated word for pasture or meadow (see FELD and ACKER in this section, and *Schindanger*, knacker's yard, under KNACK- in VIII). Anger is *die Wut* or *der Zorn* (see SPLEEN in V).

BAGGER n.m. an excavator. Some Germans may still think that bag should be pronounced like beg, but the similar English distortion of 'u' to 'a' is less familiar to German ears; a Hamburg guide pointing to a dredger working on the Elbe recently startled English tourists by exclaiming *Da ist ein Bagger!* (As a term of abuse, a bugger is *ein Scheißkerl* or *ein Arschloch*.) The confusion seems to work both ways: when Leopold Mozart heard the London street urchins calling 'Bugger French' after him and and his eight-year-old, bewigged son Wolfgang, he assured his friend Lorenz Hagenauer a trifle disingenuously (letter of 28 May 1764) that this meant 'French *Bürger*'.

BANK n.f. as in English, the bank/bench you sit on (plural *die Bänke*), or the bank you put your money in (plural *die Banken*). Also a sand-bank such as *die Doggerbank*, though not a river-bank, which is *das Ufer*.

Note that *ein Banker* works in a bank, or is perhaps a banking expert, but *ein Bankier* owns the bank, or at least sits on the board. Germany's banking system is discussed under KASSE below. See also *Bankert* under BASTARD in VI.

BAUER n.m. **1.** the normal word for a farmer – a *Großbauer* usually owns between 50 and 250 acres; a *Kleinbauer* is a smallholder; a '*Bio-Bauer*' farms without chemical fertilizers. Agriculture itself is *der Ackerbau*, wine-growing *der Weinbau*, etc., while to cultivate a crop is *bauen* (more often *anbauen*).

or else **2.** as a class term, a peasant, and used figuratively, a yokel or country bumpkin given to unsophisticated or foolish behaviour, though not necessarily the 'boorish' behaviour (*rüpelhaftes, flegelhaftes Benehmen*) once associated with the Dutch *Boers* in South Africa. On the other hand, a baby that needs to be winded is still expected to *ein Bäuerchen machen*. In the days when we were all peasants, our *Nachbar* ('neighbour') was the *Bauer* who lived nearby ('*nahe*'). In chess, *der Bauer* is the lowly pawn; in cards, the jack or knave. *Das Bauer*, however, is a bird-cage.

Nowadays, both *bauen* and *der Bau* with its many compounds are used mainly of construction work: *ich bin beim Bau*, I work in the building industry; *an einer Baustelle*, on a building site; on road-works, *beim Straßenbau*. See also *Bergbau* under BERG- below. In mil-itary slang, however, *sieben Tage Bau* is a week in the guardhouse; *er war drei Jahre im Bau*, he was 'inside' for three years (see KITTCHEN in I).

Finally, *wir haben gebaut* usually means that after years of living in a rented flat (see APARTMENT, BLOCKHAUS, DOPPELHAUS, TER-RASSENHAUS in IX), and saving a substantial amount towards the costs, we have helped design our own home and had it built.

BERATEN v. not to berate (*schimpfen, schelten, jemandem Vor-würfe machen*), but to advise. A *Steuerberater* (tax consultant), rather than a *Steuerbeamter** (tax official), advises on what is legally *absetz-bar* (tax-deductible), that is to say, the difference between *Steuer-umgehung* (tax avoidance) and *Steuerbetrug* (tax evasion). See also RAT in I and IV.

BERG- in cpds. refers either to a mountain (*der Bergführer**, moun-tain guide; *Bergsteiger*, mountaineer) or else to the mining industry, since shafts were originally driven into the side of a mountain (note, though, that a *Steiger* is a pit foreman). Coal-mining is still called *der Bergbau**, and the subject studied by a *Bergingenieur*, mining engin-eer, is *das Bergfach*. A miner (*Bergarbeiter* or *Bergmann*) who works down the mine *arbeitet im Bergwerk*, though he would probably use a more colloquial expression to describe his job: *ich arbeite im Pütt* (down the pit) or *ich arbeite unter Tage* (literally, 'below day'). The pit itself is *die Grube* or *die Zeche*. See also below, MONTAN- and HÜTTE.

Die Bergstraße, however, is the name given to an area of orchards and vineyards north of Heidelberg. Figuratively, *über alle Berge sein* is to be long gone or miles away, but *über den Berg sein* is to be over the worst or out of the wood; *mit etwas hinterm Berg halten*, to keep quiet about something.

Just as *Berg* (mountain) and *Burg* (castle) are so often etymologi-cally indistinguishable in place-names, from Bregenz to Burgund (not forgetting the 'elevated' St Brigit), so the verb *bergen* formerly meant to bring to the safety of a *Burg*; hence, *Menschen bergen* or *retten*, to rescue people, *Leichen bergen*, to recover bodies; also to hide, shelter, hold or contain, as in *das Unternehmen birgt Gefahren in sich*, it's a potentially dangerous enterprise.

BILANZ n.f. a balance sheet (*ein Bilanzprüfer* is an auditor), but also a figurative term for taking stock of a situation (*Bilanz ziehen*), as in the title of Alfred Grosser's influential account of the Federal Republic during its first decades, *Deutschlandbilanz* (1970). Financial 'balance' through redistribution is the aim of a system whereby the rich *Länder** give to the poor (*der Finanzausgleich*, see LAST below) – though never enough, as the unending litigation before the *Bundes-verfassungsgericht* indicates.

BILLION n.f. as formerly in Britain, a million million. Britain now seems to have accepted the American usage (a billion = a thousand million), whereas the Germans have their own word for a thousand million: *eine Milliarde* (French *un milliard* – which makes sense because of Latin *mille*).

BLANK adj. broke is one meaning; others include shiny, clean, bare. A blank cheque is *ein Blankoscheck*. During storms, the North Sea, *die Nordsee**, is also known poetically as *der Blanke Hans*.

BRANCHE n.f. not the branch of a store, company, bank (*die Filiale, die Niederlassung, die Zweigstelle*), but a separate branch of business or industry. So, *die Branche wechseln* means to change one's line of business, not to move to a different branch office. *Er ist jetzt in der Computerbranche*, he's in computers now; *in einer Dienstleistungsbranche**, in a service industry. *Ein Branchenverzeichnis* is a classified trade directory or 'yellow pages'.

BRÜTER n.m. not a brute (*ein brutaler Kerl*), but a nuclear breeder reactor. The verb *brüten* covers both breeding (of birds only, not animals) and brooding, facilitating a cartoon in the *Süddeutsche Zeitung* on 31 January 1987 depicting Rodin's 'Thinker' brooding over a nuclear plant and entitled *Langsamer Brüter*, Slow Brooder/Breeder.

BULLE n.m. a bull (for breeding; if castrated, *ein Ochse*, bullock; see also STIER below), and figuratively someone who is strong and beefy (as strong as an ox, *bärenstark**) or else boorish and clumsy. Colloquially, *die Bullen* are the cops, the fuzz, and *eine Bullenhitze* sweltering or boiling heat. On the stock market, bulls and bears are *Haussespekulanten* and *Baissespekulanten* (or *Haussiers* and *Baissiers*), though the English terms are also used. A papal bull or decree is *die Bulle*.

CENTER n.n. a vogue word, as in *Garten-Center, Fitneß-Center Einkaufs-Center* (shopping mall), or the more authentically German *Eros-Center* (see PUFF in VI). The Americanism has virtually replaced *Zentrum*, which now usually means town or city centre and is an alternative word for *Stadtmitte*. (For details of Bismarck's fight against *das Zentrum* – the German Catholic party – see KULTUR in II.) While in some German cities, such as Frankfurt, *die City* is both the city centre and the main business quarter, Hamburg's *City-Nord* is just one successful example of how to avoid inner-city desolation by moving firms' headquarters and administrative centres (*die Zentrale*) to the periphery.

CHEF n.m. not chef (*der Koch*), but chief or boss. Though *der Chefkoch* (or *Küchenchef*) is indeed the head cook, *ein Personalchef** is a personnel manager, not a personal chef (*ein Leibkoch*), and *der Juniorchef* is the boss's son. Similarly, *der Chefarzt* is senior consultant in a hospital and *die Chefvisite** his round of the wards; the office of a *Chefredakteur*, editor-in-chief of a newspaper, will be on the *Chef-etage*, the executive or management floor; and *Chefsache* does not mean 'the chief or main thing' (*die Hauptsache*), but rather 'a matter for the boss'. This is what *Die Zeit* meant on 28 September 1990 when describing Helmut Kohl's performance at the Strasbourg summit on 6 December 1989: *Die Einheit war von da an Chefsache* – unity from that moment on was managed by Kohl personally.

In many walks of life, *Chef* is an acceptably familiar way of addressing one's boss. In Austria (where *Herr Chef* always means the boss) a waiter who does not know his customer, and hence the title by which he should be addressed, might also call him *Chef*. Also in Austria, *die Chefin* may be the boss's wife, whereas in Germany it is only the boss herself (see MEISTER below). But the chief of an Indian tribe is *der Häuptling*, not *der Chef* – the *Indianerhäuptling* best-known to Germans being the eponymous hero of Karl May's novel *Winnetou* (1892), rather than Geronimo, on whom he was in part based. Finally, *hallo* Chef!* is a way of attracting someone's attention, rather like 'hey, guv'nor' or 'hello there, squire'.

CONTROLLER n.m. only used in the sense of 'comptroller' or specialist in costing. *Das Controlling* is control system engineering. An air-traffic controller, however, is *ein Fluglotse* (*ein Lotse* is a ship's pilot – see REALPOLITIK in II).

DEALER n.m. only a drug dealer, pusher, trafficker (*ein Fixer** is a drug addict – while the vocabulary of drugs is mainly American, the meanings may have shifted). Any other kind of dealer is *ein Händler*, though *der Handel* can mean both legitimate trade and illegal traffic (*einen guten Deal machen* is generally in drugs). To deal at cards is simply *geben*.

DEPOT n.n. can mean things deposited, as well as a depository, bank's strong room, bus depot, or ammunition dump, but the deposit you pay to reserve something is *eine Anzahlung* (see also KAUTION in IX). A Swiss *Depot* is also the deposit you reclaim when you return bottles.

DEVISEN n.p. in the singular (*die Devise*), a heraldic device or political motto; in the plural, foreign currency, including travellers' cheques payable in a foreign currency. *Der Devisenkurs** is the mean exchange rate (*der amtliche Mittelkurs*) whereas *der Sortenkurs** is the 'tourist rate'.

DIENST n.m. broadly corresponds to English 'service', but also a common synonym for work or business: *eine Dienstreise* is a business trip, *ein Dienstwagen* an official or company car; *ein Dienstjubiläum wird begangen* to mark 25, 40 and 50 years with the firm; *die Dienststelle hat jetzt Dienstschluß* simply means the office is closed. As *Feierabend** approaches, German office life frequently appears to mix business with pleasure, giving the lie to the proverb *Dienst ist Dienst und Schnaps ist Schnaps*.

New laws on late-night opening have at last been passed and should come into force in 1996. In recent years, large stores, in cities at least, were permitted to stay open on Thursdays until 8.30pm (now it will be until 8pm six days a week) and as the name *Dienstleistungsabend* ('service evening') suggested, you could avail yourself of your dentist's or lawyer's services as well. On the other hand, everything closed at 2pm on Saturdays, except for *langer Samstag*, the first Saturday in the month, when shops in winter were meant to stay open until 6pm, though in summer (at the trade unions' fierce insistence) only until 4pm. But there will still be no general Sunday opening: on Sunday mornings you can buy cakes for *Kaffee** *und Kuchen*, but little else, since neither the German concept of *Dienst* nor the law governing it extend to corner shops open at all hours. (Airports, large railway stations and petrol stations *are* welcome exceptions). For the military context, see DIENEN in I.

DIREKTOR n.m. while a film or theatre director is *ein Regisseur*, the head of most large organizations (firm, school, hospital, bank, prison) is a *Direktor*, formally addressed as *Herr Direktor*. *Die Direktion* can mean either the office of director (management, administration, headship, principalship) or else the director's office. Similarly, *das Direktorat* can be a directorship or governorship, but also the director's or governor's office. The French Directory of 1795–99 is known as *das Direktorium*, a term also used of the governing body of some institutions. Large German firms, however, are controlled jointly by a three-man executive board (*der Vorstand* – also the word for the managing director in person) and a supervisory board (*der Aufsichtsrat*) with shareholders and workers equally represented (see MONTAN- below).

EFFEKTEN n.p. stocks and bonds, trading in which dominates the German financial market. The main *Effektenbörse*, with 70% of all stock traded, is in Frankfurt. *Der Effektenhandel*, unlike the Anglo-Saxon quote-driven system, is an order-driven system which British financial commentators tend to see as evidence of 'endemic German provincialism'. Some three-quarters of the turnover is dominated by the banks, while market capitalization of publicly listed companies is only 5% of US levels. Germans put most of their surplus cash into *feste* Anlagen*, fixed-interest deposits.

ENERGETISCH adj. refers only to the science of energetics, in particular nowadays to *die Erhaltung der Energie*, the conservation of energy. Vigorous reactions, forceful protests, resolute denials are all *energisch*, whereas energetic people are *voller Energie*.

ETAT n.m. not a financial statement or return – one of the word's many French meanings – but (like *der Haushalt**) a budget, specifically the national budget. An item in the budget is known as *ein Etatposten* (besides meaning a post or job, *ein Posten* is also an individual item of stock or entry on a bill) which those familiar with Louis XIV's *l'Etat c'est moi* might misconstrue as an official position in the service of the State (*eine Beamtenstelle**).

EXTRAVAGANT adj. used of flamboyant behaviour, fantastic dress, wild claims; someone who is extravagant with money is *verschwenderisch*.

FABRIK n.f. not fabric (*der Stoff**), but a factory. *Fabrikwaren*, mass-produced articles, are often contrasted with *Handarbeit*, hand-made high-quality goods.

FABRIKATION n.f. manufacture (more commonly *die Herstellung*), but not the concoction of a false story (*pure Erfindung*). By contrast, the verb *fabrizieren* is now seldom used of manufacture (*herstellen, produzieren*), but can mean to fabricate (as in *eine Lügengeschichte fabrizieren*, to make up a whole tissue of lies); or more commonly, to make a mess of something (*was hast du da schon wieder fabriziert?*); or, ironically, to botch a job.

Britain's loss of jobs in industry during the 1980s (from 38% of the labour force to 29%, compared with Germany's 44% to 40%), might be thought an aptly ironic example of scoring an own goal (*ein Eigentor fabrizieren*), since her appetite for manufactured goods continued to rise. See also HANDWERK below, and for service industries, DIENST and BRANCHE above.

FEIERABEND n.m. not 'party night' (*der Abend der Feier/ des Feierns*), but originally 'the eve of a festival', now the end of the normal working day (*machen wir Feierabend*, let's call it a day), even if that sometimes means midday (*Freitags haben wir schon mittags Feierabend*). Also closing time, though as this is generally well after midnight, only the stragglers are thus addressed: *Feierabend, meine Herrschaften!* time, gentlemen, please. Figuratively, *jetzt ist aber Feierabend!* enough is enough.

FELD n.n. always arable land in German (like *der Acker**), except in certain combinations when it means open countryside (*auf freiem Feld*; *Feld und Wald*, woods and fields) or the field of battle (*das Schlachtfeld*; hence *der Feldherr*, military commander; *der Feldjäger*, military policeman, or else a courier, and in Austria a rifleman). A meadow is *eine Wiese*, and a field of grass used for grazing *eine Weide*.

   Note also: *ein Schachbrett hat 64 Felder*, there are 64 squares on a chess board.

FILIALE n.f. one of a chain of shops in a *Filialnetz*, network; or else a branch office (not *eine Branche**). Consequently, *der Filialleiter* is the branch manager, not the boss's son (*der Juniorchef** – 'filial' duty is *Sohnespflicht* or *töchterliche Pflicht*.) A subsidiary firm is *eine Tochterfirma* or simply *eine Tochter*, and an affiliated company *eine Schwestergesellschaft*.

FIR TREE over a quarter of Germany is wooded. *Laubbäume* (deciduous trees) make up a third of this, mainly *die deutsche Eiche* (oak furniture still distinguishes many traditional restaurants and beer halls) and *die Buche* (the beech woods outside Weimar gave their name to Buchenwald concentration camp). What the traveller mainly sees, however, are *Nadelbäume* (conifers). Of these, *die Tanne* (fir) is predominant in mountainous regions, while Brandenburg's sandy soil suits *die Kiefer* or *die Föhre* (pine); also *die Lärche* (larch) and *die Fichte* (spruce). Where we talk loosely of conifers as fir trees, the general word in German is not *Föhre* but *Tanne*.

   Ever since Hermann the German (Arminius) deprived Quintilius Varus of his three legions in the *Teutoburger Wald* in the year 9 AD, the forest has been the spiritual *Heimat** of the Germans, especially in song. Germans were singing *O Tannenbaum, O Tannenbaum, wie treu sind deine Blätter* almost a century before the Irish agitator, Jim Connell, altered the words in 1889 to: 'Though cowards flinch and traitors sneer, we'll keep "The Red Flag" flying here.' Even German Existentialism conjures up the *Schwarzwald* rather than bistros and black sweaters. Heidegger, who lived in the Black Forest, disarmingly entitled one of his books *Holzwege*, suggesting not only walks in the forest, but also the possibility of finding oneself *auf dem Holzweg*, on a logging-path leading nowhere, i.e. on the wrong track, barking up the wrong tree.

FIXER n.m. not an orchestral manager (*ein Manager*), sports organizer (*ein Veranstalter*), or someone who fixes more illicit matters (*ein Schieber*), but the most common word for a drug user (*er fixt, er gibt sich einen Fix*), whereas the fixer/pusher who supplies the drugs is *ein Dealer**. On the stock market, however, a *Fixer* is a 'bear' (who makes a *Fixgeschäft*, speculating on a fall in prices, *eine Baisse*), not someone who fixes deals for other people (*ein Makler*). The fixing of the exchange rate (*der Kurs**) is also known as *das Fixing*.

The adjective *fix* can mean fixed (*fixe Kosten* or *eine fixe Idee*), but more often means intelligent (*ein fixer Junge*, bright lad, smart chap), or else quick (service – *geht's nicht ein bißchen fixer?*). This is one sense of *fix und fertig sein* (to have polished off a job); the other is to be worn out, at the end of one's tether, ruined; *jemanden fix und fertig machen* means to drive somebody mad, or beat the hell out of somebody. The main sense of the verb *fixieren*, apart from that of specifying the *Termin** of a *Fixgeschäft* or the object of one's fixation (*auf etwas fixiert sein*), is to stare at someone (see under STARREN in X).

FOLIE n.f. not a *folie*, as in *bergère*, but a piece of foil: *die Metallfolie*, metal foil; *die Klebfolie*, adhesive cling film. But also: *Mephisto dient Faust als Folie*, Mephisto serves as a foil to Faust.

FRANC n.m., **FRANKEN** n.m. the French and Belgian *franc* is retained in German (but note: 100 *Franc*, not *Francs*), while the Swiss currency becomes *der Schweizerfranken* (1 *Franken* = 100 *Rappen*), sometimes mockingly deflated to *Fränkli* (the diminutive suffix is widespread in *Schweizerdeutsch*, from the *Rütli* meadow, the birthplace of the Confederation in 1291, to the *Bähnli*, or narrow-gauge railway, which winds its way up many an otherwise inaccessible valley).

Charlemagne thought of himself as *ein Franke* (giving the name to France and the franc), but today's *Franken* have been politically absorbed into northern Bavaria and Hesse. Frankfurt am Main, where German kings were elected from the ninth to the eighteenth century, may be Germany's business centre ('*Mainhatten*'), but Franconia is now more readily associated with rolling hills and dry white *Frankenweine* (see BOCKSBEUTEL under BOCKBIER in VIII). One memorial to the Franks' heyday as 'free' men is the phrase *frank und frei* (frankly, openly); *etwas frank und frei heraussagen* (to say something straight out). Also: *frankieren* (= *freimachen**), to stamp or frank a letter.

FUND n.m. a find (*das Fundbüro*, lost property office), not a fund. This is *ein Fonds*, while public funds are *Staatsgelder* or *öffentliche Mittel**. I am short of funds, *ich bin knapp bei Kasse**.

GRAB n.n. a grave, whereas *der Graben* is a ditch, trench or moat (*graben*, to dig), and *die Grube* a pit or mine (or else another word for the grave). The reformed Faust in Goethe's play devotes his energy to drying out a swamp (not REKLAMIEREN – see below), but, as Mephistopheles points out, the workmen he thinks are digging a ditch are actually digging his grave: *Man spricht, wie man mir Nachtricht gab, / Von keinem Graben, doch vom Grab* (ll. 11,557–8). Even more poignantly, Kurt Tucholsky, one of Germany's relatively few pacifists in the 1920s, returned repeatedly in his poetry to the proximity of graves and First World War trenches.

GRATIFIKATION n.f. not gratification (*die Genugtuung, die Befriedigung*), but a gratuity or bonus. *Ein dreizehntes Monatsgehalt als Weihnachtsgratifikation* (a thirteenth month's salary as a Christmas bonus) is common, a fourteenth instalment in the summer not unusual. Very gratifying, *sehr erfreulich!*

GROSS adj. not gross as opposed to net (*brutto – netto*), nor gross meaning vulgar (*grob*), but simply big or tall, or else great. *Friedrich der Große* was great, but he was not tall (*ein großer Mann* in its narrower sense; someone who is tall and thin is *lang*, if a real beanpole *eine lange Latte*); he might, to make the point, have acknowledged that his officers were *länger, nicht größer* (as Napoleon is said to have responded to one of his marshals who, being taller, offered to reach down a book from a high shelf: *plus grand? plus haut!*).

Der Großhandel is wholesale trade, *der Einzelhandel*, retail. Some hardware shops still advertise their sale of *Eisenwaren – en gros und en detail*, wholesale and retail, but *das Gros* is a now somewhat dated word meaning either a gross (twelve dozen), or else the bulk or greater part of something.

GUT n.n. not gut (*der Darm*), but either **1.** good in the sense of asset or possession: *ein kostbares Gut* (a precious asset); *ideelle* Güter* (intangible assets, such as goodwill or patents). In combinations, *-gut* means 'all aspects of', 'the totality of', as in *Strandgut* (flotsam and jetsam) or *Erbgut* (genetic make-up/DNA, though also anything else inherited). *Das deutsche Musikgut* (German music) speaks for itself. *Das Namensgut spiegelt häufig den historischen Gang der Besiedlung wider* means that place-names often reflect the historical process of settlement – *Au/Aue, Gau/Gäu**, *Börde* all signifying clearances, for instance, and *Hard(t)* woods and forests. In everyday material terms, *Güter* are goods or commodities (*der Güterbahnhof*, freight depot).

Or else **2**. landed property. Thus, *ein Landgut*, or simply *ein Gut*, is an estate (if inherited, *ein Erbgut*); *ein Weingut**, a wine-growing estate. *Gutsherrschaft* (demesne farming) grew up in Brandenburg, Mecklenburg, Pomerania, Prussia and Silesia in the sixteenth century, mainly through younger sons without inheritance (the word *Junker* is derived from *Jung Herr*, 'young lord') colonizing those territories on the north-eastern frontiers recently secularized by the Teutonic Knights or sold off by the princes, thereby acquiring *ein Rittergut*. Though the great Peasants' War of 1525 centred on the south-west of Germany, it was in Prussia that its effects on the ancient rights of peasants – first to move freely, then to move freely if they could find a successor – were most violated with the re-introduction of serf labour (*zweite Leibeigenschaft*). Prussia's Emancipation of the Serfs in 1807 proceeded in turn much more slowly under the partly feudalistic, partly entrepreneurial *Gutsherrschaft* system prevalent east of the Elbe ('*Ostelbien*') than under the simpler contractual arrangements of *Grundherrschaft* in the west. The Prussian Junkers, for all their growing dominance of local government (as *Landräte**) and in the army officer corps under Frederick the Great, were themselves forbidden to travel – at a time when the Grand Tour was the aristocratic norm elsewhere – on pain of forfeiting their estates.

The ironies of history are not lost on their successors today in what has become 'Germany's *Mezzogiorno*' (Imanuel Geiss). With the abolition of Prussia after the Second World War, the *Junker* – a hate figure in German history on account of his reactionary politics and militaristic arrogance (but see under GOTHA in II) – also officially disappeared. All of the 13,000 *Gutsbesitzer* in possession of more than 100 hectares (247 acres) – by no means all of them *Junker* – were dispossessed (*enteignet*) by the Soviets between 1945 and 1949, losing a total of 5.43m acres. When the irreversibility of this measure, on which the Russians were thought to have insisted as a main condition for reunification, was unequivocally denied by Mikhail Gorbachev in August 1994, Bonn found itself in the unenviable position of having to weigh multiple claims for restitution and compensation against the fears and potential for social unrest of some half a million eastern Germans who had been given smallholdings in the 1950s (subsequently collectivized) in accordance with the new maxim *Junkerland in Bauernhand**.

HANDELN v. not just to handle certain goods, but to engage in any form of trade (also to bargain or haggle). The Prussian-led

Handelsverein, for instance, was the forerunner of the *Zollverein* (tariff union – see ZENSUR in X) which dismantled most of the 1,800 customs boundaries within the German states, effectively creating what the philosopher, Johann Gottlieb Fichte, and the economist, Friedrich List – the godfather of 'national economy' – propagated as *der geschlossene Handelsstaat* (united trading nation).

But *handeln* also means 'to act'. Hamlet's enterprises, in the Schlegel/Tieck translation, *verdienen nicht der Handlung Namen*; and when Fichte declared as part of his dynamic Romantic credo: *Handeln!, Handeln! Das ist es, wozu wir da sind*, he, too, was using the word in this second, general sense: 'We are here to *do* things' (putting it another way, he declared *außer mir zu wirken**to be his overriding ambition). Goethe's *Faust* carries a similar message: you might say the play *handelt von Erlösung durch Handeln* (deals with redemption through endeavour), or that this is the play's plot, *die Handlung des Stücks*.

HANDWERK n.n. a professional trade or craft, rather than handiwork (*das Werken* is the school subject; *die Bastelarbeit*, handicraft as a hobby; *die Handarbeit*, needlework, but also any hand-made article). *Handwerk* thus means manufacture in its original sense of made by hand, as distinct from *Fabrikation**, *ein Handwerker* is a skilled manual worker or craftsman, and one unshakeable conviction of the German *Mittelstand**is reflected in the dictum *Handwerk hat goldenen Boden*, signifiying that craftsmanship is worth its weight in gold.

The local *Handwerkskammer* (trade corporation) co-operates closely with the *Handelskammer* (chamber of trade and commerce) to arrange vocational training and examinations, but it is the firms themselves which are most crucially committed (each putting 2% of its wage bill into the local training centres, while those firms which take apprentices are fully reimbursed for the first 20 months during which they see little of their trainees). German firms in 1989 spent DM28bn on apprenticeships (*die Lehre*), and the same on further training (*Weiterbildung*), always using the most modern machinery – an average of DM1,800 per worker. See also below, MEISTER.

HAUS n.n. house, also as in *das Haus Siemens*, the House of Siemens, but in addition used of the company for which one works – *unser Haus* ('our firm') – suggesting a degree of corporate identity. When telephoning a firm: *er ist nicht im Hause* means he's not on the premises, he's not in. *Das erste Haus am Platze* is either the top store in town or the best hotel. On the domestic front, *wir liefern frei** *Haus*, we offer free delivery. Note also *ins Haus stehen*, to be imminent – derived from the houses of the zodiac and one of Helmut Kohl's favourite expressions for describing an imminent threat (it also signifies a baby on the way). See also HAUSEN, HAUSHALT and HAUSIEREN in IX.

HONORAR n.n. a fee or honorarium; someone who works *gegen Honorar* is thus on a contract (an *Honorarprofessor**, for instance), whereas an honorary or unpaid post is *ein Ehrenamt*. If one's work is *schlecht honoriert*, it means it is badly paid, not that it is not highly thought of.

With *die Honoratioren*, however, the focus is solely on honour: dignitaries, notabilities, VIPs; *die Honoratioren des Ortes*, the local bigwigs.

HÜTTE n.f. either **1.** a hut or cabin: the famous revolutionary slogan *Friede den Hütten! Krieg den Palästen!* ('Peace to the hovels! War on the palaces!') was taken up by Georg Büchner (1813–1837) and Ludwig Weidig (1791–1837) as a motto for his attacks on the ruling classes in *Der hessische Landbote*. But *eine Hütte* is also **2.** an iron and steel smelting works – part of *die Hüttenindustrie* (iron, steel, and coal together constitute *die Montanindustrie**). When *Hüttenarbeiter* were being laid off in the '*Noch-DDR*' ('what was still the GDR') in 1990, Volker Braun caught both senses with his neat inversion of the slogan: *Da bin ich noch: mein Land geht in den Westen. / KRIEG DEN HÜTTEN FRIEDE DEN PALÄSTEN* ('Here I remain as my country goes west. War on the hovels and peace to the palaces' – from his poem *Das Eigentum*, 'Property').

IMPULS n.m. often better translated as impetus or momentum, or else factor – *Wachstumsimpulse* are factors encouraging economic growth. On impulse: *spontan, ohne zu überlegen.*

INTERESSANT adj. also a common term in commercial trading, meaning advantageous: *das dürfte ein interessantes Angebot für Sie sein* (roughly: that's as good an offer as you will get); *zu diesem Preis ist das nicht weiter interessant für uns* (we would no longer be interested at that price).

JOBBER n.m. not only a *Börsenjobber* on the stock exchange, but also someone doing a casual job; *jobben* is to 'temp'.

KAPITAL n.n. only the financial capital which Marx wrote about (or a figurative asset, such as beauty), not a capital city (*die Hauptstadt*, though this could also be called *die Kapitale*). The connection with 'head' is evident in the hunting term *ein kapitaler Hirsch* (a royal or prize stag), though the connotation is more often negative – *einen* *kapitalen Bock* schießen* means to make a real bloomer, *ein Kapital-verbrechen* is a serious crime (no longer a capital offence – Germany has no *Todesstrafe*).

KASSE n.f. the cashdesk or cashpoint in a bank (savings banks are called *Sparkassen* – see SPAREN below). Or a box office at the theatre; or where you pay in a shop or restaurant. It also corresponds to 'cash' in such phrases as *ich bin ziemlich knapp bei Kasse*, I'm a bit short of cash. *Getrennte Kasse machen/führen* ('separate kitty') is to go Dutch. For *Kasse* meaning a health insurance scheme, see KRANKENKASSE in VII.

KOMFORTABEL adj. convenient (but see KONVENIENZ in VII), as well as comfortable. Credit cards are often advertised as being *ein komfortables Zahlungsmittel*, a convenient way of paying, though it is only recently that garages or department stores have begun to accept them, and most supermarket check-outs still do not. Banks are now hastening to supplement their *Euroscheck* bank-cum-cash card system with credit cards, but Germans still prefer to pay for most things in cash (*bar**).

KOMMISSIONÄR n.m. a commission agent, in particular a wholesale bookseller (an intermediary between the *Verleger*, pub-lisher, and the *Sortimenter**, book retailer). An EEC Commissioner is *ein Kommissar**; a commissioner of police, *ein Polizeipräsident*; a commissioner for oaths, *ein Notar*; a commissionaire, *ein Portier* or *ein Pförtner*.

KONJUNKTUR n.f. the immediate economic situation, usually favourable (like 'getting a result' in English football parlance). Eng-lish 'conjuncture', a combination of circumstances, is better rendered as *das Zusammentreffen*, but the conjunction of the stars and planets is also *die Konjunktion*. The economic situation is likewise constantly changing, and *die Konjunkturpolitik* denotes the measures taken to prevent economic fluctuations, *Konjunkturschwankungen* or *kon-junkturelle Schwankungen*.

Die Konjunktur (like *der Kurs**) can also have the sense of literary or intellectual fashion: *die Werke von Christa Wolf haben jetzt etwas weniger Hochkonjunktur* (Christa Wolf's works are not quite as pop-ular as they once were), though when Northrop Frye first used the metaphor in his *Anatomy of Criticism* (1957, p. 18), it was to dismiss as sonorous nonsense 'the literary chit-chat which makes the reputa-tions of poets boom and crash in an imaginary stock exchange'.

KONKURRENZ n.f. not concurrence, but competition or con-test (*eine Schönheitskonkurrenz* is a beauty contest) – both the phenomenon itself and those ('concurrently') engaged in it. *Ein Konkurrent* is slightly more specific: a business competitor or sporting rival. In contrast, people who concur *sind einer Meinung* or *stimmen miteinander überein*; things which run concurrently are *gleichzeitig*, including jail sentences '*unter gleichzeitigem Vollzug beider Freiheitsstrafen*'.

KONKURS n.m. like *Bankrott*, means bankruptcy. The *Konkursmasse** (the bankrupt's estate or the insolvent firm's assets) is dealt with in a *Konkursverfahren* (a 'concourse' of the creditors or *Gläubiger*, that is to say, bankruptcy proceedings or liquidation). This is sometimes avoided by *ein außergerichtlicher Vergleich*, out-of-court settlement. Alternatively, *er hat sich durch einen Konkurs gesundgestoßen*, going into bankruptcy helped him back on his feet.

KONSISTENT adj. a technological term. *Konsistentes Material* refers to one specific consistency, namely workable (as applied to *Beton*, concrete), or thickly running (*Schmiermittel*, lubricants), or firm/solid/semi-solid (*Fette*, fats, greases). For logical consistency, see KONSEQUENT in V.

KONSTRUKTION n.f. both the process of building a machine, bridge, etc. (*der Bau*), and the technical design behind it (*der Entwurf*), so that *ein Konstruktionsfehler* may be either a design fault or a structural defect. Since *der Konstrukteur* is closely involved with the implementation of his designs, this ambiguity is less a linguistic weakness than a strength of German industry. The construction industry, in its narrower sense, is *die Bauindustrie**. Though we might call someone who uses sub-standard *Baustoffe** and has a cavalier approach to *Konstruktion* a jerry-builder (*ein schlampiger Bauunternehmer*), associations with the Federal Republic are misplaced, though they might have seemed apt enough in the GDR. See HANDWERK and MEISTER in this section.

KONSUM n.m. people in the 1950s would go *zum Konsum* (stressed on the first syllable) for their groceries, but these were soon replaced by the co-ops (though there is still a *Krupp Konsum* in Essen – originally established for Krupp employees only). In the former GDR, however, the local *Konsum* was a branch* of the monopolistic *Konsumgenossenschaften*, which had little similarity to the co-ops set up in Britain and the Weimar Republic to combat profiteering (*der Wucher*). In today's *Konsumgesellschaft* (consumer society), with its alleged *Konsumzwang* (compulsion to buy) and *Konsumterror* (materialistic pressures), *der Konsum* (stressed on the last syllable) is consumption itself.

KONTINGENT n.n. a quota or allocation, as well as a contingent of soldiers (*Truppenkontingent*). *Den Ölexport kontingentieren*, to impose oil-export quotas.

KORN n.n. *der Korn* is the drink (corn schnapps), *das Korn* either an individual seed or grain, or else the cereal crop: in the North and East, with its harsher climate and poor soil, mostly *der Roggen*, rye; in the richer soil of the South, *der Weizen*, wheat (British or US corn/ sweet-corn/maize is *der Mais*, and cornflour *Stärke/Stärkemehl*). Nevertheless, in the days when East Prussia was still properly drained, it was known as *die Kornkammer* Europas* (the granary of Europe). *Kornblumenblau** (cornflower blue) is both the title of a *Karneval** song and – since *blau** also means squiffy – the condition in which it is generally sung, in accordance with the motto: *Blau ist keine Farbe, blau ist ein Zustand.*

KURS n.m. besides a course that you attend, or the course you hold to, the rate* of exchange (*Wechselkurs* – see DEVISEN and SORTEN in this section), or the market price/share price (*Börsenkurs/Aktienkurs*), or the going rate. Metaphorically: *Karl Marx steht nun nicht mehr hoch im Kurs*, Karl Marx is no longer so highly regarded (see also KONJUNKTUR above).

LARGE adj. in Switzerland, generous (German *großzügig*) rather than large (*groß**) or wide (the French sense of *large*) – though the Swiss are not known for their *largesse*, and reputed to be a trifle *knauserig* or *knickerig*, tight-fisted.

LAST n.f. not a cobbler's last (*der Leisten*), but a load or burden, also financial, as in *der Lastenausgleich* – compensation for losses suffered in the Second World War, as well as the tax to raise it. *Die Last der Verantwortung*, the burden of responsibility, weighed heavily on Helmut Kohl after his electoral promise in 1990 that the cost of reunification would not be borne by the taxpayer, *dem Steuerzahler nicht zur Last fallen würde*. That was before the government added a '*Solidaritätszuschlag*' to people's taxes – an open-ended imposition, as it seemed to protesters in 1995. Even with increased tax revenue, *die sozialen Lasten* (welfare costs) of the eastern *Länder* are only partly met by a central *Einheitsfond*. Fears that the hitherto successful, though controversial, system of sharing financial burdens between the *Länder*, known as *der horizontale Finanzausgleich*, might become *überlastet*, overloaded (to outlast is *überdauern*), delayed the first payments from rich *Länder* such as Baden-Württemberg or Bavaria until 1995 (when Lower Saxony, for instance, relinquished 10% of its budget to the east).

Some east Germans now find that they have acquired or become *Altlast*, a new word meaning (someone with, or constituting) 'an old burden' or 'burden from the past', in that their previous political affiliations are likely to impede their future careers, perhaps even more than was the case with those designated *Belastete* at the Nuremberg Trials (see BRAUN in II).

In an ecological context, *die Belastungsgrenze* is the maximum capacity or limit, as when (Green) politicians talk of *Schwermetallbelastung* or *Strahlenbelastung*, meaning the risks from heavy metals or increased exposure to radioactivity.

Note that *der Laster* – like *Lkw*, an abbreviation of *Lastkraftwagen* (see KRAFT in II) – is a lorry, whereas *das Laster* means vice, iniquity.

LEASING n.n. a modern way of financing, mainly industrial plant or a firm's car fleet – like hire purchase (*der Ratenkauf*) in that regular payments count towards a final purchase option, and thus distinct from normal hire (*Mieten, Leihen*). In a country where it is always the car, not the driver, that is insured (and where motor insurance is correspondingly expensive for German drivers – see CAR INSURANCE in VII), visitors will find a *Mietwagen* rather good value.

To lease property or land is *pachten*, to lease out *verpachten*, while *der Pächter* is a tenant farmer, the leaseholder of a shop, pub, etc., and *der Pachthof* a smallholding.

LOCH n.n. any kind of hole. An inland loch/lough/lake is *der See**, an arm of the sea *der Meeresarm*. For holing out at golf, see AUSHOLEN in VII.

LOHN n.m. not loan (*das Darlehen*), but wage. In 1994, average monthly earnings in western Germany were DM4000 (£1,880) and in the east a third lower. Reunification has necessitated some savings on the welfare bill (see LAST above) and the average unemployment benefit (*Arbeitslosenunterstützung*) has consequently been trimmed to DM2200 (£1,030).

Der Lohnsatz, one's net daily income, is the unit on which fines are based (see BUSSGELD in I). *Es lohnt sich nicht*, it's not worth it.

LOYAL adj. as in French, also means to be faithful in interpreting a contract, *einen Vertrag loyal auslegen*, in accordance with articles 85 and 86 of the Rome treaties concerning 'level playing fields'.

MADE IN GERMANY retained by the Germans as a sign of quality, rather than the stigma intended by the British regulation of 1887 which required all imported goods to be stamped with the country of origin.

MAINLINIE n.f. not a mainline of the railway (*eine Hauptstrecke*), but the line formed by the River Main, seen before 1866 as dividing the Prussian sphere of influence from the Austrian sphere of influence (see KULTUR in II), now as dividing the North from the relatively more prosperous South, roughly as the River Trent divides England. It is also jocularly known as the *Weißwurst*-Equator*. But *das Gerede über das Nord-Süd-Gefälle ist vorbei*, talk about the north-south divide is a thing of the past (Johannes Rau, *Süddeutsche Zeitung*, 3 May 1990) – if only because the east-west debate now has obvious priority. See also *Rhein-Main-Donau-Kanal* under KANAL in VII; and FIXER in VII for mainline drugs.

MANCHESTER n.m. manufacturing centre of corduroy, where in 1826 Schinkel admired the new technology and the rural labourers' *Manchesterhosen* (corduroy breeches) as much as he deplored the 'monstrous, shapeless buildings put up by foremen without architecture'. Still a familiar name for the material: German streetsweepers, for instance, traditionally wear *braune Manchesteranzüge mit ausgestellten Hosen*, brown suits of broad-ribbed corduroy with flared trousers. Otherwise the material is known as *Cord* (*eine Cordhose*, *Cordjeans*, etc.), and in Austria also as *der Schnürlsamt* or *Struck*. For economic *Manchestertum*, which puts freedom of trade above freedom of the individual, see LIBERAL in II.

MARKE n.f. 'marque' in the sense of brand (*die Sorte*) or make (*das Fabrikat*). Thus: *die Marke war seine Konfession**, the make of car he drove was his religion (Martin Walser, *Die Brandung**, 1985, p. 87). Also a voucher (*Essensmarke*), coupon (*Lebensmittelmarke*), stamp (*Briefmarke*), token (*Pfandmarke*), or playing chip (*Spielmarke*). *Ein Markenartikel* is a proprietary article, the word suggesting some distinctive feature of excellence ('hallmark'), so *Markenbutter* means best-quality butter.

MARODE adj. *marodieren* means to maraud, but *ein marodes Unternehmen* is an insolvent and demoralized business rather than one engaged in asset stripping (*das Asset-Stripping* also in German – reflecting the fact that what one would otherwise have to describe as *Ankauf von finanziell gefährdeten Firmen und anschließender Verkauf ihrer Vermögenswerte* is not a German phenomenon). In Austria, *marode* has the sense of slightly ill, off-colour; in Germany, exhausted or washed-out.

MASCHINE n.f. also a typewriter (in full, *eine Schreibmaschine*); *das Maschinendiktat* does not in fact involve *eine Diktiermaschine* or *ein Diktiergerät* (dictaphone), but means direct dictation, as when *der*

Chef* seiner Sekretärin den Brief in die Maschine diktiert. Similarly, a type-written letter is *maschinengeschrieben* or *getippt**. However, *ein Maschinist* is not a shorthand typist (*eine Stenotypistin*), but a ship's engineer or an engine-driver. *Ich fliege mit der nächsten Maschine nach München* is the normal way of saying 'I'm taking the next plane to Munich'.

MASSE n.f. **1.** the mass in the formula $e=mc^2$ (*die Formel*, not *das Formular**; Einstein would have said *E gleich M mal C hoch 2* or *E gleich M mal C quadrat* – see POTENZ in IV). Or **2.** as in the *Arbeitermassen* (French, *les masses laborieuses*) whose social and economic enslavement the Expressionist writer Ernst Toller dramatized as *Masse Mensch* (1920), 'mass man'. Or else **3.** one's assets (*Erbmasse*, inheritance; *Konkursmasse**, a bankrupt's estate). *Die Masse muß es bringen* means 'profit only comes with quantity', i.e. it will only pay if enough people buy it or come to see it. Or finally, **4.** the negative pole on a car battery. See also MASS in II and VIII, MESSE in III and V.

MATTE n.f. **1.** the mat or matting you stand on (*er stand plötzlich auf der Matte*, he arrived out of the blue), or throw your opponent on to (*den Gegner auf die Matte legen*). Or else **2.** an alpine meadow, giving rise to such place-names as Zermatt and Andermatt. Used poetically of any meadow or pasture: the cattle grazing 'on fields and meadows green' in Haydn's *The Creation*, for instance (a fusion of the First Book of Genesis and the seventh book of *Paradise Lost*) is rendered admirably in Baron Gottfried van Swieten's sometimes rather loose translation (*Die Schöpfung*, 1797/98) as *auf grünen Matten weidet schon das Rind**; generally, though, *eine Matte* is mowed (*gemäht*) nowadays rather than left for grazing as *eine Wiese*, or cultivated as *ein Feld**.

The adjective *matt* (checkmate in chess) now also means weak, faint, matt, frosted, opaque – hence *die Mattscheibe*, the 'goggle-box' or TV, but also: *du hast wohl 'ne Mattscheibe*, you're soft in the head.

MAUL n.n. an animal's jaws (*Maul- und Klauenseuche*, foot-and-mouth disease), rather than the damage they might inflict. The verb *maulen* is used of people and means to moan or whine (also *quengeln, jammern, schimpfen*; dogs *winseln*, whimper), but 'to maul' is *zerreißen, zerfleischen* or *übel zurichten* (dogs are at least licenced in Germany).

Halt's Maul! or *Maul halten!* is about as rude as 'shut your gob' (more polite: *Ruhe, bitte!*; most polite: *wenn ich um Ruhe bitten darf*). People who are *maulfaul** do not necessarily have bad breath (*der Mundgeruch*), nor are they foul-mouthed (*unflätig, vulgär*), but merely uncommunicative. *Maultaschen* are pasta squares or ravioli – a typically Swabian dish.

MEISTER n.m. the qualification 'master craftsman' – *Bäckermeister* (master baker), *Fleischermeister* (master butcher), *Schreinermeister* (master joiner) – as well as the title by which he is still often addressed; the feminine *Meisterin* is nowadays more likely to be a fully qualified dressmaker or hairdresser than, as formerly, (a way of respectfully addressing) the wife of a *Meister*. Goethe's *Wilhelm Meister*, the archetypal *Bildungsroman**, fittingly begins with Wilhelm's *Lehrjahre* (1794), his years of apprenticeship. Today's *Lehrlinge* (apprentices, trainees), or as they are now more often called in such white-collar jobs as banking and publishing, also covered by the system, *Azubis* (short for *Auszubildende* – see BILDUNG in IV), at first earn only a third of a qualified worker's wage, but know that this will change when they have attained their *Gesellenbrief* ('journeyman's certificate' or full qualification), and after further practical and theoretical training their *Meisterbrief* (master craftsman's diploma – see HANDWERK above). Since one becomes a *Meister* by hard work rather than by accident of birth, the word is not used, even ironically, to address a young boy in the way the English use(d) 'master'.

The *Meister* has long been a figure of authority and prestige, and a central pillar of German *Kultur** in its wider sense. While Meister Eckhart's title was an academic one (a *Magister* or master's degree from the University of Paris), another great German mystic, Jakob Böhme, was in fact a *Schustermeister* (master cobbler), as was the poet* Hans Sachs. It is, of course, Wagner's Sachs who gives the most memorable defence of solid, traditional standards in both the arts and the crafts as a bulwark against changing fashion and foreign influence (see WELSCH in II), and his warning at the end of *Die Meistersinger von Nürnberg* (1868) – *Verachtet mir die Meister nicht und ehrt mir ihre Kunst*, 'Do not despise the Masters but honour their craft' – is resonant of the veneration in which the master craftsman is still held in Germany. ('Nationalistic' elements in *Die Meistersinger* reflect no more than contemporary German aspiration towards nationhood, and it would quite wrong to suppose the line *Ehrt eure deutschen Meister* could mean you should 'Honour your German Masters' in the sense of 'overlords' – one is subservient to a *Herr*, and the 'master race' is das *Herrenvolk**.)

Beethoven thought *Die Zauberflöte* was Mozart's greatest work, for with it he became truly *ein deutscher Meister*. Yet the word is equally, chillingly, apt in what is possibly the most poignant poem written in German since the war: *Der Tod ist ein Meister aus Deutschland*, 'Death is a master-craftsman from Germany' (Paul Celan, *Todesfuge*,

'Death Fugue', 1950) – a grim reminder of the smooth functioning of the death camps.

MESSE n.f. not the fine mess you can get somebody into (who might consequently complain: *du hast mir die Angelegenheit ver-masselt*), but a trade fair. Best known are the *Hannover Messe* in March and the *Leipziger Messe* in March and September. The world's largest book fair, the *Frankfurter Buchmesse*, takes place in October, and the *Leipziger Buchmesse* in May. See also MESSE in V.

MIST n.m. not what rolls in from the sea (*der Nebel*), but dung. The wealth of a farmer was often judged by the size of his *Misthaufen*, which took pride of place in the centre of the farmyard. Also, like French *merde*, a fairly innocuous expletive when you have *Mist gemacht* or *Mist gebaut* (produced rubbish): *verdammter Mist!* Somewhat stronger is *Miststück* or *Mistvieh*, bitch/bastard; or *Mistfink*, as used of muck-raking journalists; but *alter Mistkäfer* ('old dung beetle') is the cleaning lady's affectionate, though alas accurate, description of Gregor Samsa at the end of his metamorphosis in Kafka's story, *Die Verwandlung* (1912) – see also under SCHRECKEN in II, SCHULD in V.

Rolls-Royce were probably ill-advised to retain the name Silver Mist in Germany (the Jaguar SS – 'Swallow Sidecars' – obviously had to go after the war, but Ford recently decided to keep the name of their *Probe** model in spite of connotations of it being merely on trial).

MITTELSTAND n.m. the middle classes, but also small to medium-sized firms. In March 1993, Eberhard von Kuenheim, then head of BMW, warned of the problems facing those *mittelständische Unternehmen* and *mittelständische Betriebe* which supply Germany's flagship industry now that a third of the value of a German car is produced abroad. See also MITTELKLASSE in VII, MITTEL in V, STAND in I.

MONIEREN v. a traditional commercial term meaning to make a complaint: *die Firma hat sofort moniert, daß die Sendung beschädigt war*, the firm immediately made a complaint that the consignment was damaged (the goods complained about or queried are *die be-anstandete Ware**). But since Latin *monere* means to remind or advise as well as to warn (the function of a *Monitor* or a *Monument*), *wir haben bei unserem Handelspartner* bereits moniert* can mean either 'we have already made a complaint to our trading partner' or 'we have already sent our trading partner a reminder'. More generally, like *bemängeln* (see MANGEL in IX), to find fault with or criticize: *er hat* *meine schlechte Handschrift moniert* (he criticized my bad hand-writing).

MONTAGE n.f. as well as film montage, the normal word for an industrial installation such as *das Montageband*, assembly line. *Ein Monteur* may be a fitter, an automechanic, or the engineer who installs or repairs your heating (*Heizungsmonteur*), telephone (*Fernmeldemonteur*), or electricity supply (*Elektromonteur*). *Er ist auf Montage*, he's out on a job.

MONTAN- in cpds. *die Montanindustrien* are the iron and steel industries (an individual plant is called *eine Hütte**) as well as coal-mining (see above, BERG-). In 1951, the Federal Republic joined *die Montanunion*, the West European coal and steel community, as a first step towards the Common Market, and *das Montan-Mitbestimmungsgesetz* of that year gave workers in these industries important co-determination and management rights – after modification the basis of subsequent industrial relations in Germany.

MOOR n.n. not a high-lying heath such as Exmoor (in German this would be *ein Hochmoor* or *eine Heide*, such as *Lüneburger Heide*), but a bog. Lines from Gottfried Benn's poem *Gesänge* (1913), *Oh, daß wir unsre Ururahnen wären. / Ein Klümpchen Schleim in einem warmen Moor*, express a longing to return to the condition of 'our primordial ancestors, a lump of slime in a tepid swamp' – the sort of fashionable *nostalgie de la boue* which Johann Esser and Wolfgang Langhoff failed to echo in the *Lied der Moorsoldaten* which they wrote, and Rudi Goguel composed, in Börgermoor concentration camp in 1933. In parts of Schleswig-Holstein, the *Moorland* (marshland; the corresponding southern German word is *Moos*) contains a thriving *Moorkultur* (reclamation and cultivation of peat bogs, sometimes revealing *Moorleichen*, preserved bodies), and has seen a revival of *Moorkur** with *Moorbäder** – the original mud-baths and mud-pack therapy.

A Moor, however, is *ein Mohr*. One such, disgruntled that his underhand services to the conspirator Fiesco are no longer required, famously observes in Act III, Scene 4 of Schiller's play *Die Verschwörung des Fiesco zu Genua* (1783): *Der Mohr hat seine Arbeit getan, der Mohr kann gehen*, a line cited nowadays in slightly altered form (*Der Mohr hat seine Schuldigkeit getan, der Mohr kann gehen*) when one feels one has been badly used or exploited.

NATURALIEN n.p. either natural produce (*in Naturalien bezahlen*, to pay in kind), or else natural-history specimens.

OTTER n.f. an adder or viper (usually *die Kreuzotter*; the animal is *der Otter*, sometimes to avoid ambiguity *der Fischotter*). The snake is also, indeed originally, *eine Natter*: the Germans, like the English with a nuncle/an uncle, ran article and noun together, then made the split in a different place. John the Baptist – *Johannes der Täufer* in Luther, but *Jokanaan* in Richard Strauss's *Salome* (1905) – addresses the Pharisees and Sadducees in the *Evangelium des Matthäus* 3.7 as *Ihr Otterngezüchte.* 'To nourish a viper in one's bosom', *eine Natter am Busen nähren.* See also WURM in X.

PAKET n.n. either **1.** a (large) parcel or package; or **2.** a tied bundle – of newspapers, clothes, washing; or **3.** a pack or packet of some commodity such as washing powder, *ein Waschpulverpaket*; or **4.** an insurance package, *ein Versicherungspaket*, or government saving's package, *ein Sparpaket**. But the (small) packet you post is *ein Päckchen* (*das Pack*, like *die Bagage**, has come to mean a rabble). Note, too, that what you buy is *eine Schachtel Zigaretten*, what you throw away when empty *eine Zigarettenschachtel.*

PAPIER n.n. also a financial security (in full, *das Wertpapier*): *völlig risikofreie Staatspapiere* (*Die Zeit*, 1 July 1988) are not declassified state papers, but totally risk-free national bonds, which most Germans prefer to stocks and shares (see EFFEKTEN above).

PASSIV adj. *eine passive Handelsbilanz** is an adverse trade balance. Similarly, *ein Passivsaldo* is not an account which is 'inactive', but one which is in debit. *Aktiva und Passiva*, assets and liabilities. See also the special meaning of '*passiv*' voting rights in II.

PATENT adj. from *das Patent* (patent, master's ticket, officer's commission; in Switzerland, a licence to practise one's trade or profession – *Gastwirtschaftspatent, Musizierpatent, Hausierpatent*), via *eine Patentlösung* (patent remedy, ideal solution) to someone or something ingenious, clever, handy, nifty, neat (also neatly dressed). *Ein patenter Kerl* is an excellent fellow, and the *patente Witwen, schräge Vögel und knorrige Individualisten* interviewed by the *Süddeutsche Zeitung* on 15 June 1990 in defence of their Munich allotments were 'resourceful widows, oddbods and rugged individualists'. A patent remedy for hangovers, *ein Spezialrezept* gegen Kater*, is revealed under MUSKELKATER in VIII.

PERFEKT adj. note the additional meaning: settled, agreed, final. *Der Vertrag ist perfekt*, the contract is signed, sealed and delivered. *Machen wir die Sache perfekt*, let's clinch the deal.

PERSONAL n.n. staff (especially domestic – *früher, als man sich noch Personal leisten konnte*); *ein Personalchef** is a personnel manager, and *eine Personalfrage* (though also *eine personelle Angelegenheit*) a question of staffing or staffing matter, not a personal question (*eine persönliche Frage*). Germans carry a *Personalausweis*, identity card, with details of *Personalien* – their 'particulars' (see also PASS in I).

POLICE n.f. an insurance policy. The police is *die Polizei*, individual officers are *Polizisten*.

PREIS n.m. three basic meanings: price, prize, praise. This can be confusing. *Die Preisfrage* may be either a question of price, or the big question; *eine Preisangabe* is a price quotation, *eine Preisaufgabe* a prize competition. More august when it means 'praise', as in *Lobpreis*, *Lob und Preis*, or *Preis und Dank*.

While *die Preisgabe* sounds as if it should refer to prize-giving (*die Preisverleihung*), it in fact means surrender; similarly, *preisgeben* (like French *donner en prise*) is to relinquish or betray (*ein Geheimnis preisgeben*, to divulge a secret).

PRO prep. as in *Prozent* (per cent), *pro Stück* (per piece), *pro Person* (per person). When Germans give details about how much they earn (see LOHN above) – which they, like the Americans, do more freely than the British – they cite their earnings *pro Monat* (per month), not *pro Jahr* (per annum). *Das Pro und das Kontra* are the pros and cons, a golf professional/pro is *ein Profi*.

PROKURIST n.m. not a procurer/pimp (see under PIMPF in VI), but a procurator, usually the company secretary who holds a general commercial power of attorney or proxy (*die Handlungsvollmacht, die Prokura*).

PROVISION n.f. commission. *Er verdient 10 Prozent Provision auf jede Police*, die er verkauft*, he earns 10% commission on every policy he sells. But the act of providing is *die Bereitstellung, die Beschaffung, die Versorgung* (in a will, a provision is *eine Vorkehrung* or *eine Bestimmung*), that which is provided or supplied in general *der Vorrat**, and provisions of food in particular *Lebensmittel*, die Verpflegung*, or *der Proviant*.

PUMP n.m. no connection with *eine Pumpe* (pump), but credit or tick. Thomas Mann called the prodigal Wagner *ein Pumpgenie*, and this is also the title by which German readers of P. G. Wodehouse have been introduced to Ukridge, *der auf Pump lebt* (who lives by sponging). But excessive borrowing is seldom a laughing matter in Germany: in Edgar Reitz's film epic *Heimat** (1985), the credit boom which led to hyperinflation in the 1920s and helped destabilize the Weimar Republic is deplored by the older generation in the recurrent phrase *alles auf Pump* (all on tick). Similarly, critics of Chancellor

Kohl's electoral promise to finance reunification through borrowing (*Staatsverschuldung*), rather than through raising taxes (*Steuererhöhung*), speak of *Einheit auf Pump*.
Opinions differ on how Germany's most famous bread, *Pumpernickel*, got its name. Chambers imaginatively suggests it is 'possibly from its giving forth a sound like *pump* when struck'; Thackeray would have us believe, in *Vanity Fair*, that it can be traced to a town of that name on the river *Pump* (in fact, Weimar); actually, it is derived from its unfortunate effect on the digestive system. *Ein Pumps* (like *ein Furz*) is a fart (hence also *ein Pimpf*, a young squirt – the name given to the junior branch of the *Hitlerjugend*, Hitler Youth).

Note also *die Pumphose*, the baggy breeches that oriental sultans wear, or else an alternative word for *Knickerbocker* – from the wide-breeched Dutchmen in the humorous *History of New York* by 'Knickerbocker' (Washington Irving). But the narrower leather knee-breeches worn in Bavaria and Austria as part of their *Tracht*, or national dress, are known as *eine Kniebundhose*. *Der Pumps* (pronounced *Pömps*) is a light dancing shoe or pump/US court shoe, while today's running pumps/US trainers are *Turnschuhe* (see TURNEN in VII), if not already anglicized as *Trainingsschuhe*.

QUITTIEREN v. *das Amt quittieren* means to quit office. However, *er quittierte die Vorwürfe mit einem Lächeln* does not mean 'he stopped making accusations', but rather 'he answered (someone else's) accusations with a smile', paid them back in different coin. This is an extension of *quittieren* in its other basic sense, 'to give a receipt': *können Sie mir die Rechnung quittieren?* can you give me a receipt (*eine Quittung*) for the bill? – as in (archaic) English 'quittance', or the phrase 'now we are quits' (*jetzt sind wir quitt*).

QUOTATION n.f. like *die Quotierung*, only a commercial or financial quotation; to quote a price or rate is *quotieren*. Derived from *die Quote*, quota or rate – *die Quote der Arbeitslosen*, unemployment rate; *das Frauenförderungsgesetz sucht die Quote der Frauen im öffentlichen Dienst* zu erhöhen*, the law promoting women aims to increase the number of women in public service jobs. The quotation you get from a tradesman, however, is *ein Kostenvoranschlag*. On the other hand, *ich zitiere* (and I quote): *das Ewig-Weibliche zieht uns hinan* – the last line of Goethe's *Faust* is *ein Zitat*.

RABATT n.m. a rebate (*die Rückzahlung*, *die Rückvergütung*), but also a discount (*der Preisnachlaß*): *mit 5% Rabatt* (at 5% discount), *Rabatt bei Barzahlung** (discount for cash), *Rabattmarken* (trading stamps). *Eine Rabatte*, however, is a flower-bed or border.

RAIN n.m. not rain (*der Regen*), but a grassy ridge between fields, or verge in a country lane. Especially in the Alps, *der Anrainer* (French, *riverain*) is one's neighbour, the owner of the adjacent property, or else a local resident – the road sign *Anrainer frei** (German, *Anlieger frei*) means 'residents only'.

RATE n.f. though some Anglo-American usages such as *Wachstumsrate* (growth rate) and *Inflationsrate* (inflation rate) exist, the basic German meaning is instalment, as in *auf Raten kaufen*, to buy in instalments or on hire purchase (see also LEASING above).

The floor or minimum lending rate, fixed by the *Bundesbank*, which other banks have to pay when borrowing money, is *der Diskontsatz*, while the ceiling or rate for loans on security is known as *der Lombardsatz* (this long-term rate matters more in a country where, in 1994, only 15% of business borrowing was short-term, against 66% in Britain). The – essentially negotiable – interest rate ordinary borrowers have to pay, is *der Zinssatz*. The exchange rate is *der Devisenkurs** and is fixed by the markets, while 'rates', *Gemeindesteuern* or *Kommunalsteuern**, are fixed by local authorities.

REELL adj. honest, on the level. *Reelle Preise* are fair prices, good value for money, and *ein reelles Geschäft* means a solid business or sound transaction. It is thus distinct from *real*, actual or realistic – *reale Kaufkraft*, real purchasing power; *reale Werte*, tangible assets. Understanding the nuances of reality in German (see AKTUELL and REALPOLITIK in II, IDEELL in V) has become marginally less complicated with the passing of *der real existierende Sozialismus*. See also REALSCHULE in IV and REALISIEREN in X.

REFERENT n.m. sometimes 'business consultant', but also a rank in the bureaucratic structure of a public authority (*eine Behörde*), or in the hierarchy of a firm. The disillusioned hero of Martin Walser's novel *Brief an Lord Liszt* (1982, p. 92) contemplates the following promotion ladder in his firm: *Sachbearbeiter, Gruppenleiter, Hauptgruppenleiter, Referent, Abteilungsleiter, Hauptreferent, Hauptabteilungsleiter, Bereichsleiter, Direktor*. See also REFERAT/REFERENT in I and IV.

REKLAMIEREN v. not to reclaim, but to complain. *Die Rechnung reklamieren* means to query the bill, rather than to reclaim it (*das geht alles auf Spesen*, it's all on expenses). British visitors sometimes feel the customer is always wrong in Germany, perhaps because they are not used to shop assistants who know rather a lot about what they sell. While *eine Reklamation* is a complaint, *eine Reklame* (also *eine Werbung* or *ein Werbespot*) is an advertisement or TV commercial. *Reklame für etwas machen*, to advertise.

Germans are very keen on *das Recycling* – *rezyklieren* is the vogue word these days for the reclamation process applied to waste products (traditionally, *wiedergewinnen* or *regenerieren*; in the case of both paper and atomic waste, *wiederaufbereiten*) – and financial inducements and/or penalties persuade all concerned to make/sell/buy products which are *recyclebar*. To claim/reclaim luggage or baggage, however, is *Gepäck abholen*: in an airport you go to the *Gepäckabholhalle*, in a railway station to the *Gepäckausgabe* counter. Finally, to reclaim land: *Land gewinnen* (see GRAB above).

RENTE n.f. either **1.** the pension which most workers and employees collect (only *Beamte**receive *eine Pension**); or **2.** an annuity. This may be a steady income derived from an insurance policy or from investments (*der Rentenmarkt* is a market in fixed-interest securities, not in pensions funds). War, invasion, and ultimately hyperinflation (against which the *Rentenmark** was successfully introduced in 1923, converted in 1924 to the *Reichsmark*) militated against the emergence in Germany of a villainous *rentier* class living on unearned income, such as Marx described in France. The word *der Rentier*, meaning either *rentier* or pensioner, is now archaic (*das Ren* or *Rentier* – German pronunciation – is a reindeer). A pensioner is *ein Rentner* or, in the case of civil servants, *ein Pensionär*.

One, somewhat risky, way of buying a house in Germany (see under DOPPELHAUS in IX) is *auf Rentenbasis*, on an annuity basis: instead of paying the purchase price, the buyer undertakes to pay the seller an annuity for life. But most Germans still rent their flat and pay *die Miete*.

RENTIEREN v., **RENTABEL** adj. not to rent (*mieten*) or rentable (*mietbar, zum Mieten*), but to be profitable or viable: *das rentiert sich nicht* or *das ist nicht rentabel*, it doesn't pay, it's not worth doing. *Die Rentabilität* is thus profitability. The *Bundesbahn*, planning new high-speed rail track, has recently been offering attractive compensation to German farmers for *ihre unrentablen Felder**, their unprofitable fields.

ROTTENFÜHRER n.m. not a dissenting view on Hitler's capabilities as a leader. A *Rotte* (etymologically, a 'disruptive' horde) is now either a pack of wolves or dogs (not necessarily rottweilers – from Rottweil in Swabia), or a gang of youths; or else a small troop of soldiers or pair of planes/ships operating in formation; or a gang of railway workers, whose foreman is thus *der Rottenführer*.

ROUTINE n.f. also means experience, and the proficiency it brings. *Ein Routinier* is an expert, an old hand at something, though confusingly it *can* also mean someone with a routine, unimaginative approach. Similarly, *routiniert* has both the positive sense of skilled, professional, and the pejorative sense of slick, practised, purely routine.

SANIEREN v. does not evoke sanitariness or sanitation (*die Hygiene*; of a city, *die Stadtreinigung*; sewage disposal is *die Kanalisation**), but rather the civic renovation and redevelopment projects (*Altstadtsanierung*) which the Germans have been keen on since the 1960s (or, indeed, since the war, which destroyed so many ancient buildings) to restore and upgrade the original buildings or townscape (*das Stadtbild*). Thus, *ein neu saniertes Haus* is not a house that has recently had sanitation installed (*ein Haus mit neuen sanitären Anlagen*), but one which has been cleaned and restored.

Also economic rehabilitation: *Sanierungsmaßnahmen für das Pfund* are measures to restore the value of the pound, while an insurance company applies *Sanierungsmaßnahmen* by increasing premiums and reducing risks. An even more blatant euphemism for making profits is: *bei dem Geschäft hat er sich saniert*, he made a killing on the deal.

SCHWANKEN v. not to swank (*protzen*, *angeben*; *ein Angeber* is a show-off), but (like *wanken**) to vary, waver, stagger, totter, vacillate, dither. *Schwankende Börsenkurse* are fluctuating stock-market prices, and *der Schwankungsbereich* the range of fluctuation. *Ein Schwank*, however, is a humorous anecdote or a local dialect farce, especially popular in Bavaria, though also in Hamburg (see also POSSE in X).

SCHWINDEL n.m. dizziness as well as swindle. *Schwindeln* means to swindle or to be dizzy (*mir schwindelts*, *mir ist schwindlig*), and *ein Schwindelpreis* suggests both senses – it is an astronomical, exorbitant price (the opposite of a *Spottpreis**). Michael Oakeshott used to tease his left-wing students at LSE by saying that politics were *nur für Schwindelfreie**, that is, only for those who are free from lies, but equally, who do not suffer from vertigo induced by clinging to a single *Weltanschauung* (see Noel Annan, *Our Age*, 1990, p. 531).

SORTEN n.p. foreign currencies (see also *Devisen** above), including banknotes and coins (*Bargeld**). *Der Sortenkurs** is consequently the 'tourist exchange rate'.

SORTIMENT n.n. a range or assortment of wares, specifically in the retail book trade. *Eine Sortimentsbuchhandlung* sells books from a wide range of publishing houses, usually arranged first by subject area, and then under the various imprints. *Den Titel haben wir im Sortiment*, we have the book in stock.

SPAREN v. to save or economize (to spare only in the sense of sparing oneself the trouble, *sich die Mühe sparen*). *Eine Sparkasse* is a savings bank, and most towns and cities have their own *Stadtsparkasse* which offers full banking services and is often preferred to the 'big three' private banks – *Deutsche Bank, Dresdner Bank, Commerzbank* – which also have branches* in most towns.

    Ein Sparschwein is a piggy bank. 'Buddy, can you spare a dime?': *Kumpel, haste mal 'nen Groschen für mich?*

SPLENDID adj. usually means generous: the recipient of *splendide Behandlung* has been handsomely treated. Göschen's phrase 'splendid isolation' is also used in German (see also ISOLIERUNG/ISOLATION in IX).

SPOTTPREIS n.m. a ridiculously or ludicrously low price (*spottbillig*, dirt cheap), whereas a spot transaction is *ein Spotgeschäft*, on the spot market, *der Kassamarkt*, or more recently *der Spotmarkt* (the oil spot market in Rotterdam, for instance).

STALL n.m. the accommodation for most farmyard animals – *Pferdestall* (stable), *Kuhstall* (cowshed), *Hühnerstall* (hen-house), *Schweinestall* (pigsty) – hence also a filthy, untidy room. Figuratively, *den Stall tüchtig ausmisten** is to clean out the Augean stables, create order; but also, *ein ganzer Stall voll Kinder*, a whole brood/pack of children.

STAPELN v. not to staple papers together (*heften*), but to stack things one on top of the other to form *ein Stapel* (or *ein Paket**). *Stapelwaren* are mass-produced goods, but staple commodities are *Grundstoffe** (natural), *Rohstoffe* (when traded), *Bedarfsgüter* (manufactured), or *Hauptnahrungsmittel** (foodstuffs); the staple topic of conversation, however, is *das Hauptgesprächsthema*. Since *der Stapel* in nautical parlance is the stocks, *der Stapellauf* refers to the launching of a ship.

STEMPELN v. to stamp (for instance, one's ticket on a bus – see GÜLTIG in I); also, for those in employment, to clock in; for the unemployed, to sign on the dole – *stempeln gehen*.

STIER n.m. not a steer (*ein junger Ochse*), but a bull or bullock (see also BULLE above). A bull-fight is *ein Stierkampf.*

STOCK n.m. 'stock' in the sense of a firm's basic capital (*der Grundstock, das Stammkapital**), or of its stocks (*der Vorrat**, *der*

Bestand; stocktaking is *die Inventur,* figuratively *die Bestands-aufnahme*), but not the stocks and shares (*Aktien, Wertpapiere, Effekten**) traded on the Stock Exchange (*die Börse*). Also 'stick', as in a walking-stick, conductor's baton or billiard-cue; and as an intensifier, something as rigid or unchanging as a stick: *stock-konservativ,* arch-conservative; *stocksteif,* as stiff as a poker; *stockblind,* as blind as a bat; *stockfinster,* pitch-black; *stocknüchtern,* stone-cold sober; *stockbesoffen/stockvoll,* dead drunk. In addition, an abbreviation of *das Stockwerk*: *im dritten Stock* (or *auf der dritten Etage*), on the third floor or storey; *ein dreistöckiges Gebäude,* a three-storey building.

   Though 'stock' retains its original sense of trunk or stem in both languages (*der Rebstock,* vine; *der Rosenstock,* rose-bush), stocky in build is *stämmig* (from *der Stamm,* tree-trunk) whereas *stockig* is used of a musty smell or mildewed paper, and *stockend* means faltering, hesitant (*stockende Geschäfte,* business slackening or dropping off).

STOPP n.m. stop or halt. *Ein Baustopp* is a halt on building projects, and the slogan *Atomstopp* advocates a total ban on nuclear energy, but *ein Lohnstopp* is when wages are frozen, not stopped.

STORY n.f. a strange story (*eine ungewöhnliche Geschichte* – see SKURRIL in V) which, it is alleged, actually happened; or else the story of a film or novel; or a saleman's 'spiel*' – *er hat mir eine lange Story* – pronounced *Schtory* – (or *einen langen Sermon*) *erzählt,* he gave me a long sales pitch.

STÜCKARBEIT n.f. literally 'piecework' (see AKKORD above): not to be confused with either *Stuckarbeit* (stucco work) or *Stückwerk* (an unfinished or makeshift piece of work).

SUBSTANZ n.f. more often used in an abstract or general sense; a material substance is better rendered as *ein Stoff**. Thus, *der Baustoff* or *das Baumaterial* refers to bricks, mortar, etc., whereas *die Bau-substanz* is something quite different. *Die Bausubstanz der DDR gehört von Grund auf erneuert* (*Süddeutsche Zeitung,* 2 May 1990) means that all the buildings in the GDR need complete renovation.

   Also capital assets: *er lebt von der Substanz* means he is living off his capital.

SUBSTITUT n.m. not a substitute (*der Ersatz*; see also *kommissarisch* under KOMMISSAR in I), but formerly the deputy or assistant manager of a section in a department store.

SYKOMORE n.f. mulberry or sycamore fig; the sycamore tree is *der Bergahorn.*

TARIF n.m. not only Customs tariffs, but the usual word for public service charges such as *Gastarif* (gas tariff), *Stromtarif* (electricity tariff), *Wassertarif* (water tariff), *die Tarife für Telefonanschlüsse* (telephone rental).

Die Tarife für Löhne/Gehälter are basic wage rates/salary scales. These are negotiated between the *Tarifpartner* (union and management, both sides of industry) in an annual *Tarifrunde* for each industry (the twenty unions are organized on sectoral lines), generally at national level (individual companies are not involved), in which the government is not allowed to meddle because of *Tarifautonomie*. Unlike the other unions, the engineers' *IG Metall*, the biggest union in the world, reaches a collective deal in one state which is then binding on all others. In addition, individual firms' top-up agreements reflecting local skill shortages are negotiated, not with the unions, but with the elected *Betriebsrat**, a works council representing workers' interests (except on basic pay, so that unlike Britain there is no connection between a pay rise and changes in working practice). Only after lengthy arbitration procedures can the union call a strike.

Note also *Vereinigung zum Nulltarif** – German tax-payers soon had reason to be sceptical of the promised 'unification at no extra cost' (see LAST and PUMP above).

TAXE n.f. not the taxes we all have to pay (*die Steuern*), but a charge or levy, such as the *Kurtaxe** levied on visitors to a *Kurort*; also a colloquial word for *Taxi* (the fare is *das Fahrgeld*). Or else a valuation or estimate – *der Taxwert* or *der Taxpreis*; this is the only sense of the verb *taxieren*. The hero of Christoph Hein's novel *Der fremde Freund* (1982) buys a second-hand car *für den doppelten Taxwert*, for twice the estimated value. As the waiting time for a new *Trabant** in the GDR was up to fifteen years, this was not unusual. See also EXPERTISE in I and TEMPERAMENTVOLL in VI.

TECHNIK n.f. technology or engineering, as well as technique(s). *Ein Techniker* is either a non-graduate engineer or a technician (*er ist kein Techniker*, he is not technically minded). For the prestigious job and title of *Diplomingenieur* (*Dipl.–Ing.*), see DIPLOM and INGENIEUR in IV.

TENDENZ n.f. changes in price or temperature *zeigen eine steigende/fallende Tendenz*, show an upward/downward trend, but *Tendenz* is sometimes much stronger than 'tendency'. Thus, *die Tendenz eines Artikels* is the slant or bias of a newspaper article; the *Tendenzstücke* of the Young Germans (*die Jungdeutschen*, 1830–48) were the first German plays with a consistently political message, albeit implicit. *Tendenziös*, used in this context, is pejorative.

TERMIN n.m. not termination (the expiry of a contract is *der Ablauf*), but either an appointment (the person you want to see is your *Gesprächspartner*); a date (for delivery – *ein Liefertermin*); a deadline (*Termintreue* in the GDR signified, somewhat pathetically*, attempts to keep to the targets of the planned economy – see AKTIVIST in II); a sporting fixture; or a legal hearing (see HEARING in I).

Nor does the verb *terminieren* mean to terminate, but rather to put a time limit on something, especially a business deal (hence *ein Termingeschäft*, a deal on the forward or futures market), though it *is* now sometimes used in the sense of liquidating a firm's assets (*liquidieren*), and the liquidator (*der Liquidator, der Abwickler*) accordingly, and inevitably, also known as *der Terminator*.

To terminate a contract, *however*, is *einen Vertrag lösen*; a pregnancy, *eine Schwangerschaft unterbrechen* (the noun is *Schwangerschaftsabbruch* – see ABORT in VI); a friendship, *eine Freundschaft beenden*.

Terminus is only used in the sense of *terminus technicus*. A rail or bus terminus is *die Endstation**, or in the case of a railway station at the end of a line, *der Kopfbahnhof.*

TRESOR n.m. not treasure (*der Schatz* – *mein Schatz* is a term of endearment), but a strongroom, vault, or safe. The Treasury/US Treasury Department is *das Finanzministerium* (previously *Schatzministerium*); the treasurer of a club or society, *der Schatzmeister* or *Kassenwart* (see above, KASSE).

ULTIMO n.m. *per Ultimo* is not a final demand (*eine letzte Aufforderung zu zahlen*) or ultimatum (*ein Ultimatum*), but 'by the end of the month' – like 'ultimo' in archaic commercial English, rather than its more general sense in writing when 'your letter of the 31st ultimo' means 'the 31st of last month'.

UNKOSTEN n.p. expenses, not 'lack of costs'. As well as signifying negation (see UNMENSCH, monster, in II), the *un-* prefix is sometimes simply an intensifier, as in *eine Unmenge Leute*, vast numbers of people; *ein Untier*, a very beastly beast. See also UNFALL in VII.

UNTERHANDELN v. simply to negotiate, without any suggestion of underhand means (*hinterhältige Mittel*).

UNTERNEHMER n.m. an industrialist or entrepreneur. Siegfried Trebitsch's generally excellent translations ensured the early success of Shaw's plays in Germany, but one wonders what they made of 'an undertaker' becoming *ein Unternehmer* instead of *ein*

Leichenbestatter, or 'a public house' *ein öffentliches* Haus* (brothel) instead of *eine Gaststätte.*

VOLLBLÜTIG adj. thoroughbred, and hence figuratively 'full-blooded'. A thoroughbred horse is *ein Vollblut* or *ein Vollblüter.*

WALZEN v. to roll, mainly metal in a *Walzwerk* (rolling mill). To waltz is now only *Walzer tanzen,* and one no longer sees many *Wanderburschen auf der Walze,* journeymen on the road. Those who do still tramp* through Germany from job to job often wear the distinctive *Tracht* of their trade, like the joiner in black velvet and silver buttons who, having worked his way through Canada and Russia, was recently encountered hitch-hiking home to his Swabian village to settle down. See above, MEISTER.

WIRKEN v. not the normal word for 'to work' (*Arbeiter arbeiten; Maschinen funktionieren*), but to work in a more elevated sense (*als Arzt wirken; Wunder wirken*); or else to make a certain impression (*er wirkt nervös**); or to have an effect (*Alkohol wirkt berauschend,* causes intoxication; *eine stark wirkende Droge,* a strong drug). The more specific sense of *wirken* is 'to weave': *ein Wirker* nowadays works in *eine Wirkerei,* knitwear factory.

Consequently, the *Erdgeist** (Earth Spirit) conjured up by Faust uses a doubly appropriate metaphor: *So schaff' ich am sausenden Webstuhl der Zeit / Und wirke der Gottheit lebendiges Kleid,* 'And so I work at Time's whirring loom and weave the living garment of God' (*Erster Teil,* ll. 508–9). But 'to weave' is more commonly *weben,* an activity better known to German literature through Gerhart Hauptmann's moving portrayal in *Die Weber* (1892) of impoverished Silesian *Heimarbeiter** (homeworkers) confronting the new machines which have destroyed their cottage industry, now with social agitation (see under DOM in V), now with the *Weltschmerz* of Christian resignation. Their loosely or badly woven Silesian linen is the unlikely origin of what we know as 'sleaze'.

WIRTSCHAFT n.f. the economy, the business world, industry and commerce; *ein Wirtschafter* is a manager. But also a pub; *der Wirt* is the landlord. For those who frown upon '*Frollein*' (*Fräulein*) and even *Herr Ober** as non-PC terms, an alternative way of summoning waiting staff is to call '*Wirtschaft*'.

Now that Britain is showing interest in *die soziale Marktwirtschaft,* the social market economy with which Ludwig Erhard launched the post-war German *Wirtschaftswunder,* it might also ponder why, even allowing for different job specifications, Germany only needs 6,000 *Wirtschaftsprüfer* (accountants or auditors), but has 60,000 *Steuer-*

*berater** (tax consultants) often working under the same roof as the 80,000 *Rechtsanwälte* (lawyers) – a system which professional organizations in the UK oppose.

ZINS n.m. interest (*Zinzeszins* is compound interest; for interest rates, see RATE above). In southern Germany and Austria, however, *Zins* also means rent*. *Ein Zinshaus* is the Viennese equivalent of a Berlin *Mietskaserne* (tenement), and *eine Zinswohnung*, like a German *Mietwohnung*, is a rented flat.

EDUCATION
and
SCIENCE

IV

ERZIEHUNG
und
WISSENSCHAFT

ABSOLVIEREN v. Either **1**. to finish one's schooling (*die Schule absolvieren*). The leaving certificate (*das Abgangszeugnis*) at secondary school is *der Hauptschulabschluß*, taken after nine years, or the *Realschulabschluß**, more widely known as *Mittlere Reife**, taken after ten years – both comparable to GCSE. Pupils at a *Gymnasium** sit for *das Abitur*, comparable to A-Levels, in their twelfth and (in some *Länder*) thirteenth years. While those with *Realschulabschluß* then normally begin a three-year *gewerbliche Lehre* (trade apprenticeship) or *kaufmännische Ausbildung* (business training) – see MEISTER in III – it has been quite common in recent years for *Abiturienten/innen* to complete the same training schemes (albeit in two years) before going to university.

Those who pass the *Abitur* automatically qualify for university entrance. Once a general examination in many subjects, it is now based on course work and examination in two specialist *Leistungsfächer* with two subsidiary *Grundkurse* or *Prüfungsfächer*, taken in the three-year *Oberstufe* (sixth form). Apart from the new *Bundesländer**, only Bavaria and Baden-Württemberg retain external setting and marking, but their *Abitur* still tends to be more highly regarded than those set and marked by the schools themselves in more 'liberal' *Länder*. The equivalent examination in Austria and Switzerland is *die Matura*.

Or **2**. to complete a course of vocational training, *Berufsausbildung*: German industry is keen to see more *Berufsabsolventen* without *Abitur* admitted to university, though they must first undergo an *Einstufungsprüfung*; or else complete a university degree, *das Studium absolvieren*: firms advertising for *Hochschulabsolventen* mit überdurchschnittlichem Examen* want good honours graduates. By extension, to complete any task, not necessarily on the global scale of 'the work begun, how soon absolved' in Book VII of *Paradise Lost*, but more especially in the sense of discharging an obligation: *das tägliche Pensum absolvieren*, to achieve one's daily quota or target, get through the day's work; *einen Besuch absolvieren*, to make a dutiful visit.

Or **3**. in a religious context: to absolve from sin (*die Absolution*); in a legal context: to acquit or exonerate from blame (*freisprechen, der Freispruch*).

ADEPT n.m. once, like Faust, an adept or initiate in the secret arts, now a humorous term meaning a disciple or acolyte (though the word Goethe uses to describe Faust's assistant, Wagner, is *Famulus* – nowadays a medical student in clinical training). Someone who is adept at doing things is *geschickt*, or else a *Meister** or *Experte* (for instance, *im Rechnen*, at doing sums).

AKADEMIKER n.m. any graduate, not only an academic in the usual English sense of someone who teaches at a university.

This is *ein Hochschullehrer* in the general sense; in the more restricted legal sense, a *Hochschullehrer* is a *Professor** or a *Dozent* (one who has taken the *Habilitation**), while *Akademischer Rat** is a specific grade and title within the *Mittelbau* of a university (the non-professorial teaching staff).

*Jungakademiker** sucht Arbeit* therefore means 'recent graduate seeks employment', while jobless graduates are sometimes referred to as *das akademische Proletariat*. Accordingly, when Ralf Dahrendorf writes of *junge großstädtische Akademiker* in pursuit of *mehr Raum für Initiative* (*Die Zeit*, 27 March 1992), he means 'Yuppies', not young right-wing dons. Nor is it likely that the editor of *Junge Freiheit*, a right-wing weekly, was claiming a readership of '30,000 young academics' (thus Denis Staunton in *The Observer*, 1 January 1995), but rather that his subscribers were young professionals. On the other hand, to talk of *die Herren Akademiker* is not a sign of deference but rather contains a note of mockery, if not contempt, for the status-conscious graduates with their lofty ideas/ideals.

The adjective *akademisch* is used much as in English, also in its pejorative sense of worthy but turgid, theoretical, unworldly – though not with the anti-intellectual* slant of a question being 'merely academic' (*rein theoretisch*). Germans generally prefer to designate their academic books as *wissenschaftlich**. *Akademische Freiheit* (alternatively, *Lehr- und Lernfreiheit*) is both the traditional freedom of a teacher to state his opinions openly and without fear of losing his job (but see BERUFSVERBOT in II), as well as a student's right to choose what courses to attend (see SCHEIN below). It is advisable to check in the *Vorlesungsverzeichnis* or guide to all classes, published before each *Semester* begins, whether a class begins *mit akademischem Viertel* (*cum tempore* or *c.t.* for those with a more classical education – the traditional 15-minute delay while the absent-minded professor tries to find the lecture room) or *ohne akademisches Viertel* (*sine tempore* or *s.t.* – at the given time). See also AKADEMIE in X, and for academic qualifications, DIPLOM and GRAD below.

APPARAT n.m. scientific apparatus; but also a radio or television set (*Fernsehapparat*); or some other complex appliance such as *Rasierapparat* (electric razor), *Photoapparat* (only the camera; photographic apparatus – suggesting extra *Geräte* such as filters and stands – is *Photoausrüstung*, while the batteries and transformer needed for lighting are known as *das Aggregat**). Or the telephone: if a caller asks for you by name, say *Am Apparat* (speaking); *Bitte bleiben Sie am Apparat!* means 'Hold the line, please'.

Or else the administration of a large firm or government department (*Verwaltungsapparat*); or the apparatus or machinery of a political party (*Parteiapparat*, whose anonymous cogs in Communist countries were known as *Apparatschiks*); or the collection of texts regularly used on a specific university course (*Seminarapparat**, *Handapparat*); or the *apparatus criticus* so beloved of German scholarship and appended to critical editions (*kritischer* Apparat*).

BILDUNG n.f. formation – of anything from committees and governments to crystals or rust – but a key word when it refers to the formation of character: the 'classical' German concept of education, along the lines expounded around 1800 by Wilhelm von Humboldt and others and still alive today (see KLASSIK and GYMNASIUM below). Emphasis is on character development through hard work, though it might also be achieved along less orthodox educational lines in accordance with the *Spieltrieb* (play instinct) famously expounded by Schiller in his letters *Über die ästhetische Erziehung des Menschen* (*On the Aesthetic Education of Man*, 1795), or as depicted in a novel such as *Wilhelm Meister*, the much imitated *Bildungsroman** which, together with *Faust*, occupied Goethe for over 50 years (see FATAL in V).

The German *Bildungsbürgertum** finds itself most faithfully reflected in the career and works of Thomas Mann. Not to have read *Der Zauberberg* (1924), the story of a seven-year *Bildungsreise* (educational trip) which, ironically, gets no further than a Swiss sanatorium, is a serious *Bildungslücke* (gap in one's education), though like the modern *Bildungsroman* in general, the book is less concerned with its hero's assimilation into existing society than with a questioning of that society itself. *Der zweite Bildungsweg* offers a 'second chance' to gain an academic education at the local *Volkshochschule** (night school).

CHEMIKER n.m. an academic or industrial chemist, as distinct from an *Apotheker** (dispensing pharmacist) or *Drogist* (someone who sells non-prescription items in a *Drogerie**).

CLEVER adj. never simply intelligent – *ein kluger* or *intelligenter Kerl* is a clever chap, but *ein cleverer Bursche* is crafty, astute, a shrewd operator – *ein cleverer Verleger*, for instance, is a publisher with his finger on the pulse of what the public wants. Germans do not share the ancient English suspicion of brain-power, however, so someone who is clever-clever, a clever Dick, or 'too clever by half', is more robustly called *ein Klugscheißer*. A know-all or smart-aleck is *ein Schlaukopf*, *ein Pedant* or *ein Besserwisser* (someone who always knows better), a term easily adapted by put-upon eastern Germans (*Ossi*) for their big brothers from the west: *Besserwessis*. See also INTELLEKTUELLER in V.

DEKAN n.m. not a deacon (*Diakon/Diakonissin* – see KONFESSION in V), but the dean of a university faculty, who is officially addressed as *Spectabilis* or *Spektabilität*. The dean in charge of a cathedral is *der Dechant*. See also REKTOR below.

DEPUTAT n.n. either payment in kind (*in Naturalien**), or else the number of hours which a teacher has to teach. In Martin Walser's novel *Brief an Lord Liszt* (1982), for instance, we are told the narrator's wife *hatte längst wieder ein volles Deputat*, meaning that she had once again a full teaching load of some 24 lessons a week (school teachers enjoy considerable flexibility in this respect).

To deputize someone else to do something is *deputieren*, to deputize for someone *vertreten* (*Der Stellvertreter/The Representative*, 1963, was Rolf Hochhuth's controversial play about the response of 'God's Deputy', Pius XII, to Hitler), but a supply teacher is *ein Aushilfelehrer*, except in Switzerland where the word is *Vikar** (as in English 'vicarious', rather than 'vicar'). For deputy, meaning someone who is temporarily in charge, see KOMMISSAR in I.

DIDAKTISCH adj. no pejorative overtones in German, but simply, like *pädagogisch*, to do with teaching (*Pädagoge* is a synonym for *Lehrer*); or having an instructive purpose (*didaktische Spielzeuge* are toys that help children to learn). Accordingly, *ein miserabler Didaktiker* is not a dreadful pedant (*ein schrecklicher Pedant* – see CLEVER above), but someone whose teaching methods are inadequate – however unlikely this is in a country with a traditional respect for education and appropriate remuneration for those who supply it. A *Didaktiker* may formerly have taught in a *Pädagogische Hochschule* or *PH* (Teacher Training College) before it became part of a university faculty and was renamed, for example, *Seminar* für Romanische* Sprache und Literatur und ihre Didaktik*, or *Fachrichtung Didaktik*.

DIPLOM n.n. not only a diploma or certificate, but a full Degree. Germans are often addressed by the title that reflects their status and function (*Herr Professor, Herr Direktor, Herr Doktor, Herr General*, even – leaving room for flattery or irony – *Herr Kollege*). Though a person's name is otherwise sufficient in speech, you address a letter to, say, a *Diplomkaufmann* (a business school graduate in *Betriebs-*

wirtschaft): *Herrn Dipl.–Kfm. Franz Schmidt*; or to a *Diplomvolkswirt* (an economist who has graduated in *Volkswirtschaft*): *Herrn Dipl.– Volksw. Hans Müller.* The same formality holds for most professions: *Dipl. Chem.* is a *Diplomchemiker* (graduate chemist); *Dipl.–Ldw.* a *Diplomlandwirt* (graduate from agricultural college); *Dipl.–Dolm.* a *Diplomdolmetscher* (qualified interpreter); *Dipl.–Ing.* a *Diplomingenieur** (graduate engineer).

DISSERTATION n.f. specifically refers to that nineteenth-century German invention, the doctoral dissertation (Ph.D.), also known as a *Doktorarbeit*, and supervised – the name suggests paternalistically – by a *Doktorvater*, though nowadays there is, of course, no theoretical objection to calling one's female supervisor *meine Doktormutter.* (A medical doctor, like a doctor of philosophy, is addressed as *Herr* or *Frau Doktor*, but by profession he/she is *ein Arzt/ eine Ärztin.*) Any other form of academic dissertation is *eine wissenschaftliche Arbeit.* See also PROMOTION and HABILITATION below.

DUMM adj. not literally dumb (*stumm*), but stupid. *Dummerchen*, silly billy; *sei kein Dummkopf!* don't be a fool; *mach bloß keine Dummheiten!* just don't do anything stupid. *Der dumme August* is a circus clown.

ELEMENTAR adj. both elementary, as in education (*Elementarunterricht*, provided by the *Grundschule*), and elemental (*Elementargewalt*, elemental force; *Elementarteilchen*, elementary particles). 'Elementary, my dear Watson', *Ganz einfach, mein lieber Watson!*

EXEMPLAR n.n. not necessarily something or someone to be imitated (an exemplar of that sort is *ein Musterbeispiel* or *Vorbild*), but a specimen, sample, or – especially of books – a copy (not *eine Kopie*, which is a replica, print or reproduction, as in *Photokopie*). Hence: *ein schönes Exemplar* (a fine specimen); Onkel Toms Hütte *war der erste Roman, von dem mehr als eine Million Exemplare verkauft wurden* (*Uncle Tom's Cabin* was the first novel to sell over a million copies).

The adjective *exemplarisch*, however, as in English: offering an illustration (*eine exemplarische Lösung*, a model proof); an example to be followed (*ein exemplarisches Leben*, an exemplary life); or an example to be avoided (*eine exemplarische Strafe*, exemplary punishment). The noun *Exempel* is mostly used in this latter sense (*ich werde an Dir ein Exempel statuieren, mein Junge! sagte der Direktor**, 'I'm going to make an example of you, boy', said the headmaster), just as it was in the original *Volksbuch* account of *Faust* (1587) – a terrible warning against necromancy rather than a heroic example of the questing spirit. Such an example is simply *ein Beispiel*, and a prime example *ein Paradebeispiel**.

FEHLER n.m. not a failure (*das Stück war ein Mißerfolg*; *das Scheitern der Ehe*; *menschliches Versagen*), but a mistake or fault. The *Prädikat** awarded to homework or a written test with too many *Fehler* might be *mangelhaft** (unsatisfactory); *er ist durchgefallen* means he failed his exam (but: *er hat Durchfall*, he has diarrhoea). The verb *fehlen* (to be lacking, missing, absent) is often used impersonally: thus, *mir fehlen die Worte*, words fail me; *du hast mir gefehlt*, I missed you (not: you failed me, *du hast mich enttäuscht* or *im Stich gelassen*); but *das hat mir gerade noch gefehlt*, that's the last thing I need. Failure to do something may be simply rendered by the prefix *Nicht-* (*wegen Nichtbeachtung der Verkehrsvorschriften*, for non-observance of the traffic regulations).

Conversely, an involuntary Freudian slip* (parapraxis, more imaginatively rendered by Walter Kaufmann as 'mischievement') is a *Freudsche Fehlleistung*. One of Freud's patients confessed to him: *Dann sind die Tatsachen zum Vorschwein** (a nonsense word) *gekommen* instead of *zum Vorschein** *gekommen* – the facts that had come to light, Freud deduced, were clearly of a 'swinish' nature (other examples, such as *Apopos* for *à propos* – *Popo* being a nursery word for 'bottom' – are recounted in the third of the five introductory lectures entitled *Einführung in die Psychoanalyse*, 1916).

FREQUENZ n.f. as in radio frequency (*Frequenzmodulation*, FM); or the frequency of trains (*die Frequenz der Züge*), though the more common German word for frequency of occurrence is *Häufigkeit*; but also used in the (older English) sense of numbers, as when *die Frequenz* refers to the volume of traffic (*die Verkehrsdichte*). *Die Klassenfrequenz* is the size of classes (Austrian and Swiss schools keep a *Frequenzliste* instead of the German *Anwesenheitsliste*, attendance register, though *Schule schwänzen*, truancy, is not a major problem); similarly, *die Frequenz des Elternabends* is not the frequency of PTA meetings, but (like French *fréquentation*) the number of parents who attend.

GELERNT adj. not learned (*gelehrt*; *ein Gelehrter* is a scholar; viewed humorously: *hochgelahrt*, highly erudite), but trained, skilled. Similarly: *er lernt noch* or *er ist noch in der Lehre* or *er ist noch Lehrling*, he is still doing his apprenticeship. But the implication of *er ist gelernter Tischler* or *er hat Tischler gelernt* (he is a joiner by trade/training) is invariably that, although he has finished his apprenticeship and become *ein Geselle* (journeyman) or even *ein Meister** (master craftsman), he no longer works as a joiner.

GRAD n.m. not grade, but degree – either a unit of measurement: *40 Grad Fieber** (a temperature of 104°), *ein Winkel von 45 Grad* (an angle of 45°); or else a university degree. An essay grade or degree classification is *die Note**or *das Prädikat**(for grade = school class, see PRIMA below).

To take a degree: *einen akademischen Grad erlangen* or *graduieren*, after which one can call oneself a *Graduierter, Akademiker** or *Hochschulabsolvent* (but see also DIPLOM above). Less formally: *ich studiere* means quite specifically 'I am a university student' (*während des Studiums*, while I was a student; *der Studiengang**, course of study, curriculum). *Examen machen* is to take Finals (*mit einer Eins*, to get a First); this usually refers to the *Staatsexamen*, the (first) state examination taken by those aspiring to employment in the broadly based 'public sector' (see ASSESSOR, BEAMTE and REFERENDAR in I), especially budding teachers. The *Magister* is an alternative first degree – like the Scottish Masters degree; in Austria, the *Magister* is bestowed at a ceremony called *die Sponsion*, and *er wurde an der Universität Salzburg spondiert* means he received his MA there. *Er hat die Uni ohne Abschluß verlassen*, he left university without taking his degree – something which happens quite often in Germany, where the time taken to complete a degree course is commonly still some fourteen semesters or seven years, where anyone with the *Abitur* is entitled to matriculate, and where there are no fees (but substantial financial advantages to having student status).

GRANT n.m. German students have never enjoyed full maintenance support, though there are various forms of *Stipendium* (scholarship, grant; see MODELL below) and, increasingly, of interest-free state loans.

Ich habe einen Grant, however, is an Austro-Bavarian expression meaning 'I'm cross'. This does less than justice to that 'uniquely Middle European blend of melancholic dissatisfaction and choleric tetchiness' known as *Grant* (Iain Bamforth, 'Bile with style', *Times Literary Supplement*, 6 October 1995) which the Austrian writer Thomas Bernhard (1931–89) raised to an art form, though the word also fits the misanthropic spleen* of both author and hero of *Look Back in Anger*. The adjective is *grantig*: grumpy, grouchy, querulous.

GYMNASIUM n.n. not a gymnmasium (*die Turnhalle*), but a grammar school, of which there were formerly three basic types: *mathematisch-naturwissenschaftlich** (also called *Realgymnasium**), *neusprachlich*, and *altsprachlich* (*humanistisch*), though most are nowadays designated *naturwissenschaftlich-neusprachlich* and teach common core subjects – German, history, maths, and at least one scientific subject and one foreign language – leading to the *Abitur* (see under ABSOLVIEREN above).

Educational policy is controlled by the *Kultusministerium* in each of the *Bundesländer*. Feeling ran high among German parents at earlier moves to replace the *Gymnasium* with the *Gesamtschule* (comprehensive school), an innovation strongly resisted in conservative Bavaria and Baden-Württemberg, with Hessen taking a more progressive approach, but comprehensivization fully accepted (at least, in theory) only in Berlin and Hamburg. More commonly, new *Gymnasien* were created, or the existing ones adapted and expanded to become more 'comprehensive'. The churches, both *evangelisch** and *katholisch*, also run denominational grammar schools (*Konfessionsschulen** or *Bekenntnisschulen*) with partial *Land* funding, a secular version of these being the *ökumenisches Gymnasium*. Another option is the prestigious *bilinguales Gymnasium*, which uses English (in some instances, French) when practicable as the language of tuition. Among today's seventeen to nineteen-year-olds, almost one in three attends a *Gymnasium*, takes the *Abitur*, and applies for a *Studienplatz* (see HOCHSCHULE below).

There are three standard types of secondary school: *Hauptschule* (secondary modern), *Realschule**(secondary intermediate, without an *Oberstufe* or upper school/sixth form), and *Gymnasium* (grammar, with an *Oberstufe*), these divisions sometimes existing within a single school. Entry criteria vary from the formal *Eingangsprüfung* (entrance examination) which *Gymnasien* in Bavaria and Baden-Württemberg use to select ten-year-olds in their fourth year of *Grundschule* (primary school), to continuous assessment by teachers during the fifth and sixth years in what is known as the *Orientierungsstufe*. Under this latter system, the *Lehrerkollegium** (teaching staff) proposes, though it is the parents who, at least initially, dispose, parental pressure tending to push for the *Gymnasium*. However, the reality of examination marks ultimately counterbalances such flexibility, since pupils still have to satisfy their teachers at the end of each school year before being permitted to move up to the next form (*versetzt werden*) and 'resume the stranglehold on learning they relinquished at the beginning of the long vac', as Wodehouse puts it, though this is no laughing matter for ambitious parents. Having to change school (most often from academic to vocational education), combined with *Sitzenbleiben* (having to repeat a year), are effective deterrents against an unsuitable initial choice of school. In East Germany, the *Einheitsschule* or unitary school offered less *Chancengleichheit* (equality of opportunity) than was claimed, since entry into the sixth form was restricted to a small *Bildungs- und Gesinnungselite*:

an élite selected as much on the basis of political attitude as educational achievement.

As Germany has no public (in the English sense of private) schools, nor any need for them – though some *Internate* (boarding schools) cater for special needs – children are generally unfamiliar with the ethos and rituals of boarding-school life, though also, regrettably, with the school stories which have grown up around it in England. Local *Gymnasien* function much as grammar schools did in Britain in the 1960s, but there is no school uniform and no tradition of games playing. Mind is cultivated at school (still often mornings only, six days a week, though afternoon classes and free Saturdays are on the increase), and the body outside it. The Battle of Tannenberg was not won on the playing fields of Schulpforta – Germany's most famous *humanistisches Gymnasium* (in fact, a Protestant *Internat*), where Klopstock, Fichte, Ranke, Wilamowitz and Nietzsche all received a brilliant classical* education.

HABILITATION n.f. the qualification to give lectures at a German university (unlike French *habilitation*, which is the ministerial validation of university degrees). In practice, an academic, *der sich habilitiert hat*, has completed a second, postdoctoral thesis and is on the threshold of a professorial career (see ORDENTLICH and PRIVAT-DOZENT below). Professors* delegate much of their teaching to those who have not yet the official *venia legendi* ('privilege of reading', i.e. lecturing/*Vorlesen*) – mainly *Assistenten*, who generally have doctorates (see PROMOTION below) and are working towards their *Habilitation*, or colleagues in the non-professorial teaching staff or '*Mittelbau*' (*Lektoren* and *Akademische Räte**).

HANG n.m. although *hängen* means to hang, *ein Hang* is either **1.** a mountain slope (*der Nordhang der Zugspitze*, the north face of Germany's highest mountain, is a particularly dramatic location for *Hangsegeln*, hang gliding, though the sport is now usually called after kite-flying, *Drachenfliegen*); or **2.** a (figurative) leaning or inclination, generally towards something considered undesirable – in spite of the fact that *an jemandem hängen* means to be devoted to someone. *Der preußische Hang zum bedingungslosen Gehorsam*, for instance, is the (alleged) Prussian tendency towards unquestioning obedience. This tendency is not a characteristic of German schoolchildren today. If their academic progress is unsatisfactory, however, they have to repeat the year – *hängenbleiben* or *sitzenbleiben* (to 'remain hanging' or 'sitting'). He is poor at Latin, *er hängt in Latein*. Hang it! *so ein Mist!*; *verflixt noch mal!* Now he's got the hang of it, *jetzt hat er es kapiert*; *jetzt ist er dahintergekommen*; *jetzt hat er's 'raus*.

HAUSARBEIT n.f. either **1.** the housework of a *Hausfrau* (or nowadays a *Hausmann*); or **2.** although schoolchildren do regular homework – *Hausaufgaben* (for which they have plenty of time as the school day in Germany often ends at 1pm, depending on the time-table; see GYMNASIUM above) – this only occasionally takes the form of *eine Hausarbeit*, a major essay. Teachers, who enjoy considerable flexibility in choice of themes, materials and methodology, set some five to ten written tests a year in each subject; these are known as *Arbeiten* (*Klausurarbeiten*) in the *Unterstufe* and *Mittelstufe*, but as *Klausuren* in the *Oberstufe*. *Abschreiben* (*mogeln, spicken, schummeln*) is not unknown, but those who crib or copy are seldom thought of as morally degenerate by their peers, whatever the alternative term, *tricksen*, might suggest.

HOCHSCHULE n.f. not a US high school (*die Oberschule* = *Gymnasium**), but another word for *Universität*. Nor is a *Technische Hochschule* (*TH*) a 'technical high school' or 'technical college' (*Technische Fachschule*), but a synonym for *Technische Universität* (*TU*), a university specializing in technical subjects (the first was established in Karlsruhe in 1825). So Peter Ackroyd was wrong to say that when Einstein formulated the theory of relativity 'he was neither a graduate nor an academic – merely the product of a technical college' (*The Independent*, 18 March 1993); in fact, he had graduated in 1900 from the prestigious *Eidgenössische Technische Hochschule* (*ETH*) in Zurich, later becoming one of its 21 Nobel laureates.

Fachhochschulen (*FHs*) with shorter (on average four-year) courses still provide what British Polytechnics were set up to do before their recent *Gleichstellung* with universities (or as it seemed to some in the universities, *Gleichschaltung*). Local *Volkshochschulen* offer adult education classes, mainly at night school, and excellent opportunities ('*auf dem zweiten Bildungsweg**') for achieving the *allgemeine Hochschulreife/Abitur* needed for university entrance, or, more commonly, the *Fachhochschulreife* (see ABSOLVIEREN above).

German universities are free (*man zahlt keine Studiengebühren*; for maintenance grants, see MODELL below) and open to anyone who has passed the *Abitur*, or any foreigner with a comparable qualification, though with a student population that has grown to almost two million (in 1990, for the first time, there were more students than apprentices), most departments require a specific overall grade which – as with individual subject grades in England – varies from university to university. The *Zentralstelle für die Vergabe von Studienplätzen* (*ZVS*) in Dortmund allocates free places in increasingly popular subjects such as *Volkswirtschaft, Betriebswirtschaft, Jura* or *Informatik*; for subjects where demand traditionally far outstrips capacity

(*Medizin, Zahnmedizin, Tiermedizin*) it uses additional criteria such as *Eignungstests* (suitability tests), the waiting time since the initial application, and the relevance of the applicant's occupation in the intervening period.

Effectively, then, there often is restricted entry, but the very notion of a *numerus clausus* (a term which *never* implies discrimination by race or sex, as it sometimes does in England) is resisted as *ein Elitegedanke*, especially by SPD-controlled *Länder**. With seminars of two to three hundred participants common, however, they have some way to go before appearing élitist in the Oxbridge sense. The *Universität Erlangen-Nürnberg*, for instance, introduced Sunday lectures in 1987, Saturdays being already full. This has led to an open market in mid-course *Studienplatztausch*, or even a black market of the kind that recently caused Hamburg to abolish its *Tauschbörse* (where those studying the same subject at different universities could exchange places) after a student of *Betriebswirtschaftlehre* (business management) offered an additional DM10,000 for a *BWL* place in Hamburg.

Though the ancient universities in picturesque towns such as Tübingen or Heidelberg have obvious attractions, others are equally ancient, or attractively situated, or more prestigious in selected subjects, or simply closer to home, so that student preference is seldom based simply on traditional prestige.

HOSPITANT n.m. not a hospital patient, but someone sitting in on a university lecture – *Gasthörer* is the more common word – or, as a trainee teacher, on a school lesson without taking an active part. University numbers are such that unofficial *Gasthörer* (those who are not *immatrikuliert* – registered) are unlikely to be challenged, though equally unlikely to find a seat in the crowded lecture theatres unless they adopt the recent practice of attending the lecture on Persian pottery which precedes the one on the latest management techniques.

Like *Hospitant*, the verb *hospitieren* derives from the same Latin root (*hospitare*, to be a guest) as our word 'hospital' and German *Hospital** – a connection to which Ludovico Settembrini, an admirer of the German *humanistisches Gymnasium**, is slyly alluding in his advice to Hans Castorp to leave the sanatorium on the Magic Mountain as soon as possible: *Sie sind gesund, Sie hospitieren hier nur, wie Odysseus im Schattenreich* ('You are healthy, you are only an onlooker here, like Odysseus in the Realm of Shades' – Thomas Mann, *Der Zauberberg*, 1924; see also SOMMERTHEATER, SCHRECKEN in II).

INGENIEUR n.m. used only in the sense of a graduate engineer, a non-graduate engineer being *ein Techniker**. Thomas Mann made the hero of *Der Zauberberg* (see HOSPITANT above) an *Ingenieur* in accordance with Oswald Spengler's famous dictum in *Der Untergang des Abendlandes* (see GANG in II) that the *Zeitgeist* belonged not to poets but to engineers. *Diplomingenieur** (*Dipl.–Ing.*, graduate engineer) is a prestigious title reflecting the respect shown in German society to someone who both designs and makes things (see KONSTRUKTION in III) – together with the *Diplomkaufmann* (*Dipl.–Kfm.*, graduate in commerce), who sells things, one of the pillars of Germany's *Wirtschaftswunder* in the 1950s and 1960s.

KAPAZITÄT n.f. besides capacity in its usual English senses, also an expert or specialist: *eine Kapazität auf dem Gebiet der Raumforschung*, an authority on space research. Conversely, *ein Fachidiot* is a crank who, though not an idiot in his or her subject, can think of nothing else.

KLASSIK n.f. the Classics – *Latein* and (to a lesser extent) *Griechisch* – are still taught in the German *humanistisches Gymnasium**, and at university as *klassische Philologie** or *Altphilologie*. Both the *Odyssey* and its author(s) are *Klassiker*; so, too, are Goethe and Schiller in the sense that they are established authors, but also because the works they wrote in little over a decade – after Goethe's Italian journey and before Schiller's death in 1805 – are synonymous with *Weimarer Klassik*, so called after the small Thuringian town to which Goethe had moved in 1775 (and to which the German government was to move in 1919 to reshape Germany's political culture). Although *klassischer Stil* is broadly applicable to a whole century of German music – from Bach (a *Vorklassiker*) and Handel (in Germany, Händel) through Haydn and Mozart to Beethoven and Schubert (who is usually counted a *Romantiker*) – here, too, *die deutsche Klassik* (or *Wiener Klassik*, Viennese classicism) in its narrower sense is the period from the 1780s to the 1810s, framed by the *Sturm und Drang* (Storm and Stress) and *Romantik* movements. See also ANTIKE in IX.

KOLLEG n.n. either **1.** a university class or course of lectures (also *der Kurs*); *Telekollegs* are the equivalent of Open University programmes. Or else **2.** a theological college. Or **3.** a *Studienkolleg* (such as the *Braunschweig-Kolleg*) which provides the necessary pre-university training for those who have not got the *Abitur* or have insufficient German. Only exceptionally is it a student residence with collegiate activities (Münster's *Aaseehaus-Kolleg*, for instance), for most students live in digs, *in einer Studentenbude*, or in a *Studentenwohnheim* without the formal social dimension, and *das College-Leben* on the Oxbridge model – with tuition – is unknown.

Nor is there a general word for college in such expressions as 'going to college' (simply *studieren*), or 'starting college' (*das Studium beginnen*). A technical college or agricultural college is *eine Fachhochschule**, an art college or music college *eine Kunstakademie* or *Musikakademie*. Professional people might still, somewhat formally, address their colleagues as *Herr Kollege* or *Frau Kollegin*, and sign letters *mit kollegialem Gruß*; students commonly address their fellow-students, especially on leaflets or posters (see NOTIZ below), as *Kommilitonen/Kommilitoninnen*. See also KOLLEGIUM below.

KOLLEGIUM n.n. 'college' only as in the College of Cardinals – a collective noun for people in the same profession. Thus, *das Lehrerkollegium* is the teaching staff of a school, not a teacher training college (see DIDAKTISCH above). Latinisms are widespread in an educational context, but it is early music ensembles such as the *Collegium Aureum* of Cologne that have appropriated the spelling *Collegium*, harking back to the *Collegium Musicum* which Telemann founded and Bach conducted in Leipzig.

KOMMENT n.m. not a comment (*eine Bemerkung*), or a commentary (*ein Kommentar**), but the code of conduct in a student fraternity (see KORPORATION below). *Der Komment* or *der Comment*, like so many student terms, comes from the Latin (sometimes via French), and may be used with a touch of irony to suggest how (French *comment?* – which is also the German pronunciation of *Komment*) those in the public eye are meant to behave. *Wäre es nicht absolut gegen den Comment, die Offiziere hätten ihn beklatscht* (if it had not been absolutely against the rules, the officers would have applauded him) – thus *Die Zeit* on 1 June 1990 when Rainer Eppelmann, a pacifist and Lutheran minister who nevertheless became East Germany's last Minister of Defence, announced that only one army officer in three would become redundant. More controversial still was the call (*der Appell**) on 13 July 1990 by Ulrich Greiner, literary editor of *Die Zeit*, for a more open appraisal of the erstwhile East German literary establishment: *der Flüsterton ist offenbar der Komment* (hushed tones are apparently the accepted norm). It was widely considered *nicht kommentgemäß* (unfair, not cricket) to criticize Christa Wolf for not having published her mild indictment *Was bleibt?* (*What remains?*) until after the regime had collapsed.

KOMMERS n.m. not commerce or trade (see HANDELN in III), but the meeting of a student fraternity involving *Bundesbrüder** (see KORPORATION below) in much drinking, singing from the *Kommersbuch*, and toasts of *Schmollis!* between songs – all of which is conducive to a warm sense of belonging and identity, though equally to being lampooned: *Draußen bin ich nur ein armes Luder, / Hier bin ich ich – und Bundesbruder* (Tucholsky).

KONVIKT n.n. a seminary (also known as a *Seminar**); or else, mainly in Austria, an *Internat* or boarding school. While the most famous Protestant seminary-cum-boarding school in Germany was known as the *Tübinger Stift* (where Hegel, Hölderlin and Schelling were friends and contemporaries from 1790 to 1793), Schubert attended the principal boarding school in Vienna, the *Stadtkonvikt*, from 1808 to 1813 (where his teachers included Salieri).

A convict, however, is *ein Sträfling, Strafgefangener* or *Zuchthäusler* (though *das Zuchthaus* itself, with its harsh penal regime, was abolished in the 1960s).

KORPORATION n.f. a somewhat dated term for a student fraternity (*eine Verbindung*), specifically one whose members – *Korporierte, Korpsstudenten, Korpsbrüder* or *Bundesbrüder* – participate in fencing bouts (*Mensuren*). Also (formerly) known as *eine Burschenschaft* or, to distinguish it from other *Studentenverbindungen*, as *eine schlagende Verbindung*. Mark Twain was much taken by the *Korpsgeist* (*esprit de corps*) – 'the dignified gravity and repression maintained at all times' – of the *Korpsstudenten* at Heidelberg (eighty in all, members of five different *Korps*, out of a university population of 750), who were obliged, in accordance with their *Komment**, to duel (*eine Mensur schlagen*) twice weekly, thereby collecting at least one duelling scar (*der Schmiß*) as a distinctive badge of honour (*A Tramp Abroad*, 1878; also discussed in Jerome K. Jerome's *Three Men on the Bummel*, 1896 – see KISSEN in VI and BIER in VIII).

Nowadays, duelling has all but died out, and even non-duelling fraternities with names such as *Germania, Teutonia, Alemania, Franconia, Bavaria, Sauerlandia, Langobardia, Cheruskia, Aenenia, Tusconia* or *Winfriedia*, though widespread and useful as life-long old-boy networks, are considered at best reactionary by most students. As the names indicate, some are *Landsmannschaften*, that is to say, élitist corporations of students from the same region (including those from territories lost after 1945 – an old taboo which the radical right in emergent east German student groups has begun to break: see HEIMAT in II), whereas others look back to the more liberal *Burschenschaften* which spearheaded the moral and cultural revival of the German states after the Napoleonic wars. At the time Mark Twain was writing, this distinction was already blurred by the trend to strident nationalism which students shared with their professors: *Studenten sind so dumm**was Nietzsche's verdict in a letter to his sister in April 1885, but *Professoren sind noch dümmer*. No such critique was evident in Wilhelm Meyer-Förster's extraordinarily successful play *Alt-Heidelberg* (1901), or Sigmund Romberg's musical version of 1924 with Richard Tauber, later to become the ultimate Hollywood kitsch of *The Student Prince* (1954), in which Mario Lanza provides Edmund Purdom's singing voice when courting Kathie, the landlord's daughter, with 'Deep in my heart', 'Golden days', and other maudlin and patriotic songs – see KOMMERS above. The best known, 'Gaudeamus igitur', provides a rousing climax to the Academic Festival Overture which Brahms composed in 1881 to express his gratitude when the University of Breslau awarded him an honorary doctorate.

LABOR n.n. a science laboratory: *im Labor*, in the lab. A woman in labour *hat die Wehen*.

LEKTÜRE n.f. not a lecture (*eine Vorlesung*), but reading as an activity, or else the reading matter itself. Thus, *englische Lektüre* is the reading of English texts at school; *Karl May ist immer noch eine Lieblingslektüre der Jugend*, children still love reading Karl May. But note that while English students 'read' German or Physics or Economics, the verb is reserved for the teaching staff of German universities: *Professor Maier liest dieses Semester über Fontane* means he is lecturing on Fontane.

MAPPE n.f. not a map (*eine Landkarte** or *ein Stadtplan*), but a large, flat satchel (*Schulmappe*); or else a document case (*Aktenmappe*), slimmer than the heavy leather briefcase (*die Aktentasche*) use of which in Germany is by no means confined to academics, or even *Akademiker**. Also a folder or portfolio for drawings or papers, as in Adalbert Stifter's *Die Mappe meines Urgroßvaters* (three versions: 1841, 1844, 1867) – a superb *Bildungsroman** in which the narrator's great-grandfather has chronicled the small-scale events and gradual re-evaluations which constitute his own *Bildung**.

MENSA n.f. a university refectory (Latin *mensa*, table) – thus unconnected, at least linguistically, with the society for those with high IQs (Latin *mens*, mind).

MINE n.f. an explosive mine; or an underground mine, especially an underground shaft or seam of metal ore (for the more specialized vocabulary of coal mining, see BERG- and MONTAN- in III); and by extension also the lead in a pencil or a ball-point refill.

MODELL n.n. as in *das Humboldtmodell* – the educational ideal which Wilhelm von Humboldt tried to realize when he founded Berlin University in 1810. This model of a self-governing, élitist institution in which each *Ordinarius* or professor* was free to pursue *die Einheit von Forschung und Lehre* (the unity of research and teaching) is now slowly making way for more vocational and democratically run *Hochschulen**.

German university students never enjoyed the full (means-tested) maintenance grants to which British students were until recently entitled; instead, the *Honnefer Modell* – administered from Bad* Honnef, near Bonn – provided widespread partial (means-tested) support, known since 1971 after the relevant law (*das Bundesausbildungsförderungsgesetz*) as *BAföG*.

MUTATION n.f. nothing to worry about, unless you are, say, one of the *Wiener Sängerknaben* (see WANDERN in VII), since it means that your voice has broken: *er hat die Mutation gerade hinter sich*; in Austria: *er hat schon mutiert.*

NASSAUER n.m. originally an inhabitant of Nassau, now a sponger or scrounger. In the early nineteenth century, students at the University of Herborn in the Duchy of Nassau received free meals from the state and could invite friends to take their place. *Nassauern, schnorren, schmarotzen, abstauben* all mean to sponge or scrounge. An alternative nickname for a scrounger is *Salzsäure* (hydrochloric acid), since 'he eats his way through everything' (*er frißt sich überall durch*).

NOTE n.f. in schools and universities, a mark or grade. In descending order: *Eins* (*sehr gut*), *Zwei* (*gut*), *Drei* (*befriedigend*, satisfactory), *Vier* (*ausreichend*, adequate*), *Fünf* (*mangelhaft** – a fail, but one which can be compensated for by good marks elsewhere), *Sechs** (*ungenügend* – an irredeemable fail). Assessment is therefore *die Benotung*. See also PRÄDIKAT below.

In addition, a musical note: Germans say *nach Noten spielen* and *Noten lesen* where we would say 'to play from music' and 'to read music'; however, the great tradition of German *Lieder* consists mainly of Romantic poems which have been *vertont**, set to music (see HEIMAT in II). Also a banknote, *eine Banknote* (see SCHEIN below), but not (except for a note in the margin or a diplomatic note) a written note, which is *eine Notiz** or *ein Zettelchen*.

Note, too, the figurative sense of *Note* – tone, character, trademark – as in *Bad Ems hat eine ganz besondere Note* (Bad Ems has an atmosphere all its own); *seinem Vortrag fehlte die persönliche Note* (his lecture lacked the personal touch); *ein Parfüm mit einer herben Duftnote* (a perfume with something tangy about it).

NOTIZ n.f. a note* (in a *Notizbuch*, on a *Notizblock*, or as a *Notizzettel* or *Zettelchen*, reminder; *sich Notizen machen* or *notieren* means to make a note of something), rather than a notice. Exceptions are a brief newspaper notice – of a wedding, for instance, or a job vacancy (*eine Anzeige*); or else in such phrases as *nimm keine Notiz!* (take no notice), though even here *Notiz* may be better rendered as 'note': *bitte nehmen Sie davon Notiz, daß das Rauchen verboten ist* (please note that smoking is forbidden).

For the full range of notices, from public notices (*Ankündigung, öffentliche Bekanntmachung, Wandanschlag, Plakat, Warnschild, Warntafel*), to those posted *am Schwarzen Brett* in schools and universities, and those of a more personal kind (*Zahlungsaufforderung, Zahlungsbefehl, Anzeige, Bescheid, Benachrichtigung, Mitteilung*), including notice to quit (*Kündigung*), see dictionary.

OBJEKTIV n.n. the lens or combination of lenses in an optical instrument, especially a camera lens; hence *Tele-Objektiv*, telephoto lens. An individual lens is *eine Linse* (so called because it is lentil-shaped; *Linsensuppe* is a favourite soup), or in spectacles simply *das Glas*. To attain one's objective: *das Ziel erreichen.*

ORDENTLICH adj. an *ordentlicher Professor* is not necessarily orderly, neat and tidy (*ein ordentlicher Mensch*); nor is he necessarily a thorough and precise worker (*jemand, der ordentlich arbeitet*); nor even respectable (*jemand, der sich ordentlich benimmt, der ein ordentliches Leben führt*). He is, however, or rather was until the title was recently abolished, a full professor or *Ordinarius* with his own chair (*Lehrstuhl*), assistants and secretary – that is to say, ordinary in the same sense that the Physician-in-Ordinary to the Queen occupies a regular, established position, whereas an *außerordentlicher Professor* (like a Lady of the Bed-Chamber Extraordinary) did not – his status was approximately that of a Reader/US associate professor (see also PRIVATDOZENT below). *Unordentliche* (disorderly) *Professoren* exist primarily in the pages of Heinrich Heine, who in his *Harzreise* (1826) recalls with distaste *alle ordentlichen und unordentlichen Professoren* he had encountered as a student in Göttingen.

Note also the sense 'in order': *dieser Wein ist recht ordentlich* (quite a decent wine; a 'very ordinary' wine would be *mittelmäßig*); *ordentliche Preise* are reasonable prices, good value for money. As an intensifier, often best rendered as real or proper: *ordentlich essen* (to eat heartily, have a proper meal); *der Schreck ist mir ordentlich in die Glieder gefahren* (gave me a real shock). See also ORDINÄR in V.

PAUSEN v. not to pause (*Pause machen*; *die große Pause* is the main mid-morning break at school), but to trace (*durchpausen – auf Pauspapier*, on tracing paper).

PHILOLOGIE n.f. whereas English 'philology' is primarily the science of language or linguistics (*die Sprachwissenschaft**, *die Linguistik*), *die Philologie* resembles the much wider American usage: the study of language and literature, often embracing the general culture of a people, as undertaken in traditional university departments of modern languages with names such as *das Seminar* für englische Philologie*.

A century ago, during the *Kaiserzeit*, a teacher at a *humanistisches Gymnasium** was also called *ein Philologe* (now *ein Gymnasiallehrer*), and the Association of German Grammar School Teachers is still called *der Deutsche Philologenverein*.

PHYSIK n.f. physics. The eponymous physicists of Dürrenmatt's play *Die Physiker* (1962) merely wear the mask of madmen, their physician (*Arzt*) really is mad. Medical students have to pass *das Physikum* at the end of their pre-clinical courses before learning how to prescribe a medicinal physic (*eine Arznei*). A person's physique is *die Statur* or *die Erscheinung*.

POTENZ n.f. potency (*schöpferische Potenz* is creative power), or potentiality in philosophy, but also the normal mathematical term for the square (*die zweite Potenz*), cube (*die dritte Potenz*), etc., of a number. 'Two to the power of eight' can be expressed as *die achte Potenz zu zwei* or *zwei potenziert mit acht*, though more simply as *zwei hoch acht*.

PRÄDIKAT n.n. a university examination classification or grade: the final *Prädikat* is given to one decimal place (*1,0* is best; see NOTE above), and a *Doktorarbeit* awarded *summa cum laude* or *cum laude*, with distinction. Films are also given a *Prädikat* (rating) such as *wertvoll* or *besonders wertvoll*. For wine classification, see PRÄDIKAT in VIII.

Since German schools still teach the syntactical function of words as basic grammar, it is common knowledge that *das Prädikat* also means everything 'predicated' or said of the subject of a sentence. The idea is generally expressed differently in English: *Feuerbach beseitigte das Subjekt der religiösen Prädikate, Gott, jedoch nicht die Prädikate selbst* means that Feuerbach got rid of God as the source of religious attributes, but retained the attributes themselves.

PRIMA n.f. the sixth form in a German *Gymnasium**, but the first form in Austria – *ein Primaner* is thus a sixth-former in Germany, a first-former in Austria. German pupils take their *Abitur* after finishing the *Oberprima*, the ninth year of attendance at secondary school, having started in the *Sexta* and eventually progressed up to *Unter-*

sekunda, Obersekunda and *Unterprima*. The order is simply reversed in Austria, so that pupils take their *Matura* in the *Sexta*. This automatically entitles them, like German *Abiturienten*, to a place at university. (Except for *Abitur/Matura*, this terminology is now somewhat obsolete in most schools, though nostalgic literature bristles with it). See also under PROMOTION below.

Prima! is also one of the more durable slang expressions of pleasure or approval ('great', 'fantastic', US 'swell').

PRIVATDOZENT n.m. a lecturer recognized by the university but not on the salaried staff (thus occupying a *nichtbeamtete Stelle* – see BEAMTE in I), generally someone who has completed his *Habilitation** but not yet been appointed to a chair.

Formerly one had to wait for 'the call' (*er hat einen Ruf nach Freiburg erhalten*), now all *Professorenstellen/Professuren* (on an upward scale from C2 to C4) must first be advertised (*die Ausschreibung ist gesetzlich vorgeschrieben*), and the Minister of Higher Education (*der Wissenschaftsminister**) of the *Land** offers the chair (*spricht den Ruf aus*) on the recommendation of the university (*auf Vorschlag der Hochschule**) to one of the candidates interviewed – there are usually three on the short-list (*üblicherweise aufgrund einer Dreier-Liste*). See also ORDENTLICH above and HEARING in I.

PROFESSOR n.m. in Austria, a grammar school teacher in a tenured post (*Gymnasialprofessor**; see PRAGMATISIERUNG in I) as well as a university professor. In most German *Länder**, a *Studienprofessor* was until recently a grammar school teacher in charge of teacher training (*Fachdidaktik**), and Bavaria still bestows this prestigious-sounding title on senior secondary school teachers (*Studienräte**), but the *Bundesverfassungsgericht* (see CONSTITUTION in I) now recognizes only *Universitäts-Professoren* in universities, *Fachhochschulprofessoren** in colleges of applied science/vocational training, and *Akademie-Professoren* in art or music academies.

Unlike an *Ordinarius* (see ORDENTLICH above), an *Honorarprofessor** is an associate professor who, though salaried, is *nicht beamtet*, that is to say, not appointed on a permanent basis to an established post and without a voice in faculty affairs (nowadays, the term may also be bestowed as an *Ehrentitel*, honorary title).

PROMOTION n.f. the attainment of a doctorate. 'She did her doctorate on Broch': *sie hat über Broch promoviert* or *sie hat ihre Doktorarbeit über Broch geschrieben*. Formerly also the move into the next form at school (now *Versetzung*) – failure to get his *Promotion*, for instance, is one of the reasons for the main character's suicide in Wedekind's play *Frühlings Erwachen* (1891). Promotion in the sense of advancement in rank is *die Beförderung*, but in the sense of fostering, *die Förderung*. Hence, *die Förderstufe* (or *Orientierungs-stufe*) refers to the fifth and sixth classes in German secondary schools (see GYMNASIUM and PRIMA above) which are of mixed ability and intended to promote the particular talents of all pupils, while a university student who is *förderungswürdig* or *förderungsberechtigt* is eligible for a grant, *eine Förderung* (see MODELL above). A sales promotion is *eine Werbung*.

RAT n.m. a *Studienrat* is a fully qualified teacher at a secondary school, someone who has been first *Referendar** (and then, though this civil service grade no longer exists in schools, *Assessor**). A graduate teacher (*der auf 'höheres Lehramt' studiert hat*) may go on to become an *Oberstudienrat* (a senior teacher entitled to teach *Abiturienten ab der II. Klasse*, sixth-formers) or *Oberstudiendirektor** (headmaster). In the German university system, *Akademischer Rat* is the equivalent of lecturer in a British university/US assistant professor. See also RAT in I and BERATEN in III.

REALSCHULE n.f. an intermediate or secondary school, special-izing in modern as opposed to classical subjects, in which the school-leaving examination, *die Realschulreife*, approximates to GCSE. There is wide divergence in the types of school system since education is determined at *Land**level, and controversy has been renewed with the accession of the five East German *Länder*. Those who favour *ein leist-ungsorientiertes System* (achievement-orientated system) advocate the preservation of *Gymnasium**, *Realschule* and *Hauptschule* (secondary-modern); others prefer a single *Gesamtschule* (comprehensive).

In Austria, however, a *Realschule* is what the Germans used to call a *Realgymnasium** – a grammar school specializing in science (*realia/Realien** were formerly the 'real facts' of science) and preparing for university entrance. Note also Austrian *Realbüro* or *Realkanzlei**, estate agency (US realtor); Austrian *Realitäten* are German *Immobil-ien** ('immovables', real estate).

REFERAT n.n. a seminar paper or school project. Someone who presents a *Referat* orally (*über etwas referieren, ein Referat über etwas halten*) is a *Referent*, though this is more commonly a consultant or expert in an administrative department (see REFERAT and RESSORT in I), whose report is *ein Gutachten*, while the testimonial one needs when applying for a job is *eine Referenz* or *ein Zeugnis*.

REKTOR n.m. not a rector of the Church (*Pfarrer/Pastor*; see under VIKAR in V), but a university vice-chancellor, whom one may address as *Magnifizenz* and who is usually a professor on short-term secondment (some universities have a full-time *Präsident*, not necessarily an academic). The *Deutsche Rektorenkonferenz* is the equivalent of the British Committee of Vice-Chancellors and Principals. See also DEKAN above.

SCHEIN n.m. an end-of-semester certificate or credit (*Seminarschein**) – in spite of also meaning pretence or sham (see SCHEIN in V), giving rise to the pun of a *Scheinstudium*, i.e. being concerned with accumulating the necessary credits without any interest in the subject. As the Germans know how to take their fun seriously*, anyone wanting to sail will need a *Segelschein**, and to hunt, sensibly* enough, a *Jagdschein* (though *er hat den Jagdschein* also means, colloquially, 'he's certifiable'); even an *Angelschein* requires three months' attendance at evening classes and the right answer to questions on hydrography, piscine law and the number of roe produced by a roach. Other forms of *Bescheinigung* (certification) are *Fahrschein* (bus/tram/train ticket) and *Geldschein* (banknote). See also *Giftschein* under GIFT in II.

SECHS n.f. six – the fail mark in an examination (*ungenügend*, unsatisfactory – see NOTE above). But *einen Sechser im Lotto haben* is to win first prize in the German national lottery, while *ein Vierer* also wins with four correct numbers.

SEGELN v. to sail, though *durch eine Prüfung segeln* does not mean to sail through an exam (*mit Glanz und Gloria bestehen*, *spielend schaffen*), but to fail it resoundingly.

SEMINAR n.n. both a seminar and the university department in which it takes place (*das Englische Seminar*, *das Seminar für Germanistik*). In Germany's overcrowded universities, a *Proseminar* (introductory seminar course) will generally have several hundred participants, a *Hauptseminar* (main seminar) often just as many, and only the advanced or doctoral students in an *Oberseminar* will be expected, or able, to contribute to the discussion regularly. Trainee teachers (*Refendare**) attend a *Lehrerseminar* (this now means an in-service course with regular seminars; formerly it meant only a teacher training college, and this is still the meaning in Switzerland – see DIDAKTISCH above). A *Priesterseminar*, like a *Konvikt**, is a theological seminary.

STATIK n.f. the science of statics, but also structural engineering (*ein Statiker* is a structural engineer), whereas the static which some materials give off when rubbed is *die Reibungselektrizität*, and the atmospheric disturbances which interfere with radio reception *atmosphärische Störungen*.

STICKSTOFF n.m. not 'sticky stuff' like glue (*Klebstoff, Kleber* for short; in the south also *der Papp*), but nitrogen (hydrogen is *Wasserstoff*). However, the weather or the air in a room may be *stickig*, sticky, humid, stuffy, stifling. To be in a sticky situation, *in einer heiklen Situation sein, in der Klemme sein*. See also STICKEN in IX.

STUDENT n.m. a student of human nature *studiert die menschliche Natur*, but is not necessarily *ein Student*. This is only somebody undergoing tertiary education (*das Studium* – see GRAD above), except in Austria where it is also a schoolboy at secondary school (German *Schüler**), where he will be taught by *Professoren**.

SUMMEN v. not to do sums (*rechnen*, though 2+2 is indeed *eine Summe*), but to hum (*eine Melodie*) or to buzz (*es summt*, there's a buzzing noise) – an example of *Lautmalerei* (onomatopoeia).

TRAMPELN v. the literal meaning is to tramp along, or else to destroy by trampling something or someone flat (*platt trampeln*), or to death (*zu Tode trampeln*). *Ein Trampeltier* is a camel, but in addition a clumsy, awkward person (also simply *ein Trampel*, a 'country bumpkin' – usually a woman). Trampling on people's feelings becomes *auf den Gefühlen anderer herumtrampeln*, though sometimes *trampeln* signifies just the opposite: *die Zuschauer trampeln* means the audience literally stamp their feet in approval (alternatively, *Studenten klopfen*, rap their desks).

UHR n.f. not an hour (*die Stunde*), but a clock or watch (or gauge or meter*). *Wieviel Uhr ist es, Liebling?* is usually rendered as 'What's the time, darling?', though more memorably by the German couple practising their English in *Casablanca* as '"What watch?" "Ten watch." "Such watch!"'

UNTERSTEHEN v. not to understand (*verstehen*), but to be under the control of someone or something. *Das Militär untersteht der Exekutive* (is subordinate to, under the jurisdiction of). By extension, *untersteh dich!* is not a philosophical dictum (*erkenne dich selbst!* 'know thyself!'), but a warning 'you just dare!'. *Was unterstehen Sie sich!* means 'how dare you!'

The opposite (to be in charge of) is *vorstehen* (+ dat.), not *Überstehen*, which means to survive or pull through (as in Rilke's memorable line: *Wer spricht von Siegen? Überstehn ist alles*, 'Who speaks of victory? Survival is all' – *Requiem für Wolf Graf von Kalckreuth*, 1908). The constituent parts of compounds, though readily identifiable, do not always combine to give the same meaning as in English – see especially *unter-* and *über-* in Index.

VOKABEL n.f. (in Austria usually n.n.) not vocabulary (*das Vokabular, der Wortschatz*), but an individual word, especially a new or foreign one. Thus, the main character in Ingeborg Bachmann's story *Das dreißigste Jahr* (1961), recognized by the *Kaffeehaus**waiter after many years' absence from Vienna and brought his regular newspaper (*die Phrase* bleibt ihm erspart, ein Lächeln genügt*, 'he doesn't have to say a word, a smile is enough'), notices that 'here and there a new word had clumsily crept in': *hier und da hat sich unbeholfen eine neue Vokabel eingeschlichen* (pp. 54–5). Often used of hackneyed words and expressions (also *Phrasen**), such as *die großen Vokabeln der Politik* which politicians use.

WISSENSCHAFTLICH adj. 'scientific' in the context of *die Naturwissenschaft* (generally used in the singular – the natural sciences), but 'academic'* when used of the *Geisteswissenschaften**, the arts or humanities (not, *pace* Arthur Koestler, a scientific study of ghosts – see GEIST in V). The word rose to its present ubiquity in the days when (as Lord Acton put it in the first issue of the *English Historical Review* in 1886) the typical German *Wissenschaftler* complained that the public library allowed him only thirteen hours a day to read.

It also implicitly refutes any notion of a 'two-cultures' division in Germany. Each of the four books that Hegel published contains a reference to *Wissenschaft* in the title, while the 'gay science' which Nietzsche advocated in *Die fröhliche Wissenschaft* (1882) has nothing to do with chemistry or biology, but with fearless intellectual experimentation in general (asking specifically, is morality a function of the *Wille zum Leben* working for the preservation of the species?), directed in turn against such systems as Hegel's which Nietzsche thought were corrupting the minds of German youth. Historically, however, British respect for *Wissenschaft*, connoting the highest possible academic culture based on systematic investigation, like our good opinion of most things German, was never fully recovered after the First World War (see EMPIRIE and INTELLEKTUELLER in V).

ZIRKEL n.m. as well as a circle, a pair of compasses or dividers – as in the symbol of the erstwhile German Democratic Republic: *Hammer und Zirkel im Ährenkranz*, hammer and compasses (not sickle, *die Sichel*) in a garland of corn. A circle is more commonly *der Kreis*, but one talks of the squaring of the circle as either *die Quadratur des Zirkels* or *des Kreises*; of an *hermeneutischer Zirkel*; or of a *Zirkelschluß* – a circular argument, not the 'closing' or completion of a circular movement (*eine Zangenbewegung*, pincer movement, in military parlance). A *Zirkel* is also a clique* or coterie.

PHILOSOPHY,
RELIGION
and MORALS

PHILOSOPHIE,
RELIGION
und MORAL

AFFEKT n.m. emotional agitation, or in William James's words 'a general seizure of excitement, which Wundt, Lehmann, and other German writers have called an *Affect*, and is what I have all along meant by an emotion' (*Collected Essays and Reviews*, 1920, p. 358). *Eine Affekthandlung* is thus a crime motivated by anger, fear, despair, etc., and *eine im Affekt begangene Tat* a deed committed in the heat of the moment – a *crime passionnel*. Behaviour may be *affektiv* (affective) or *affektgeladen* (impassioned); it may also be *affektiert* (affected); but *die Affektion* (affection, fondness) is – linguistically – old-fashioned and has given way to *Wohlwollen, Zuneigung* or *Gunst*.

AFTER- in cpds. has two meanings, both related to 'after' or 'behind': **1.** (now very dated) *die Afterrede* (calumny) and *jemandem afterreden* (to speak ill of someone, talk behind their back) are now *die Nachrede* and *jemandem nachreden*, while *der Aftermieter* has become *der Untermieter* (tenant, lodger). This may be because of meaning **2.** the anus (*der After*). Schopenhauer's contempt for what he called Hegel's *Afterphilosophie* was exacerbated when, as a *Privatdozent** drawn to what he called Berlin's *höhere Geisteskultur**, he attempted to lecture at the same hour as the famous professor – Monday to Friday 5–6pm – and drew only a handful of students (*der bittere Nachgeschmack*, the bitter aftertaste, of this experience never left him). Though quite a fruity term of abuse – Schopenhauer did not mean Hegel's ideas were merely derivative – it can still be used in polite society, and *Afterwissenschaft* is no worse than so-called or pseudo-science. None of which has prevented after-shave (*das Rasierwasser*) from being marketed as *das After Shave*.

ARGUMENT n.n. not the kind of argument one gets involved in (*eine hitzige Diskussion*; if more heated still, *eine Auseinandersetzung, ein Streit*), but rather the argument one advances (*argumentieren*) in support of a proposition (*seine Argumente waren nicht stichhaltig*, were not sound). This, and not 'overly fond of arguing' (*streitsüchtig*), is similarly the sense of *argumentativ* (*der Wahlkampf wurde argumentativ geführt*, the election was fought on the basis of reasoned argument).

While the Argument with which each Book of *Paradise Lost* begins is also *das Argument* (as is the summary, plot, or 'argument' of a

Greek or Latin play), a philosophical theme or claim is more commonly called *die These*. Sometimes *das ist kein Argument* means 'that's no excuse'.

ARRIVIERT adj. successful, often in the pejorative sense of being an upstart, parvenu, arriviste (for Yuppies, see LIBERAL in II).

BETBANK n.f. no connection with betting (*wetten*) or banks*, but a praying-stool or prie-dieu (also *ein Betstuhl*). An overzealous church-goer or churchy type is known as a *Betbruder* or *Betschwester* (see DEVOT below).

BLAMIEREN v. not to blame (*beschuldigen* or some other combination with *Schuld**), but to cause embarrassment, usually to oneself: *sie hat sich ganz schön blamiert*, she made quite a fool of herself, she really let herself down. *Du blamierst die ganze Innung* means 'you're letting the side down'. But to let others down in the sense of leaving them in the lurch is *im Stich lassen*, as when Captain Grimes in Evelyn Waugh's *Decline and Fall* says: 'That's the public-school system all over. They may kick you out but they never let you down' – for the German old-boy network, see VITAMIN B in III and KORPORATION in IV.

After it was recently discovered that two of the big banks had lent enormous unsecured loans (*Großkredite ohne Sicherheiten*) to building contractors, *Die Welt* observed, on 23 April 1994, *daß sich die beteiligten Banken* gnadenlos blamiert hatten* (that the banks involved had irredeemably disgraced themselves – not that they had blamed each other).

Correspondingly, *blamabel* means shameful rather than culpable (*schuldig*). For instance, when Germany acquired only some swamps in the Congo out of the second Morocco crisis of 1911: *das Ergebnis wurde als blamabel empfunden* (the outcome was considered shameful – *Die Zeit*, 7 July 1989). *Eine furchtbare Blamage* (though the term is unknown to the French) is a dreadful *faux pas* or terrible disgrace.

CHRIST n.m. *ich bin Christ*, I am a Christian. Christ is *Christus*.

DÄMONISCH adj. demonic, appertaining to the Devil. Alternatively, relating to man's innate, creative genius*, or inspired by a good genius. In this sense, Goethe (like Socrates) is said to have been *von seinem Dämon getrieben*, though it was not for him (as it had been for Socrates) a negative force like his Mephistopheles, but rather, however incalculable and contradictory, a source of positive energy (*Tatkraft*) in great men. He had his own – providential – relationship with Schiller in mind, often described Frederick the Great as both *genial** and *dämonisch*, and equally admired *das Dämonische* in

Napoleon, his 'daemonic' nature. For the Romantic generation (notably E. T. A. Hoffmann, Pushkin, Kierkegaard), it was Mozart's Don Giovanni whose daemonic impulses supremely embodied this amoral, elemental force.

DEFTIG adj. not 'deft' in the sense of handy, dexterous, nimble (*flink, geschickt, gewandt, hurtig**), but often just the opposite. *Deftiger Humor*, for instance, is crude and lacking finesse rather than neat and clever. Or else solid and substantial, as in *ein deftiger Bauer** (a powerful, hard-working farmer), *eine deftige Ohrfeige* (a hefty clip round the ear), *eine deftige Lüge* (a whopping lie), *deftige Preise* (high prices) or *deftige Einsparungen* (huge savings). Often used of plain, substantial food: *Grünkohl* (curly kale) is a good example of *deftige Kost**.

DEVOT adj. obsequious, rather than devout (*fromm*) or devoted (*ergeben, treu*). New visitors to Demel, Vienna's famous *Konditorei* and café (see TORTE in VIII), may still be asked '*Wurden schon bedient?*', an address which according to Friedrich Torberg constitutes a discreet compromise between the *abrupt zupackenden* (brusque and businesslike) '*Wurden Sie schon bedient?*' and the *allzu devoten* (abjectly ingratiating, cringingly sycophantic) '*Wurden Herr Baron schon bedient?*' (*Die Tante Jolesch*, 1977, p. 227). More unexpected is the way those who once served in the secret police headquarters in Erfurt reacted to its occupation by the people. As Wolf Biermann recalled in *Die Zeit* on 4 May 1990: *einzelne Stasis schlichen vorbei und baten devot um Einlaß* (individual members of the *Stasi* sidled past and grovelled to be let in).

DEZENT adj. a matter of decorum rather than moral decency: *dezente Farben* are subdued, restrained colours, *dezente Musik* soft, muted music, and *ein dezentes Kleid* an unobtrusively elegant dress. Since the Germans once admired both English tailoring and the English character for their quiet self-assurance and understatement, the *Süddeutsche Zeitung*, on 13 August 1987, could even allude to the *dezente Brutalität* of the *Ur*-James Bond, Sean Connery. By contrast, when *Die Zeit* reported on 22 June 1990 that the *RAF** terrorists given new identities in the German Democratic Republic had been *dezent überwacht* by the *Stasi*, it meant only that they had been unobtrusively watched over by the secret police – a judicious reticence that had little to do with decency.

This is *der Anstand.* Decent behaviour is *anständiges Benehmen* – whether in accordance with the ordinary decencies of everyday life or inspired by what the Germans call *das Fair play* ('having no word that denotes what the English call "fairness"', according to Theodor

Heuss, soon to be the Federal Republic's first President, in a lecture in 1946 – *Aufzeichnungen 1945–1947*, 1966, p. 207) – whereas *dezentes Benehmen* is merely tactful and discreet.

DOM n.m. not the dome of a building (*die Kuppel*), but (like *die Kathedrale* and *das Münster*) a cathedral, such as *der Kölner Dom*. Forty years of vigorous activity by the *Dombauverein** were crowned in 1880 by the completion of Cologne Cathedral, a central focus for antiquarian, Rhenish, and nationalist sentiment. But Heine had poured scorn on the project (in *Deutschland. Ein Wintermärchen*, 1844, Caput IV), and Bettina von Arnim's widely reported remark that the King of Prussia should build a new cathedral in Silesia instead, to alleviate the poverty and unemployment there, is said to have touched off the uprising of the starving Silesian weavers in 1844 (who were given heart by Heine's revolutionary poem, *Die schlesischen Weber* of the same year, and subsequently mourned in Gerhart Hauptmann's famous play, *Die Weber*, of 1892 – see WIRKEN in III).

An exception is *der Hamburger Dom*, an annual carnival and fair, held not far from the *Reeperbahn* – anything but a holy place.

EBEN adv. the adjective *eben* means 'even' (smooth, flat, level), but the adverb *eben* means 'precisely', 'exactly', 'just'* ('even' only in the archaic Biblical sense of 'even so have I also sent them into the world', John xvii, 18). Thus, *eben das weiß ich nicht* (that's precisely what I don't know), as distinct from *auch das weiß ich nicht* (I don't even know that); *er ist nicht eben klug* (he's not exactly clever), but *er ist nicht einmal klug* (he's not even clever); *ich wollte ihn eben schlagen* (I was on the point of hitting him), but *ich wollte ihn sogar schlagen* (I even wanted to hit him).

EMPIRIE n.f. not the British Empire, *das Empire*, but the empiricism which the Germans see as essentially British. Thus, Egon Friedell in his *Kulturgeschichte der Neuzeit* (1928; 1974 ed., p. 630) described David Hume's philosophy as *echt englisch** (which might have seemed somewhat bizarre to readers in Edinburgh), because he equated Hume's 'English' empiricism with 'mistrust of all metaphysics and idealism' (*das Mißtrauen gegen alle Metaphysik und Ideenlehre*), 'deep-rooted conservatism which explains everything away as custom' (*der tiefgewurzelte Konservatismus, der alles aus Gewohnheit erklärt*), and 'unremitting shallowness' (*die unerbittliche Flachheit*) which 'almost becomes profundity, so estimable is its clarity and energy' (*die in ihrer bewunderungswürdigen Schärfe und Energie fast zum Tiefsinn wird*). (More recently, Derrida has said much the same thing, if less clearly.)

Appropriately enough, Eustace Barnack in Aldous Huxley's

Time Must Have a Stop (1945, p. 63) remarks on 'how appallingly thorough the Germans always managed to be, how emphatic! In sex no less than in war – in scholarship, in science. Diving deeper than anyone else and coming up muddier'. This certainly fits Herr Diogenes Teufelsdröckh ('Devil's droppings'), Professor of *Allerley-Wissenschaft** (Quodlibetical Scholarship – or Things in General) at the University of *Weißnichtwo* (Know Not Where), whose labyrinthine whimsy and extravagant germanicisms Thomas Carlyle made the perfect vehicle for his own championship of German idealism (*Sartor Resartus*, 1835). But a more typically English view of the 'subjectivistic madness' which Bertrand Russell found characteristic of most modern, and especially German, philosophy (*History of Western Philosophy*, p. 773), is provided by that confirmed anglophile, Schopenhauer. Himself an Idealist, he thought that Idealism in its more extreme, solipsistic form was to be found *nur im Tollhause*, only in the madhouse: *als solche bedürfte es dann gegen ihn nicht sowohl eines Beweises, als einer Kur**, in which case what was needed was not so much a reasoned refutation as a cure – *Die Welt als Wille und Vorstellung* (*The World as Will and Representation*), 1819, I,ii,19.

ENGLISCH adj. English (*der Engländer* is frequently used, *pars pro toto*, for *die Engländer*, the English), but also angelic (modern German, *engelhaft*; an angel is *ein Engel*). This can be confusing: *der Englische Gruß* is the Angelic Salutation or Ave Maria, not an English counterpart to the raised-arm salute which the Nazis called *der deutsche* Gruß*. Similarly, when Faust's servant Wagner warns him that the evil spirits he has invoked *lispeln englisch, wenn sie lügen* (l. 1141), he means that they 'speak with the tongues of angels when they tell their lies', not that they indulge in the English vice of hypocrisy (*die Heuchelei*). For Heine (*Memoiren des Herrn von Schnabelewopski*, 1834), the manners in anglophile Hamburg were *englisch* in both senses – an originally Latin pun (*non Angli, sed Angeli*) which goes back at least as far as Pope Gregory the Great's instruction to Augustine of Tarsus in AD 597 to convert the *Angli* into *angeli* (which, as readers of *1066 And All That* know, means 'not Angels, but Anglicans').

The fact that *ein Engländer* is also an adjustable spanner or monkey-wrench (oddly, so is *ein Franzose**, which the French themselves call *une clé anglaise*) is doubtless a throwback to pre-war days when Europe still used British imperial measures, as East Germany continued to do up to reunification. Before *die englische Krankheit* came to mean strikes (which the Germans called *Streiks* after the English, albeit much less often), it meant rickets, and before that, melancholia – see SPLEEN below; also ENGLISCH in II and VIII.

EVANGELISCH adj. not 'evangelical', but Protestant in general – in practice, Lutheran, *evangelisch-lutherisch* (*ev.–luth.*); or Reformed, *evangelisch-reformiert* (*ev.–ref.*) – as distinct from Roman Catholic. In so far as an evangelical revival exists in Germany alongside the 'liberal' theology – which, with its concerns for peace, ecology and the Third World, is more in evidence – the word used is *evangelikal*, and the tendency includes traditional *Pietisten* as well as those influenced by American Evangelicalism and the Charismatic Movement. Thus, it is not *ein Evangelischer* but *ein Evangelikaler* who takes a fundamentalist stance on the literal truth of *das Evangelium* (the Gospel) and the total depravity of unregenerate human nature, while the word *Fundamentalist* refers primarily to Islamic fundamentalists, or else to the radical wing of *die Grünen* (the Green Party, once irreconcilably divided between '*Fundis*' and more pragmatic '*Realos*' – but see LIBERAL in II). The four evangelists are *die vier Evangelisten*.

Given the long tradition of Protestant *Landeskirchen* with regional autonomy (see KONFESSION below), *die Deutschen Evangelischen Kirchen* (German Evangelical Churches) are most obviously united in the length of their sermons and their magnificent repertoire of sixteenth- and seventeenth-century chorales, which the congregation sings while seated, only rising to pray.

For the times of *Evangelischer Gottesdienst* and *Römisch-katholischer Gottesdienst*, see the adjacent purple and yellow signs posted on the roads into most German towns. Catholic churches usually have a weathercock (*ein Wetterhahn*) on top, Protestant churches do not.

EXALTIERT adj. not exalted (the ranks of the exalted are *die Ränge der Erhabenen*), or even dignified (*ehrwürdig*), but effusively enthusiastic. This is exactly the quality which Goethe captured in his *Werther* (1774), and which then became known as *Schwärmerei* (see SCHWARM in VI), but which he himself came to consider unhealthy. He was seventy-seven when he nevertheless decided that his Faust, a *Schwärmer* when he had lost Gretchen fifty years earlier, should wake more than merely refreshed from his long sleep to win Helen of Troy (*tritt exaltiert hervor* is the stage direction); and his own elation matches that of his creation when he writes to Sulpiz Boisserée on 22 October 1826: *Verzeihen Sie, mein Bester, wenn ich Ihnen exaltiert scheine.*

Nowadays, *ein Exaltierter* is closer to what the French call *un exalté* (and what Walter Bagehot thought a typically French trait: 'exaltable') – that is, someone over-excited by his own opinions – while *exaltiertes Benehmen* is extravagant, exaggerated, or hysterical behaviour.

EXISTENTIELL adj. has taken on the sense of 'vitally important', as in *das Problem der Umweltverschmutzung* (environmental pollution) *ist existentiell.* Nowadays *ein Existentialist* is unlikely to owe much to Heidegger or Sartre, more to *eine extravagante* Lebensführung*: a flamboyantly eccentric life-style. Note that *die Existenz* means not only existence or way of life, but also a person's living or income – *er hat seine Existenz im Krieg verloren* means he lost his livelihood, not his life; or else the person himself, as when someone whose life has gone to pieces is called (usually with an element of disapproval) *eine verkrachte* or *gescheiterte Existenz.*

FATAL adj. either exceedingly embarrassing, awkward (*peinlich**); or else fateful, dire (*verhängnisvoll*), or ominous (*ein fatales Lächeln*, an ominous smile); but seldom 'fatal' (*tödlich*), and then only in a figurative sense. When Novalis called Goethe's *Wilhelm Meister** (1794) *ein fatales Buch*, he was not thinking back to *Werther* (1774) and the suicides that earlier novel was said to have inspired (see EXALTIERT above), but, on the contrary, of the way Goethe seemed to have turned away from *Innerlichkeit* (inwardness) towards social activity and integration in the latter stages of the novel, thereby allegedly offering a less exemplary model to German writers. Novalis conceived his own *Heinrich von Ofterdingen* (1801/2) – the key Romantic *Bildungsroman** – as an '*Anti-Meister*'.

Similarly, *eine Fatalität* is a great misfortune, not a fatality (*ein Todesfall**, *ein Todesopfer**, or, in the sense of inevitability, *die Unabwendbarkeit*). Willy Brandt criticized Germany's participation in the general arms build-up of the late 1970s as *eine fatale Kontinuität oder doch eine deutsche Fatalität* (*Die Zeit*, 12 August 1988), which suggests only that it was the continuation of a familiar and fateful policy, and at the very least an unfortunate development for Germany.

GEIST n.m. broadly has three meanings: **1.** mind/intellect (and wit); **2.** spirit (of friendship, of the law, of alcohol, and much else); **3.** ghost.

In practice, this is less confusing than it sounds – rather like French *esprit*. Those who have grappled with Hegel's *Phänomenologie des Geistes* (1807) might find it surprising that a *Freigeist* like Nietzsche (a free-thinker *and* a free spirit) thought Hegel embodied *eine ihnen 'erlaubte' Form des* esprit ('the only form of *esprit* "permissible" to the Germans' – *Morgenröte*, para. 193; see also WISSENSCHAFTLICH in IV). In Hegel's influential use of the word (no excuse here for translating *Geist* as 'mind' instead of 'spirit', says Walter Kaufmann in *Hegel, A Reinterpretation*, 1965, p. 89), *Geist* is that which strives to realize itself 'subjectively' through advancing self-consciousness (see SELBSTBEWUSSTSEIN below), and 'objectively' through history as the *Zeitgeist* of one era confronts its antithesis. Appropriately enough, it was while Napoleon (*der Weltgeist zu Pferde*, 'the world spirit on horseback', according to Hegel) was finishing off the Holy Roman Empire and inflicting the greatest defeat the Prussians had ever suffered at the Battle of Jena, that Hegel was in the city finishing his book.

On a similar dialectical note, Mephistopheles is Faust's divinely sanctioned Spirit of Negation (*der Geist, der stets verneint*), though Faust at first seems sceptical of the historical dimension introduced by his assistant: *Was ihr den Geist der Zeiten heißt, / Das ist im Grund der Herren eigner Geist* ('What you call the spirit of the times is really nothing but the gentlemen's own spirit' – *Urfaust*, ll. 224–5). For Karl Marx, both mind and spirit are inseparable from economic reality, and the spectre haunting Europe in 1848 is merely the sort of *Geist* which adults use to make children's flesh creep (this third meaning of *Geist* also appears as *der Spuk* or *das Gespenst*, which is the word actually used in the opening sentence of the *Manifest der Kommunistischen Partei*).

The adjectival form of meanings 1. and 2. is *geistig* or *Geistes-* (and *geistreich*, witty), but neither is used of meaning 3. Instead, 'ghostly' is *Geister-*, as in the *Geisterfahrer* who drives down the wrong side of the motorway. An intriguing headline in the Munich *Abendzeitung* on 5 January 1988, *Theologie-Professor als betrunkener Geisterfahrer*, concerned one such 'ghostdriver', who appears to have been under the influence of spirits – perhaps *Himbeergeist*, raspberry brandy – rather than attempting to exorcize them. (The *Geisterfahrer* phenomenon is a continuing mystery, since German road signs all conform to a pattern of exemplary clarity, though recent research into the functions of the the hemispheres of the brain suggests we should continue driving on the left.) Other examples are the *Geisterbahn* at a funfair, the *Geisterschiff* of Wagner's *Der fliegende Holländer*, or indeed the *Geisterbann** (Senta's *Liebestod*) which exorcizes it. Thus, *Geisterwelt* is the spirit world, but *Geisteswelt* the world of the intellect, and *die Geisteswissenschaften* the humanities (as distinct from *die Naturwissenschaft**, the natural sciences). Hamlet's father's ghost is a *Geist* who appears at the *Geisterstunde*, the witching hour; but so, too, is Hamlet himself in Horatio's lament (in the standard Schlegel/ Tieck translation): *O welch ein edler Geist ist hier zerstört* ('O! what a noble mind is here o'erthrown').

For all the overlapping, then, *geistig* is quite distinct from *geistlich* (spiritual, sacred, religious, ecclesiastical – *ein Geistlicher* is a clergyman).

GENIAL adj. *eine geniale Erfindung* is a brilliant invention, *ein genialer Gedanke* an ingenious thought, *ein genialer Künstler* a creative/artistic genius (*ein Genie**), who might also be called *genialisch* if his behaviour suggests he disdains convention (genius being *antiautoritär, anti-normativ, anti-traditionell*). A simple genius for doing what comes naturally is what distinguishes a real woman (at least in Karl Kraus's aphorism, best left untranslated) from a high-born, if low-minded, blue-stocking: *das Weib* koitiert genialisch . . . die Dame kogitiert genitalisch* (*Sprüche und Widersprüche*, 1909).

So, *genial* is emphatically not 'genial' in the sense of agreeable – *ein freundliches Lächeln* (genial smile), *angenehme Gesellschaft* (genial company), *ein leutseliger Vorgesetzter* (genial superior), *wohltuender Einfluß* (genial influence) – and most examples of German *Genialität* suggest it is no more compatible with geniality than is English genius or French *génie*. In young people's slang, however, with its tendency to hyperbole, *genial* is often used where the older generation might simply say *toll**.

GENIE n.n. whereas Aladdin's genie is *ein dienstbarer Geist** or *ein Dschinn* (but see PANTOMIME in X), *das Genie* is the phenomenon of genius, or its embodiment.

We think of Beethoven – frightening the maids when he emerges, wild-eyed and dishevelled, from nocturnal struggles with his *Dämon** – as the first great composer self-consciously aware of his genius. By contrast, Leopold Mozart never called his son's extraordinary talents 'genius' in the modern sense until Wolfgang was a grown man, for the idea of *Originalgenie* in its full-blown form emerged, in Germany and Austria, only in the 1770s (some sixty years after Addison had written the first rudimentary typology of genius). This was *die Geniezeit* (synonymous with the *Sturm** *und Drang* period), and the related Romantic idea of music as the highest of the arts came later still. So a word such as *Geniestreich**, signifying the sort of wild escapade you might expect of a genius, was topical when Schiller used the term in a letter of 1 November 1790 to his (and Mozart's) friend, Christian Körner, to describe Goethe's proposed marriage to Christiane Vulpius. Leopold felt much the same way about Wolfgang's marriage to Constanze Weber, but Goethe might have been speaking for both himself and Mozart when he observed at the age of almost eighty: *geniale Naturen erleben eine wiederholte Pubertät, während andere Leute nur einmal jung sind* (men of genius go through several puberties, others are only young once).

One can say *Goethe war ein Genie* or prefer the more rarified *ein Genius* (or speak of *Goethes Genie* or *Goethes Genius*), but *Genius* is also used in the original sense of a protective spirit (of a person: as when Macbeth says of Banquo 'Under him my genius is rebuked, as it is said Mark Antony's was by Caesar'; or of a place: the *genius loci*); or in the sense of a defining quality: *der Genius der deutschen Sprache* (the spirit or essence of the German language).

In the Swiss army, fittingly, *die Genietruppe* is the engineering corps (in French, *le Génie*).

GLÜCKLICH adj. happy as well as lucky, but when used predicatively it always means happy, and *unglücklich* unhappy. *Unglücklich das Land, das keine Helden hat* ('Unhappy the land that has no heroes'), declares Galileo's disillusioned disciple in Scene 13 of Brecht's *Leben des Galilei* (written in 1938/39) after Galileo has recanted on being shown the instruments of torture by the Inquisition. *Unglücklich das Land, das Helden nötig hat* ('Unhappy the land that needs heroes') is the reluctant hero's reply.

Schwarze Katzen sind glücklich (black cats are happy), but *schwarze Katzen bringen Glück* (black cats bring good luck), though only when they cross in front of you from right to left; otherwise they bring *Pech*, bad luck: *Von links nach rechts, da pecht's, / Von rechts nach links, das bringt's*. An encounter with a *Schornsteinfeger* – chimney-sweeps traditionally wear all black, incl·ding a top hat (see ZYLINDER in IX) – is thought to bestow similar benefits.

GRAZIÖS adj. not gracious, but graceful. *Eine graziöse Tänzerin* is a graceful dancer, but 'Long live our gracious Queen' becomes *Es lebe unsere gnädige Königin* (from *die Gnade*, mercy), and a gracious smile *ein gütiges* or *liebenswürdiges* (or, if condescending, *huldvolles*) *Lächeln*. Goodness gracious!: *du meine Güte!* or *du lieber Himmel!* To say grace: *das Tischgebet sprechen*.

HEMMEN v. not to hem a dress (*ein Kleid säumen*), but akin to English 'to hem in' meaning hinder, check, block. Hence such key terms in modern psychology as *gehemmt* (inhibited) and *Hemmung* (inhibition); conversely, *hemmungslos* means unrestrained or unscrupulous.

HUMAN adj. humane, or else considerate, but human only in such contexts as *Humanmedizin* or *Humangenetik*. Otherwise, human is *menschlich* and humanist/classical *humanistisch*, which between them cover Nietzsche's main areas of investigation – see his *Menschliches, Allzumenschliches* (*Human, All-Too-Human*, 1878–80), also UNMENSCH in II, GYMNASIUM, KLASSIK, WISSENSCHAFTLICH in IV, GEIST and SCHULD in this section, ROMAN in X.

IDEELL adj. not 'ideal' in the everyday sense of 'perfect' (*ideal*), but 'concerning or based on ideas': *ideelle Ziele* are non-material goals, *ideelle Bedürfnisse* spiritual needs. In a novel like *Der Zauberberg* (1924), Thomas Mann once said, *alles Detail ist langweilig ohne ideelle Transparenz* (all detail is tedious if the idea behind it is not transparent), but he also made it clear that his great novel of ideas was *ein musikalisch-ideeller Beziehungskomplex* (a musical complex of ideas) in which the ideas themselves, like musical *Leitmotive*, might well be very simple, even banal (see also KULTUR above and ROMAN in X).

Though not an exclusively philosophical term (derivatives from Idealism are either *idealistisch* or *ideal* – see EMPIRIE above), it alludes to that which exists only in the mind, as 'ideal' once did in English too: "'The idea of Ghosts is ridiculous in the extreme; And if you continue to be swayed by ideal terrors. . .' 'Ideal?' exclaimed the Nuns with one voice; "Why we heard it ourselves, Segnor!"' (M. G. Lewis, *The Monk*, 1796, 1973 ed., p. 362).

The distinction between *reell** and *real-** is analogous, but misleading.

INSTANZ n.f. an extension of the legal and administrative sense of *Instanz* (see Section I) is that of a moral authority. Freud's use of the term to describe the development of conscience during childhood is particularly apt: *Als Niederschlag der langen Kindheitsperiode, während der der werdende Mensch in Abhängigkeit von seinen Eltern lebt, bildet sich in seinem Ich eine besondere Instanz heraus, in der sich dieser elterliche Einfluß fortsetzt. Sie hat den Namen des Über-Ichs erhalten.* (As a residue of the long period of childhood during which the individual evolves while still dependent on its parents, a special *Instanz* develops within the ego in which this parental influence endures. It has been given the name *super-ego*. – *Abriß der Psychoanalyse*, 1938, chapter 1). Freud himself considered the Latin terms – *id, ego, super-ego* – adopted by his translator, James Strachey, needlessly obscurantist, though he offered no alternatives.

Those responsible for *Bild*, Germany's mass-circulation daily, see the paper as some such *Instanz*: readers should not only submit to its 'male authority and power to get things done' (*männliche Autorität und Durchsetzungskraft*) but also to its 'maternal solicitude and understanding' (*mütterliche Fürsorge und mütterliches Verständnis*); it aims to be a sympathetic *Instanz* in which they can freely confide (*eine verständnisvolle Instanz, der man sich unbesorgt anvertrauen kann*). The suspect nature of these claims was revealed in the investigative journalist Günter Wallraff's inside account of *Bild*'s violation of privacy and other gutter-press methods in *Der Aufmacher* (*The Lead Story* – 1977, p. 206).

Tabloid ethics are also the subject of Heinrich Böll's story *Die verlorene Ehre der Katharina Blum* (*The Lost Honour of Katharina*

Blum, 1974), a sharp attack on the irresponsibility of *Bild* and other tabloids by a writer regarded by many as a *moralische Instanz* – the moral conscience of Germany. And when Ralf Dahrendorf, writing in *Die Zeit* on 1 December 1989, described its longtime editor, Marion Gräfin Dönhoff, as *eine verehrte Instanz*, he was referring to the high regard in which she too – the *grande dame* of German liberalism* and something of an institution – is held.

INTELLEKTUELLER n.m. enjoys higher standing than his or her Anglo-Saxon counterpart, though still less than the French intellectual. There are good historical grounds for this discrepancy.

Whereas *Le manifeste des intellectuels en faveur de Dreyfus*, organized by Emile Zola in 1898 in support of the Jewish army captain wrongly accused of spying (a sort of French *Kulturkampf**, except that the aggression was aimed against the state), famously demonstrated the moral prestige and political effectiveness of the intellectuals, the *Manifest der deutschen Intellektuellen*, drawn up by the great classicist* Ulrich von Wilamowitz-Moellendorff in October 1914, did just the opposite. In proclaiming that Germany was a *Kulturnation** fighting for the legacy of a Goethe, a Beethoven, and a Kant (the 'ideas of 1914'), the original ninety-three, and finally four-thousand signatories – virtually the whole of academia – made manifest only their political naivety. (British academics, as Stuart Wallace has shown in *War and the Image of Germany*, 1988, did little better.) And again after the war, while Julien Benda's polemic *La trahison des clercs* (1927) was directed primarily against interference by right-wing French intellectuals in the process of government, their German counterparts stood aloof or even attacked political involvement in the Weimar Republic as *der Verrat des Geistes** (betrayal of the intellect). '*Geistige Menschen*' were encouraged to withdraw into the ivory tower, a sphere finally rejected by the reluctant republican, Thomas Mann, as *machtgeschützte Innerlichkeit* (power-protected inwardness), whence some, such as the philosopher Martin Heidegger, the sociologist Werner Sombart and the poet Gottfried Benn, emerged in 1933 to flirt, or worse, with Nazi ideology and in consequence quarrel with others who by that time were literally rootless *Intellektuelle*, the literary émigrés. For the Nazis, the word was something of a *Schimpfwort*, a term of abuse often combined with *zersetzend* (subversive) or adorned with the prefix *Links-*. Against this they set their own terminology with *Arbeiter der Stirn und der Faust* (recalling the English brawn-brain distinction – see INTELLIGENZ in I).

Purged by confrontation with the horrors to which such attitudes had contributed, post-war German intellectuals revived a healthier critical tradition with their rediscovery of that *Protointellektueller*,

Heinrich Heine. Günter Grass and Heinrich Böll, Alexander Mitscherlich and Jürgen Habermas led public debate in the Germany of Willy Brandt and Helmut Schmidt – themselves intellectuals. By the late 1970s, however, Kurt Sontheimer in *Das Elend unserer Intellektuellen* (*The Poverty of our Intellectuals*, 1976) and Arnold Gehlen in *Das Engagement der Intellektuellen gegen den Staat* (*The Intellectuals in Contention with the State*, 1978) signalled a conservative reaction or '*Tendenzwende*', leading to the political *Wende** of 1982.

Such anti-intellectualism in turn gives rise to that 'doubt as to practical sagacity' which the English, too, attribute to intellectuals (see CLEVER in IV), along with a deep scepticism towards their habits: 'To the man-in-the-street who, I'm sorry to say, / Is a keen observer of life, / The word *intellectual* suggests right away / A man who's untrue to his wife' (W. H. Auden, *Shorts*, 1939–1947).

JUST adv. like *gerade* or *ausgerechnet* means 'just' in the sense of 'exactly', 'precisely', not in the sense of 'only' (*nur*). Thus: *es sind just nicht die Besten, die zum Reichtum kommen* (it is precisely not the most worthy people who get rich). *Und just dieser Mann gefiel meiner lieben alten Mutter* ('And that was the very man my dear old mother had taken to' – Joseph Roth, *Die Kapuzinergruft*, 1938, p. 111). See also EBEN above, HALT in VII, EXTRA in VIII, and for justice, RECHT in I.

KLERIKAL adj. clerical only in the ecclesiastical sense (Austria before the Second World War was referred to as *der klerikale Ständestaat**): an unambiguously pejorative term nowadays, used frequently in public debate to denounce, for instance, the Catholic stance on abortion (see ABORT in VI). The neutral word is *geistlich* (not to be confused with *geistig**). A clerical worker or clerk is *eine Schreibkraft* or *Bürokraft* (see under TIP in VIII).

KLOSTER n.n. not the cloisters of a cathedral, etc., which is *der Kreuzgang*, made up of four *Arkaden*, but a monastery (also *Mönchskloster*) or convent (*Nonnenkloster*). Rather as people once said the BBC was run by Queers, Commies and Catholics, the national journalism school at Leipzig University was popularly and aptly known as *das rote Kloster* (echoing *Das graue Kloster*, one of the most prestigious independent schools in pre-war Berlin, but perhaps also the Communist underground during the Third Reich, *die rote Kapelle**).

KONFESSION n.f. religious denomination or persuasion, rather than the confession one makes to a priest (*die Beichte*).

When the Church failed to reform after Luther (1483–1546) nailed his Ninety-Five Theses to the church door in Wittenberg on 31 October 1517, he eventually supported a system known as *Landesherr-*

*liches Kirchenregiment** (Government of the Church by Princes) as a temporary solution to the perceived *Notstand**(emergency situation). Then, at the Peace of Augsburg (1555), which recognized the *Augsburger Konfession* (Lutheranism) along with Roman Catholicism as the two religions of the Reich, the principle of *cuius regio, eius religio* established the right of the ruler of each of Germany's 300-odd principalities (*Duodezstaaten*, so called because they were so small) to determine how his subjects should worship. *Landesherrliches Kirchenregiment* ended with the abolition of the remaining ruling houses in 1918, but the map of Germany still reflects the results of *cuius regio, eius religio*. One notable exception was *Sachsen* with its Protestant population (Bach in Leipzig, for instance) and its Catholic ducal, later royal, family (in Dresden) who had converted in order to make possible their accession to the Polish throne.

Before reunification, four-fifths of the population of the Federal Republic belonged nominally, and in equal numbers, to one *Konfession* or the other; with the addition of the overwhelmingly Protestant East Germany (where the eight *Landeskirchen* had come to a mutual understanding with the regime in 1969, but – as became splendidly evident during the events of 1989 – retained their democratic autonomy and integrity), there are now some 29 million Protestant and 27 million Catholic church members. Though numbers are in decline, especially among the young, all still pay a *Kirchensteuer* (church tax) of some eight per cent of their income tax (exemption is possible if one leaves the Church, but to do so one must first make a statement in court to that effect, *eine Erklärung vor Gericht abgeben*), so that clergy are quite well paid and the churches run many hospitals and charitable institutions (*'Diakonisches Werk'*).

What we know as the Confessing Church is *die Bekennende Kirche*; this grew out of another emergency, the *Pfarrernotbund** (Pastors' Emergency League) founded by Martin Niemöller (1892–1984) and others in 1933 when the Nazis attempted to establish a single *Deutsche Evangelische** *Kirche* under a *Reichsbischof*. In Dietrich Bonhoeffer (1906–1945), the Confessing Church produced a further hero of the 'Protestant' tradition.

KONSEQUENT adj. or adv., **KONSEQUENZ** n.f. suggests consistency, logical rigour or single-mindedness, rather than mere consequence. The distinction can be crucial, especially in a legal context: *sie war stur und sagte konsequent 'nein'* (she was stubborn and said 'no' every time/consistently), but *sie war stur und sagte folglich 'nein'* (she was stubborn and consequently said 'no'). The idea of strict necessity remains even when *die Konsequenzen tragen* is translated as 'to take the consequences', or *die Teilung Deutschlands war* *eine Konsequenz des verlorenen Krieges* as 'the division of Germany was a consequence of its having lost the war'.

Ein konsequenter Realist is a thorough-going realist; *sei konsequent!*, be consistent; *er zog den konsequenten Schluß*, he drew the logical conclusion.

KORREKT adj. as in 'George III and his very correct Queen Charlotte' – *korrekt* is used of people (*ein korrekter Beamter*), their behaviour (*korrektes Benehmen*) and their dress (*in korrektem Abendanzug* – cf. French *une tenue correcte*); or else the accuracy with which they give information (*eine korrekte Auskunft*) or speak a language (*korrektes Englisch* – 'Farmer George' was the first of the Hanoverians to manage this). But the more common way of saying correct/incorrect is *richtig/falsch*: that is correct, *das ist richtig* or *das stimmt*; you are incorrect: *du hast unrecht, das stimmt nicht*.

KREATUR n.f. 'creature', generally in its pejorative sense: *eine Kreatur des Chefs** is not a 'creation of the chef' but the boss's stooge or minion; *eine armselige Kreatur*, a miserable, wretched creature. But also, though rarely, 'creation' in the sense of all created things, as when Gurnemanz explains the magic of Good Friday (*Karfreitagszauber*) in Act III of Wagner's *Parsifal*: *Nun freut sich alle Kreatur* ('now all creation rejoices'), whereas the act of creation itself is *die Schöpfung* (for Haydn's oratorio, see MATTE in III).

LIST n.f. not a list (see LISTE in II), but a ruse or wile (*eine gemeine List*, a mean trick; *eine raffinierte** *List*, a clever stratagem); or else cunning: *List der Frauen* (feminine guile); *mit List und Tücke* (by low cunning; sometimes used more figuratively to mean: with a bit of ingenuity, by dint of much trying). What Hegel called *die List der Vernunft* (the cunning of reason) allegedly harmonizes individual selfishness with the progress of the whole by turning men's passions to its own inscrutable ends (in another famous phrase of Hegel's, *die Individuen holen dem Weltgeist** *die Kastanien aus dem Feuer*, individuals pull the world spirit's chestnuts out of the fire) – a faith in the inevitability of change which, in its Marxist form, doubtless kept many going in East Germany before November 1989.

LUMPEN n.m. a rag (in the south also a cleaning cloth, *ein Lappen*). Since fine feathers make fine birds (*Kleider machen Leute* – see DIENEN in I) while wretched clothes (*lumpige Kleidung*) unmake the man, *ein Lump* has come to mean a rogue or scoundrel (of children, less disapprovingly, a little rascal), and *dieses Lumpenpack* or *dieses Lumpengesindel* is very much a term of censure: 'that rabble', 'that riffraff'. This led Marx, in *Die Klassenkämpfe in Frankreich* (1850), to describe as the *Lumpenproletariat* that impoverished under-class in a capitalist society too 'lumpen' to develop class consciousness by recognizing where its true class interests lay, thus incapable of political struggle. He went on to say that the financial aristocracy was nothing but the reborn *Lumpenproletariat* – the rabble on the heights of bourgeois society.

When D. H. Lawrence ran off to Germany with Frieda Weekley (*née* von Richthofen) in 1913, he seems to have experienced some of the opprobrium meted out to his fictional *alter ego*, Gilbert Noon: 'an *ungebildeter Simpel*, a *gewöhnlicher Lump*: very nasty things to be called: uneducated simpleton and common lout. *Common* lout is especially nasty' (*Mr Noon*, written 1920–22, 1985 ed., p. 215; see also under GAFFER in VI). Even nastier, and more physical, is *Erröthe, Klumpe schnöder Mißgestalt* (*Richard III*, Act I, Scene 2 in the Schlegel/Tieck version), though it does not quite have the force of the original 'Blush, blush, thou lump of foul deformity', or even of Faust's comparable reaction to Mephistopheles: *Du Spottgeburt von Dreck und Feuer!* (l. 3536). On the other hand, one might call 'a lump of a man' *ein Fettkloß/Fettsack** or *ein (richtiger) Brocken* without impugning his character (see also FEIST in VI).

Eine lumpige Tat is a shabby deed; *lumpige zehn Mark*, a measly ten marks. It is said of someone who does not wish to be thought *ein Lump* and who is consequently* generous: *er hat sich nicht lumpen lassen* (as well as 'to splash out', the Austrians still use *lumpen* to mean 'to be out to all hours' – *tu nicht zu lange lumpen!*). Other lumps include *ein Brocken Erde* (a lump of earth), *eine Beule am Kopf* (a lump on the head), *ein Knoten in der Brust* (a breast lump), *ein Kloß im Hals* (a lump in one's throat), *ein Stück Zucker* (a lump of sugar; cube sugar: *Würfelzucker*).

MERKWÜRDIG adj. nowadays means 'worthy of remark' only in the sense that someone or something is odd, curious, strange (*seltsam*). *Merkwürdige Gestalten treiben sich dort herum*: there are some very suspicious characters hanging around. *Denkwürdig* is used of remarkable/momentous events (also ironically: 'an evening to remember', *ein denkwürdiger Abend*); *beachtlich* of a remarkable talent: *ein ganz beachtlicher Tennisspieler*.

MESSE n.f. as in *Paris vaut bien une messe* (German: *Paris ist eine Messe wert*), as well as the accompanying sacred (*geistlich**) music. Heinrich Mann's novels on the first *Abgesandte der Vernunft und des Menschenglücks* ('herald of reason and human happiness') to wear a crown – *Die Jugend des Königs Henri Quatre* and *Die Vollendung des Königs Henri Quatre* (1935/38) – are eloquent testimony to the birth of that civilization which his brother Thomas thought inimical to German *Kultur** (see ROMAN in X).

Eine Messe is also a trade fair (see MESSE in III) or a ship's mess (but see KASINO in I). *Das Maß** and *die Masse** have quite different meanings.

MINISTER a minister of the church is *ein Priester* (*katholisch*) or *ein Pfarrer* (*katholisch, evangelisch**). Only a government minister is *ein Minister* (see also STAATSSEKRETÄR in I).

MITTEL n.n. unlike the adjectival 'middle' of *Mittelklasse**, *Mittelstand** or *Mitteleuropa**, a means, way, method, device, etc. – as in Kant's maxim: *man dürfe den Menschen immer nur als Zweck, nie als Mittel behandeln* (one must always treat others as ends in themselves, never as means); or Schopenhauer's counter-argument that, since the law should be concerned solely with deterrence, the lawbreaker must become *das Mittel zur Erfüllung des Gesetzes* (the means of fulfilling the law – *Die Welt als Wille und Vorstellung*, I.4, section 62); or Clausewitz's dictum that war should be seen as *die fortgesetzte Staatspolitik mit andern Mitteln* (the continuation of politics by other means); or the Machiavellian, perhaps also Bismarckian, principle, *daß der Zweck die Mittel heiligt* (the end justifies the means – see REALPOLITIK in II). Karl Kraus adapted this in order to draw attention to the discrepancy between Kantian idealism and the more commercial impulses behind the First World War, wittily observing *daß das Lebensmittel nicht Lebenszweck sei* (that foodstuffs/groceries should not be the purpose of life – *Die Fackel*, 5 December 1914). *Lebensmittel* are literally the 'means of life', just as *die Mittel* (plural) are also funds or resources.

MOMENT n.n. whereas *der Moment* is now simply a moment of time, *das Moment* still means either **1.** momentum (in mechanics, the product of a force on an object, as in *das Drehmoment* – the torque of an engine); or else **2.** by extension, a crucial factor or decisive circumstance in a development. In a play or novel, for instance, *ein Spannungsmoment* is not a tense moment, but a suspense-creating factor such as the use of retardation: *das retardierende Moment*; detectives might say: *wir haben keine Verdachtsmomente gefunden* (found no suspicious circumstances), or: *das wichtigste Moment zu seiner Verurteilung waren die Fingerabdrücke* (his fingerprints were the crucial element or critical factor in bringing about his conviction).

In Hegel's philosophy, the word has a special meaning: *These, Antithese* and *Synthese* are *Momente* in the 'dialectic' of history, the most interesting such *Moment* being the birth of *Selbstbewußtsein** (self-consciousness). Here *das Moment* is usually translated as step or stage, but when Marx applies Hegel's three *Momente* – first to food, drink, and shelter; then to new needs when these are satisfied; and finally to the family – he specifies that they are 'not of course to be taken as three diferent stages, but just as three aspects or, to make it clear to the Germans, three "moments", which have existed simultaneously since the dawn of history' (Part I of *The German Ideology*, 1846).

MORAL n.f. either **1**. morals/morality; or **2**. moral (*die Moral von der Geschichte*, the moral of the story); but also **3**. morale. German uses the same French word for *die Moral des Kämpfens* (the question whether or not it is morally right to fight) and *die Kampfmoral* (the morale of the troops), whereas English added the 'e' to look French and convey this latter sense of discipline, confidence, fixity of purpose and faith in the cause fought for – qualities we might now think of as German rather than French.

Germans associate *die Moral* with Kant (1724–1804) and with Schiller (1759–1805), his foremost disciple. Kant's essential tenet is that it is not self-interest, however well disguised, but logic which should lie at the root of all our moral precepts, and that *Pflicht* (duty) and *Neigung* (inclination) can ultimately be reconciled. Yet his celebrated *kategorischer Imperativ* is often thought to amount to no more than 'do as ye would be done by', and to rest on the assumption that *Sollen* (what we should do) and *Wollen* (what we want to do) are inevitably at odds. Schiller made gentle fun of such rigorism in the poem *Gewissensskrupel* ('Pangs of Conscience'): *Gerne dien ich den Freunden, doch tu ich es leider mit Neigung, / Und so wurmt* es mir oft, daß ich nicht tugendhaft bin.* 'I serve my friends gladly, but alas, I do it from fond inclination, so it often rankles with me that I am not being virtuous.' His solution: *Da ist kein anderer Rat; du mußt suchen, sie zu verachten, / Und mit Abscheu alsdann tun, wie die Pflicht dir gebeut.* 'So you must try to loathe them, and then do with abhorrence as duty dictates' – a 'charming *reductio* of Kant' which Karl Popper thought as good as anything ever written on ethics since Plato (*Unended Quest*, 1976, p. 193).

The more austere reading is nevertheless shared, if Shaw is to be believed, by Englishmen who think they are being moral only when they feel uncomfortable; also by Wilhelm Busch's terrible twins *Max und Moritz* (1865) and their fellow mischief-maker *Die fromme Helene* (1872) before they all come to a sticky end: *Das Gute – dieser Satz steht fest – / Ist stets das Böse, was man läßt!* 'Virtue – this is always so – is but the evil you must forgo.' See also PRANKE in VI, COUPLET and STREICHINSTRUMENT in X.

Schopenhauer's supreme moral value was *Mitleid*, compassion, which we should derive from an awareness that we are all subordinate to the same inexorable will* – a deduction which notably Nietzsche rejected, arguing for the replacement of such *entartete* Mitleidsmoral* with a philosophy of will designated *moralinfrei** or morality-free (the *-in* suffix suggests morality is some pathogenic substance – *Werke* III, 739, 1211). The metaphor underlying his ironically robust demonstrations of *Wie man mit dem Hammer philosophiert* (the subtitle of *Götzen-Dämmerung*, 1888) – *Hammer oder Amboß?* 'hammer or anvil?' – seems to mean 'do before it is done to you'. In anti-Christian vein, Goethe encapsulated identical pragmatic advice in his second *Cophtisches Lied* (1787–89): *Du mußt herrschen und gewinnen, / Oder dienen* und verlieren, / Leiden oder triumphieren, / Amboß oder Hammer sein* – a defiance vividly conveyed in Hugo Wolf's setting (1888–89). But firmer support for Karl Kraus's thesis that violent language entails violent deeds came from Chancellor von Bülow, who used the same metaphor to describe Germany's options as it embarked on *Weltpolitik*.

Schiller had dealt only with moral heroism, while those who did not share his lofty ideals spoke of him as a *Moralheld und Tugendschwätzer* ('blethering about morality': Nietzsche, adapting a popular ballad, was also to call him *der Moraltrompeter von Säckingen*). The reaction set in most strikingly with Büchner's *Woyzeck* (1837), a totally unidealistic account of one of nature's underdogs who knows that virtue (like legitimate children) is a luxury only the rich can afford: *Wer kein Geld hat. Da setz einmal einer seinsgleichen auf die Moral in die Welt* ('Just try bringing a child into the world on the back of morality if you've no money'). And Brecht, in Scene 6 of *Die Dreigroschenoper* (*Threepenny Opera*, 1928), conveys a similar realism: *Erst kommt das Fressen, dann kommt die Moral*, which Auden renders as 'Grub first, then ethics'. For Brecht's *Moritat von Mackie Messer*, see HAI in VII.

OPFER n.n. Bach wrote *Das musikalische Opfer* in 1747 as a gift-offering for Frederick the Great – a secularized version of the *Messopfer** (Sacrifice of the Mass, gift to the gods) or *Brandopfer* (burnt offering). But a *Brandopfer* is also, literally, a fire victim – the other sense of the word 'holocaust'. That is to say *ein Opfer* can also be the person on the receiving end, as in Fritz von Unruh's haunting evocation of the inferno of Verdun in *Opfergang** (*The Sacrificial Path*, 1918), itself a bitter allusion to the notion of willing sacrifice (the German General Staff's version of Kitchener's pointed finger appealed to *Opferbereitschaft*, *Opfermut* or *Opfergesinnung*). Rilke, too, who like most European intellectuals had equivocal feelings soon after the war started, was sensitive to this fatal* ambiguity while regretting that the German language had no equivalent of the French word *offrande* (see HEIMSUCHEN in IX). The worst was yet to come: as J. P. Stern points out in *Hitler: The Führer and the People* (1975, p. 33), 'it is as though the German language itself, in its inability to distinguish between "victim" and "sacrifice", were an accessary to the ideology'. See UNMENSCH in II.

ORDINÄR adj. of people, never means ordinary (an ordinary chap is *ein ganz normaler Typ** or *ein ganz gewöhnlicher Mensch*), but common, coarse, vulgar or downright rude. The lovers disturbed by the voyeuristic heroine of Elfriede Jelinek's novel *Die Klavierspielerin* (*The Pianist*, 1983, p. 184; see SPANNER in VI) make *eine internationale ordinäre Geste* (with one finger – a '*Stinkefinger'* – rather than two, one supposes, for Europeans use both the backhand and forehand V-sign in the sense of Churchill's Victory sign). In a similar vein, the husband in Max Frisch's novel *Mein Name sei Gantenbein* (*Call me Gantenbein*, 1964, p. 155) who mentally addresses his errant wife *mit Wörtern, die ihm umso wohler taten, je ordinärer sie ausfielen*, does not simply relish using any old words, 'the more ordinary' the better, but rather 'the more obscene'.

Apart from *ordinäre Menschen*, their *ordinäres Benehmen* (common behaviour), *ordinäre Redensarten* (vulgar language) and *ordinäre Witze* (dirty jokes), *ein ordinäres Parfüm* denotes a cheap and nasty perfume and *ein ordinärer Brillantring* a flashy diamond ring, but other things deemed *ordinär* may, somewhat confusingly, be simply ordinary, that is to say, unprepossessing – *eine ganz ordinäre Kiste* is a perfectly ordinary box. There is a further meaning, specific to the book trade: *Ordinärpreis DM19,80* is a book's retail price in the shop, as distinct from what a *Kommissionär** (wholesale bookseller) charges.

Though the upper classes do not have what it takes to be *ordinär*, they have their own way of being brash, rude and offhand, for which Ralf Dahrendorf found a good word – *die Schnoddrigkeit* (arrant snobbery, contemptuous superiority) *der englischen Oberschicht* – when describing to readers of *Die Zeit* on 20 July 1990 Nicholas Ridley's anti-German outburst in the *Spectator* a week before (see also DEUTSCH in II).

ORIGINAL German *original* means real, genuine, going back to the origins; *originell* suggests something new, striking, sometimes witty. Curiously, the distinction between French *original* and *originel* is exactly the opposite: original sin, for instance, is *le péché originel* – though Germans call this *die Erbsünde* or *Ursünde*. Only *Original-* is used in compounds, but since the cult of the *Originalgenie** in the 1770s and 80s, *ein Original* has come to mean a real character, even (as in French) an eccentric.

A useful alternative to *Original-* is *Ur-*. The usage is both *uralt* and *urdeutsch* – typically, essentially German (cf. *echt deutsch*, genuinely German) – and suggests either the original occasion on which something happened (*die Uraufführung*, première), or else something ancient, so that *die Urzeit*, primeval times, is quite different from *die Uhrzeit*, the time of day. Thus: the *Urvogel* (archæopteryx) is on display in Eichstätt; the *Urbewohner* of Europe in their *Urwald* (primeval forest) supposedly spoke an *Ursprache* known as Indo-European. Most German *Lokale** are still *urig* in the best sense – atmospherically traditional without horse-brasses and plastic-wood beams.

PARTOUT adv. a *faux ami*, for in German it is an intensifier meaning 'at any price', 'absolutely' or 'simply': *er will partout nicht mitkommen* (he absolutely refuses to come with us); *er will partout nicht gehorchen* (he simply will not obey) – generally in negative expressions where *unbedingt* does not fit (*er will unbedingt kommen*, he insists on coming; *ich muß unbedingt gehen*, I really must go).

Das Passepartout is not what is known in English as passe-partout – a roll of sticky paper, one of whose many uses (French *passe partout*, 'fits everywhere') was once to frame pictures (this is *Papierklebeband** in German) – but rather a cardboard surround which serves the same function. *Ein Passepartout* is also a master key (*ein Haupt-* or *Generalschlüssel*), while a skeleton key, having undergone the same process of naming by personal association as a burglar's 'jemmy', is known as *ein Dietrich*, and in the Rhineland as *ein Klaus/Kläuschen*.

PHANTASIE n.f. the primary sense is simply imagination – *in seiner Phantasie* (in his mind), *er singt ohne Phantasie* (unimaginatively); but the plural, *Phantasien*, suggests imaginings of a more trivial, capricious, unobtainable sort (a singular exception being *das ist reine Phantasie*, that's pure fantasy). On the other hand, *phantastisch* can mean fantastic or incredible also in the literal sense of unbelievable, as one might expect from a *Phantast* (a dreamer, visionary, someone who fantasizes), though when Karl Böhm once said he looked forward to hearing in heaven *wie Mozart phantasiert*, he meant improvising (a musical fantasia is *eine Fantasie*).

PHRASE n.f. usually pejorative in everyday parlance, especially so when applied to politicians: *alles nur Phrasen*, just empty words, mere platitudes; *abgedroschene Phrasen*, the outworn clichés of a *Phrasendrescher*, windbag. What characterizes Ernst Gombrich, according to *Der Spiegel* on 15 August 1994, is precisely the *Phrasenlosigkeit* of his writings, their lack of that high-sounding but fatuous jargon which Karl Popper called, ironically, 'elevated depth' – a virtue which Ralf Dahrendorf, in his obituary of Popper for *Die Zeit* on 23 September

1994, found equally characteristic of the philosopher's own writings. See also *Kanzleistil* under KANZLEI in I.

POPE n.m. the Pope is *der Papst*, but *ein Pope* is a priest in the *griechisch-orthodoxe/russisch-orthodoxe Kirche*, and sometimes a pejorative term for any priest or cleric (see KLERIKAL above).

PRINZIPIELL adj. either **1.** *aus Prinzip*, on principle (*das tue ich prinzipiell nicht*, I won't do that on principle – German bureaucracy has its fair share of *Prinzipienreiter*, sticklers for their principles, i.e. the rules). Or else **2.** *im Prinzip*, in principle (*prinzipiell bin ich einverstanden*, I agree in principle – which does not always imply the subsequent serious objections of a Frenchman who says *en principe, oui*). 'Principally': *vornehmlich* or *in erster Linie*.

RAFFINIERT adj. refined, polished, sophisticated, but only when used predicatively, as in *sie kleidet sich sehr raffiniert*, she dresses very stylishly. Otherwise cunning or crafty: *ein raffiniertes Weib** is a derogatory term for a woman 'who knows every trick in the book' (definitely not a 'refined' lady, *eine vornehme Dame*, or one with refined taste, *ein erlesener Geschmack*).

When Albert Einstein carved the words *Raffiniert ist der Herr Gott, aber boshaft ist er nicht* above the fireplace in Princeton University's Fine Hall, he meant 'God is subtle but not malevolent' – sometimes rendered as 'God's sly, but he ain't mean' or 'God's devious, but he ain't bloody-minded' – a variation on 'God does not play dice with the universe'.

RATIO n.f. the faculty of reason (*die Vernunft*), not the ratio of men to women (*das Verhältnis von Männern zu Frauen* – but take care when using *Verhältnis* as it is also a sexual affair; see under FALL in II).

SÄKULAR adj. either **1.** secular, worldly; or **2.** 'occurring every 100 years' (*die Säkularfeier*, centenary celebration). The first words of Schiller's Karl Moor, the archetypal angry young man of the *Sturm und Drang*, set the tone for the greatest scandal in German theatrical history: *Mir ekelt vor diesem tintenklecksenden Säkulum, wenn ich in meinem Plutarch lese von großen Menschen*, 'I'm sick of this inksplattering century when I read about great men in my Plutarch' (*Die Räuber*, 1781, Act I, Scene 2), though it is his villainous brother Franz who remains defiantly *säkular* in the first sense. Or **3.** timeless, exceptionally rare. Heinrich August Winkler, writing in *Die Zeit* on 28 September 1990 about National Socialism *und seine säkularen Verbrechen*, meant that its crimes were unique (happening only once in each *saeculum*), not that they were a consequence of its godforsaken ideology.

It was Napoleon, however, who brought about the greatest *Säkularisation* in German history when what is known as the *Reichsdeputationshauptschluß* transferred almost all the remaining spiritual or clerical territories (in total an area as large as Bavaria) to secular princes at the last *Reichstag* of Regensburg in 1803.

SCHEIN n.m. appearance as distinct from reality (*Sein*). German drama of the classical period (no mere *Scheinblüte*, illusory flowering, but a wonderful counterpoint to philosophers of the day who held, more austerely, that all *Schein* was deception), nevertheless generally turns on the play of *Schein und Sein*. In Act II, Scene 5 of Schiller's *Maria Stuart* (1800), for instance, Elisabeth, faced with the dilemma of whether to sign Mary's death warrant, *kann den Schein nicht retten*, 'cannot save appearances' (or her reputation), and observes ruefully: *Was man* scheint, *hat jedermann zum Richter, was man* ist, *hat keinen*, 'Everyone judges what one *seems* to be, no one what one *is*'. However, Schiller's Elisabeth is revealed to be a *Scheinheilige* (a 'sham saint' or hypocrite).

There is an anti-Marxist joke which plays on another meaning of *Schein* (a banknote – in which context *eine Blüte* is a dud or counterfeit note) as well as on the Marxist belief *daß das Sein das Bewußtsein bestimmt*, that being determines consciousness, and not the other way round (see SELBSTBEWUSST below): East Germans travelling to the Mediterranean for the first time in 1990 realized it was the *D-Mark-Schein* which determined their *Sein*. For further meanings, including the *Seminarscheine* students need to accumulate as evidence of having attended the appropriate number of classes, see SCHEIN and SEMINAR in IV.

SCHULD n.f. either **1.** blame/fault; or **2.** guilt; or **3.** debt. Nietzsche argues in *Zur Genealogie der Moral* (1887, II, 4) that the moral concept of 'guilt' originated in the all-too-material concept of 'debts' (*daß jener moralische Hauptbegriff 'Schuld' seine Herkunft aus dem sehr materiellen Begriff 'Schulden' genommen hat*) – which is perhaps less far-fetched than his etymological derivation of 'good' and 'God' from the Goths (I, 4). Kafka was to transpose Nietzsche's influential critique of morality into the hellish business and family setting of *Die Verwandlung* (*Metamorphosis*, 1912 – see also SCHRECKEN in II, MIST in III), in which we are told that the unfortunate Gregor Samsa has inherited *die Schuld der Eltern* – parental guilt as well as their debts towards an all-powerful boss (these would normally be *Schulden* in the plural). In a similar way, the religious dimension of Dostoevsky's novel is better expressed by its German title *Schuld und Sühne* (literally *Guilt and Atonement*) than by the English title *Crime and Punishment* (literally *Verbrechen und Strafe*).

In an everyday context, *was bin ich Ihnen schuldig?* means 'what do I owe you?' But: *daran bist du selber schuld*, 'you've nobody to blame but yourself'.

SCHÜLER n.m. a schoolboy; or a pupil/student in the sense that *Berg und Webern waren Schüler Schoenbergs* or *Schoenbergschüler*; but not a scholar, which is *ein Gelehrter* or *ein Wissenschaftler**, or if more specific *ein Kenner* (*ein Shakespearekenner*; *ein Kenner der Antike**).

Writing in anglophile (and increasingly anglophone) Hamburg, Lessing pointed out in the second of his *Briefe, die neueste Literatur betreffend* (January 1759) that a new translation of the still enormously popular Alexander Pope had nonsensically rendered 'Scholar' as *Schüler*. The passage was from the Preface of 1717, where Pope had recommended 'imitation of the Ancients', considering it just as unreasonable 'that people should expect us to be Scholars, and yet be angry to find us so' as to complain that 'our faces are not our own, because they are like our Fathers'. This, Lessing thought, was a *feine* Anmerkung*, yet for all his championship of English poetry as a suitable model for the Germans, he had reservations about Pope as a thinker, and in *Pope ein Metaphysiker!* (1755) cast doubt on the facile optimism which Voltaire was soon to satirize in *Candide* (1759).

SELBSTBEWUSST adj. while Mrs Thatcher once described the German character as 'swerving unpredictably between aggression and self-doubt' (see DEUTSCHLAND in II), the Germans sometimes say the English are *selbstbewußt*. This does not mean 'self-conscious' or 'self-aware' in the English sense of being embarrassed and unsure of oneself (*befangen, gehemmt**), but rather in the opposite sense of being self-assured, confident, proud. Hegel (in *Phänomenologie des Geistes**, Part IV – a section greatly admired by Marx) made much of the *Selbstbewußtsein* of the slave, whose self-reliance and independence grows while his master becomes increasingly reliant on the slave's labours to sustain a life of leisure and consumption – leading to the 'dialectical' turning-point at which the slave vanquishes his oppressor.

Sometimes, however, the word suggests smugness (see SÜFFISANT below) or self-importance rather than the self-realization of a free agent. When the Christian Democrats defeated Germany's first coalition between Social Democrats and Greens in the state of Hesse, their leader Walter Wallmann naturally (being a German politician) informed the *Süddeutsche Zeitung* on 8 August 1987 of his philosophical position – one which, not surprisingly, inverts Marx's: *eine*

Position der idealistischen Philosophie, der ich anhänge: es ist die Überzeugung, daß das Bewußtsein das Sein und nicht das Sein das Bewußtsein bestimmt (the Idealist philosophy to which I subscribe: the conviction that consciousness determines being, not the other way round). But then he added: *ich bin Ministerpräsident, und ich habe es nicht nötig, an jedem Tage zu bekunden, welches Selbstbewußtsein ich habe* (I am the prime minister and I do not need to give a daily account of just how self-confident I feel).

SENSIBEL adj. not sensible (*vernünftig*), but sensitive – the adjective from *die Sensibilität* (sensibility), either in an emotional sense (*sie wirkt* sehr sensibel*, she seems very sensitive – 'oversensitive' is sometimes associated with the flower: *mimosenhaft*), or in a physical sense (*eine sensible Haut*, sensitive skin). Also used of a sensitive issue, as when the demolition* of buildings along the route planned for an experimental high-speed train between Fulda and Würzburg – *die 42 sensiblen Objekte* entlang der neuen Bahnstraße* – presented the government with a delicate or tricky problem (*Die Zeit Magazin**, 12 August 1988). See also SENTIMENTALISCH below and ADÄQUAT in VI.

SENTIMENTALISCH adj. a word associated with Schiller, whose *Über naive und sentimentalische Dichtung* (1796) is arguably the greatest work of German criticism. Usually translated as 'reflective', that is, self-consciously aware of man's 'modern' separation from the notionally prelapsarian state of a Homer, but also of a Shakespeare, a Molière, and (for the reflective Schiller, the crucial contrast) a Goethe, who are nostalgically perceived as *naiv* in their instinctive harmony with life and nature. In practice, works designated *sentimentalisch* are recreations of an earlier mode (thus, Romance returns as Romanticism), while *naiv* is often synonymous with classical.

Schiller probably took the word from the enormously popular *Sentimental Journey* (1768), though this is known in Germany as *Eine empfindsame Reise durch Frankreich und Italien* – the title given it by Lessing (who said he would have given five years of his life for another book by Sterne) – and the fashion for sentiment and sensibility which it ushered in as *Empfindsamkeit*. Today, Germans use *sentimental* in its (often derogatory) English sense.

SINN n.m. has several meanings, including 'sense' (*der Tastsinn**, the sense of touch; *ein Sinn für Gerechtigkeit*, a sense of justice); 'mind' (Heine's *Die Lorelei* of 1827 recounts *ein Märchen aus alten Zeiten, das kommt mir nicht aus dem Sinn*, 'I can't get it out of my mind'); and 'meaning' itself. This wide range facilitates rather hackneyed word-play, as when the *Süddeutsche Zeitung* observed on 25

January 1986: *wir sind ja als Deutsche dauernd faustisch mit allen Sinnen auf Sinn-Suche* (like Faust, we Germans are forever searching with all our senses for meaning), to which one might add that the Faust who rediscovers the pleasures of life is also *ein sinnlicher Mensch* or *Sinnenmensch*. In spite of the distinction often drawn between *sinnlich* (sensuous or sensual) and *sittlich* (moral), there is no connection with sin (*die Sünde*), and *sinnvoll* means meaningful or sensible*, not sinful (*sündig* or, most often figuratively, *sündhaft* – as in *sündhaft teuer*, wickedly expensive).

SKURRIL adj. not as in a scurrilous accusation (*eine Verleumdung*) or a scurrilous joke (*ein unflätiger, gemeiner Witz*), but droll, sometimes eccentric – both attributes of the great Munich comedian, Karl Valentin (1882–1948), and of the traditional *Schwank** in which he appeared. When Odo Marquard, president of the professional association of German philosophers, accused his fellow-thinkers of having *skurrile Züge* (*Süddeutsche Zeitung*, 19 September 1987), he meant only that their views were odd. And after a well-known urban myth resurfaced in Germany – that of the hitch-hiker's severed hand, subsequently found on the doorhandle by a driver who had had second thoughts and driven on – the paper commented on 18 July 1990: *es ist so abwegig und skurril, daß schon die Erstfassung erfunden zu sein scheint* (so bizarre and grotesque that even the original version was surely invented). A further instance – after someone had emptied a chamber pot over his neighbour's head – highlights the growth of private legal actions in Germany: *Die Zeit*, on 19 August 1988, was dismissive of such *skurrile Auswüchse des deutschen Rechts-Triebes und nachbarlicher Impertinenz* (ludicrous excrescences of the Germans' instinctive recourse to litigation and their impertinent – or impudent, perhaps even 'scurrilous' – behaviour towards their neighbours). See also SPLEEN below.

SOLIDE adj. as in 'a solid citizen': sound, solvent and – something especially prized by German landladies – leading a morally unobjectionable life, *ein solider Lebenswandel* (respectability is *die Solidität*). Shaw's Mrs Warren, 'a good sort but a bad lot', might charitably be described as *lieb aber unsolid*. Furniture made of solid wood (or cutlery of solid silver) is *massiv**, and only *solid* if it is also sturdy and of good quality. *Solide Bedienung* is good, honest service in a restaurant, while *solide Preise* means that the prices are reasonable.

SPINNER n.m. from *spinnen* (the lilies of the field *arbeiten nicht, auch spinnen sie nicht – Ev. Lukas/Luke*, xii.27 – and the sentiment expressed in John Ball's revolutionary sermon at Blackheath during Wat Tyler's Rebellion of 1381 – 'When Adam delved and Eve span, /

Who was then the gentleman?' – becomes in German *Als Adam grub und Eva spann, wo war denn der Edelmann?*). *Garn spinnen* means literally to spin yarn, figuratively to spin a yarn (*Seemannsgarn* is a tale of the sea, usually a creepy or spooky one). But to call someone a *Spinner* is often more disparaging than to say they are 'spinning a yarn' (*du erzählst vielleicht Geschichten!*). Thus, *du bist ein Spinner!* or *du spinnst!* means 'you're crazy', 'you're talking rubbish'; *spinn doch nicht!*, 'come off it!'

The spider (*die Spinne*) can even suggest deadly enmity to the Germans (*einander spinnefeind sein*) rather than the perseverance which inspired Robert the Bruce. In Act II, Scene 2 of *A Midsummer Night's Dream*, the Fairies are simply arachnophobic: 'Hence, you long-legg'd spinners, hence!' (Felix Mendelssohn-Bartholdy, who always gets his full name in Germany, was only seventeen when he wrote the incidental music to the play in 1826.)

Spinnen is confined to these two contexts. To spin round is *sich drehen*, a washing machine *schleudert*, and to explain what a spin bowler does (see GULLY in VII) one would have to say: *er gibt dem Ball einen Dreh* or *einen Drall* (German tennis players use *Topspin*, though, and quite effectively).

SPLEEN n.m. Nowadays, the word tends to mean a crazy idea or quirky behaviour, as in the phrase *du hast ja einen Spleen!* (what's got into you? / you're in a funny mood). On 29 January 1988, *Zeit Magazin* took a nostalgic look at those British cars which are still made by hand *für Fahrer mit Spleen*, for drivers who want something different. More eccentric still, the mysterious masked stranger who commissioned Mozart to write a Requiem was Graf von Walsegg-Stuppach, who had the odd and obsessive habit – *der den Spleen hatte* – of buying other people's compositions which he would pass off as his own (see *Der Spiegel*, 14 July 1986).

No longer used of those afflicted with morose melancholia, though the Germans and the French – if only from reading in Burton's *Anatomy of Melancholia* about the ill-humour produced by black bile in the spleen – long thought of the English as splenetic. Egon Friedell, for instance, once described Jonathan Swift as *ein Genie* des Spleen*. German visitors in the latter part of the eighteenth century attributed the prevalence of *Spleen* and the high suicide rate in England to the poor climate and too much red meat. Nor did travel – at least, not to Germany – lift the spirits. Heinrich Heine (in *Deutschland – Ein Wintermärchen*, 1844, canto XIX) imagined the Duke of Cumberland languishing in Hannover: *An großbritannisches Leben gewöhnt, / Sei es ihm hier zu enge, / Ihn plage der Spleen, er fürchte sich schier, / Daß er sich mal erhänge* ('Used to the British way of life, as broad as Germany's is narrowing, a prey to spleen he's half afraid he'll hang himself, it's so harrowing'). During the vogue for Existentialism* in the 1940s, the term *Angst**acquired many of the associations of nineteenth-century *Spleen* – as when Cyril Connolly wrote in *The Unquiet Grave* (1944) that 'the secret of happiness lies in the avoidance of *Angst* (anxiety, spleen, noia, fear, remorse, cafard)'.

Spleen in the sense of anger is *der Zorn* (John Osborne's play is known in Germany as *Blick zurück im Zorn*). To vent one's spleen, *seinem Ärger Luft machen*; in a fit of spleen, *in einem Wutanfall.*

STADIUM n.n. not a stadium (*das Stadion*), but a stage of development, as of an illness (*im vorgerückten Stadium*, at an advanced stage). The plural of both words is *Stadien.* As the German title of Kierkegaard's famous book, known in English as *Stages on Life's Way*, this is somewhat misleading, for the 'stages' – aesthetic, ethical, religious – are overlapping 'existential' modes rather than the historically progressive *Momente** which Kierkegaard attacked in Hegel's philosophy. See also STATION in VII.

SUBLIM adj. suggests awe-inspiring grandeur (Duden is surely wrong to ignore this sense altogether), though also eloquently subtle or refined (*eine sublime Ironie*), something to which only the most acute minds or senses have access – originally tragedy and the epic (*genus sublime*) which ancient rhetoric distinguished from 'lower' literary genres.

Burke's *Philosophical Enquiry* (1757) spoke of sublimity's 'delightful horror' turning on pain rather than pleasure – a step beyond the distinction he had already made in *On the Sublime and the Beautiful* (1750) between mere sensual delight and the noble exaltation* of sublimity. This influential treatise is known in Germany as *Über das Erhabene und das Schöne*, and *erhaben* is precisely what Kant, too, felt when he contemplated *den gestirnten Himmel über uns und das moralische Gesetz in uns* (the starry heavens above us and the moral law within). In his case, it was the night sky above Königsberg, now Kaliningrad, a city which he never left, and which some of its Russian citizens now want to rename Kantgrad.

What Kant felt when he contemplated blondes is less well known (see JUNGFRAU in VI). He suggests in his own essay on the Beautiful and the Sublime (1764) that *Blonde**(or *Blondinen*) are no more than undisturbingly appealing (they evoke *eine angenehme Empfindung, die aber fröhlich und lachend ist*), while *Brünette* occasion a mixed agitation in the beholder, pleasing but also creepy (*Wohlgefallen, aber mit Grausen*) – an unusual example of sublimity. Mozart's Blonde does her best to refute it in Act II, Scene I of *Die Entführung aus dem*

Serail (1782), when she reveals herself to be sublimely plucky and resourceful in the face of dire threats. But then, she is *eine Engländerin, zur Freiheit geboren*, a freeborn Englishwoman, and more than a match for Osmin (harem-keeper, eunuch, but also, with comic incongruity, basso-profundo).

SÜFFISANT adj. complacent, mockingly arrogant (from French *suffisance*, self-satisfaction). At a reception to mark completion of a major refit on the *Queen Elizabeth II* at the Lloyd shipyard in Bremerhaven, the sound of hammering was heard: *süffisant merkte ein Vertreter der Werft an, dies seien fast ausnahmslos britische Firmen, die der Zeit noch ein wenig hinterherhinkten* (a representative of the yard observed smugly that almost without exception this would be British firms which were a bit behind – *Süddeutsche Zeitung*, 27 April 1987). The Christian Democrats' election slogan (*Parole**) in the 1986 election campaign: *Weiter so, Deutschland* ('Keep it up' or 'More of the same, Germany') was also widely seen as *süffisant*. But a 'sufficient'/suitable/valid policy would be *eine adäquate* Politik*. See also SELBSTBEWUSST above.

No connection with *süffeln* – 'to like one's drink'. *Ein süffiger Wein* is light and quaffable; *er hat sich dem stillen* Suff ergeben* is a joking reference to a secret drinker (by contrast, *der stille Zecher* in the popular Viennese song of that name, far from being *still**, simply refuses to be hushed up), all of which allows the punster (smugly) to lament the woes of '*Süffilis*', rather as a fellow-spirit once traced the course of civilization to the spread of syphilisation.

SUGGESTION n.f. used only in the psychological sense of an implanted idea or underhand representation. *Jemandem etwas suggerieren* means to subject someone to suggestion, to insinuate or get someone to believe something without realizing it, while *dem Angeklagten Suggestivfragen vorlegen* means to ask the accused leading questions (a suggestive/indecent question, joke, remark, etc. is *zweideutig* or *anzüglich*). To suggest a visit to the theatre, however, is *einen Theaterbesuch vorschlagen*.

SUPERINTENDENT n.m. not a senior policeman (*ein Kommissar**), or the person in charge of, say, a hostel (*ein Heimleiter*), or a high-profile theatre-manager (*ein Intendant* – the '*Super-*' might be added in jest), but a presiding minister or dean in the *Evangelische* Kirche* (like the 'superintendent' which John Wesley introduced within Methodism; it is worth noting that while 'Free Church' is the global name given by Nonconformists to many major non-established churches, a German *Freikirche** is merely a sect). See also DEKAN and REKTOR in IV.

SYMPATHISCH adj. like *sympathique* or *simpatico* – nice, like-able, charming. Note the construction: *sie war mir sympathisch* (I took to her), whereas 'she was sympathetic (towards me)' becomes *sie hatte Mitleid mit mir*. Similarly, *ein Zeichen der Sympathie* is a sign of affection. Alfred Andersch probably meant only that he felt well-disposed towards Idris Parry when he sent him one of his books inscribed 'with all my simpathie'. *Ich möchte Ihnen mein herzliches Beileid aussprechen*, May I offer you my heartfelt sympathy?

VIKAR n.m. a curate, whereas a vicar is *ein Pfarrer* or *Pastor*. Catholics distinguish between the *Pfarrer/Pastor* who runs the parish (*die Pfarre, die Pfarrei, die Gemeinde*), and the *Kapläne* (chaplains – the lowest rank) or *Vikare* (curates) who assist him. For the Swiss sense of *Vikar* (supply teacher), see DEPUTAT in IV.

VIRTUOS adj. virtuoso, masterly. Virtuous is *tugendhaft* or *tugendsam*.

VORSICHT n.f. caution or prudence rather than 'foresight' (*der Weitblick*; in the foreseeable future, *in absehbarer Zeit*). As an exclamation, *Vorsicht!* (at sea: *Wahrschau!*) means 'watch out!', 'be careful!' 'attention!'.

WALLFAHRT n.f. a pilgrimage. No connection with a wall, though Heinrich IV's famous pilgrimage did end before the walls of Canossa (see BUSSGELD and WALL in I). Germany's numerous *Wallfahrtskirchen* today attract more tourists than pilgrims.

WILL a false friend and a key word. *Ich will kommen* means 'I (strongly) want to come' (from *wollen*), whereas 'I will come' – simple future tense – is *ich werde kommen* (from *werden*).

The question of the freedom of the will, *die Willensfreiheit*, has been central to German thought at least since Kant (whose intoxication with the notion of human autonomy was wryly echoed by Isaac Bashevis Singer: 'We have to believe in free will, we've got no choice'). In *Über das Erhabene* (1801; see SUBLIM above), Schiller put the Idealist credo most succinctly: *alle andern Dinge müssen; der Mensch ist das Wesen, welches will* ('all other things are subject to necessity; only man *wills*'). By way of reaction, Schopenhauer argued that the only freedom, granted to few, was to understand the unrelenting will, which he equated with Kant's thing-in-itself and which, he thought, manifests itself in all appearances (*Die Welt als Wille und Vorstellung*, 1818), and to renounce it. Nietzsche turned his mentor's philosophy of the will on its head, but his own notion of the *Wille zur Macht* (will to power) in the 1880s was already sceptical of universal claims, while Leni Riefenstahl's film *Triumph des Willens*

(1936) vividly illustrated the view that some men cannot avoid striving to dominate others. Later on, when Hitler's *eiserne Willensnatur* (iron will) was no longer in the ascendant, he claimed it was the will of the German people which had let him down. *Die Willkür*, finally, is arbitrariness, despotism.

WISCH n.m. not a wish (*ein Wunsch*), but a pejorative word for a scrap of paper or piece of 'bumf'. It is the word the Kaiser used to describe the Great Powers' guarantee to Belgium 'for whose sake England could not possibly go to war'; rather more accurately, it conveys what Hitler is likely to have thought of the piece of paper bearing his signature which Chamberlain waved after securing 'peace in our time' at Munich in September 1938 (an example of *Wunschdenken*, wishful thinking – see PLAKATIV in X).

Die Scheibenwischer, windscreen wipers. *Wisch ihm eins!* Clout him one!

WITZ n.m. either **1**. wit (*Geist**, *Esprit*), or the wits one is born with (*Mutterwitz, Schläue*); or **2**. figuratively 'the important point', as in *der Witz der Sache ist der, daß. . .*, the great thing about it is that. . .; or **3**. an individual joke. The English title of Freud's *Der Witz und seine Beziehung zum Unbewußten* (1905) is *Jokes and their Relation to the Unconscious*. In Karl Kraus's *Die letzten Tage der Menschheit* (1922), the generals and ministers who spend the First World War in Viennese *Kaffeehäuser* shout for the waiter to bring them *das Witzblatt*, 'the comics' – an apt illustration of Freud's theory on the function of jokes as codified references to forbidden subjects. *Das ist doch wohl ein Witz!* suggests something is utterly unbelievable.

WUNDERN v. generally translates as 'surprise' rather than 'wonder': *das wundert mich*, I'm surprised (baffled); *das würde mich nicht wundern*, I shouldn't be surprised; *da wirst du dich aber wundern!* you're in for a surprise; one exception, though, is *ich hab' mich schon gewundert, wo du bleibst*, I've been wondering what was keeping you. More idiomatically: *nicht ärgern, nur wundern!* don't get worked up; *da staunt der Fachmann, der Laie wundert sich*, that's a real turn-up for the book.

'Wonder' is variously conveyed: 'I wonder why?' *ich frage mich, warum?* or *ich möchte gern wissen, warum?*; what next, I wonder? *ich bin gespannt, was jetzt kommt*; oh, I was just wondering, *ach, nur so.*

While *das Wunder* is either a divine miracle or (merely) a surprise, the sense of wonder/awe is *das Staunen* or *die Verwunderung*. Distinguish also between *wunderbar* (wonderful, marvellous) and *wunderlich* ('wondrous', strange, odd – see MERKWÜRDIG above).

SEX
and the
FAMILY

SEX
und die
FAMILIE

VI

ABORT n.m. either **1.** (medically) a miscarriage – more commonly *eine Fehlgeburt**; or **2.** the formal legal term for an abortion or termination (also *der Abortus*) – the usual word is *die Abtreibung*, while doctors refer to the operation as *der Schwangerschaftsabbruch*; or **3.** with the stress on the *Ab-*, a homonym meaning a public lavatory ('off-place') – see KLOSETT in IX.

Though *der Pillenknick** (the slump in the birth-rate caused by the pill) affected the GDR as well as the Federal Republic (where 1,065,000 babies were born in 1964, but only 582,000 in 1979), East German women, unlike those in the West, could have an abortion if they so chose. After reunification, and much acrimonious debate, the new law which came into force on 1 January 1993 was less liberal than the GDR's *Fristenlösung/Fristenregelung* (permitting termination of any pregnancy within the first three months) though also less restrictive than the old Federal Republic's *Indikationslösung/Indikationsregelung* (abortion only on ethical, eugenic, medical, or social grounds) – still interpreted with controversial strictness in such predominantly Catholic regions as Bavaria. See PARAGRAPH and SENAT in I.

ADÄQUAT adj. the primary meaning is suitable – *eine adäquate Stellung*, a suitable job; *adäquates Verhalten*, fitting behaviour; *eine adäquate Darstellung*, an appropriate, well-conceived interpretation of a theatrical part. Also used in our sense of adequate – *adäquate Belohnung*, adequate or sufficient remuneration; *eine adäquate Übersetzung*, a 'very adequate' or competent translation – though never grudgingly (a pupil's performance which is 'just adequate' is *genügend* or *ausreichend*, that is, less than *befriedigend*, satisfactory).

A doubly confusing advertisement which appeared in *Die Zeit* on 18 May 1990 illustrates this important distinction: *Junger Professor*, dynamisch und doch sensibel*, sucht adäquate frauliche Partnerin.* This means: 'Young professor, dynamic yet sensitive ('sensible' would be *vernünftig*), seeks compatible (not 'adequate') female partner'. Readers who felt he was not what they were looking for might call him *inadäquat* without giving offence – personal inadequacy is *Unzulänglichkeit*, and such a person *ein Versager* (failure, flop), colloquially *eine Flasche**.

ALLÜREN n.p. not allure (*der Reiz*, *der Sex-Appeal*; to allure: *anziehen*, *anlocken*, *verlocken*), but conceited behaviour, as in *Star-allüren** – the affectation, airs and graces, of a star.

ÄNGSTLICH adj. 'anxious', but mainly as a character trait (someone who is timid, easily frightened, is *ein ängstlicher Typ** or *ein Angsthase*). To be anxious about, say, one's children, is *um die Kinder besorgt sein* or *sich um die Kinder Sorgen machen*; to be anxious to do something, *darauf aussein*, *bestrebt sein*; an anxious time waiting, *eine Zeit voll bangen** Wartens*. At the thought of having to pronounce a word said to contain more consonants in sequence than any other German word: *mir brach der Angstschweiß aus*, I broke out in a cold sweat. See also SCHRECK in II and *Angst* under SPLEEN in V, NERVÖS in VII.

ANIMIERDAME n.f. a hostess* in an *Animierlokal* or *Animier-kneipe* (ranging from a hostess bar to a clipjoint), *die dich zum Trinken animiert* (encourages you to drink). Someone who is *animiert* may be slightly tipsy ('tired and emotional', *rührselig*; non-euphemistically, 'he was very animated' is better rendered as *er war sehr angeregt*), but the verb *animieren* commonly means to enliven (a conversation, *ein Gespräch animieren*), stimulate, prompt, or inspire to action; or else to animate a cartoon film (*ein Zeichentrickfilm*) – an animator is ein *Animator*.

ANTIBABYPILLE n.f. whereas the East German *Wunschkind-pille* ('wish-child-pill') focused on the positive side of family planning, West Germans with their *Antibabypille* opted to call a spade a spade (the German equivalent of this expression – *das Kind beim Namen nennen*, to call the child by its name – might seem inappropriate in the context). Unlike *ein Wunschkind*, the Austrian *Wahlkind* is the 'child of one's choice' only in the sense that it is adopted; in Germany, this is *ein Adoptivkind* (and *Wahl-* is confined to such combinations as *Wahlheimat*, one's country of adoption). Note that the Germans call the rhythm method of contraception *die Knaus-Ogino-Methode*. See also ABORT above.

BANGEN v. not 'to (go) bang', which is *knallen* (*Peng, peng!* or *paff!* are both curiously muted versions of 'bang, bang', *Kladder-adatsch!* a more resonant 'crash-bang-wallop'), but a somewhat dated way of expressing fear for oneself: *mir bangt vor ihm* or *er macht mir/ mich bange* (he frightens me), or anxiety about others: *die Mutter bangt um ihr Kind* (the mother fears for her child); in the south, however, *sie bangt nach dem Kinde* or *ihr ist bange nach dem Kinde* means she longs or frets for the child, yearns to be with it. This is not

what Sophie feels for her husband-to-be, that incomparable *Lump**
Baron Ochs auf Lerchenau, when in Act II of *Der Rosenkavalier* (1911)
he anticipates how keenly she will feel his absence by day – *Ohne
mich, ohne mich, jeder Tag dir so bang* – and his presence by night –
mit mir, mit mir keine Nacht dir zu lang – a sentiment he soon
redirects towards the Marschallin's pretty maid Mariandl, alias Octavian. *Nur keine Bange!* Never fear! Sophie gets her Octavian in the
end. See also LIEBHABER below and ÄNGSTLICH above.

BASE n.f. formerly one's cousin (*die Kusine*), or else some other
female relative or friendly neighbour (famously, the Virgin Mary's
Base Elisabeth). Mozart called his favourite cousin, Maria Anna
Thekla Mozart, '*Bäsle*' – the diminutive conveys additional affection
– and his delightfully ribald letters to her (an 'incontinence of the
emotions' characteristic of Tourette's syndrome, according to one
recent theory) are known as the *Bäsle-Briefe*.

BASTARD n.m. historically, the bastard son of a nobleman. Graf
Dunois in Schiller's *Die Jungfrau von Orleans* (1801) is addressed as
Bastard von Orleans by Johanna without her casting any aspersions on
his honour or his character; indeed he is later accepted as a worthy if
ultimately rejected suitor. Moreover, the Dauphin Karl is greatly
reassured by her picking him out from his courtiers as the rightful
heir to the French throne, thus confirming that he is not a mere
Bankert (though given his mother's lifestyle, this is not at all unlikely;
the pejorative term *Bankert* applied originally to a child conceived on
the maid's *Schlafbank** rather than the matrimonial *Ehebett**). Edmund, 'Bastard Son to Gloucester', is similarly held in esteem by his
father, who declares in the opening lines of *King Lear* that 'there was
good sport at his making, and the whoreson must be acknowledged'
– an attitude shared by Augustus the Strong, whose acknowledge-
ments of this kind are the most prodigious and prodigal known in
German lands (see LAND in I).

By contrast, the ultimate insult that Schiller makes his Maria Stuart
hurl against her cousin Elisabeth (in the entirely fictional but dramatically most effective meeting between the two rival queens in Act III,
Scene 4 of his tragedy *Maria Stuart* – see SCHEIN in V) is: *Der Thron
von England ist durch einen Bastard / Entweiht*. In the context, this
would still be rendered as 'The throne of England has been desecrated
by a bastard', but English 'bastard' as a simple term of abuse is
nowadays *Scheißkerl* or *Arschloch*; 'poor bastard', *armes Schwein**.

BETT n.n. not a bet (*die Wette*) but a bed. The traditional 'marital
bed' is usually made up of two adjacent but separate *Ehebetten*
(sometimes, in older versions, with a dividing gap in between –

humorously referred to as a *Besuchsritze*), each consisting of a *Bett-kasten* (wooden bed-frame) into which is slotted an interior sprung base in three parts with an additional wedge under the pillow. This arrangement, with separate duvets, has now made way for *das französische Bett*, a divan bed with one continuous mattress – the French connection reflecting a different *Bettkultur**. But the traditional German *Federbett* (also *Daunenbett* or *Daunendecke*: duvet), unlike a *Steppdecke** (continental quilt, with the padding sewn into compartments), is still a voluminous affair which in the old days was aired every morning over the window-sill (*das Bett lüften*).

Some compounds are unexpected: the Swiss call a duvet cover *ein Bettanzug* (in German, *ein Bettbezug*), which sounds as if it might mean the same as *ein Schlafanzug* (pyjamas – also *der Pyjama*, Swiss *das Pyjama*). Neither breaks down into *Bett-an-Zug* or *Schlaf-an-Zug*: the sleeping compartment on a train is *der Schlafwagen*.

BRAUT n.f. a bride on her wedding-day, but also (like *die Verlobte*) a fiancée; similarly, *der Bräutigam* is either a bridegroom or (like *der Verlobte*) a fiancé. *Kennen Sie meine Braut?* Have you met my fiancée?

The best man, *der Trauzeuge*; bridesmaid, *die Brautjungfer*; wedding day, *der Hochzeitstag*; honeymoon, *die Hochzeitsreise* or, more humorously, *die Flitterwochen*. To get married in a registry office, *standesamtlich heiraten* or *sich standesamtlich trauen lassen*, as distinct from in a church, *kirchlich*, etc., but note that by law a registry wedding, the only legally binding form, has to precede any church ceremony. *Der rote Wedding*, however, is not a variation on a white wedding (*eine Hochzeit in Weiß*), but a working-class and traditionally left-wing district of Berlin ('red Wedding'; for trickier colour symbolism, see SCHWARZ in II).

BRAV adj. not brave, which is *tapfer* or *mutig*, but either **1.** well-behaved – nowadays mainly used of children (*sei schön/hübsch brav!* be a good boy/girl), or pets (*braver Hund!* good dog!); or else **2.** worthy and honest. After Faust has put paid to Gretchen's chances of remaining *ein braves Mädchen* (respectable), he compounds the injury by killing her brother Valentin, who dies *als Soldat und brav* (l. 3775) – the one context in which correct behaviour 'as befits a soldier' might be thought synonymous with 'brave'. In a more pejorative sense, an actor of whom it is said *er hat das Stück brav heruntergespielt* has done his best but was uninspired, even dull.

BUMSEN v. from the onomatopoeic *bums* (thud! bang!) – *ein Bums* is the sound of one thing bumping or banging against another: *mit dem Kopf gegen den Balken bumsen*, to bang one's head against the beam; *es hat gebumst* is the polite way of saying someone has bumped into your car, or used when two people have had a row. But as *bumsen* is also the most common jocular euphemism for having sexual intercourse (more socially acceptable than *vögeln* or *ficken* and in use long before the English tabloids came up with 'bonking', its nearest slang equivalent), it needs to be handled with care. For Heinrich Böll, for instance, this ambiguity becomes deadly serious when he makes his shrinking violet heroine Katharina Blum fend off the unwanted advances of an 'investigative' journalist with a gunshot: *Er wollte doch bumsen, und ich habe gebumst* (see INSTANZ in V). *Ein Bumslokal* is so called because it is the sort of pub or night-club that plays loud and vulgar *Bumsmusik* (and, if *bumsvoll*, is full to bursting).

CLIQUE n.f. not only what those on the outside consider an exclusive coterie or special interest group (*die Cliquenbildung*, the forming of cliques; *die Cliquenwirtschaft*, a cliquey set-up), but also a criminal gang, or else (more familiar than pejorative) a group of friends: *die ganze Clique war da*, the whole crew was there.

DOGGE n.f. specifically a mastiff (*die englische Dogge*) or a great Dane (*die deutsche Dogge*). All dogs are *Hunde*. A *Dachshund* or *Dackel* was originally bred to hunt badgers (Germans also call a silly clot *ein Dackel*) and the much-maligned *Schweinehund**to hunt wild pigs (*den inneren Schweinehund überwinden* means to overcome one's innate tendency to cowardice and/or sloth). Long before *Schweinehund* became familiar to us through war films as a term of abuse, Shaw observed that German shepherd dogs were already being renamed Alsatians and dachshunds stoned in the street in a fit of misplaced patriotic zeal ('Common Sense about the War' – a supplement to the *New Statesman* on 14 November 1914 – which concluded that 'both armies should shoot their officers and go home').

DRACHEN n.m. the mythical beast itself is *der Drache*, but *ein Drachen* is nowadays a kite or a hang-glider (also *ein Drachenflieger*; a dragonfly is *eine Libelle*), or else the sort of domestic dragon or battleaxe (also referred to as *Xanthippe*, after Socrates' allegedly shrewish wife) whom the husband, in his role as *Wurm**, traditionally appeases with *Drachenfutter* ('dragon's food' – usually roses). The classic credo of the hen-pecked husband was given by Karl Valentin but resists translation: *Mögen täten wir schon wollen, aber dürfen haben wir uns nicht getraut.*

DRESSMAN n.m. not a transvestite (*der Transvestit*), but a male model, or else – and one suspects the pseudo-anglicism reflects declining respect for English fashion rather than the activities of Anglo-Saxon *Gastarbeiter* – a *Strichjunge* or rent boy/ male prostitute.

The newspaper columns which advertise such services are sometimes euphemistically headed: *Hostessen* und Kavaliere**, but for the general openness of contemporary German society, see PUFF below. Also DRESS and MODE in IX.

EPITAPH n.n. a memorial stone (*der Gedenkstein*), commemorative plaque (*die Gedenktafel*), or gravestone (*der Grabstein*), as well as the inscription on it (*die Grabinschrift, der Grabspruch*) or a composition in the form of a tombstone inscription. Hence, one can say either *aufKleists Epitaph am Wannsee lautet der Grabspruch...* or else *aufKleists Grabstein am Wannsee lautet das Epitaph...* The actual words commemorating the *Freitod** (suicide) in 1811 of Germany's arguably greatest dramatist are: *Er lebte, sang und litt / in trüber, schwerer Zeit; / er suchte hier den Tod, / und fand Unsterblichkeit.* More cryptic is the famous epitaph Rilke wrote in 1925, inscribed a year later on his gravestone at Raron overlooking the Rhône valley: *Rose, oh reiner Widerspruch, Lust*, / Niemandes Schlaf zu sein unter soviel / Lidern* ('Rose, oh pure contradiction, desire to be nobody's sleep under so many lids').

ERST adj. not erstwhile, but first: *er hat seine erste Liebe geheiratet* (he married his first love), but *er hat eine ehemalige Freundin geheiratet* (he married an old flame). *Fürs erste* and *vorerst* both mean 'for the time being', 'for the present', while *zuerst* means 'first of all'. This, and not 'next' (*als Nächstes*), is also the sense of *zunächst* (as in the Romanian recipe joke: *zuerst/zunächst stehlen Sie Ihr Huhn*, 'first steal your chicken'). The adverb *erst* means 'only': *der Junge ist erst fünf.*

FAMILIÄR adj. not familiar in the sense of usual (*üblich*), or well-known (*wohlbekannt, vertraut*), but either **1.** (concerning the) family: *familiäre Sorgen*, family worries; *eine familiäre Krankheit* (more commonly, *Familienkrankheit* or *Erbkrankheit*), hereditary disease; or **2.** over-familiar, unceremonious: *der familiäre Ton* deutscher Schüler* ihren Lehrern gegenüber*, the very casual/informal/free and easy way in which German schoolchildren talk to their teachers (though this rarely stretches to use of the familiar '*du*'; teachers themselves make a point of switching to the adult '*Sie*' in the sixth form, sometimes earlier): *ein familiärer Ausdruck* is a colloquialism – see also below, PLUMP, ORDINÄR; or **3.** intimate: *mit jemandem familiär verkehren*, to be on (very) close terms with somebody.

FEIST adj. not what the Americans call feisty – aggressive, excitable, touchy, gutsy (*ein angriffslustiger Terrier, eine temperamentvolle* Frau*), but simply fat (*dick*, fett**), as in *ein feister Dackel* (fat dachshund). When applied to people, as it sometimes was to the bull-necked Franz Josef Strauß ('*dieser feiste Nacken*'), it suggests bulk combined with power.

FETE n.f. another word for *eine Party* (party), not a garden or village fête (see FEST in VIII, also under PARTIE in VII).

FIDEL adj. jolly, merry (intensified as *quietschfidel*, happy as a sandboy), but no longer associated with fidelity, which is *die Treue* (the main exception in German is, of course, Beethoven's *Fidelio* – see WEIB below; and for infidelity, FREMDGEHEN). First coined by students (in Jena, c.1750), along with other latinisms such as *Fidibus* – borrowed from Horace and applied to the paper spills they used to light their pipes (*et ture et fidibus*, 'with incense and the playing of stringed instruments' – *Odes* I, 36). No link with *die Fidel/Fiedel* (fiddle), which is stressed on the first syllable, unlike *fidel*, which is stressed on the second. *Immer fidel sein!* keep smiling.

FLASCHE n.f. While a Cockney with 'bottle' is brave, a person colloquially referred to as *eine Flasche* is a real washout, a dead loss. As with the French use of Italian *fiasco*, there is also a sexual innuendo – less colourful than *ein Schlappschwanz**, more expressive than *ein Versager*. One pithy version of the Peter Principle (much admired in Germany, though in inverse ratio to its relevance there – see KOMPETENZ in I), is *Flaschen fallen nach oben*, failures flop to the top, or as Swift put it, they climb by creeping.

FLATTERN v. not to flatter (*schmeicheln – mit Schmeicheln kommst du nicht weiter*, flattery will get you nowhere), but to flutter or flap (of birds, sails, flags, trousers, etc., and idiomatically, when a letter lands on your desk: *ein Brief flatterte mir auf den Schreibtisch*). Hence, to be called *flatterhaft* or *ein Flattergeist* is not flattering: it means you are fickle, flighty, a flibbertigibbet, someone who 'flits and sips' like a butterfly (Wodehouse), or indeed a bat, as in Johann Strauss's operetta *Die Fledermaus* (1874) – another word for the 'fluttering mouse' being *das Flattertier*. Nor does *einen Flattermann haben* mean you have an admirer (*ein Verehrer*): it's the shakes, stage-fright, butterflies in your stomach; and *Flatterzunge* is not the flattering tongue condemned by the Psalmist (*Der Herr wolle ausrotten alle Heuchelei und die Zunge, die da stolz redet*, 12.4), but the technique used by flautists to produce a rolled 'r' or gargling sound, originally employed by Strauss in *Don Quixote* (1898) to depict the bleating of sheep.

FLIRT n.n. flirtation; someone who is a flirt *flirtet gern* (or might be called *eine Kokette* or *ein Charmeur*). But *ein alter Flirt von mir* is simply an old boy-friend/girl-friend; *sie ist sein neuester Flirt*, she's his latest.

FLUIDUM n.n. for eighteenth-century scientists, a hypothetical element – the fluid equivalent of phlogiston. Nowadays (like *Flair**) means aura, charisma: *von Garbo ging ein geheimnisvolles Fluidum aus* (Garbo was surrounded by an air of mystery); *Wien hat ein gewisses Fluidum* (Vienna has an atmosphere all its own). A fluid is *eine Flüssigkeit*.

FRANZÖSISCH adj. 'French' – code for oral sex, and thus at least medically unconnected with '*die Franzosen*' (syphilis) and *ein Pariser** (which, like *Gummi** and *Präservativ**, is a condom; *ein französischer Brief* is only the sort of letter one writes or receives). Because of the greater openness to sexual matters there is no need to resort to such euphemisms as 'French lessons'. *Ein französisches Bett** is a divan.

FRAUENZIMMER n.n. originally the rooms of a household in which the women lived; then the occupants themselves. Thus, in the first masterpiece of German comedy, Lessing's *Minna von Barnhelm* (1767), Sergeant Werner who is smitten with Minna's lively young maid (see JUNGFRAU below) describes her as *kein unebenes Frauenzimmerchen* (not an ill-looking lassie). Now only used disapprovingly (*dieses Frauenzimmer!* that woman!) or humorously (female/US broad).

FREIER n.m. now only a prostitute's client/US john; formerly, a suitor (someone who goes a-wooing *geht auf Freiersfüßen*). The verb *freien* is used only in this latter sense, as in Wotan's farewell to Brünnhilde in Act III of *Die Walküre*: *Denn einer nur freie die Braut*, der freier als ich, der Gott* ('For one alone shall win the bride, one freer than I, the God'); or else in the sense of 'to marry off', as when the protagonist in Schiller's ballad *Die Bürgschaft* (see BUND in I) asks for a stay of execution: *Ich flehe dich um drei Tage Zeit, / Bis ich die Schwester dem Gatten gefreit.*

Frei* generally as in English 'free': historically, *der Freie/ein Freier* was a freeman, not a serf. The motto of '*Turnvater*'* Jahn, who advocated popular physical education at the time of the first nationalist stirrings in Germany, was *Frisch, fromm, fröhlich, frei* ('lively, devout, cheerful, free') – nowadays used humorously of a hearty, outdoor type. *Frei aber froh* ('free but joyful') was the somewhat more misanthropic motto which Brahms, an increasingly confirmed bachelor (with a penchant for young sopranos), encapsulated in the FAF theme of his Third Symphony – a response to Joseph Joachim's lament at the time of his divorce, when Brahms sided with Joachim's wife: *frei aber einsam* or FAE ('free but solitary').

FREMDGEHEN v. to be unfaithful (i.e. *untreu sein* – of a husband, wife, or lover, while a friend or servant is said to be *treulos*, and an inaccurate translation *ungenau*). Also referred to as *einen Seitensprung machen*, side-stepping. To 'go abroad' literally, however, is *in die Fremde ziehen*, now more commonly *ins Ausland gehen*, and the sign *Fremdenzimmer*, 'rooms for strangers', the equivalent of our 'Bed and Breakfast' (*frei*, vacancies).

FREUND n.m. the Germans tend not to overstate friendship, so that *eine Bekannte/ein Bekannter* (acquaintance) is often the equivalent of 'friend', while *ein Freund* is generally a real *Kamerad* (pal, not comrade in the political sense, which is *Genosse*). If somebody addresses you as *mein liebes Freundchen*, however, you should feel forewarned rather than sentimentally touched. Former East Germans have been called *unsere teuren Freunde*, but this of course is also ironic ('our dear friends', but also 'our expensive/costly friends' – see PUMP in III).
    Or else one's boyfriend (*hat sie schon einen Freund?*), girlfriend (*meine Freundin*), or lover. The non-committal 'escort' is *ein Begleiter* (*eine Eskorte* is only a military escort).
    Ein Freund is also a 'lover of' whatever word it is attached to: *ein Wanderfreund* is a keen hiker, rather than a friend you take on walks; *ich bin kein Fußballfreund*, I don't like football (alternatively, *ein Fußballmuffel* – see MUFF in IX). The main exception is *ein Brieffreund*, which is now a penpal rather than a keen letter-writer (still less could Kafka's uniquely obsessive five-year correspondence with Felice Bauer be called *eine Brieffreundschaft* – see REKOMMAND-IEREN in I). See also LIEBHABER below.

FRIVOL adj. indecent, as well as frivolous, flippant, flighty. *Frivole Witze* are suggestive, risqué jokes, as are *Frivolitäten* (though this is also a term in needlework, meaning tatting). To avoid ambiguity: *leichtsinniges Benehmen*, frivolous/careless behaviour; *ein leichtfertiges/albernes Ding*, a silly little creature.

FRUST n.m. (from *die Frustration*) a vogue word signalling general dissatisfaction, as in *ich habe einen Frust*; *das ist der totale Frust*; or the perception of modern life as a choice *zwischen Frust und Streß**. Also sexual frustration, nicely rendered as *Lust* gepaart mit Frust*.

GAFFER n.m. not one's foreman or boss (*der Boß, der Chef**), or an elderly rustic (*der Alte*), but someone who gawps/US rubbernecks (especially those at the scene of an accident who are often described as being *sensationslüstern*, sensation-seeking). The Germans do not avoid eye contact with strangers quite as assiduously as the English do, but *gaffen*, *glotzen* (*die Glotze* is the gogglebox) and *anstarren* (see STARREN in X) are just as rude as 'to gape'.

D. H. Lawrence noticed this, though the autobiographical hero of *Mr Noon* (see LUMPEN in V) finds himself 'glotzing, if we may borrow the word' even before he exchanges English provincialism for first-hand experience of 'Germanic Over-Allness' (pp. 116, 232). Had Lawrence returned to Munich in 1919 for *Trommeln in der Nacht*, he would have seen Brecht already exhorting his audience (via signs in the auditorium): *Glotzt nicht so romantisch!*

GUMMI n.m. & n.n. *der Gummi* is a contraceptive sheath/US rubber, also known as a *Präservativ** or a *Pariser**. *Das Gummi* is rubber as a material; to avoid misunderstandings, specify *ein Gummiband** if you mean a rubber band, or *ein Radiergummi* if an india-rubber eraser (Austrian schoolchildren call this *ein Radex*, and by association *ein Radetzky*, possibly in memory of the fact that Austria's most famous field-marshal managed to rub out so many soldiers, so to speak, including even some of the enemy). Chewing gum, *Kaugummi*, is not usually abbreviated. Cf. also *der Gummimantel*, plastic mac; *der Gummisauger*, rubber teat. Sticking gum is *der Klebstoff.*

HUSCH interj. not 'hush' (*sei still!* or *pst!* – for Mozart's lullaby, see PARAGRAPH in I), but 'shoo' (at animals) or 'come on'. *Und husch, weg war er*, he was gone in a flash. Accordingly, *das geht nicht so husch-husch, wie Sie meinen* means 'these things can't be done all in a rush, you know' (*Die Entführung aus dem Serail*, Act 1, Scene 4), whereas 'all very hush hush' is *streng geheim.*

JUNG adj. can mean recent as well as young – *die Jungverheirateten* are the newly-weds, *ob sie früh geheiratet haben, oder nicht* (whether or not they married young), *die jüngsten Nachrichten* the latest news, *die jüngste Vergangenheit* the most recent past. Also: *der Jüngste Tag* (Doomsday); *das Jüngste Gericht* (The Last Judgement) – which gave rise to the title of a political revue, *Das jüngste Gerücht* (the latest rumour/gossip).

JUNGFRAU n.f. while *eine junge Frau* is a young woman, *eine Jungfrau* is a virgin (with figurative connotations such as the mountain of that name, or *ein jungfräulicher Wald*, virgin forest), though *ich bin Jungfrau* can also mean 'my astrological sign is Virgo'.

Nowadays, *eine alte Jungfer* is an old maid (*jüngferlich*, old maidish, spinsterly); formerly *eine Jungfer* was either a maidservant (*eine Kammerjungfer*; a maid of honour is still *eine Brautjungfer*) or a maiden. In Act II, Scene 2 of *Minna von Barnhelm*, for instance, which Lessing wrote in a spirit of reconciliation at the end of the

Seven Years' War, the Saxon ladies' maid, Franziska, humours rigid Prussian officialdom by insisting on the crucial distinction which makes it clear she is as eligible for marriage as her mistress, Minna: *Nun, Herr Wirt, so setzen Sie anstatt Kammerfrau* Kammerjungfer. – Ich höre, die Polizei ist sehr exakt.* See also FRAUENZIMMER above and PLUMP in VII.

Nowadays, *eine unverheiratete Frau* avoids any ambiguity or *double entendre*, but there is no need to hesitate between *unverheiratete Männer* and *Junggesellen*. Both are neutral descriptions of the unmarried state, while a confirmed bachelor is *ein eingefleischter Junggeselle* or *ein Hagestolz*. Such a one was Immanuel Kant, but as Nietzsche pointed out in *Zur Genealogie der Moral* (III, 7), none of the great philosophers were married – *Heraklit, Plato, Descartes, Spinoza, Leibniz, Kant, Schopenhauer: sie waren es nicht* (asceticism in this one instance furnishing the optimal creative state) – while Socrates had married solely to provide ironic proof of the rule ('dying', as every schoolboy used to know, 'of an overdose of wedlock').

KAVALIER n.m. now used humorously for boyfriend, or perhaps with a touch of irony of someone who is chivalrous towards women – *ein Kavalier der alten Schule*, a gentleman of the old school; *er ist immer Kavalier*, he is always the perfect gentleman; even *der Kavalier genießt und schweigt*, one does not boast about one's conquests. Similarly, *ein Kavalier der Landstraße* or *Kavalier am Steuer* is a 'knight of the road', i.e. a considerate driver, though this is at odds with *ein Kavalierstart* – an ironic term for starting your car or driving off at traffic lights as if you were at Le Mans, accompanied by screeching tyres.

From the old-fashioned *die Damen und ihre Kavaliere* (the ladies and their escorts), the word has now also come to mean a prostitute's client (more commonly *ein Freier**) and *eine Kavalierskrankheit* is a venereal disease. *Ein Kavaliersdelikt**, however, is not usually a sexual peccadillo, but any petty or trivial offence (especially one which is not thought dishonourable by the offender).

In general, then, *kavaliermäßiges Benehmen* is the opposite of 'cavalier' behaviour. If free-and-easy or off-hand, this is *unbekümmert, ungezwungen, salopp**; if showing little regard for others, *keck, ungeniert*; if supercilious, cool as you like, *kaltlächelnd;* if presumptuous, *anmassend.* Someone with a cavalier approach to a matter *geht leichthin darüber hinweg.*

KISSEN n.n. is a cushion, whereas a kiss is *der Kuß* (and the verb *küssen*). In Middle High German the same word (*küssen*) served both meanings and the *Minnesänger* make great play of this ambiguity when they ask their lady for a *küssen* as a token of affection – and even offer to put it back where it belongs if she protests too much. But George is simply confused when he insists on buying a 20 *Mark Küssen*, 20 marks worth of kissing ('If you get it, will you go?' the shop-assistant enquires) in Jerome K. Jerome's *Three Men on the Bummel*, 1896, p. 166 (see also KORPORATION in IV and BIER in VIII).

LEEREN v. to empty, not to leer (*anzüglich grinsen*). Hence, *mit leerem Blick* means with a vacant expression, not leeringly (*lüstern*). *Den Toiletteneimer leeren*, to 'slop out' (though this would be unconstitutional in Germany – see TASTEN in I).

LEICHT adj. light. *Leichte Mädchen*, however, are not anorexic but 'easy', and (according to a film title) have their ideal complement in *schwere Jungs* (hard men).

LIEBHABER n.m. while *ein Liebhaber* is a connoisseur, collector, or enthusiast (often amateur: *eine Liebhaberaufführung* is either a performance for connoisseurs, or else one put on by amateurs), *mein Liebhaber* or *meine Liebhaberin* is 'my lover'. In addition, a theatrical 'type': *mit 50 spielte er noch den Romeo und andere jugendliche Liebhaber* (at 50 he was still playing Romeo and other romantic leads). The verb is also tricky: a letter beginning *Lieber John, ich hab dich sehr lieb* (I'm very fond of you) is crucially different from one which declares *Ich liebe dich*. On the other hand, there can be no doubting the nature of the emotion which both the Marschallin at the beginning of Richard Strauss's *Der Rosenkavalier* (1911) and the young lovers at the end wish to convey through the fittingly restrained phrase *Ich hab' dich lieb* (see BANG above).

LIFTING n.n. a face-lift (also *der Lift*; the operation is *das Gesicht liften lassen*) – one of an increasing number of borrowings from English or American which lose something in transit.

LOCKEN v. not to lock or lock up (a prisoner, *einsperren*; a shop, *abschließen*; a locker is *ein Schließfach* or *ein Spind*), but to tempt or entice. *Die lockende Ferne* is the allure of far-away places, *ein Lockvogel* a decoy bird (but *ein lockerer Vogel* is a bit of a lad – someone whose morals are *locker*, loose). Since *Locken* are curls, *locken* also means to curl hair.

LUST n.f. seldom as strong an emotion as lust (perhaps *Kauflust* comes close – the desire of *Kauflustige* to go on a spending spree – but the *Staulust* or 'traffic-jam joy' to which one in five Germans admitted in a survey seems simply perverse, whatever their feelings of camaraderie and endurance). Lust is *die Begierde* or *die Wollust*, as in a verse of Schiller's *An die Freude* which the somewhat prudish Beethoven did not use in his Choral Symphony: *Wollust ward dem Wurm* gegeben*, 'lust was granted even to the worm'. *Ich habe Lust, ins Kino zu gehen* means only that I feel like going to the cinema (youngsters increasingly use *Bock* instead of *Lust*, especially the negative *Null-Bock** instead of *keine Lust*); only when you cannot think what else is meant should you weigh the possibility that *Hast du Lust?* might mean 'Your place or mine?'

Though *ein Lustspiel* is simply a comedy and not what the Germans refer to as *eine Sex Show*, the plural *Lüste* invariably evokes sexual desire, as does *lüstern* (lecherous) and *Lüsternheit* (lasciviousness), and *ein Lustknabe* has kept its old meaning of catamite, now rent-boy. (He is also referred to as *ein Strichjunge*, while *ein Strichmädchen* is what the French call *une femme de la rue*; *ein Freudenmädchen* is also a direct transliteration of *une fille de joie*.) On the other hand, *Jenseits des Lustprinzips* (1920) is accurately translated as *Beyond the Pleasure Principle*, a useful corrective to the view that Freud's work is all about sex.

Lustig means jovial, amusing, cheerful, funny (but one's funny bone, as violinists will appreciate, is *der Musikantenknochen*). The merry widow of Lehar's *Die lustige Witwe* (1905) is also lusty (*gesund und munter, voller Leben*) – never more so than when accompanied on old recordings by Richard Tauber's *herzhafte, kräftige Stimme*, lusty voice. *Sich über jemand lustig machen*, however, is to make fun of someone – if this becomes malicious glee (as when the *Irish Times* printed its 'German Diary' in Gaelic), the Germans have a fine word for it: *Schadenfreude*. Heine (whom it is tempting to call a *Schadenfreudian*) meant something similar when he talked of *britische Spottlust**, the British love of mockery. *Streitlust* signifies an argumentative or aggressive disposition, and *Lebenslust* joie de vivre, zest for living, while *Tendenz lustlos* indicates a slack or dull period on the stock exchange.

MAN pron. one uses *man* in German much more often than one uses, or should use, 'one' in English. Moves to introduce *frau* as a feminine form have made little headway, as *Die Zeit* reported on 18 August 1989 in a feature facetiously entitled: *Warum heiratet frau einen Diplomaten?* Why marry a diplomat?

MANN n.m. man, but also husband. A woman no longer talks of her husband as *mein Ehemann* but simply as *mein Mann*. *Frau steht ihren Mann* (an ironic newspaper headline) is a variation on *seinen Mann stehen* (to hold one's own) – without any sexual innuendo. Note that the word has two plural forms: while *die Männer* simply refers to the male of the species, *die Mannen* singles them out as members of a (football) team or a band of warriors. *Mann!* is also a common exclamation: *Mann, oh Mann!*, boy, oh boy! *Mann, laß mich doch in Ruhe!* for heaven's sake, leave me alone!

MENSCH n.n. *das Mensch* (often combined with *liederlich*), as distinct from *der Mensch*, has come to mean 'slut', 'cow', 'whore' (*Dirne, Schlampe*). Thus when in Büchner's *Woyzeck* (see MORAL in V) Marie asks *Bin ich ein Mensch?* she is not wondering about her humanity (see under UNMENSCH in II) but wants to pre-empt any suspicion of having prostituted herself (which, of course, she has).

NECKEN v. to tease, not to neck, for which activity the Germans have two splendidly onomatopoeic words: *knutschen* and *schmusen* (*Schmus*, though, is not canoodling: *das ist alles Schmus* – a line from a famous Max Pallenberg song in the 1930s – means 'don't soft-soap me', 'that's all nonsense'). *Die knutschen sich in den Gängen ab!* vividly conveys a teacher's surprise that permissiveness was quite so open in the corridors of her school. By contrast, *was sich liebt, das neckt sich* means only that teasing is a sign of affection. See also FOPPEN in IX.

NUMMER n.f. a number, including a number/act/spot in a show, hence perhaps the additional slang sense of a prostitute's 'trick' or 'turn' (*eine Nummer machen* or *schieben*). But *auf Nummer Sicher gehen* means to play it safe.

ÖFFENTLICH adj. 'public'. However, *ein öffentliches Haus* is not a public house (*eine Gaststätte, eine Kneipe, ein Wirtshaus*) but a brothel (see PUFF below and UNTERNEHMER in III). It was this euphemism which unfortunately occurred to most people listening when a newly appointed minister recently said *ich bin doch eine öffentliche Person* to describe her more restricted life since becoming a 'public figure' (*eine öffentliche Figur*), though it is not quite as obvious as when Frankfurt's best-known prostitute in the 1950s, Rosemarie Nitribitt, was referred to as *die Frankfurter Allgemeine*.

PARISER n.m. a condom (also *Gummi** or *Präservativ**), as well as a Parisian.

PERVERS adj. not perverse in the sense of obstinate or contrary (*querköpfig* or *verstockt*), but perverted. The proclivities of the Marquis de Sade and Leopold von Sacher*-Masoch might still be called *pervers*, but nowadays deviation from the sexual norm would need to be more marked than when Karl Kraus wrote, in *Sprüche und Wider-*

sprüche (1909): *Perversität ist entweder eine Schuld der Zeugung oder ein Recht der Überzeugung,* 'perversion (by which he meant homosexuality) is either a fault in one's begetting or one's right by conviction' (alternatively: 'wrong at birth or birthright'). *Überzeugung* also nicely suggests the 'super-procreation' of a Nietzschean *Übermensch**, in the same way that Kraus in *Die demolirte* Literatur* (1897) had punningly alluded to Hofmannsthal's descent from many '*Degenerationen*' of aristocrats. See also *Abart* and *entartet* under ART in X.

PIMPF n.m. not a pimp, *ein Zuhälter*, but a junior member of the Hitler Youth, and still used in Austria to mean 'a young squirt'. See also under PUMP in III.

POLLUTION n.f. only in the sense of a seminal emission, not environmental pollution (*die Umweltverschmutzung*), pollution of the atmosphere (*die Verpestung* der Luft*), or any other kind of dirtying, soiling, fouling or defiling (*die Verunreinigung*) caused by a pollutant (*ein Schadstoff*).

PRÄGNANT adj. a succinct formulation or pithy remark is *prägnant*, terseness or precision *die Prägnanz*. A pregnant woman, however, is *schwanger*, and pregnancy *die Schwangerschaft*. A pregnant pause might also be rendered as *eine bedeutungsschwangere Pause*; a look pregnant with meaning, *ein bedeutungsvoller Blick*.

PRANKE n.f. an animal's paw, not a child's prank. This is *ein Streich**, and German children still enjoy those perpetrated (in rhyming couplets) by Wilhelm Busch's inveterate pranksters, *Max und Moritz* (1865): *dieses war der erste Streich, / doch der zweite folgt sogleich* ('that's the end of their first lark, but on to number two now, hark!'). See also MORAL in V.

PRÄSERVATIV n.n. not what you would expect to find in German bread, since *ein Präservativ* is a condom – though you will not find many preservatives either (these are *Konservierungsstoffe**). Other words for this form of *Verhütungsmittel* (contraceptive) are *ein Kondom* or *ein Prophylaktikum*, colloquially *ein Gummi** or *ein Pariser**, and in (unmistakably) Swiss German, rather charmingly, *ein Verhüterli*.

PUFF n.m. or n.n. a brothel. As these are legal and officially regulated in German towns with a population over 20,000, some small towns at census-time become as interesting as Clochemerle. *Puff*, like *Bums/ bumsen**, is an onomatopoeic word (German children also once called their toy steam engine a *Puffpuff*, and machine guns go *piff, paff, puff*), but for good measure etymologists add that men in the eighteenth century enjoyed playing *Puff* with the ladies (a game, similar to backgammon, named somewhat improbably after the sound of the dice on the board), and that *zum Puff gehen* soon became synonymous with more intimate games. *Die Puffmutter*: bawd, madame; *die Puffgegend*, red-light district (also *das Milieu**, *die Strichgegend*, *das Nuttenviertel*; or as applied to a designated erogenous zone in a German city, *Eroszentrum*). Though it sounds rather like 'poof', *ein Puff* has no connection with the gay scene (*ein Schwuler* is the most widespread euphemism for *ein Homosexueller*). *Ein Puff* is also the pouffe you sit on, and *Puffärmel* are puffed sleeves.

As a verb, however, *puffen* is no longer one of the numerous euphemisms for having sexual intercourse (see BUMSEN above), but means to nudge, prod or dig – usually with one's elbows; or else to puff smoke (*der Schornstein pufft*, but *man pafft eine Zigarette*, puffs a cigarette); or to make a puffing noise like a steam engine or a coffee machine. See also PUFFER in VIII.

RASSE n.f., **RASSIG** adj. denotes the (figurative) pedigree of, in particular, wine, women, and horses. Alma Mahler (*née* Schindler) was by all accounts *eine rassige Frau* – not 'racy', but a fiery, spirited, hot-blooded woman who turned the heads of Klimt, Zemlinsky, Kokoschka, Gropius and Werfel, to name but a few. When she noted in her diary the merits of a more glamorous suitor than her first husband-to-be: *er hat Rasse, was man von dem guten Mahler nun wirklich nicht behaupten kann*, she was not thinking of his race (or of the fact that Mahler was Jewish), but that he was handsome and had a forceful personality, 'which is more than you can say for poor Mahler' (Françoise Giroud, *Alma Mahler*, 1989, p. 47).

Alma could also be *eine raße Frau*, however. *Raß* or *räß* is a southern term meaning prickly or touchy, as in *eine raße Kellnerin*, a brusque, sharp-tongued waitress. Similarly, while *ein rassiges Pferd* is sleek and spirited (though not necessarily *ein Rassepferd*, a thoroughbred), *ein raßes Pferd* is vicious and unmanageable. And whereas *rassig* as a wine *Etikett** signifies young and 'lively', fruit wines (*Most*, *Obstwein*) and schnapps (*Obstler*) often taste *raß*: sharp, pungent, spicy. This is also the sense of *räße Witze*, racy jokes (in Switzerland *rässe Witze*, since the Swiss do not use *ß*; nor are they known for their quick-wittedness or *Schlagfertigkeit*, a word which originally meant 'preparedness for battle' – on which quality they do pride themselves); the Germans call such humour *gewagt*, *derb*, *frivol** or *deftig**.

SALOPP adj. closer to English sloppy – of manners, dress, language – than to the French *une salope* (bitch, slut, tart – this is *eine Schlampe* or *ein Mensch** in German, or perhaps *ein Flittchen*, a 'floozie', while *eine Fluse* is a bit of fluff only in the literal sense). Characteristically, Germans use the more disapproving word *schlampig* for sloppy work (*das ist eine Schlamperei!*). A sloppy joe is *ein Schlabberpullover*.

SCHARF adj. either **1.** sexy: *sie kleidet sich scharf* does not mean she is a sharp or natty dresser, but specifically that she is wearing a sexy dress. Or **2.** sexually attracted to someone: *sie ist scharf auf ihn*, she fancies him (like mad); *scharf wie Nachbars Lumpi*, a randy sod. See also SCHARF in I and VIII.

SCHIKANIEREN v. not merely to indulge in chicanery (*Machenschaften*) or sharp practice at law (*Winkelzüge*) or quibbling/hairsplitting (*Haarspalterei*), but to bully or harass *aus reiner Schikane* (out of sheer bloody-mindedness). One favourite *schikanöse Maßnahme* formerly employed by border guards in East Germany was *die Verzögerungstaktik* (delaying tactics); in motor racing, *eine Schikane* (chicane) has of course the same function. *Ich lasse mich nicht mehr von diesem Weibsbild*schikanieren*, I won't let that female mess me around any more.

SCHLAPP adj. While *eine Schlappe* is a 'slap in the face', a defeat, *schlapp* means generally listless, worn-out: *ich bin ganz schlapp*, I'm shattered; *Mensch, machen Sie jetzt nicht schlapp*, don't let us down now. Hence, figuratively, 'wet': *ein Schlappschwanz* ('floppy tail') is a real wash-out, also perhaps in a sexual sense (see FLASCHE above), though the first image that comes to mind is *der eingezogene Schwanz* of a dog with its tail between its legs.

SCHWARM n.m. a swarm (of bees: *Bienenschwarm*), but also the object of one's infatuation. Thus, *sie hat einen Schwarm von Anbetern um sich* (she's surrounded by a host of admirers), but *er ist ihr Schwarm* (she has a crush on him, he's her heart-throb). One might also say *sie schwärmt für ihn*, though such *Schwärmerei* is distinctly gooey. *Schwärmerei*, and the *Schwärmer* who indulges in it, more often suggests religious rapture or zealotry (its original sense in Luther's day), or some passionately invoked fancy or unfeasible vision (*Sonderbarer Schwärmer!* is King Philipp's response to the Marquis Posa's famous plea for freedom of thought – *Geben Sie Gedankenfreiheit!* – in Act III, Scene 10 of Schiller's *Don Carlos*, 1787). It is not a word one would apply to Napoleon, though he said he had read Goethe's *Werther* (1774) seven times – the story of an archetypal *Schwärmer* whose effusive sentiments towards children, nature, and his friend's fiancée, made extreme sensibility*, and even suicide, fashionable. See also EXALTIERT in V and HEFTIG in X.

VI   SEX & THE FAMILY

SERIÖS adj. in personal relationshps, as in business, means respectable, reliable, sound (*ernstzunehmend*), but not necessarily earnest or solemn (*ernst*), let alone given to the mere affectation of gravity as 'a *French* wit [La Rochefoucauld] had long ago defined it, – *viz. A mysterious carriage of the body to cover the defects of the mind*; – which definition of gravity, *Yorick*, with great imprudence, would say, deserved to be wrote in letters of gold' (Laurence Sterne, *Tristram Shandy*, Book I, Chapter II) and which the Germans might call *feierlicher Ernst* (or, frivolously, *Bierernst*).

The *Importance of Being Earnest* therefore resists direct transliteration (it is popular in Germany under the title *Bunbury*), and a German audience hears Lady Bracknell dismiss both Jack Worthing and Cecily Cardew as insufficiently *seriös* – not to be taken seriously, either as a suitor or as a good match – that is, until she learns of Cecily's financial assets, 'the really solid* qualities, the qualities that last, and improve with time' (someone with 'serious' money is *schwerreich* or *steinreich*). Similarly, advertisements in the *Heiraten und Bekanntschaften* columns of German newspapers appeal for *seriöse Zuschriften*, replies that are seriously intended, while the words *seriöser Herr* or *seriöse Dame* suggest that the person is of an age when serious intentions are ensured.

As an alternative definition, something which is *seriös* deserves to be taken seriously but only by declining to be *seriös* (in its occasional sense of pompous, self-important). Friedrich Torberg points out in *Die Tante Jolesch* (1977, p. 114) that the much-loved *Prager Tagblatt* of the pre-Hitler era was *ein seriöses Presseerzeugnis* (a serious newspaper), *die mit dem Begriff 'seriös' so gut wie nichts zu tun hatte* (which had almost nothing to do with the term '*seriös*' in its normal sense); *Seriosität figurierte im internen Sprachgebrauch der Redaktion als 'tierischer Ernst' und war streng verpönt* (*Seriosität* was used internally by the editorial staff to signify something 'deadly earnest' and was seriously frowned upon). The determination of the Viennese between the wars to continue whistling in the dark was similarly exemplified by the saying *die Lage ist hoffnungslos aber nicht ernst* (the situation is desperate but not serious). On the other hand, when the *Süddeutsche Zeitung* on 17 May 1990 criticized Chancellor Kohl's plan to finance German reunification by borrowing (*Einheit auf Pump**) as *unseriöse Schuldenmacherei*, it did not mean that the debts incurred would be trivial, but that the policy was irresponsible.

SPANNER n.m. a peeping Tom – who presumably finds the activity *spannend* or *voll Spannung* (thrilling, full of suspense – from *spannen*, to make taut or tense). Voyeurism is a humanizing activity for the lonely hero of Heimito von Doderer's comic novel

Die erleuchteten Fenster (*The Lighted Windows*, 1951), less so for the *überspannt* (over-excited, hysterical) heroine of Elfriede Jelinek's harrowingly masochistic tale *Die Klavierspielerin* (*The Piano Player*, 1983 – see ORDINÄR in V); in both cases (Freudians might think, appropriately) the city is Vienna.

Ein Spanner is also a tennis-press, trouser-hanger or shoe-tree, but not the spanner you use to tighten a nut (*ein Schraubenschüssel*; see ENGLISCH in V) or to throw in the works (*jemandem Knüppel/einen Knüppel zwischen die Beine werfen*).

SPLITTING n.n. *Das Splittingsystem* is the separate taxation arrangement whereby husband and wife each pay income tax on half their combined incomes. Also job sharing, as when *Gymnasium** teachers opt for 12-hour or 18-hour contracts, rather than a full-time contract of 24 hours per week (*Grundschullehrer/innen* teach 30 hours per week).

STRIPPE n.f. nothing to do with a *Stripteasetänzerin/Stripperin*, but a colloquialism for the telephone: *sie hängt dauernd an der Strippe*, she's constantly on the phone; *ich hab ihn an der Strippe*, I have him on the line/blower.

TEMPERAMENT n.n. non-specific (as to whether one is by nature a *Choleriker, Melancholiker, Phlegmatiker* or *Sanguiniker*) in such phrases as *es ist alles Temperamentssache*, it's all a matter of temperament. Someone who is temperamentally suited/unsuited is *veranlagungsmäßig* or *charakterlich geeignet/ungeeignet*. Used absolutely, however, *sie hat vielleicht ein Temperament* means she is very vivacious, even hot-blooded, with a bit of a temper. Accordingly, *temperamentvoll* means spirited or lively (not specifically *sexy*), as when the East German *Trabant** was advertised as *ein schnittiges, elegantes, temperamentvolles Fahrzeug*.

By reputation, the *Trabant* was certainly 'temperamental' (*launisch*). This comes from *die Laune* (mood, temper, whim: caused, according to astrologers, by the moon, *luna*) – fickle fortune, changeable weather, capricious moods are all *launenhaft*, while *launisch* is generally just 'moody', but the now somewhat dated *launig* means just the opposite: good-humoured or witty.

TRAVESTIE n.f. travesty, but sometimes used (under the influence of French *en travestie*, in drag) instead of *der Transvestismus* or *der Transvestitismus* (transvestism).

TRUBEL n.m. derived from French *troubler*, but now means commotion, hubbub, disturbance, bustle, confusion (often used in combination: *Jubel, Trubel, Heiterkeit* describes the perfect *Sylvester*-

feier or Hogmanay celebration). Thus the *Süddeutsche Zeitung* on 2 May 1990 reported that the head of Europe's longest-ruling family, the Wittelsbachs (1180–1918), spent his 85th birthday abroad, *um sich dem Trubel der Gratulationen zu entziehen* (to escape all the hurly-burly of the celebratory festivities). *Der Trouble*, however, is a straightforward anglicism: *jetzt gibt es Trouble!*, here comes trouble, now you're for it.

TYP n.m. distinguish between *ein Typ* – as in *sie ist genau mein Typ* (she is just my type), *ein netter Typ* (a nice bloke, guy), or *eine Machine* vom Typ Boeing 707* (model) – and *eine Type*, a curious character or oddball (without further qualification, though an adjective such as *seltsam*, *komisch* or *originell* is often added). For other types or sorts of things, use *die Sorte* or *die Art**.

UNTERHALTEN v. as with so many German compounds, the meaning can be partially deduced (to 'hold underneath' or support), but not totally deduced (*unterhalten* is also to entertain). *Sie unterhält ihn* might mean she provides for him financially, but also that she entertains him. *Unterhalt zahlen* is to make maintenance payments, and maintenance/upkeep is one sense of *die Unterhaltung*, but *eine Unterhaltung* is also a chat or conversation, and *Unterhaltungsmusik* (*U-Musik* in the jargon, as distinct from *E-Musik*, *ernste Musik* or serious* music) *Unterhaltungsliteratur*, *Unterhaltungsfilme*, *und so weiter*, all provide easy listening, reading, viewing, and so on. However, a nation that has been taught (by Schiller) to view *die Schaubühne als eine moralische* Anstalt* (theatre as a moral institution) finds it difficult to take *ein Unterhaltungsstück* (by Noël Coward, for instance) seriously and might dismiss it as mere *Boulevardtheater* (commercial entertainment).

VERKEHR n.m. use with care: like 'intercourse', it may be either social or sexual (see also *Verhältnis* under FALL in II), or else means traffic (see TACHOMETER in VII). This ambiguity does not extend to the verb, however: *er verkehrt in Künstlerkreisen* (he moves in artistic circles, mixes with artists); *er verkehrt mit/in den besten Familien* (he has access to the best families). Banish all thoughts of *Gruppensex*.

VISAGE n.f. whereas English 'visage' or 'countenance' generally suggests something as beautiful or noble as *das Antlitz* in German, *die Visage* is always derogatory. Thus, *jemandem die Visage polieren* means 'to smash someone's ugly mug in', and *eine fiese/glatte/ekelhafte Visage* corresponds to what Pope calls a 'vile visage' in his *Iliad* translation (11.331). Even so, *ein Visagist(e)/eine Visagistin* is a beautician.

WANKEN v. no connection with the sin of Onan (*onanieren*, *masturbieren*, colloquially *wichsen*), but either **1**. physically, to sway, reel, stagger, totter, wobble, etc.; or **2**. figuratively, to waver, vacillate, falter. Osmin *wankt und schwankt** (the two words mean much the same) because he has been slipped a Micky Finn to facilitate the abduction from the seraglio, but the mere thought of meeting the abducted Konstanze in Act I, Scene 5 of *Die Entführung aus dem Serail* is sufficient to make Belmonte, too, admit: *Schon zittr' ich und wanke, Schon zag' ich und schwanke* ('I'm trembling and quaking, shivering and shaking'). It is a more resolute Tristan who drinks what he believes to be poison in Act I of Wagner's opera: *Vergessens güt'ger Trank, dich trink ich sonder Wank!* ('The kindly cup of oblivion I drink without hesitation'), while Beethoven's Leonore/Fidelio resolutely declares in her great aria: *Ich wanke nicht!* (see WEIB below).

Sonder Wank or *ohne Wank* is now archaic (though the Swiss still say *ich tue keinen Wank* meaning 'I won't lift a finger', and *einen Wank tun* in the sense of embarking on an undertaking). *Wankelmütig* means fickle or inconstant. When shares in NSU collapsed in 1960 after the firm tried to launch the rotary *Wankel* engine (named after Felix Wankel, its inventor), *Der Spiegel* could not resist the pun: *wankelmütigstes bundesdeutsches Wertpapier** – the most unpredictable Federal stocks.

WEIB n.n. 'wife' only when used ironically (*mein Weib*, 'my woman'), or in certain archaic-sounding set phrases (*zum Weib nehmen*; *Mann** und Weib; Weib und Kind verlassen*). Otherwise generally disparaging (female/US broad), though with some exceptions (*ein tolles* or *rassiges** Weib* is 'quite a woman'). This was not yet the case when Beethoven adapted Schiller's words both in the Choral Symphony and in the closing scene of *Fidelio*: *Wer ein holdes Weib errungen, / Stimm' in unsern Jubel ein* ('whoever has won a fair woman, let him join our hymn of praise') – an appeal not to the libertinage of *Wein, Weib, und Gesang* ('Wine, women and song') but to the sacred bonds of marriage triumphantly proclaimed by Leonore in Florestan's dungeon: *Töt' erst sein Weib!* ('First kill his wife' – see also BAND in X).

By contrast, Nietzsche's famous line: *Du gehst zu Frauen? Vergiß die Peitsche nicht!* ('Don't forget the whip when you visit women' – from the section *Von alten und jungen Weiblein* in *Also sprach Zarathustra*) is often used to brand him a misogynist. William Archer, in *Fighting a Philosophy* (1915), even thought it would help persuade the suffragettes to support the British war effort. In fact, Nietzsche originally inscribed the words *Wenn du zum Weibe gehst, vergiß die Peitsche nicht* on a photograph of himself and fellow-philosopher

Paul Rée between the shafts of an ox-cart containing Lou Salomé (whose subsequent admirers included Rilke and Freud); she is the one brandishing the whip.

WILD adj. generally as in English – *wilde Leidenschaft*, wild passion. However, *in wilder Ehe leben* does not mean one's marriage is a riotous affair, though whether derived from *wild* meaning 'in the natural state', or from *wild* meaning 'lawless' (*ein wilder Streik*, unofficial, 'wildcat' strike; *wild parken*, illegal parking), either way it does sound more fun than 'living in sin' (though we have it on the best authority that that is the only way to live). Note the similar French usage in *grève sauvage* or *camping sauvage*.

WINFRIED a man's name only (the young Nazi in Edgar Reitz's *Heimat**, for instance; Hitler's beloved Winifred Wagner – Wagner's daughter-in-law – was, of course, English by birth). Curiously, Kevin joined Daniel and Alexander as the most popular boys' names in Germany in the early 1990s, with Peggy and Doreen top among the girls. Among biblical names, Samson may not be immediately recognizable as Simson, nor Isaiah as Jesaja, nor the Queen of Sheba as *die Königin von Saba*.

WINK n.m., **WINKEN** v. *ein Wink* is not a wink, but either **1.** a signal, such as a nod or a wave; or else **2.** (like *der Tip* or *der Hinweis*) a hint – *jemandem einen Wink geben*, to tip someone the wink; *praktische Winke für die Hausfrau*, practical tips for the housewife. A wink, however, is *das Zublinzeln/Zuzwinkern*, more common as a verb: *er blinzelte mir zu* or *er zwinkerte mir zu*. Accordingly, *er winkt mit den Augen* might mean he raises his eyebrows or frowns (some such silent or secret sign is *ein stummer* or *heimlicher Wink*), but not that he winks, while *einem Taxi winken*, like the Royal wave (*die Königin winkte ihren Untertanen huldvoll zu*, the Queen graciously waved to her subjects), requires no more than a wave of the hand. Figuratively, *der Frieden winkt*, peace beckons; *ihm winkt das Glück*, luck is smiling on him; I did not sleep a wink, *ich habe kein Auge zugetan*; forty winks, *ein Nickerchen**. For winking lights/traffic indicators, see BLINKER in VII.

WOCHENBETT n.n. 'lying in' – derived from the six weeks which a young mother was expected to remain in bed. *Wöchnerinnenstation**, maternity ward.

ZWINGEN v. not to swing, but to compel: *ich zwang mich zur Ruhe*, I forced myself to be calm, not I rocked myself to sleep. Freud investigated *Zwangsneurosen*, obsessional neuroses, and a crime committed in such a state might earn you 10 years *Zwangsarbeit* (forced labour). *Kein Weinzwang* means that there is no compulsion to purchase or drink wine.

Der Zwinger is the outer ward of a castle (*eine Zwingburg*, stronghold, fortress) or the defensive ditch around a city wall, once stocked with wild animals, subsequently where guard dogs were kennelled. It is also the name of Dresden's superb Baroque palace, commissioned by Augustus the Strong in 1710, destroyed in the air raid of 13 February 1945, but now largely restored to its former splendour.

ZWIST n.m. not twist, but feud, as in Grillparzer's pessimistic response to the revolutions of 1848: *Ein Bruderzwist in Habsburg* (*Fraternal Feud in the House of Habsburg*).

TRAVEL,
HEALTH,
SPORT

VII

REISEN,
GESUNDHEIT,
SPORT

AFRIKANER n.m. not an Afrikaner – (white) South Africans who speak *afrikaans* are *Afrikander* or *Buren* (Boers) – but a (black) African.

ALLEE n.f. as in French, a tree-lined avenue or boulevard, such as Düsseldorf's glitzy *Königsallee* ('*die Kö*') or Berlin's *Kurfürstendamm**, or the *Schloßallee* leading up to a castle, palace or stately home. A distinctive feature of the east German landscape is the *Pappelallee* – also known as *eine Chaussee* and hauntingly evoked by the poet Peter Huchel in *Chausseen, Chausseen* (1963) – whose poplars are now endangered by western juggernauts but defended by the *ADAC* (the main motoring organization), the *Fremdenverkehrsverband* (Tourist Board) and the *Schutzgemeinschaft Deutscher Wald* (Society for the Protection of the German Forest). Their *Aktion**, known as *Rettet die Alleen*, envisages a *Deutsche Alleenstraße* from the Baltic island of Rügen to Lake Constance, even if it means planting new trees along the west German stretches.

Many German towns and cities have an *Altstadt*, its narrow, winding, cobbled streets lovingly restored (*saniert**) – this sort of alley, lane or passageway is *ein Durchgang, eine Gasse* or *ein Gäßchen*. (In Austria, however, *die Gasse* is more broadly used to mean 'the street outside': *eine Gassenwohnung* is a flat overlooking the street; *über die Gasse* or *Gassenverkauf*, 'take-away'). For obvious reasons, Germans take their dog 'walkies' (*Gassi gehen*) to the nearest *Allee*. For bowling alleys, see BOWLING below.

AMBULANZ n.f. an ambulance is normally *ein Krankenwagen*, and *die Ambulanz* (or *Poliklinik*) the out-patients' department of a hospital (hence *ambulante Behandlung*, out-patient treatment, as distinct from *stationäre** *Behandlung*, in-patient treatment). In addition, *die Ambulanz* is the emergency ward, and by extension an ambulance with a doctor and specialized equipment on board for going to emergencies (the other meaning of *ambulante Behandlung*). In a military context, it is a field hospital (*das Feldlazarett*). See also KRANKENHAUS below.

ANGINA n.f. pharyngitis or tonsillitis as well as *Angina pectoris*. As the serious heart condition is not usually abbreviated in German, *ich* *habe eine fürchterliche Angina* means only 'I have a terribly sore throat'. See also KATARRH below.

APOTHEKE n.f. a chemist's shop/pharmacy which, unlike *eine Drogerie**, also dispenses those drugs (*Arzneimittel, Medikamente*) which are *rezeptpflichtig** or *apothekenpflichig*, i.e. need a doctor's prescription. It is also a medicine cupboard (*Hausapotheke*) or first-aid box (all vehicles must carry *eine Autoapotheke*), and is used jokingly – since most *Drogerieartikel* cost more in an *Apotheke* – of a shop or restaurant that charges fancy prices. For the formalities of visiting the doctor or having drugs prescribed (*verschrieben*), see KRANKENKASSE below.

APPENDIX n.m. of a book. The part of the body is *der Blinddarm*, and appendicitis *die Blinddarmentzündung* (redundant-gut or supernumerary-gut inflammation), though there is also a medical term, *die Appendizitis.*

AS n.n. an ace (tennis, cards); also a top player in any sport; in music, A flat (for other unfamiliar musical notations, see TON in X). It is less offensive to say someone is *ein Esel*, a (silly) ass, than to call him *ein Aas* (from *das Aas*, carrion), a sod, bugger.

AUSHOLEN v. not, despite the proliferation of anglicisms and transliterations in German sporting vocabulary, to 'hole out' at golf (*einlochen*), but to swing your arm – or the club – back. Hence, *er holt weit aus*, he takes a long backswing. In the figurative sense of starting a story at the beginning, this could be applied to the Oldest Member in P. G. Wodehouse's golfing stories when he waxes expansive. For holing out in one, German falls back on *ein Hole in One spielen.*

AUTOCAR n.m. not a car (*der Wagen, das Auto*), though it is often abbreviated to *Car*, but – in Swiss German only – a coach for excursions (in Germany, *ein Reisebus*). The basic form of rural transport in Switzerland is *das Postauto* (elsewhere it delivers only the post), which signals its approach on the bends of mountain roads by sounding on its horn the distinctive opening bar of a song familiar in war-time Britain: 'Over here.'

BACKBORD n.n. the port side of a boat or ship, i.e. the side to which the *Steuermann* (steersman) formerly turned his back (see *Backe**below) in order to hold the *Steuerruder* (rudder) to the right of the stern, which is accordingly the *Steuerbord* or starboard side. Many maritime terms are related in English and German, some even share a figurative sense: *die Segel back bekommen*, for instance, meaning that a boat's sails have been pressed back against the mast by the wind, also means to be taken aback, or have the wind taken out of one's sails. Oddly, though, *die Back eines Schiffes* is not the back of a ship (*das Achterdeck*, afterdeck; *achteraus*, astern) but the foc's'le at the front, where *die Backmannschaft*, the crew, mess together (*die Back* is also a dixie or mess-kit), while *die Backen** are the curves on either side of the prow.

BACKE n.f. once cognate with English 'back' (*der Rücken*), but now only used of the cheek (*die Wange*) or buttock (*Hinterbacke*, *Arschbacke*, *Pobacke*). For other curves fore and aft, see BACKBORD above.

BAD n.n. either **1.** a bath, *or* the bathroom (*das Badezimmer*), *or* the bathtub (*die Badewanne*); or **2.** a bathe; or **3.** a (public) swimming pool/baths (*das Schwimmbad*, *die Badeanstalt*; if outdoors, *ein Freibad*; indoors, *ein Hallenbad*); or **4.** a seaside resort (*das Seebad*) or spa (*das Heilbad*). Germans of the older generation make full use of medically prescribed *Badereisen* to Bad Kissingen or Bad Ems, Bad Homburg or Baden-Baden, to take the waters and therapeutic baths (*Bäderkur* – see KUR below) paid for by their medical insurance schemes as a normal entitlement (and adjunct to their holidays, sometimes referred to as *Kururlaub*).

BAGAGE n.f. baggage/luggage is now more commonly *das Gepäck*, whereas *die ganze Bagage* is a rabble or riff-raff, 'the whole bloody lot of them' (*das Pack* means much the same; see PACKEN below). It is always used of a crowd, not – as in English – of a single disreputable, or else pert and saucy, woman. *Eine Frechheit!* (what a cheek), said the parvenu's wife to her husband on arriving at the Gare du Nord and hearing the porters' shout, *Bagages*.

BALD adv. not bald (*kahl*), but soon, almost, nearly.

BANDAGE n.f. a bandage (more commonly *der Verband*), but also the steel tyre on the wheel of a railway engine or coach. Used figuratively: *die Kontrahenten clinchen* (properly, *kämpfen*) *mit harten Bandagen* (referring to a boxer's bandaged hands), the opponents grapple with no holds barred (*Die Zeit*, 19 August 1988); *das sind harte Bandagen*, that's tough luck, hard cheese.

BLESSIEREN v. not to bless (*segnen*), but to wound (from French *blesser*): *blessierte Frauenherzen*, wounded female hearts; 'The ladies, God bless 'em!' – *Es leben die Frauen!*

BLINKER n.m., **BLINKEN** v. you do not normally *blinken* or *winken** with your eyes (*ihr Auge blinkte* actually means 'her eyes gleamed'), but rather *zwinkern* (to wink, but often to twinkle), or else *blinzeln* (to blink when dazzled or tired, nervous, surprised, etc.; or squint in order to see better; or, in *jemandem zublinzeln*, to wink at someone).

The usual sense of *blinken* is to flash or signal, and a car's *Blinker* are its direction indicators/winkers/flashers. When overtaking on the *Autobahn*, especially in *zähfließender Verkehr* (slow-moving traffic), leaving one's *Blinker* or *Blinklicht* on betrays a certain impatience, though it is more acceptable than use of the now illegal *Lichthupe* (full-beam flashing). Blinking idiot! *Verflixter Idiot!* People with a blinkered attitude to life *laufen mit Scheuklappen* (horse blinkers) *herum*.

BOWLING n.n. ten-pin, American bowling, as distinct from *Kegeln/Kegelschieben*, the more popular traditional game of ninepin skittles. Large firms often have their own automated *Kegelbahn*, as do many pubs in which the *Kegelbrüder*, bowling fraternity (in practice, one's drinking pals), can work up a thirst playing *Sechs-Tage-Rennen*, *Hol' den Bauer*, *Totenkiste*, *Kackstuhl* and other challenging permutations on a concave bowling-lane in the shape of an elongated Y.

CAR INSURANCE in Germany it is always the car, not the driver, which is insured, which means that *Vollkaskoversicherung* (fully comprehensive cover) is very expensive. *Die Prämie* (premium) for *Teilkaskoversicherung* (third party, fire and theft insurance, so named because it excludes liability for *Kaskoschaden*, damage to one's own vehicle) is about half as much – roughly the same as for comprehensive insurance in Britain. In spite of the unlimited speed, *unbegrenzte Geschwindigkeit*, still allowed on most German autobahns thanks to the powerful automobile industry lobby, and though Germany provides transit roads for the rest of Europe (unlike France, Switzerland and most of Austria, free of charge for cars; for lorries, see VIGNETTE below), the accident rate of 5.5 fatalities per billion kilometres compares favourably with 11 in France and 18 in Italy, both of which have 130km/h limits.

CARAVAN n.m. either a caravan/US trailer, mobile home (more usually *ein Wohnwagen*), or estate car/US station wagon (also *ein Kombiwagen* or simply *ein Kombi*). A caravan of camels is *eine Karawane*.

CATCHER n.m. a catch wrestler. Free-style *Catch-as-catch-can* or *Catch* wrestlers *catchen*, but anglers *fangen Fische* (though the *Fangnetz* used to land them is known also as a *Kätscher* or *Kescher*) and goalkeepers *fangen den Ball*. Holden Caulfield's dream of catching children before they plunge into a chasm is probably more indebted to baseball than wrestling, so J. D. Salinger's *Catcher in the Rye* (1951) is appropriately known in Germany as *Der Fänger im Roggen*.

CHECKEN v. 'to check' in the sense of verify (*überprüfen*) or compare (*vergleichen*), but also 'to understand' in such colloquial expressions as *hast du es endlich gecheckt?*, have you got it/caught on at last?; *er hat das nicht gecheckt*, he didn't cotton on, wise up (though English 'check?' in the sense of 'got it?' is *verstanden?* or *kapiert?*). German airports have adopted *das Check-in* and *die Check-liste*, but passports are no longer checked (*kontrolliert*) at *Checkpoint Charlie*.

DAMESPIEL n.n. literally 'a game for ladies' (not a 'spiel* for the dames'!), in fact draughts/US checkers.

DECKE n.f. a blanket, or the ceiling – like *das Deck* of a ship (or level of a multi-storey carpark), which we tend to think of as something underfoot, but which all derive from the notion of covering (*decken*), and figuratively, of security (*eine Deckadresse* is a cover address). Thus: *unter dem Deckmantel eines Deckpassagiers* (in the guise of a first-class passenger) *lag er im Deckstuhl* (he lay in a deckchair) *unter einem Deckbett* (under a quilt).

Esmond Romilly relates how, during the Spanish Civil War, '*Fliege, Decke!* . . . warning of approaching planes, soon became a familiar phrase in our vocabulary' (*Boadilla*, 1937, 1971 ed., p. 67). *Flieger* would have been more correct (*eine Fliege* is a fly), and '*runter!* (down!) or *Deckung!* (take cover!) rather than *Decke* (echoing 'hit the deck', perhaps), but it was not a time for grammatical niceties.

DEPENDANCE n.f. either the branch office of a company (also *die Zweigstelle* or *die Filiale**), or an hotel annexe. Dependence on someone or something is *die Abhängigkeit*.

DICK adj. thick, large, big, etc. Of people, fat (but not thick in the sense of stupid, which is *dumm**, *doof*, *blöd*; Laurel and Hardy are known, in reverse order, as *Dick und Doof*). In World War I, *die dicke Berta*, Big Bertha, was the Germans' 42cm mortar (named after Frau Bertha Krupp von Bohlen und Halbach, owner of the Krupp steel works from 1903 to 1943); popularly, the epithet has also stuck in the phrase *einen dicken Mercedes fahren* (Daimler-Benz certainly do not use the phrase in their advertising campaigns). Widespread figurative and colloquial usages include: *dicke Freunde*, those who stick together, *durch dick und dünn*, through thick and thin; *das ist ein dicker Hund*, that's a real howler, or that's a bit much; *das schaffst du dicke*, you'll manage it easily; *er hat es dicke*, either 'he's had enough of it' or 'he's enough and to spare', but *er hat es dicke hinter den Ohren*, he's cunning, astute. See also FETT and PLUMP below.

DISPATCHER n.m. not, as now in England, an air-traffic/flight controller (*der Fluglotse*), but a production supervisor in industry; or else (and this is something of an oddity: an East German americanism) someone who co-ordinates the movements of trains, such as the hero of Uwe Johnson's novel *Mutmaßungen über Jakob* (1959). Dispatch riders in German cities such as Stuttgart or Frankfurt manage with bicycles rather than motorbikes and are consequently known as *Fahrradkuriere*.

DRASTISCH adj. drastic (*drastische Maßnahmen ergreifen*, to take drastic measures), but also graphic or vivid – *ein drastischer Beweis*, a strikingly convincing piece of evidence; *eine drastische Schilderung*, a realistic (often amusing) account. *Ein Drastikum* is a vigorously effective purgative or laxative.

DROGERIE n.f. a chemist's shop/US drugstore. *Der Drogist*, unlike *der Apotheker**, is not qualified to dispense a doctor's prescription, but often specializes in *homöopathische Mittel* (homeopathic preparations) as well as toiletries and cosmetics. These days, *Drogen* are mainly narcotic drugs (see DEALER in III).

ELF n.f. not an elf (*der Elf* or *die Elfe*), but the number eleven, and hence also the word for a (football) team. *Ein Elfmeter* is a penalty kick. Wolf von Lojewski's definition of cricket: *als bestünde Fußball aus einem stundenlangen Elfmeterschießen* (as if football consisted of taking penalties for hours on end) is, he admits, *ein etwas plumper* Vergleich* – a somewhat crude comparison (*Die Briten sind anders*, 1988, p. 25).

FAHRT n.f. a journey or trip, not a fart (*der Furz* – see PUMP in III). Families travelling in Germany will have noticed that children find the *Ausfahrt* (exit) signs on the *Autobahn* amusing for much the same reason that British brass players have renamed Leopold Mozart's *Schlittenfahrt* (sleigh-ride) to reflect the rude-sounding noises made by their instruments – much in the spirit of his son Wolfgang's own scatological leanings (see BASE in VI). Figuratively, *in Fahrt geraten* means to get going (about something); *auf Fahrt sein*, to be angry, livid.

FANG n.m. an animal's fang/canine tooth/tusk (though poisonous snakes have a *Giftzahn**), hence: *sie hat ihn in ihren Fängen*, she's got him in her clutches. But **also** what a hunter or fisherman has caught – the catch*, bag, haul (Scottish poachers are still sometimes 'caught with the fang'), and the hunting, fishing or trapping itself: *auf Fang gehen.* The *Fangschuß* is the shot that kills the quarry, given abominable notoriety by concentration camp guards (in which context 'coup de grâce' scarcely fits). Also: *Fangen spielen,* to play tag; *Feuer fangen,* to catch fire – and to fall in love.

FERN- in cpds. not the plant (*der Farn/das Farnkraut*), but a key word meaning distant or long-distance, either **1.** in the context of travel: *der Fernverkehr,* long-distance/transit traffic; *der Fernfahrer,* long-distance lorry driver; *der Fernpendler,* long-distance commuter; *das Fernlicht,* full beam; *der Ferne Osten,* the Far East (the Middle East is known as *der Nahe* (near) *Osten*); *Fernweh* is another word for *Wanderlust* – the opposite of *Heimweh* (see HEIMAT in II).

or **2.** in communications: *der Fernsprecher,* public telephone; *das Fernmeldeamt,* telephone exchange; *das Ferngespräch,* long-distance call; *das Fernsehen* or *der Fernseher,* television; *die Fernlenkung, die Fernsteuerung* or *die Fernbedienung,* remote control; *das Fernstudium,* Open University.

FIEBER n.n. *ich habe Fieber* means only 'I'm running a temperature' or 'I'm feeling a bit feverish'– *ich habe 39° (39 Grad*) Fieber,* I've a temperature of 102; *der Patient ist seit drei Tagen fieberfrei*,* for the last three days the patient's temperature has been back to normal. *Fieber,* then, is usually less drastic than fever, which is best rendered as *hohes Fieber.* Yellow fever is *das gelbe Fieber/Gelbfieber*; scarlet fever, *das Scharlachfieber/der Scharlach*; hay fever, *der Heuschnupfen.* See also ANGINA above.

FLANKEN v. in football, to centre the ball – *die Flanke* is both a cross (*ein Flankenball*) and the wing. See KICKER below.

FLEET n.n. a canal or narrow waterway in northern Germany. Fleet Street, as Swift and Pope already observed, lived up to its name, which originally meant an open sewer. But a trip today through the network of *Fleete* surrounding Hamburg's impressive *Speicherstadt* (the warehouses of its free port) and linking the Alster lakes to the river Elbe, affords the best views of the green-roofed *Jugendstil* (art nouveau) and *Backsteingotik** ('clinker brick gothic') of the city's *Kontorhäuser* (Hanseatic merchants' offices) and *Gründerzeit* villas (built in the boom years after 1871). Further west, it is from the shallow *Fleete* along the Frisian coast that 'multitudes of sea-going lighters, carrying full loads of soldiers' are to launch an invasion of England in Erskine Childers' thriller *The Riddle of the Sands* (1903, p. 266; see WATT below) – a book which chimed with warning prophecies in the British press as Germany began to build up her *Schlachtflotte* (battle fleet).

FLIPPER n.m. a pinball machine: enthusiasts *flippern*.

FLUT n.f. 'flood' (*die Überschwemmung, das Hochwasser*) is one sense of the word, as in the biblical *Sintflut*, or the unmetaphorical *Sturmflut* which devastated the north German coast in February 1962. Helmut Schmidt, then Hamburg's *Senator* für Inneres*, made his name (literally, as *der Macher*: doer, man of action) directing the rescue operation (*der Katastropheneinsatz*), though Franz Josef Strauß, later his Bavarian rival for the Chancellorship, claimed credit for having sent the helicopters: *was Schmidt damals bei der Sturmflut an Ruhm geerntet hat, verdankt er alles mir. Ich habe ihm die Hubschrauber nach Norden geschickt* (see *Die Zeit*, 7 October 1988).

In the matter of aquatic opportunism, one notable precedent is that tide in the affairs of men, which, taken at the flood, leads on to fortune – aptly translated by August Wilhelm Schlegel (1797–1845) as *Nimmt man die Flut wahr, führet sie zum Glück* (*Julius Caesar*, Act IV, Scene 3), since the primary meaning of *die Flut*, at least for a north German, is an incoming tide (*es flutet*), or else high tide (culminating in *Hochwasser*). Likewise, *es ist Ebbe* means either 'the tide is going out', or 'it is low tide', but there is no common word for tides (*die Gezeiten* is somewhat literary) which does not specify ebb or flow. *Die Fluten* is likewise poetic: 'the waters', as in *ein Bad* in den kühlen Fluten des Sees**.

Note also: *der Fluß fließt* (the river flows); *das Floß schwimmt* (the raft floats – only the pound *floatet*); *die Flosse* (fin, flipper*, paw); and *flott*, with all its figurative connotations of being afloat: light, brisk, fun-loving, in funds (whereas *Ebbe in der Kasse** means at a pretty low ebb, hard up). Coleridge, a great admirer and popularizer of German culture, wrote in his *Table Talk* that he 'should like the words *verflossen* and *zerflossen* to be naturalised' so that he might write 'Now feels my soul creative throes, and now all joy, all sense zerflows' (the prefix itself suggesting a flowing apart), though it was also his impression that 'nature seems to have dropped an acid into the language when a-forming which curdled the vowels and made all the consonants flow together'.

GARAGE n.f. the garage which services your car (*die Wartung, die Inspektion*), or repairs it (*die Reparatur*), is *eine Werkstatt*, and you go to *eine Tankstelle* for petrol. *Eine Garage* is for parking in, either at home, or in the city (*Hochgarage*, multi-storey, *Tiefgarage*, underground – follow the international blue '*P*' sign).

GOLF n.m. *der Golf* is a gulf/the (Persian) Gulf; *das Golf/das Golfspiel* is the game. *Seit der Golfstrom die Westdeutschen erfaßt hat* (*Die Zeit*, 25 August 1989) is, of course, a pun (*ein Wortspiel*) – in a similar

vein one could say that the Germans' craze for golf makes Germany
one of the *Golfstaaten*. But the export market for our golfing *Profis* is
limited since there are still only some 300 private courses, though
things are changing quickly since the *Wende** when the *Süddeutsche
Zeitung* reported: *CSU und Grüne lehnten einen SPD-Antrag ab,
öffentliche Golfplätze in Bayern einzurichten*, the CSU and the Greens
rejected a proposal by the SPD to build public golf courses in Bavaria
(3 May 1990).

GULLY n.m. or n.n. not a mountain gully (*die Schlucht*), rut or
groove (*die Furche, die Rinne*), but a drainage channel by the side
of the road. The other English sense of the word – a position on the
cricket field between point and third slip* – is, of course, unknown to
most Germans, as are the game's other terminological niceties. 'Who
watered the wicket at Melbourne?' (in Act II of *The Birthday Party*)
needs some explaining to a German audience, but Goldberg's question received an even more Pinteresque twist in a recent Munich
production: *Wer hat in Melbourne am Pförtchen gepinkelt?* ('Who
peed against the wicket-gate in Melbourne?').

As yet there is little sign of cricket joining football, tennis and golf
as British exports to Germany, though 'rejoining' might be more
accurate since the game already had a foothold in Berlin by the 1880s.
When the Kaiser wrote to the Prince of Wales in 1900 of 'the great
Cricket Match between England v Australia, in which the former
took the victory of the latter quietly and with chivalrous acknowledg-
ment of her opponent', the moral he drew was that England should
admit defeat in the Boer War with equal grace. In 1911, the captain of
the English tourists predicted that cricket was just as likely to improve the character of the Germans as it had already improved the
character of the English, but such hopes were dashed when the
Englishmen returned to Berlin in 1938. All the German fielders yelled
AUS! after every ball, and *Reichskricketkapitän* Thamer, having delegated a spectator to field at deep mid-off, felled him with a single
blow for dropping the ball. Commented *Reichssportsführer* von
Tschammer und Osten: 'Yes, I have heard of the incident, but I
understand it was a very simple catch.'

HAI n.m. a shark. So what might sound like a greeting (see also
HALLO and HEIL below) is in fact a warning, though one rarely heard
in German waters: *Hai!*

Colloquially, *Miethaie* ('rent sharks') are landlords who rip you
off. The shark in *Die Dreigroschenoper* (1928) is of course Mackie/
Macheath himself. But just as Gay had had the temerity to satirize
Walpole as both Peachum and Macheath in the original *Beggars'*

Opera, so it was Bavaria's political boss that 'nothing could be proved against' in a 1970s adaptation of Brecht and Weill's famous *Moritat* (street ballad, generally about a gruesome deed) by the satirical songsters, *die Biermösn Blasn*: *Und der Haifisch, der hat Zähne / Und die trägt er im Gesicht, / Und Franz Josef ist ein Haifisch, / Doch beweisen kann man's nicht* (see *Strauß* under SENIOR in I, AKTION, FALL, MASS, UNION in II).

HALLO interj. used when answering the phone, say, or summoning a waiter, but also when drawing attention to some infringement of the Germans' sense of *Ordnung* (orderliness) or *Gründlichkeit* (thoroughness), on which occasions it may be stressed forcefully (to English ears, gratingly, or even vindictively) on the first syllable.

HALT adv. an emotive particle conveying resignation in such expressions as *das ist halt so*, that's simply the way it is; *da kann man halt nichts machen*, I'm afraid it can't be helped; *wir müssen es halt versuchen*, we'll just have to try it. Rather different, then, from the imperative so beloved of writers of war film dialogue: *Halt*!*! Stehenbleiben!*

HALTEN v. 'to halt'; but also 'to hold' (*Kurs halten auf Helgoland*, to hold course for Helgoland; a knot, etc., which holds fast, *hält*), also in the sense that one might hold certain truths to be self-evident (always in the combination *halten für*); or else 'to keep' (*Abstand halten!* keep your distance – see TACHOMETER below, also MASS in II).

Thus, *Halten verboten* means no stopping, but *halten Sie sich rechts* keep to the right. Motorists turning right should not forget that pedestrians and cyclists crossing the road you are entering have a green light at the same time as you – and the right of way.

Note the odd use of the present participle: *ein haltender Wagen**, like *ein parkendes Auto* but unlike 'a stopping car', is already stationary.

HARSCH n.m. & adj. rarely used of harsh words or harsh treatment (*Churchill, der harscheste Kritiker Chamberlains – Die Zeit*, 23 September 1988), but rather to describe ice-encrusted or frozen snow (*der Harschschnee*; *der Schnee harscht/ist harsch/ist verharscht*). The harsh winters (*die harten Winter*) and harsh weather conditions (*das rauhe Wetter, das rauhe Klima*) which produce it are more familiar to skiers in Scotland than in the Alps, where *der Firn* (granulated icy snow) still provides good skiing for several weeks in spring ('*die Firnwochen*').

HEIL n.n., adj. & interj. the main sense of the adjective – hale, unscathed, intact – is reflected in a wide range of compounds signifying **either 1**) health: *ein Heilpraktiker* uses *Heilkräuter* and *Heilpflanzen*, herbs and plants, as alternative medicines; *Whisky nur zu Heilzwecken*, for medicinal purposes only; **or 2**) salvation: *der Heiland*, Saviour; *der Heilige*, saint; *die Heilsarmee*, Salvation Army.

As a greeting or salutation (though not in the Hail Mary – *das Ave Maria* – which starts with the words: *Gegrüßt seist du, Maria*), several combinations are still historically resonant. Had the customs official Alois Schicklgruber not arranged for belated legitimation* in 1877 (when he was almost forty) through his foster father, one Hüttler, things might have turned out differently: as has often been remarked, *Heil Schicklgruber!* just hasn't got the same ring. But *Sieg Heil!* ('hail victory', or in Cassell's German Dictionary's innocent, not to say culpably naive, pre-war rendering, 'hurrah!') is clearly still infected, perhaps less so the Kaiser's favourite anthem *Heil dir im Siegerkranz* ('Hail to thee in victor's laurels'). Even the simple *Heil* – quite a common greeting among fellow students and close friends in the 1960s and one far removed from being an expression of revisionist Nazi leanings – could still cause a certain frisson reflecting this loss of linguistic innocence, even though it merely echoes the hearty *Ski Heil!* (good skiing!) with which skiiers greet each other, or hunters' *Weidmannsheil!* (when enquiring if their companions have had any luck: *kann man Weidmannsheil wünschen?*)

HOSPIZ n.n. not primarily a hospice for the long-term or terminally ill (though *die Hospizbewegung*, hospice movement, was recently founded on the English model), but either **1.** (like *die Herberge*) a refuge for travellers, such as those traditionally rescued by *Bernhardiner*, revived by their brandy flasks, and offered hospitality (*Gastfreundschaft*) by the monks of the *Hospiz am Großen Sankt Bernhard*; or else **2.** a hostel for foreigners, funded and run by the Protestant church: *ein Hospizhotel* is the equivalent of the YMCA. The main such Catholic institution is *das Kolpinghaus*. Neither institution can cope with the recent waves of *Asylanten** from eastern Europe and the Balkans. See also HOSPITANT in IV and KRANKENHAUS below.

HOSTESS n.f. a flexible job description: the woman at the information desk, a guide at exhibitions or trade fairs, a travel courier, and what most people call an air hostess (also *die Stewardeß*), as well as a nightclub hostess, and (euphemistically) a prostitute. But the hostess at a private party or reception is *die Gastgeberin* (or *die Hausherrin*, or *die Dame des Hauses*, 'the lady of the house').

HUB n.m. not the hub of a wheel (*die Radnabe*), but the piston stroke of an engine; hence *der Hubraum*, cubic capacity; *der Hubschrauber*, helicopter.

HURTIG adj. has long since lost all connection with 'hurt' – *ein Wespenstich tut weh*, a wasp sting hurts; I hurt my arm, *ich habe mir den Arm verletzt*; but surely a little drink won't hurt, *aber ein kleines Gläschen kann doch wohl nicht schaden*; hurt/pain is *der Schmerz.*
Hurtig, instead, means quick or nimble (see also DEFTIG in V). Thus, a review in the *Frankfurter Allgemeine* on 10 April 1995 of Botho Strauss's play *Das Gleichgewicht* (*Equilibrium*) describes the actors nimbly dancing their way through his palatial linguistic edifice: *hurtig tanzen die Schauspieler durch den pompösen* Sprachpalast des Botho Strauß*, the possibility of them losing their balance adding a distinctive thrill (*ein aparter* Kitzel*) to the proceedings.

INSPEKTION n.f. most sorts of inspection, but especially having one's car serviced, *das Auto zur Inspektion bringen.*

IRRITIEREN v. 'to distract', seldom 'to irritate' (*jemanden ärgern, jemandem auf die Nerven gehen, jemandem lästig sein*). This can be confusing, even to Germans, especially since something off-putting might also get on one's nerves (*Musiker werden durch Digitaluhren irritiert; die Photographen* irritierten John MacEnroe*).
Other nuances of *irritieren* are to puzzle, to disconcert, or to disorientate. Reviewing a recent production of *Der zerbrochene Krug* which dwelt on the characters' mutual bafflement, one critic wrote: *Eva wird die im tiefsten irritierte Schwester Penthesileas, Alkmenes und Käthchens*, meaning that she was shown to suffer from the same profound existential confusion as Kleist's other heroines (*Kleist Jahrbuch*, 1991, p. 87; see also FALL in II). *Der irritierte Bürger** is a study of the ways in which the middle classes are becoming 'unsettled' in the novels of Fontane and Raabe, while those who call Kafka's stories *irritierend* mean only that they are enigmatic. Even further removed from irritation was the characteristic response of an East German returning from his first Mediterranean holiday: *da war ich völlig irritiert von der ganzen Bläue*, 'I was completely overwhelmed by all that blue'.
This is the original, physiological sense of *irritieren/die Irritation* – to stimulate/stimulation. *Goethe irritierte das Unheimliche, das Flamme und Rauch zum Leben brachte* is Wolfgang Koeppen's description (in *Nach Russland und anderswohin*, 1958) of the way Goethe's imagination was fired by the eerie effects of torchlight and smoke during his visit to the Vatican art collection – these were *optische Irritationen angenehmster Art*, optical stimuli of the most pleasant kind.

KANAL n.m. either **1.** – a canal, such as *der Rhein-Main-Donau-Kanal*, the canal linking the rivers Rhine, Main and Danube, and thus the North Sea with the Black Sea, begun under Charlemagne in 801 AD and now nearing completion. The Kiel Canal is known in Germany as the *Nordostseekanal*, having had to shed, for obvious reasons, its original name of *Kaiser-Wilhelm-Kanal*; or **2.** a water channel (the English Channel is *der Ärmelkanal*), ditch, drain, or sewer. *Die Kanalisation* is most likely to refer to the sewerage system (it also means canalization) and *ein Kanalarbeiter* is specifically a sewerage worker. Drawing on these meanings, *den Kanal vollhaben* is a fairly vulgar way of saying one is canned, one has had a bellyful (see BLAU in VIII); or **3.** a TV channel, radio channel.

KARTE n.f. includes most kinds of card (a pack of playing cards is *ein Kartenspiel**; cardboard *der Karton**), ticket, voucher, coupon, invitation, etc.; but also a map or chart; or the menu (in full, *die Speisekarte*; the wine list is *die Weinkarte*). One way of describing a *Rückfahrkarte*, return ticket, is *Hin und zurück?* (literally 'there and back?'). This is the question which catches out the escapees in the film *The Colditz Story* – they only wanted singles, *einfache Karten*.

KATARRH n.m. synonymous with a cold (*der Schnupfen*), rather than specific symptoms such as a blocked or runny nose (*mir ist die Nase verstopft*; *mir läuft die Nase*). Similarly: *Rachenkatarrh*, pharyngitis; *Darmkatarrh*, enteritis; *Magenkatarrh*, gastritis.

KERBE n.f. not the kerb/US curb (*die Bordkante*, *der Bordstein*, *der Randstein*), but a groove or notch. *Kerben* is 'to carve' ('to curb' is *zügeln*). A German might put someone graphically in his place by threatening to 'iron out the cleft in his arse': *ihm die Kerbe aus dem Arsch bügeln*.

KICKER n.m. any footballer: *die Stuttgarter Kicker* did not choose their name to reflect a particularly robust style of play, and *Norman Hunter kickte für Leeds United* means only that he was a Leeds United player. One who kicks his opponent's shins rather than the ball *tritt dem Gegner gegen das Schienbein* or *haut auf den Gegner ein. Foul!* Table football is also known as *Kicker*.

It may seem rather odd that while *der Torschütze* is the player who has scored a goal (*der Schütze* is a marksman, as in *Der Freischütz* – see under FREI in X), the verb *schützen* means 'to defend'; in football, though, defenders *verteidigen das Tor*.

KLAPS n.m. a gentle slap or smack (for clapping, *Beifall klatschen*, see KLAPPEN in X), but *einen Klaps haben* is to have a screw loose (to be fit for *die Klapsmühle*, the nut house or loony bin), and 'the clap' is *der Tripper**.

KLIMATISIEREN v. what *eine Klimaanlage* (air-conditioning) does. To acclimatize oneself to a place is *sich akklimatisieren.*

KOFFER n.m. not a coffer (*die Truhe*; the 'national coffers' are *der Staatssäckel*), but a suitcase. *Der Kofferraum* is the boot/US trunk of a car, or its luggage capacity.

KOLONNE n.f. not a pillar such as Nelson's Column (*eine Säule*), but a column of numbers/figures; or a gang of outdoor workers (*eine Arbeitskolonne*); or a detachment of troops (*eine Rettungskolonne*, rescue party); or a military convoy – still a fairly frequent sight on German autobahns despite the gradual departure of '*unsere amerikanischen/britischen/sowjetischen Freunde*'. *Achtung Kolonne!* on the back of a jeep warns of more military vehicles ahead, but with gaps for overtaking; *ein Kolonnenspringer*, however, creates his own gaps in a queue of slow-moving traffic (also *eine Kolonne*) by forcing his way in.

KOMMA n.n. Germans (like the French and Italians) use the comma where we use a decimal point – they will tell you, for instance, that the permissible alcohol level when driving is *nullkommaacht Promille*, which they write as 0,8; similarly, *DM 15,95* is 15 marks 95 pfennigs – but where we use a comma in large numbers, they use a point or simply leave a gap above 10,000 (thus: 5 617 500 or 5.617.500; 10 000 or 10.000; but 9999, etc.). See also NULL in II.

KONTROLLIEREN v. the main sense is to check/inspect/monitor/supervise (*Paßkontrolle*, passport control; *Zollkontrolle*, customs), rather than to have control/mastery/power over something – a distinction which also holds for *die Kontrolle* (the most common exceptions being *außer Kontrolle geraten*, to get out of control, and *unter Kontrolle halten*, to keep under control). *Ein Kontrolleur* is primarily a ticket inspector. For the nuances of controlling a machine (*steuern*, *bedienen*, *regeln*), or air-traffic (the province of a *Fluglotse*), or oneself (*sich beherrschen*), see dictionary.

KONVENIENZ n.f. a dated term meaning what is decent, appropriate, socially acceptable (*die Schicklichkeit*), as well as what is convenient (*die Bequemlichkeit*). It is, however, still possible to speak of a *Konvenienzehe*, marriage of convenience. A 'public convenience' is *eine öffentliche Toilette* (indicated by the sign 00).

KRANKENHAUS n.n. a general hospital – no connection with cranks (*Spinner**), a lunatic asylum (*eine Irrenanstalt*), or psychiatric treatment (*psychiatrische Behandlung*, for a mental illness, *eine Geisteskrankheit**). According to Karl Kraus in *Nachts* (1918): *die Psychoanalyse ist jene Geisteskrankheit, für deren Therapie sie sich hält,* 'psychoanalysis is the mental illness for which it thinks itself to be the cure'.

The word *Hospital* is found in proper names, such as *Sankt-Johannes-Hospital*, and occasionally signifies what we call a hospice (*ein Hospiz** is something different again) – except in Austria and Switzerland, where the abbreviated form *das Spital* is synonymous with *Krankenhaus. Eine Klinik* is either a private hospital or a specialized clinic (the one which featured in the popular TV soap *Schwarzwaldklinik*, Black Forest Clinic, was more like a hotel), or else a teaching hospital (*Universitätsklinik*), but see also *Poliklinik* (outpatients' department) under AMBULANZ above.

KRANKENKASSE n.f. often abbreviated to *Kasse**, is a national or private health-insurance scheme. The sign *Alle Kassen* denotes a general practitioner, *ein praktischer Arzt* or *Hausarzt*, who will treat people from all insurance schemes, or refer them to the appropriate *Facharzt* (specialist). UK nationals intending to visit Germany should obtain an EIII form entitling them to free medical and dental treatment under mutual agreements between EC countries. Except in emergencies, if you need to see a doctor or a dentist, you should first go to the *Allgemeine Ortskrankenkasse* or *AOK* (local health office) to be issued with a *Krankenschein* (medical voucher). Take prescriptions to an *Apotheke**, not a *Drogerie**.

KUR n.f. 'cure' in the sense of a remedy is more commonly *das Heilmittel*, a course of remedial treatment *das Heilverfahren*, and recovery *die Heilung. Eine Kur* is primarily a health cure at a *Kurort* – one of the many small spa towns scattered throughout Germany, where the *Kurgast* 'takes the waters' in the morning (see BAD above) and whatever else is prescribed by the many *Kliniken* (each as specialized as the *Kurort* itself), before settling down to coffee and cakes and a *Kurkonzert*, strolling along the *Kurpromenade* to the assembly rooms of the *Kurhaus*, a flutter in the *Kursaal* casino, or an amorous rendezvous in the *Kurpark* (one's *Kurschatten* may still 'cast a shadow' when spouses are reunited after the usual four weeks).

Nowadays, most, if not all, of the costs are borne by private or corporate insurance schemes (see KRANKENKASSE above), *um für den Arbeitsprozeß zu regenerieren*, as one brochure puts it – that is to say, for the important objective of getting people back to work. This is reminiscent of Tolstoy's Levin who wanted 'to enrich medicine with a new word: *Arbeitskur*' (*Anna Karenina*, vol. 1, New York, 1939, p. 309); consequently, 'the cure' is not only what a youthful Katherine Mansfield observed during her stay at a Bavarian *Kurort*: 'something the Germans do when they're too fat to work' (*In a German Pension**,

1911). Like Brighton or Bognor, the *Kurort* was once a place to see and be seen: Goethe bowed to the Empress Maria Ludovica at Bad Teplitz in 1812 while Beethoven, famously, strode on. In spite of such associations (Franz-Joseph and Bad Ischl, Bismarck and Bad Ems), the connection of a *Kurfürst* with a *Kurort* is not linguistic: the word derives from the obsolescent verb *küren* (to elect) and means an Elector in the Holy Roman Empire – one such being the ruler of *die Kurpfalz* (the Electoral Palatinate).

LINIEN- in cpds. indicates a regular service (bus, ship, train, tram, etc.): *ein Linienflug* is a scheduled flight, as distinct from *ein Charterflug*. Otherwise, *eine Linie* is a line, such as *die Linie Hamburg-Bremen*, the Hamburg-Bremen line; or a bus/tram route: *fahren Sie mit der Linie 5*, take a number 5. In a political context, someone who is *linientreu* tows the party line.

LOS n.n. **either** fate or lot in life (*ein bitteres Los, ein leichtes Los*) – the fated role of Weimar, for instance, dwarfing its 3,000 inhabitants: *O Weimar! dir fiel ein besonder Los! / Wie Bethlehem in Juda, klein und groß* (Goethe, *Auf Miedings Tod*) – see KLASSIK in IV, RAT in I; **or else** a lottery ticket. *Ein Klassenlos* has nothing to do with Marx's *klassenlose Gesellschaft* (classless society – *los* here meaning '-less', 'free of', 'loose'), but is one of various categories (*Klassen*) of ticket for the popular *Klassenlotterie*. The draw in *Lotto* * is made on television from a *Lostrommel* (a mnemonic for old Desert Rats?). *Losen* is to draw lots, to lose is *verlieren*.

LOTTO n.n. the children's game, also the national lottery. *Das Große Los* * *ziehen* means to win the first prize (*der Hauptgewinn*), if not necessarily the *Jackpot* (now a German word since the draw has been televised). The football pools are known as *Toto*, but there is no equivalent to bingo. Ludo is fittingly called *Mensch-ärgere-dich-nicht* (don't get angry).

MEILE n.f. an English mile (= 1.609 km), but also the internationally recognized nautical mile of 1.852 km (the approximate linear equivalent of one minute of latitude).

Still used figuratively (*meilenweit verfehlen*, to miss by a mile; *meilenweit entfernt*, miles away), occasionally also in its former, un-English, sense of a league (4.8 km). 'The Charge of the Light Brigade' sounds more like a canter in German: *Eine halbe Meil', eine halbe Meil', eine halbe Meile weiter*. More authentically German are *Siebenmeilenstiefel*, seven-league boots, while *eine preußische Meile*, at 7.532 km, is getting on for an Irish mile. Since *der Meiler* is a charcoal kiln, and now also an atomic pile (*Atommeiler*), that specialist in anglophone athletics, the miler, is circumscribed as *ein Läufer im Meilenrennen.*

MITTELKLASSE n.f. indicates middle quality or mid-range rather than middle-class. The middle classes are *das Bürgertum** or *der Mittelstand**; Wahrig's dictionary now omits the sociological sense of *Mittelklasse* altogether (as in *die gehobene Mittelklasse/die gehobene Mittelschicht,* the bourgeoisie).

Die Mittelklassen are the middle forms in school (see PRIMA in IV); *ein Mittelklassewagen* is a medium-sized, medium-priced family saloon; and when the *Hamburger Abendblatt* (19 April 1991) predicted *die ersten Mittelklassehotels* in the new eastern *Länder*,* it was not envisaging the re-emergence of class distinctions but rather of what used to be known as family hotels in England (and which are still common and affordable in western Germany). In the 1994 *Which?* guide to hotels, a medium-quality double room costs on average £80 in the UK, £48 in Germany; a basic room is £50 in the UK, £30 in Germany – prices which mean German hotels are close to full most of the time with ordinary travellers as well as businessmen, whereas the UK's low-occupancy hotels depend on 60 per cent conference and business trade.

MURMELN v. to mumble or mutter (*etwas vor sich hinmurmeln*) as well as the somewhat more polite 'to murmur'. Also to play marbles (*die Murmeln*). Somebody who has lost his marbles *hat den Verstand verloren.*

NECESSAIRE n.n. as in French, a vanity bag, toilet bag, manicure set, cosmetics pouch, etc. – here, at least, the requisites of civilization and culture appear to coincide (see KULTUR in II) since *ein Kulturbeutel/eine Kulturtasche* fulfils the same function.

NERVÖS adj. *das macht mich ganz nervös* may mean 'that makes me quite nervous' (fearful, *ängstlich**), but the more likely sense is jumpy, twitchy, jittery, on edge. Similarly, *nerven* means 'to get on one's nerves' or (usually of a child) 'to pester'. When *Die Zeit* on 24 February 1989 described Ernst Nolte as *einen sichtlich genervten Hochschullehrer,* it meant that the historian who had sparked off the *Historikerstreit* (see SOGENANNT in II) was visibly *unnerved* by the resulting furore.

NOT n.f. neediness; affliction; trouble; necessity; but in compounds often means 'emergency': *im Notfall**, in an emergency – *Notruf* o, ring o (not 999); *der Notausgang* is the emergency exit. *Nothung* ('Needful') is the sword which Siegmund has been promised should he find himself *in höchster Not* (in dire distress) – it is one of Wagner's favourite words. In fact, few poets can resist it: *Beschütze mich in aller Not, / Mach meine Eltern noch nicht tot* ('Keep me safe from fear and dread and please don't make my parents dead' – Joachim Ringelnatz (1883–1934), *Drittes Kindergebetchen*). See also NOTSTAND in II, but for musical notes NOTE in IV.

OLDTIMER n.m. primarily a machine – a veteran car (vintage car: *ein Vorkriegsmodell* or *Vintage-Car*), classic steam engine, or old plane/crate – rather than characters like Walter Huston in *The Treasure of the Sierra Madre* (see SENIOREN in I). Most English cars in Germany, especially the lovingly restored MGS and Jaguars, probably fall into this category.

ORDINATION n.f. besides the ecclesiastical sense, also a doctor's consultation hours (*Sprechstunden*), or in Austria the surgery itself.

PACKEN v. **1.** to pack (*das Gepäck*, luggage); but also **2.** to grab (*an der Kehle packen*, to seize by the throat). Many figurative usages include: *packen wir's!* let's go; *packt euch!* skedaddle, clear off; *wir packen's gerade noch*, we can just about make it; *von Entsetzen gepackt*, terrified; *ein packender Film*, an enthralling film; *hast du die Prüfung gepackt?* did you manage to get throught the exam?; *jetzt hat er's endlich gepackt*, he's got the hang of it at last. See also PAKET in III, and *Pack* under LUMPEN in V.

PARTIE n.f. not a party. A political party is *eine Partei*; a birthday party *eine Party* or *ein Fest**; a party of soldiers *ein Trupp* or *ein Kommando**; a party of tourists, etc., *eine Gruppe*. Only in the phrase *da bin ich mit von der Partie* (count me in, I'm game, I'm with you) does the word suggest a party of people – except in Austria, where *eine Partie* is also a gang of labourers and *der Partieführer* their foreman (in Germany, *der Vorarbeiter*).

Otherwise, *eine Partie* is either **1.** a part or section of the whole (*die 'Fränkische Schweiz' gehört zu den reizvollsten Partien Bayerns*, 'Franconian Switzerland' is one of the most charming parts of Bavaria); or **2.** a musical part or theatrical role (*die Partie des Lohengrin hat Paul Frey berühmt gemacht*, Paul Frey made his name singing Lohengrin); or **3.** the playing of a game (*die Partie endete unentschieden*, the game ended in a draw; an adjourned *Schachpartie* or chess game is called *eine Hängepartie* – no connection with *ein Lynchmob*); or **4.** a good catch, if not necessarily a good match; *eine gute Partie machen* is thus to marry 'well' (or into money) – Vikram Seth's novel *A Suitable Boy* (1994) is known in Germany as *Eine gute Partie*; or **5.** in commerce, a batch or consignment – though *Partiewaren* are specifically sub-standard goods, discontinued lines, or 'seconds' sold cheap; in printing, *Partiestücke* or *Partieexemplare** are the extra free copies added to a *Partie*.

PATT adj. or adv. stalemate in chess (*die Partie* endete patt*), but also a feature of coalition politics, when proportional representation leads to *ein politisches Patt*. Someone who always has an answer pat *hat immer eine Antwort parat*; to know the rules off pat: *die Regeln in- und auswendig kennen*, or *aus dem Effeff kennen*.

PEINLICH adj. painful only in the sense of painfully embarrassing, awkward (though often synonymous with 'capital' in the old, legal sense whereby *peinliche Befragung*, for instance, was interrogation under torture). If your arm hurts, tell the doctor: *mein Arm tut mir weh* or *ich habe Schmerzen im Arm*. Only if you have forgotten your EIII form or cannot pay in cash (see KRANKENKASSE above) will you say *wie peinlich!*, for *die Pein* is already one stage removed from physical pain: *die Schmerzen machten ihr das Leben zur Pein*, pain made her life a misery, one long torment. *Mir gäb' es keine größ're Pein, / Wär ich im Paradies allein* (Goethe, *Sprüche in Reimen*).

PENSION n.f. either **1.** the pension civil servants (*Beamte**) enjoy when they retire (*ein Pensionär* – in Austria, *Pensionist* – *geht in Pension*) in place of a normal *Rente**; or **2.** a guest-house (which is not a *Gasthaus**); or **3.** 'board' – either *Halbpension* (breakfast with either lunch or dinner) or *Vollpension* (full board); for bed and breakfast only, see GARNI in VIII. What was once known as *ein Pensionat* (boarding school) is now generally called *ein Internat* (see GYMNASIUM and KONVIKT in IV). Figuratively, in defence of more robust manners: *ein Fußballverein ist kein Mädchenpensionat!* A football club is not a finishing school.

PFLASTER n.n. not what a plasterer (*der Gipser, der Stukkateur*) puts on houses (*der Putz*), or a surgeon on broken legs (*der Gips*), but a sticking plaster, or else the surface of a road. *Ein Pflasterer* is thus a road worker, either one who works the enormous machines which lay, and eventually resurface, the high-cost, long-life, good-value motorways with asphalt (Hitler's old concrete autobahns in eastern Germany are next in line to be *neu gepflastert*); or else one who lays *Pflastersteine*. These are either *Steinplatten* (paving stones), or *Kopfsteinpflaster* (cobbles) in town centres that are being *saniert** (restored). Figuratively, an expensive (high-rent) city – like Munich, Stuttgart or Hamburg – is called *ein teures Pflaster*. Note also: *sie hat ihm eine gepflastert*, she socked him one, but for getting plastered, see KANAL above and BLAU in VIII.

PLANE n.f. not an aeroplane (*das Flugzeug*) or a planetree (*die Platane*) but a tarpaulin, such as is used, for instance, to cover a lorry's load. Brecht's Mother Courage draws a *Planwagen* (covered wagon) during the Thirty Years' War – like those of the American pioneers who crossed the Great Plains (a plain is *eine Ebene*, though it is also one meaning of *Plan* which survives in the phrase *auf dem Plan erscheinen*, to arrive on the scene. Otherwise *der Plan*, as in English, means a street-map, blueprint, timetable.)

Note also the distinction between *die Planung* (planning – *Stadtplanung*, town planning) and *die Planierung* (levelling off), as when *Die Zeit* on 31 March 1989 reported *Pläne* (plans) for the demolition of a nuclear power station and the subsequent *Planierung des Geländes* (flattening of the site by bulldozers – *Planierraupen*). To plane wood is *hobeln*.

PLUMP adj. physically awkward (*plumpe Bewegungen*, clumsy movements; *ein plumper Gang*, ungainly walk), rather than plump. A plump child or girl is *pummelig*, a plump woman *mollig* or *rundlich*. Falstaff imagines himself – in the standard Schlegel/Tieck translation – *ein wackrer stattlicher Mann, in der That, und wohlbeleibt* ('a goodly, portly man, i' faith, and corpulent'), but the simple *dick** still renders the final pathos best: *den dicken Hans verbannen, heißt alle Welt verbannen* ('Banish plump Jack, and banish all the world' – *Henry IV Part I*, II,iv). See also FETT above and FEIST in VI.

Figuratively, *plump* means unrefined, uncouth. To insist on translating *corriger la fortune* as *betrügen* (to cheat) is the sign of '*ein plump Sprak*' (a barbarous language) according to Riccaut de la Marlinière, Lessing's memorable portrait of a French soldier of fortune and gambler in his comedy, *Minna von Barnhelm* (see JUNGFRAU in VI). Falstaff's humour may not strike us today as noticeably *plump* (crudely obvious, unsubtle), but along with his *plump vertrauliche Art** (embarrassingly overfamiliar manner) and *plumpe Anbiederungsversuche* (clumsy attempts to ingratiate himself) it contributes to his banishment. Little wonder that Friedrich Wilhelm Plumpe, director of the classic film *Nosferatu* (1922) and something of a dandy, changed his name to that of the picturesque Bavarian village beloved of the *Blauer Reiter* school of painters: Murnau.

POLITESSE n.f. far from meaning courtesy, is the official designation for a female traffic warden. Motorists with a smattering of French have been heard to sigh: *toujours la politesse*.

PRANGEN v. not to 'prang' a car or aeroplane (*ramponieren*; in a car, this is *ein Bums**, in a plane *eine Bruchlandung*), but to be resplendent (*in voller Schönheit prangen*) or to boast (*mit etwas prangen*). But *jemanden an den Pranger stellen* or *jemanden anprangern* means to pillory someone (*der Pranger*, pillory or stocks).

PROSPEKT n.m. an advertising prospectus/leaflet/brochure. A back-drop in the theatre and an historical print showing the elongated panorama of a landscape, town, town square, avenue, etc., are also called *ein Prospekt*, but 'where every prospect pleases', the Prospect of Whitby, or the prospect of a job are all *die Aussicht*. For the equivalent of Nevsky Prospekt, see ALLEE above.

PSYCHISCH adj. as a medical term means psychic as distinct from physical (*eine psychische Störung*, a psychic disorder), and in common parlance mental (*psychische Leiden*, mental suffering) or psychological (*psychisch überbelastet sein* or *psychisch unter großem Druck stehen*, to be under great psychological strain). *Psychoterror* is an extreme form of emotional blackmail. 'To be psychic', however, is *übersinnlich* or *spiritistisch veranlagt sein*.

QUEUE n.n. or n.m. curiously, the Germans have adopted only one sense of this French word – that of a billiard cue. To stand in a queue is *Schlange stehen*, though in spite of an otherwise highly developed *Sinn* für Ordnung* (exemplified by patient waiting for the 'green man' at road crossings) the practice is less common than in Britain. But so too are *Autoschlangen* (literally 'car snakes'), partly because German holidays are sensibly staggered *Land* by Land*.

RAGE n.f. rage, fury (*in Rage geraten*, to get worked up; *jemanden in Rage bringen*, to infuriate somebody), though something done *in der Rage* is merely a consequence of being rushed or flustered: *in der Rage habe ich meinen Regenschirm vergessen* (I was in such a state I forgot my umbrella). *La rage* also means rabies in French, but for this German combines *die Wut* (the more common word for rage) with *toll* (meaning crazy or wild – see TOLLHAUS below): *Tollwut*. When walking in woods/forests, one might come across warning signs such as *Tollwutbezirk!*

To rage is *wüten*, *toben* or *rasen*, but not *ragen*, an unconnected verb meaning to tower, loom, rise up (also figuratively – *eine hervorragende Leistung* is an outstanding performance; *von überragender Bedeutung*, of paramount importance).

RASCH adj. or adv. the old, in Schiller's view, may criticize, *wenn sich die rasche Jugend kühn vergißt* ('when rash youth boldly forgets itself'). In the main, however, *rasch* does not mean rash or overhasty (*voreilig*, *überstürzt*, *unbesonnen*), but simply prompt, speedy, quick: *ein rascher Entschluß*, a quick decision; *in rascher Folge*, in quick sequence; *ein bißchen rasch, bitte!* (make it snappy – see also DALLI in

I). The aged Goethe told his secretary and diarist Johann Peter Eckermann with some justice, if a trifle smugly, that he would be a difficult act to follow: *So rasch macht mir das keiner nach.*

RESTLOS adj. or adv., **RASTLOS** adj. the restless activity which secures Faust's salvation is *rastlos*. Goethe thought of his own early years as being *ohne Rast und Ruh*, while Carlyle's favourite motto from Goethe was *Ohne Hast, aber ohne Rast*, 'Without haste, but without rest' (the Latin *festina lente* is translated into German as *Eile mit Weile*). But *Rast' ich, so rost' ich* ('To rest is to rust') is a maxim which does not apply when driving, so stop for a rest, *eine Ruhepause*, at a *Raststätte*.

Rest in the sense of what remains is *der Rest*. For Hamlet, *der Rest ist Schweigen* ('the rest is silence'), and when *seine irdischen Reste* (his mortal remains) are borne off, we suppose that his father, too, will cease to be *ein rastloser Geist** and find his rest. *Samstag ist Restetag* means Saturday is the day we eat all the leftovers; if completely satisfied, one is *restlos befriedigt*. Also: *der Rest ist für Sie*, keep the change; *seine Schulden restlos begleichen*, to pay off all one's debts.

REZEPT n.n. the medical prescription you take to an *Apotheke**; also a figurative cure or remedy such as *ein Rezept gegen die Langeweile* (against boredom); or else a recipe. In a hotel, *die Rezeption* or *der Empfang* is the reception, and the receipt you receive after payment *eine Quittung**.

RINGEN v. to wrestle, not to ring. Participants in the sport (named after the *Ring* in which it takes place) are thus *Ringer* (or *Catcher**, or *Schwinger**), but *ein regelrechter Ringkampf* – as when boys *miteinander ringen* – is one which dispenses with the rules. *Man klingelt an der Tür* or simply *man klingelt* (rings the doorbell), *man ruft seine Frau an* (rings one's wife), and on Sundays *man läutet die Kirchenglocken*, though for all its fine churches the art of change ringing (*Wechselläuten*) is virtually unknown in Germany.

ROLLER n.m. a motor scooter or a child's scooter. The roller used to make a lawn or a road level is *eine Walze*, and what German women wear only *beim Friseur* are *Lockenwickler*. Roller-skates are *Rollschuhe*, ice-skates *Schlittschuhe*, but Germans use the English words for roller-blades and skateboards.

ROWDY n.m. more often someone who indulges in wanton violence or destruction than mere rowdy behaviour – widely applied in the wake of visiting English football supporters (*Schlachtenbummler*, away fans 'going into battle') to all sorts of vandals or hooligans, even to roadhogs (*Verkehrsrowdys, Straßenrowdys*).

RÜDE adj. rude, but also coarse-mannered (*rüde Burschen*, rough types), or physically rough (*ein rüdes Foul* is a bad tackle in football – see ROBINSONADE in X). *Der Rüde* is a male dog/fox/wolf, or else a hunting dog.

SANITÄT n.f. in Switzerland the military medical corps, in Austria the medical service in general, and, colloquially, an ambulance (*das Sanitätsauto, der Rettungswagen*). Standard German uses such derivatives from the original *Sanität* meaning health as *der Sanitäter* (paramedic, first-aid attendant, medical orderly, ambulance man) and *sanitär* (*ein Haus sanitär ausstatten*, to install sanitation). The narrower English sense of sanity (*mens sana*) is usually rendered in German by the words Kant used for reason – at its highest metaphysical level *die Vernunft*, as mere empirical understanding or intelligence *der Verstand* – reminding us of his conviction that insanity (*der Wahnsinn, die Geisteskrankheit*) is first and foremost a form of irrationality, and that all men are autonomous human beings who would prefer prison to hospital. German law does, of course, recognize that men are either *zurechnungsfähig* (of sound mind, *compos mentis*) or *unzurechnungsfähig*. See also SANIEREN in III, and for public sanitation, KANAL above.

SCHLIMM adj. not slim (*schlank*; a slimming diet is *eine Schlankheitskur**), but one of the three main words for bad: *schlimm, schlecht* or *übel*. *Ich habe einen schlimmen* (never *schlechten*) *Finger* means 'I have a sore finger', or *schlimme Mandeln* (inflamed tonsils), or *eine schlimme Wunde* (a nasty or infected wound). But 'I don't feel well' or 'I feel sick' is *mir geht's schlecht, mir ist übel*.

SCHNAPPEN v. 'to snap' (closed) in most contexts except photography, where the verb is *knipsen* (though a snapshot is indeed *ein Schnappschuß*), and when snapping one's fingers (*schnippen, schnalzen*). *Er hat mir meine Brieftasche weggeschnappt* (he snatched my wallet); *er wurde bald von der Polizei geschnappt* (he was soon caught by the police). Also the origin of schnapps, *der Schnaps*, which you throw back in one gulp in accordance with the motto: *erst nippen**, *dann kippen** (alternatively, in the north, *nicht schnacken, Kopf im Nacken*). The card game 'snap' is *Schnipp-Schnapp* ('snip, snip' – the sound of scissors), but snappy play is *flott* or *zackig*. See also KLAPPEN in X.

SCHÜTTEL- in cpds. shudder, not shuttle, so that *ein Schüttelbecher* is a cocktail shaker, *der Schüttelfrost* a fit of the shivers, and *der Schüttelreim* a couplet in which the consonants of the rhyming syllables are amusingly transposed, for instance: *ich wünsche, daß mein Hünengrab ich später mal im Grünen hab'* ('when I die, I want to be buried like a hero, out in the country'), or *es soll der Mosel Sonnenwein uns Inbegriff der Wonnen sein* ('wine from the sunny Moselle shall be for us the epitome of bliss'). But the shuttle of a loom is *das Schiffchen*, a shuttlecock *ein Federball*, commuter traffic as well as a shuttle service *der Pendelverkehr* (people *pendeln;* goods *werden hin- und hertransportiert*), and a space shuttle *ein Raumtransporter* (although 'space shuttle', or simply, 'shuttle' is almost a naturalized German word now).

SCHWESTER n.f. all female nurses are *Krankenschwestern*, addressed as *Schwester*, while a male nurse is a *Krankenpfleger*. The ward sister is *die Stationsschwester** and the senior* nursing officer or matron *die Oberschwester* (or *Oberin*, though this also means Mother Superior). Also a sister company (see FILIALE in III).

SCHWINGER n.m. in Switzerland, a wrestler; *ein Schwingfest** is a kind of wrestling gala. The Swiss in particular are not noted 'swingers': though *schwingen* also means to swing, even to vibrate, the attitudes of '*die swinging sixties*' are best designated *locker* or *flott*, rather than *schwingend* (*das Tanzbein schwingen*, 'to shake a leg', hardly catches the mood). See also SCHWUNG in X, and for taking a swing at the ball, AUSHOLEN above.

SEE n.f. & n.m. *der See* is a lake, *die See* (or *das Meer*) the sea. Goethe wrote *Auf dem See* in a boat on Lake Zürich (*Aug, mein Aug, was sinkst du nieder? / Goldne Träume, kommt ihr wieder?*), but crossing to Palermo, the only occasion on which he was *auf der See*, or simply *auf See*, he was sea-sick.

SEEHUND n.m. a seal. A 'sea dog' is *ein alter Matrose* or *ein Seebär*, and *eine Seekatze* a catfish.

SKATING n.n. (pronounced as in English) is not skating, but skate-boarding. Ice-skating is *das Schlittschuhlaufen* (world champions in figure skating, *Weltmeister** im Eiskunstlauf*), roller-skating *Rollschuhlaufen*. Something different again is *skaten*: to play the traditional, three-handed card-game *Skat* (the most popular card game in Germany), usually after work at one's local *Stammlokal*, where *Skatbrüder* or *Skater* meet on their *Skatabend* for a *Skatpartie** or *Skatrunde*.

SPEDITION n.f. an abbreviation of *die Expedition* in its second sense of 'expediting' goods, 'speeding' them on their way. Also the firm which undertakes such transportation, or else a firm's own dispatch department (but see *Dispatcher** above). *Ein Spediteur* is thus a carrier, haulage contractor, furniture remover, shipping agent.

SPLITT n.m. loose stone chippings (*Rollsplitt*, as on a resurfaced road), or else grit (when it turns icy). On such occasions, Germans leave a sensible* gap between their car and the vehicle in front: even if the windscreen is *splitterfrei** (shatterproof), the bodywork is still vulnerable. *Ein Splitter* is a fragment or splinter (the *Splitter im deines Bruders Auge* as distinct from the *Balken* in one's own – *Ev. Matthäus* 7.3); hence also *Splitterpartei* or *Splittergruppe*, a political splinter party or group (see FRAKTION in II), and *splitternackt* or *splitter-fasernackt* meaning 'stark* naked' – though nobody quite knows why.

SPORTWAGEN n.m. a sports car, but also a child's push-chair or baby-buggy.

SPRINGEN v. either **1.** a multi-purpose verb meaning to jump, leap, vault, skip, hop, bounce, pounce, dive, (and regionally also) run. The act itself is *der Sprung* (the springs in a mattress or a car are *die Federn* – 'feathers' – or *die Federung*), and the performer *der Springer* (as is the knight in chess – the other *Steine** being *König, Dame, Turm, Läufer* and *Bauer**). Or else **2.** used when a violin string snaps (*eine Violinsaite springt*) or china cracks (*die Tasse hat einen Sprung*). Note also: *es ist nur ein Sprung*, it's only a stone's throw; *der springende Punkt*, the crucial point; *so dürfen Sie nicht mit den Menschen umspringen*, you can't push people around like that (a stronger form of *umgehen*, to handle).

SPRIT n.m. the colloquial term for petrol (*Benzin*) or diesel (*Diesel*), like 'gas' or 'juice'. Formerly an alcoholic spirit such as *Weingeist** (Latin *spiritus*, French *l'esprit de vin*), still used in the plural, *Spirituosen*. An inscription in the Wiesbaden *Ratskeller: Was man beim Baufach* nötigst haben muß: / Der Maurer Schnaps, der Meister* Spiritus* implies that the master builder needs something more refined than mere schnapps.

SPUR n.f. when Robinson Crusoe finds *die Spur eines Menschen im Sande*, this is not a spur (*der Sporn*; plural *die Sporen*), but a spoor, sign, track, clue (hence, *die Spuren verwischen*, to cover one's tracks; *die Leute von der Spurensicherung*, the forensic people). *Von Kultur* keine Spur!* is a sentiment modern-day Robinsons* attach not to savagery, but to the philistinism and vulgarity they hope to leave behind. *In der Spur bleiben!* means to follow in the lead skier's tracks off piste, and even more vitally, to stay in lane on the autobahn, in the *Kriechspur* (crawler lane) if necessary, and in the *Überholspur* for overtaking only. The car which appears in your rear-view mirror one moment may be *spurlos verschwunden* (disappeared without trace) ahead the next.

STAR n.m. either **1.** as in film star or pop star (*mit Starallüren**, *Stargage**); or **2.** a starling; or **3.** an eye disease – *der graue Star* (cataract), *der grüne Star* (glaucoma or 'white-eye'), *der schwarze Star* (amaurosis). Sirius is *ein Stern.*

STARK adj. not stark, but strong (also big or, euphemistically, stout), with numerous figurative uses as an intensifier. *Das ist stark* or *das ist ein starkes Stück!* is a reproof (that's a bit thick) – the opposite of what the young mean when they say *das ist echt stark* or *ich finde den Typ* irre stark* (great, fantastic). This is *ein krasser Gegensatz* (a stark contrast), whereas a stark landscape is *kahl*, stark colouring *grell*, stark staring mad *total verrückt*, stark naked *splitternackt**, etc. *Die Stärke*, meaning either strength or starch, points to the common ancestry of both words (stark=stiff=strong).

STATION n.f., **STATIONÄR** adj. a railway station or bus station is now *ein Bahnhof*, though the station-master is still known as *der Stationsvorsteher*, the stops as *Stationen*, and the terminus as *die Endstation* (the destination of *A Streetcar named Desire* is also the play's German title: *Endstation Sehnsucht*). Both literal and figurative phases or stages on life's way are also *Stationen* or *Stadien*, including the occasional *freie Station* (free board and lodgings). Since the second sense is a hospital ward, *stationäre Behandlung* means in-patient treatment, as distinct from *ambulante* Behandlung*. Otherwise *stationär* is contrasted with *mobil* only in formal, mainly scientific contexts; a stationary car is *ein parkendes* or *haltendes* Auto*, stationary traffic *steht still* or *bewegt sich nicht*.

STRASSE n.f. a street, of course (*Verkauf über die Straße*, take-away; and as a metonym, *die Herrschaft der Straße*, mob-rule); but also any road; or straits (*die Straße von Dover/Gibralter*); or a production line (*eine Fertigungsstraße*).

STREIFE n.f. not 'strife' (*die Zwietracht*), but a police patrol – any association is fortuitous. *Ein Polizist auf Streife* is a policeman on the beat; *im Streifenwagen*, in a patrol car.

STRESS n.m. when Germans say *ich bin sehr im Streß*, *ich bin gestreßt* or *das streßt mich* – which they are quite fond of doing – they generally mean only that they feel harassed by the hectic daily grind (*der Alltagsstreß*), not that they are literally in need of a *Kur**. Even less concerned with mere passive endurance was the period known to us as 'Storm and Stress', which takes its name from Friedrich M. Klinger's drama *Sturm und Drang* (1777) and its *Temperament** from music such as Haydn's Symphony No 49, '*La Passione*' (1768). The angry young men of the 1770s did indeed lay great stress on living life to the full (Klinger became a Russian general), though this is not *der Streß*, but *der Nachdruck, das Hauptgewicht, der Akzent* or *die Betonung.* This should be stressed, *das muß man betonen.* (The stress in a poetic line is *der Ton**, a stressed syllable *eine Tonsilbe* or *eine Hebung.*)

TABLETT n.n. a tray. The tablet you swallow is *eine Tablette* or *eine Pille.*

TACHOMETER n.m. or n.n. speedometer, not tachometer (*der Drehzahlmesser*). *Mindestabstand ist mindestens halber Tacho* means that if you are driving at 160km/h, you should keep a minimum distance of 80m between you and the vehicle in front. Instead of the patrol cars which cause such panicked braking on British motorways, video cameras record *Drängler* (those who drive too close to the car in front) as well as those who exceed the speed limit (*die Geschwindigkeitsgrenze, das Tempolimit**). Most drivers assume they might be prosecuted for even a slight transgression on urban roads, but may risk driving up to 20km/h faster than the occasional limit on the autobahn (the reason for which, such as a steep incline or narrow lanes, is transparently obvious); very few ignore limits entirely. *Alle Verkehrssünder* werden in Flensburg registriert* (a record of all traffic offenders is kept in Flensburg, in the *Verkehrszentralkartei* or *Verkehrszentralregister*).

TEAMLEADER n.m. not a team or group leader (*der Gruppenführer*), but what the Austrians and Swiss call the team at the head of the table, the league leader (German: *der Tabellenführer*).

TEMPO n.n. not only musical tempo, but speed/pace in general. Calls for a *Tempolimit* on the autobahn are as regularly countered by the powerful lobby of German car manufacturers and by the most influential *Bürgerinitiative** of all, German car owners, with their ironical, last-ditch slogan – *freie* Fahrt* für freie Bürger** – demanding 'freeways for free citizens' ('free' also in the sense of toll-free – see VIGNETTE below) or 'an open road for an open society'. *Das Arbeitstempo*, the rate of work in industry, has been another novelty for those who once built Wartburgs and Trabants*: *ein bißchen Tempo bitte!* (get a move on! – see also DALLI in I).

TICK n.m. more commonly used of a quirk than of a nervous twitch (*ein nervöses Zucken**). Thus, *er hat einen Autotick*, he's got a thing about cars (see also SPLEEN in V). But *er hat einen gewaltigen Tick* or *er tickt nicht ganz richtig* (he's a bit crazy) took its meaning from the ticking of a clock. For buying 'on tick', see PUMP in III.

TOLLHAUS n.n. not a tollhouse (on Swiss and some Austrian motorways *das Mauthaus*, signalled simply as *Maut*), but an old word for *eine Irrenanstalt*, lunatic asylum. This is now only used figuratively (*hier geht's wie im Tollhaus zu*, it's like a madhouse here), as is the adjective *toll*, which basically means mad, rabid (hence *die Tollwut*, rabies – see RAGE above), silly or daft, but is nowadays used in such expressions as: *es ging toll her* (there were wild goings on), *das war ein tolles Ding* (that was a crazy stunt), *er fährt wie toll* (he drives like a maniac). Above all, *toll* belongs with *prima*, *super*, *genial**, *Klasse* and *Spitze* as a ubiquitous expression of approval or admiration ('great', 'fantastic', US 'swell').

TOR n.n. not a tor, but a gate such as the *Brandenburger Tor*, also a gate in slalom skiing, or a goal (in football, etc.). Hence, *ein Felsentor* is not a rock tor (*ein felsiger Hügel, ein schroffer Fels*), but a gateway in the rock – an arch or gap, such as the place where Tell ambushes Geßler (though the famous soliloquy in Act IV, Scene 3 of Schiller's play (1804) uses a different expression: *Durch diese hohle Gasse muß er kommen* – see ALLEE above). *Der Tor* is a fool.

TOUR n.f. trip, outing, excursion, as well as a longer tour – hence, *eine Tour machen* may mean no more than to go for a walk/drive/ride/hike/climb. Indeed, before tourism (*der Fremdenverkehr*) became widespread, *ein Tourist* was generally someone who climbed mountains, *und wenn er auf hohe Berge stieg, war er ein Hochtourist* ('and if he climbed high mountains, then he was a high altitude tourist' – Friedrich Torberg, *Die Tante Jolesch*, 1977, p. 80). Nowadays, *auf Hochtouren* signifies at full speed, flat out, also raging mad – from *Tour* meaning the revolution of an engine: *der Tourenzähler*, rev counter (not to be confused with a *Tageskilometerzähler*, trip counter); *auf Touren kommen*, to get into top gear, also to get worked up; *er redet in einer Tour*, he talks incessantly. A third meaning of *Tour* is ploy: *krumme Touren*, sharp practices; *komm mir nur nicht auf die schmeichlerische Tour!* flattery will get you nowhere.

A tour of Germany is *eine Deutschlandreise*; of Munich, *eine Rundfahrt durch München*; of Heidelberg castle, *ein Rundgang durch das Heidelberger Schloß* (if guided, *eine Schloßführung**). Popstars, orchestras, football teams, etc. *gehen auf Tournee*, but the cricket tourists are *die Besuchermannschaft*.

TRAINER n.m. in team sports, especially football, the manager (assisted by *der Coach* – though with usage in both languages changing fast, the coach/*Coach* may now be the manager); otherwise *der Trainer* is a horse trainer, tennis coach, etc. Nowadays also a tracksuit (*der Trainingsanzug*), but the trainers you wear on your feet

(*Trainingsschuhe, Turnschuhe**) are not abbreviated. The verb *train-ieren* can also mean to practise some specific skill, such as one's golf swing, *seinen Schlag im Golf trainieren.*

TRAMPEN v. to hitch-hike. *Tramper* are tolerated at service stations on the autobahns, and – if they use their discretion – at the end of the slip-road (*die Auffahrt*) furthest from the autobahn itself. It is probably helpful not to look like a tramp – this is *ein Land-streicher* or *Tramp* (vagabond) in the countryside, *ein Stadtstreicher* or *Penner* (down-and-out, hobo) in town; for further nuances, as when the tramp is a lady, see SALOPP in VI. *Fahrendes Volk* (all kinds of 'travelling people') are again more in evidence since 1989; one also occasionally encounters true gentlemen of the road *auf Wander-schaft**, keeping alive the journeyman tradition in their often flam-boyantly traditional gear (see MEISTER and MANCHESTER in III).

But hitch-hiking has largely been replaced by agencies for arrang-ing lifts. Through their local *Mitfahrzentrale* drivers find potential passengers, who pay a small commission and – at the driver's discre-tion – a third or less of the petrol costs for their *Mitfahrgelegenheit*, an additional attraction being automatic insurance cover. A comparable centre for finding accommodation is called *eine Mitwohnzentrale.*

TRIBÜNE n.f. a speaker's rostrum (*Rednertribüne*), or raised stand* for spectators (*Haupttribüne*, grandstand). A tribune of the people like Coriolanus, Wagner's Rienzi or Tony Benn is *ein Volks-tribun.*

TRIMMEN v. most familiar in the injunction *trimm-dich!* (keep fit), either by *Trimmtrab* (jogging, also *das Joggen*) along a *Trimm-Pfad* (keep-fit trail) or by using a *Trimmgerät* (keep-fit apparatus), all aimed at making oneself – as Wahrig puts it in a key phrase – *körperlich leistungsfähig* (see KUR above). Used non-reflexively: to trim a ship, or a poodle, train a pet or a child (*auf Ordnung trimmen*), 'soup up' an engine (cf. TUNING below), or alter something's appear-ance (*ein auf rustikal getrimmtes Restaurant*, done up in the rustic style).

TRIPPER n.m. gonorrhoea. Derived from 'drip' rather than 'trip' (a day tripper is *ein Tagesausflügler*), but see also KLAPS and TOUR above.

TUNING n.n. *ein Tuner* 'soups up' the engine (to 'tune' it in the sense of adjusting the carburettor is *einstellen*), but also restyles the bodywork. Though the words are English, it is the German car industry which has sensibly* learnt to incorporate aspects of *die gestylten Modelle* developed by *Tuningfirmen.*

TÜV n.m. the '*TÜV*' (an abbreviation of *Technischer Überwachungs-verein*) is responsible for the technical supervision of everything from cars to nuclear power stations. All vehicles must display a current *TÜV-Plakette* (MOT disc) on the numberplate.

ÜBERHOLEN v. to overtake (*rechts überholen ist verboten*, no overtaking on the inside) as well as to overhaul (*der Motor ist neu überholt worden*), but *überholt* used adjectivally means obsolete, passé, antiquated (*das sind völlig überholte Anschauungen*, totally out-dated views).

UNTERARM n.m. forearm rather than underarm. An exception is *Unterarmhaare*, the hair in one's armpit (*die Achselhöhle*). To serve underarm in tennis is *von unten aufschlagen*; overarm, *über Kopf.*

UNTERLIEGEN v. to lose a game: *Borussia Dortmund unterlag dem HSV* (*mit*) *0:2*, but not 'to underlie': *dem Spiel der Kölner lag kein Konzept* zugrunde* (the Cologne team's game had no underlying strategy). Also to be subject or liable to: *es unterliegt keinem Zweifel, daß...*, it's not open to any doubt that...; *starken Schwankungen* unterliegen*, to be subject to violent fluctuations.

VIGNETTE n.f. not a character sketch (*eine Skizze, eine kurze und prägnante Darstellung*), but the wispy tendrils of *Jugendstil* decoration, or else a template used by photographers – from which is derived the more recent meaning of a tax disc (as in French). On 7 August 1987, the *Süddeutsche Zeitung* conveyed German dismay at *die angedrohte Autobahnvignette* which the Belgians were threatening to impose on foreigners using their motorways, and a reader's letter on 19 August 1989 complained that, in Switzerland, not only the autobahns but other main roads, too, were liable: *auch Autostraßen seien vignettenpflichtig*. The paper proposed: *daß in ganz Europa das straßenräuberische Mautwesen unterbunden wird* (that road tolls should be abolished throughout Europe as a form of highway robbery). Periodic attempts to limit the number of cars using German autobahns by charging a toll have been fiercely resisted, but on 1 January 1995 *Vignetten* came into operation for foreign lorries. See TEMPO and CAR INSURANCE above.

VISITATION n.f. a formal visit by ecclesiastical or academic authorities, but *eine Leibesvisitation* is the sort of body search to which suspect smugglers are subjected. For visitations by plagues of locusts, etc., see HEIMSUCHEN in IX.

VISITE n.f. not any kind of visit (*der Besuch*), but specifically the doctor's rounds in a hospital (see CHEF in III), or a private house call (*ein Hausarzt* is either a GP/family doctor or a 'houseman'/resident intern in a hospital).

VITAL adj. as with *die Vitalität*, used primarily of people who are (still) vigorous, energetic, full of life (*ein vitaler alter Herr*, a sprightly old gentleman), though also of a person's vital needs (*vitale Bedürfnisse*), or a country's vital interests (*vitale Interessen* – see EVENTUELL in II). Otherwise, vital is usually rendered as *unerläßlich*, *lebenswichtig* or *unbedingt notwendig* (but for vital statistics, see MASS in II).

WAGEN n.m. a car (*Personenwagen*) – *ein offener Wagen* or *Kabriolett/Kabrio* is a convertible – with many further combinations also abbreviated to *Wagen*, such as *Eisenbahnwagen* (railway carriage; *der Waggon* is a goods wagon), *Straßenbahnwagen* (tramcar), *Lieferwagen* (van), *Kinderwagen* (pram), *Einkaufswagen* (shopping trolley), even *Schreibmaschinenwagen* (typewriter carriage). And, of course, a wagon such as the green gypsy caravan which epitomizes bohemianism for Thomas Mann's Tonio Kröger (*Wir sind doch keine Zigeuner im grünen Wagen*), or the covered *Planwagen**of Brecht's Mutter Courage; an agricultural wagon is *ein Fuhrwerk* – which distinguishes it from the farmer's BMW or Mercedes (see DICK above). *Der Große Wagen* is something different again: the constellation of the Plough or the Big Dipper.

WANDERN v. a serious business in Germany, though also, of course, *des Müllers Lust** ('the miller's joy' – and Wilhelm Müller's own, no doubt, whose poems Schubert set in *Die schöne Müllerin*). But the traditional wanderlust evoked by the Vienna Boys' Choir (see MUTATION in IV) in its rendering of *Mein Vater war ein Wandersmann* tends to have a goal. To convey a sense of aimless wandering, one needs to add a *ziellos*, or else use the word *umherirren*, or *bummeln* for an extended *Stadtbummel* taking in a café or *Kneipe* or two as well as window-shopping. Indeed, *Bummelei* is seen by some as mere dawdling, idling, or loafing: *ein Bummelzug* (slow train), like *Three Men on the Bummel* (see KISSEN in VI), may have an itinerary, but it is not a very pressing one. On a school *Wandertag*, however, there is an organized hike or ramble. German students were once obliged to follow their professor from university to university, just as successful apprentices embarked as journeymen on their *Wanderjahre*, and the *Völkerwanderungen* across Europe were doubtless as purposeful as the movements of migratory birds – or their namesakes who took to the hills *en masse* in the 1910s and between the wars in the *Wandervogel* movement, prototypes of today's *Wandervereine*, ramblers' associations.

WARTEN v. to wait (*der Warteraum, der Wartesaal,* waiting room; *die Wartehalle,* departure lounge), but note the additional meaning: to service a car (*das Auto zur Wartung bringen*) or maintain a machine (*wartungsfrei,* maintenance-free). Hence *der Wärter,* meaning warder, keeper, attendant, guard, and *der Wart* which now appears mainly in combinations such as *Hauswart* (caretaker), *Torwart* (goal-keeper), *Tankwart* (petrol pump attendant). An example of German schoolboy humour: *der Kellner heißt auf englisch* 'waiter', *weil man so lange auf ihn warten muß.*

WATT n.n. besides the unit of electrical power, means mud-flats, especially the *Wattenmeer* separating the Frisian Islands from the north German coast, across which it is possible to wade (*waten*) at low tide (the key to Erskine Childers's thriller *The Riddle of the Sands* – see FLEET above). As the north coast of Germany is known by the *plattdeutsch* term *Waterkant,* the scandal surrounding the suicide (if it was that) of Schleswig-Holstein's prime minister, Uwe Barschel, in 1988 quickly came to be known as *Waterkantgate.*

WETTER n.m. while *das Wetter* is the weather, *der Wetter* is a gambler (from *wetten,* to bet). *Schlagende Wetter,* however, are not disappointed gamblers who have gone berserk, but an outbreak of explosive gases in a mine.

Simply add *Wett-* to signify a *Wettkampf* or *Wettbewerb* (competition): *Wettsingen* (singing competition), *Wettschießen* (shooting contest), *Wettschwimmen* (swimming race), even *Wettrüsten* (arms race). Nor is *wettmachen* what a bed-wetter (*ein Bettnässer*) does, but means to make up for something (*den Verlust wettmachen,* make good a loss).

WIMPER n.f. eyelash; *ohne mit der Wimper zu zucken*,* without batting an eyelid. The whimpering of a child is *das Wimmern,* of a dog *das Winseln.*

ZUCKEN v. not to suck (*lutschen*), but to twitch (see TICK above).

ZUCKER n.m. sugar (*die Zuckerwatte,* candy floss), but also an abbreviation of *Zuckerkrankheit,* diabetes.

FOOD
and
DRINK

ESSEN
und
TRINKEN

VIII

AROMA n.n. aroma (more commonly, *der Duft*) but also flavour/ flavouring, as in ice cream. For smelling and tasting, see TASTEN in I, PROBE in X, DEGUSTATION, KOST, RIECHEN below.

BACKEN v. to bake, though also to fry – pancakes, doughnuts, fish, etc. – usually in deep fat (*Backfett*). *Sie bäckt gern* (she likes baking) is unambiguous, as is *ein Konditor backt Kuchen* (a pastry-cook makes cakes) or *frisch gebackene Brötchen vom Bäcker* (fresh crusty rolls from the baker's). But the Austrian *Backhendl* is deep-fried chicken in breadcrumbs (a speciality of the Wienerwald '*Backhendlstationen**') as distinct from *Brathendl* (German *Brathuhn* or *Brathähnchen*) which is oven-roasted on a spit. Confusingly, *braten* too can mean to bake or fry as well as to roast (for roast potatoes, see also RÖSTI below). *Bratwurst** (sausage fried on a hot plate) is as much a standby in Germany as the *Fish and Chips* most Germans associate with England (baked beans also remain *Baked Beans*, but are not readily available in German supermarkets). The German for fried fish would be *gebackener Fisch* or *Backfisch*, but remember that a German *Backfisch* is also an inexperienced teenage girl (fusing the Latin word for a freshman student, *baccalaureus*, with a young and tender fish – English 'flapper' – as in the old adage suggesting the age when a girl was ready for marriage: *Vierzehn Jahr und sieben Wochen / ist der Backfisch ausgekrochen*). If in doubt, ask if something has been cooked *im Ofen* mit Fett* (roasted), *im Ofen ohne Fett* (baked), *am Spieß* (grilled* on a spit), *in der Pfanne* (fried), *paniert** (bread-crumbed) or *natur** (without breadcrumbs).

Backerbsen (not 'baked peas' but small round noodles added to soup, known in more elongated form as *Nockerln*, in Swabia as *Spätzle*) are another Austrian speciality. What the Germans call *feine Backwaren* – pastries (*Gebäck*) and biscuits (*Kekse*, not *Biskuit**) – are known in Austria as *Bäckerei*, which is also the shop in which they are made and sold. Germans call an oven *ein Backofen*, sometimes (usually in restaurants) *eine Backröhre*; Austrians call it *ein Backrohr*.

Backstein is brick (literally: baked stone) – the traditional building material in the north of Germany. The Nikolaikirche in Wismar is one outstanding example of the heights to which Hanseatic *Back-steingotik* soars – Gothic architecture built in red brick.

Note that something home-made is *hausgemacht*, not *hausbacken**.

BAISER n.n. meringue, as in the Viennese speciality *Eisbaiser mit Schlagobers**(ice-cream topped with meringue and whipped cream) – from French *baiser* in its more innocent sense, though the French themselves make no connection between their *meringue* and (French) kissing. Also known as *der Schaumkuß* ('frothy kiss'; *ein Negerkuß* is a chocolate marshmallow) as well as *die Meringue* (pronounced 'may ringa').

BALLASTSTOFFE n.m.p. roughage: the essential components of a balanced diet rather than worthless stuff constituting ballast (*der Ballast*; see also STOFF in IX and LAST in III).

BAR n.f. not an ordinary pub. This is *eine Kneipe, ein Lokal*, eine Wirtschaft** or (especially in the country) *ein Wirtshaus*, and if food is also available, *eine Gaststätte* or *ein Gasthaus**. 'My local' is *meine Stammkneipe*; regulars may sit at their own *Stammtisch**, which it is tactful to respect (there is sometimes a sign on the table). *Eine Bar*, on the other hand, is a more intimate, or pretentious, establishment, sometimes a sort of nightclub (*Nachtlokal*) where you might drink cocktails, usually pay more, and sit directly at the raised bar, *an der Bar*. Alternatively, the low life beckons in *ein Bumslokal*, eine Kaschemme* or *eine Spelunke*, all of which are 'dives'. Note also the unconnected *Bargeld* (cash), as in the question *Zahlen Sie bar oder per/mit Scheck?*

BEDECKEN v. not 'to bedeck' in the sense of to decorate or ornament (*schmücken*), but simply 'to cover'. *Man deckt den Tisch* (lays the table), but *man bedeckt den Tisch mit einem Tuch* (covers the table with a cloth). The young Goethe's defiant, rather than tragic, reading of the Prometheus myth begins: *Bedecke deinen Himmel, Zeus, / Mit Wolkendunst!*

BEEFSTEAK n.n. *deutsches Beefsteak* is usually a meatball, sometimes topped by a fried egg, while *Beefsteak* (relatively) pure and simple is what goes into a beefburger or hamburger. (Since *ein Hamburger* is primarily a citizen of Hamburg, Germans tend to pronounce the now ubiquitous fast-food inspired by their city in the American way). Proper beefsteak is *das Steak*, but so, too, is *argentinisches Beefsteak* or *schottisches Beefsteak*, though *ein Steaklet* is, once again, merely a fried mince patty. A German *Metzger* puts meat through his fearsome-sounding *Fleischwolf* to produce *Hackfleisch* or *Gehacktes* (*Hackepeter* in Berlin, though in southern Germany this is seasoned raw meat loaf); an Austrian *Fleischhauer** calls his best mince *Faschiertes*, while Swiss *Geschnetzeltes* is beef cut into thin strips (fried with onions in butter or oil).

BEKOMMEN v. not to become (*werden*), but to get, receive, obtain, etc. – *ein Kind bekommen*, for instance, is to be pregnant or to have a child, not to become one, and the saying of Franz Josef Strauß recalled by the *Süddeutsche Zeitung* in its obituary on 4 October 1988: *er habe oft recht gehabt, aber selten recht bekommen*, means that he was often right but seldom got credit for it. In *Goodbye to All That* (1929), Robert Graves recalls a touching exchange between the trenches: 'You little dog ran over to us and we keep it safe; it became no food with you so it run to us'. The German soldier was probably thinking of how he would say in his own language *es bekam bei Euch nichts zu fressen* (you gave it nothing to eat). Thus, *ich bekomme Hunger* (I'm getting hungry), or, when ordering food or drink, *ich bekomme eine Gulaschsuppe* or *ich bekomme noch ein Bier*.

Only in the sense that *Mourning Becomes Electra* (German title: *Trauer muß Elektra tragen*) does *bekommen* occasionally mean to suit, befit, agree with – again mainly in the context of food and drink, as when proposing the toast* *wohl bekomm's!* or complaining *das Essen bekommt mir nicht*, that it does not agree with me, or that it is *keine leicht bekömmliche Kost**, not easily digestible. But when Cecily Cardew says 'I look quite plain after my German lesson . . . it isn't at all a becoming language', this is best rendered as *die deutsche Sprache ist keine vorteilhafte Sprache* – Wilde himself proposed to take up German in Reading Gaol, 'the proper place for such a study'.

BIER n.n. not a bier (*die Bahre*), but beer. The Bavarian *Reinheitsgebot* (purity regulation) of 1542 was adopted by the rest of Germany in 1906 (though any Bavarian will tell you that acceptance of their 'Real Ale' standards was their price for agreeing to join a united Germany in the first place). It decrees that beer should contain nothing but hops, malted barley, yeast and water (*Hopfen, Gerste, Hefe, Wasser*). This clearly distinguishes it from most English beers since 1880, when Gladstone permitted brewers to use starch sources other than malt to bring the price of beer down. A sophisticated *Bierkultur** will probably ensure that the EC directive insisting that beer with chemical additives can be sold under the name of *Bier* will remain a dead letter. Resistance to foreign imports found some sympathy in a judgement of the *Europäischer Gerichtshof* (*EuGH* for short – the German exclamation of disgust, however, is *igitt!*) which on 12 March 1987 recognized *die auf der Welt einzigartige Bierlandschaft Bayerns* (Bavaria's unique beer culture).

Yet Dortmund produces even more than Munich of the 150-odd litres of beer drunk annually by each German (*Urgroßmütter und Säuglinge statistisch eingeschlossen*, statistics include old grannies and babes in arms) – a world record. The people of Munich (see MASS

below) drink *Weißbier*, which is a light beer made with top-fermen-
tation yeast, as is *Weizenbier*, a 'breakfast beer' with a somewhat
tangy wheat and malt taste traditionally accompanied by *Weißwurst**,
coddled veal sausages. *Berliner Weiße* is also light and effervescent,
with a *Schuß* of raspberry juice added (or woodruff syrup which turns
it green); in *Düsseldorf* they drink *Alt* (a top-fermented dark beer), in
Cologne *Kölsch*, and there are some 4,000 other local varieties. Until
quite recently, most German beer drinkers ordered *ein Helles* (pale
ale) or *ein Dunkles* (brown ale), and the slightly more expensive *Pils*
only on special occasions – and when they did not mind waiting the
seven minutes or more for it to be fastidiously drawn, *gezapft*. This
again distinguishes *Pils* (the method originated in Pilsen) from our
lager (a word derived from German *Lagerung* – cold conditioning
during fermentation – though Germans use *Lager** only in the sense
of a store or camp).

   'Is it not possible,' Jerome K. Jerome wondered, 'that these placid,
gentle folk may in reality be angels, come down to earth for the sake
of a glass of beer, which, as they must know, can only in Germany be
obtained worth the drinking.' The last chapter of *Three Men on the
Bummel* (1896; see also under KORPORATION in IV and KISSEN in
VI) is a sustained homage to this 'amiable, unselfish, kindly people
. . . the best people perhaps in the world'.

BISKUIT n.n. as in biscuit ware ('twice-fired', unglazed pottery or
porcelain) but not a biscuit/US cookie, which is *ein Keks** or *ein
Plätzchen*, while Germans might describe a US biscuit/English scone
as *ein brötchenartiges Buttergebäck*. German *Biskuit* or *Biskuitteig*,
however, resembles English 'sponge' in such combinations as *Biskuit-
rolle/Biskuitroulade* (Swiss role) or *Löffelbiskuit* (sponge finger) – a
sponge mixture made of eggs, flour and sugar, but without the fat
which is added to make the base of a flan (*der Tortenboden**). See also
SANDKUCHEN below.

   Like a biscuit, *der Zwieback* has been 'twice-baked', but is in fact a
rusk such as children eat when poorly.

BLAU adj. *au bleu*: a characteristically German way of preparing
freshly caught fish. In *Forelle blau*, the trout is placed in a pan of
boiling fish-stock (water, wine, onions, thyme, bayleaves, parsley,
peppercorns, salt), taken from the heat and left for five minutes (the
traditional Christmas Eve dish of carp, *Karpfen blau*, simmers a little
longer). 'Blue' derives from the distinctive shimmer the fish acquires
when boiling tarragon or wine vinegar is poured over it and it is left
in a draught for ten minutes before cooking. But see also CORDON
BLEU below.

Colloquially, *blau* also means tipsy, sloshed – presumably the source of *einen blauen Montag machen* (to skip work on a Monday). In his *Germania*, Tacitus seems to have been impressed that the Germans discussed all important decisions twice, once drunk and once sober (or as the old maxim has it: *Bedacht im Rat*, bedacht im Wein, / Wird euer Spruch ein weiser sein*).

BLENDEN v. not to blend ingredients in the kitchen (*mixen*, in a *Mixer* or *Mixgerät*, or by hand, *einrühren*), or types of tea (*mischen*, to produce *eine Teemischung*) or whisky (*mischen*, to produce *ein Blend* or *ein Blended*), but to dazzle or blind. Hence, *eine Blende* is a sun blind or visor, or in photography an aperture, filter, or 'fade' (TV). *Das war eine blendende Rede*, that was a brilliant speech; *ihm geht es blendend*, he's in the pink; but Chaucer would have recognized the 'envye that blendith the hert of man' as *ein Blendwerk des Teufels*, a deception of the devil.

BLOND adj. *ein Blondes* or *kühles Blondes* is another word for a glass of beer (see BIER above), sometimes jocularly called *blondes Gift** ('blond poison') though this is primarily 'a blond bombshell*'. For Kant's views on *Blonde*, see SUBLIM in V.

BLUTIG adj. synonymous with *englisch** when ordering steak, that is to say, rare. Used figuratively: *ein blutiger Anfänger* is a complete beginner, not a bloody beginner (*ein verdammter Anfänger*). *Das ist mein blutiger Ernst*, I'm deadly serious.

BOCKBIER n.n. a strong dark beer, traditionally drunk with *Bockwurst* in Bavaria to celebrate Corpus Christi (*Fronleichnam*) ten days after Pentecost. When German brewers tried to introduce it to the suspicious French before the Franco-Prussian War they served it in wine glasses, and it is this measure, rather than the beer itself, which the French call *un bock* – a quaint eccentricity in the eyes of visiting Bavarians accustomed to drink beer by the litre or *Maß**.

Ein Bocksbeutel, by contrast, is a distinctively round, flattened bottle – named after its alleged resemblance to a ram's scrotum – which contains good *Frankenwein*, wine from Franconia, especially the Würzburg region.

Though a *Stein** is also a measure, *ein Steinbock* has no connection with beer, but is an ibex, and in astrology, Capricorn.

BROILER n.m. the East German word for a *Brathendl* or *Brathähnchen* (roast chicken: see BACKEN above), known there colloquially as a *Gummiadler* (rubber eagle) and served in *Hähnchen-Grillrestaurants* with names like *Zum Goldbroiler*.

BROT n.n. bread in general, a loaf of bread (varieties galore of *Weißbrot, Schwarzbrot, Graubrot*), a slice of bread (with butter: *ein Butterbrot*), or a sandwich, usually open (*ein belegtes Brot, ein Käsebrot, ein Wurstbrot*). South Germans call their tea-break, as well as a mid-morning or mid-afternoon snack, *Brotzeit* (see also VESPER below), but their breakfast rolls *Semmeln* (or *Wecken/Weckerln*) rather than *Brötchen*, while in Berlin rolls are known as *Schrippen*. Not long after reunification and the influx of all things western, East Germans rediscovered (along with *Eberswalder Wurst*, Rotkäppchen Sekt*, Cabinet* and *Club* cigarettes) the charms of their own *Ost-Schrippen*, which are heavier than western *Luftbrötchen* and only half the price.

For *Pumpernickel*, see PUMP in III.

BÜFETT (also **BUFFET** or **BÜFFET**) n.n. still means a sideboard (also *die Anrichte*, and since the Germans discovered English antique shops, *das Sideboard*), as well as a counter or bar, a buffet meal (*kaltes Büfett*), or a station buffet (see also RESTAURATION below), but not the buffet or buffet car on a train (*der Speisewagen*).

BULETTE n.f. a meat ball or rissole (especially in Berlin with its Huguenot tradition), also known as *die Frikadelle, der Fleischkloß* or *der Klops* (note that *Königsberger Klopse* are boiled not fried).

BÜRGERLICH adj. the sign *gutbürgerliche Küche*, like its French counterpart *cuisine bourgeoise*, advertises good, homely cooking, almost invariably prepared by a professionally trained German *Bürger** to a consistently high standard. The burger you eat has no umlaut, so a *Spießbürger**, for instance, has no connection with a *Spießbraten* (joint roasted on a spit) or *Schaschlik am Spieß* (kebab). Several cities have given their name to the local *Wurst** or sausage – *Frankfurter, Wiener, Nürnberger, Braunschweiger* – but *ein Kasseler* is a lightly smoked pork loin chop much like English gammon, *ein Berliner** a doughnut, and the connotations of *Hamburger* are discussed under BEEFSTEAK above.

BUTTERBOHNEN n.f.p. not the large, white and very filling variety once served with school dinners in England ('butter beans'), but tender runner beans, lightly boiled and tossed in butter, constituting a separate dish.

CHIPS n.m.p. as in American English, potato crisps. 'French fries' are *Pommes frites*, often abbreviated colloquially to *Fritten* or *Pommes* (to rhyme with 'promise'), and eaten with *Tomatenketchup* (*Pommes rot*) or *Mayonnaise* (*Pommes weiß*); it would be considered eccentric to ask for *Essig*, vinegar. The Belgians may be Europe's true *hommes frites*, but it was German advertisers who invented the cartoon character Fritz Pomm to rehabilitate the homely virtues of the chip.

Since tennis became popular in the 1960s and golf in the 1970s, Germans have also mastered such terms as *ein Chipshot* and *er hat den Ball gechippt*. Computer chips and gambling chips are likewise *Chips*.

CORDON BLEU n.n. a veal schnitzel 'cordon bleu' is breadcrumbed and filled with cheese and ham. This is not 'cordon bleu' cookery, *feine* Küche**, but a staple of *gutbürgerliche* Küche*.

DANKE interj. 'thank you' (when it is generally followed by (*Aber*) *Bitte!* don't mention it), but also 'no, thank you' – the normal, polite way of rejecting a second helping: *Noch eine Portion? – Danke! (es hat sehr gut geschmeckt/es war ausgezeichnet*, it was excellent). To accept, say *Bitte!* or *Ja, bitte!*

DEGUSTATION n.f. (cf. French *dégustation*) – a tasting, especially in Switzerland and especially wine (German *Weinprobe**), though sometimes cheese. Hence *degustieren*, like *kosten**, means to taste or sample – best before buying, since there is no disputing about tastes: *über Geschmack läßt sich nicht streiten (de gustibus non est disputandum)*. It tastes disgusting, *es schmeckt widerlich/ekelhaft*. See also FAUL and KOST below, PROBE in X.

DELIKATESSE n.f. either **1.** a delicacy such as *Delikateßhering* (marinaded herring). Though a shop sign might advertise *Delikatessen*, the shop itself is a *Delikatessengeschäft* or *Feinkostgeschäft**, abbreviated only in East Germany (where the choice of goods on offer was equally abbreviated) to *ein Deli*. When a new store was about to open in East Berlin, *Die Zeit* on 8 July 1988 suggested that the first floor was likely to contain *ein 'Delikat'-Laden für Lebensmittel besserer Qualität* (a delicatessen for fine foods), the second *ein 'Exquisit'-Laden für Kleidung besserer Qualität* (a boutique for luxury clothes), and the third *eine ständige Photoausstellung: Obst und Gemüse* (a permanent photo exhibition of fruit and vegetables); or **2.** delicacy of feeling (though a more likely rendering of *quelle délicatesse* in the traditional story of the widowed Frenchman who wears black underwear to visit his mistress would be *welches Feingefühl!*).

The adjective *delikat* usually refers to delicious food, sometimes to delicate hints, problems or issues, but delicate health is *zart*, delicate tea-cups are *zerbrechlich*, and delicate fabrics *empfindlich* (the setting for 'delicates' on a German washing-machine is *Feinwäsche**.)

DOSE n.f. not a medicinal measure (*die Dosis*), but a can or tin (*eine Blechdose*, never *eine Kanne**) – of canned beer (*Dosenbier*) or tinned food (*Konserven**, *in Dosen*; thus, a *Gemüsekonserve* is a tin of vegetables, while you might find that your supermarket only stocks *Champignons in Dosen* or *als Konserve*). Or else a sugar bowl (*Zuckerdose*), or the condensed milk (*Dosenmilch*) which Germans add to their coffee – and also (*igitt!* ugh!) to their tea; mercifully, *Frischmilch* is available for breakfast cereals. In addition, a jewellery box (*Schmuckdose*), a powder compact (the distinctive additions to Berlin's ruined *Gedächtniskirche* are known familiarly as the *Lippenstift* and *Puderdose*), or an electrical socket (as the pins on a standard two-pin German *Stecher* are slightly further apart than on an English plug, use an *Adapter* to prevent your electric razor or hairdrier getting stuck in the *Steckdose* on the wall).

The plural of both *Dosis* and *Dose* is *Dosen*, so *Pillen in kleinen Dosen* can mean either pills in small boxes or in small doses.

DRINK n.m. usually a mixed drink such as a *Gin-Tonic*, a *Whisky-Soda*, or (as the Germans also say, *last not least*) the *Cocktail* one orders in a *Bar**. Less specific when inviting friends in for a drink, *auf einen Drink einladen*. The normal word is *das Getränk*, and *die Getränkekarte** the wine list or list of beverages.

EIS n.n. ice-cream (*die Eisbombe, bombe glacée*) as well as ice (*der Eiskaffee*, iced coffee; *Eis am Stiel*, ice lolly). The famous *Fürst-Pückler-Eis* (see ENGLISCH in II) is made with whipped cream divided into three vertical portions: one mixed with macaroon biscuits and cherry liqueur, one with strawberry puree, one with grated chocolate and maraschino.

EISBEIN n.n. a North German dish: cured knuckle of pork, boiled and served with *Kartoffelpüree* (mashed potatoes) and *Sauerkraut** (pickled cabbage). No connection with the frozen legs and feet (*Eisbeine*) you get from standing around in the cold, though it *is* derived from the fact that the shin bone of large animals was once used to make ice skates (*Schlittschuhe zum Eislauf*). The Bavarians eat their knuckle of pork or veal roasted, and call it *Schweinshaxe* or *Kalbshaxe* respectively.

EISWEIN n.m. not chilled wine, but a naturally sweet, sticky wine made from grapes which have been exposed to the first frost. The grapes are so shrivelled it takes a whole vine to produce one glass. See ETIKETT, LESE and PRÄDIKAT below.

ENGLISCH adj. when ordering steak: *englisch*, or to be even more emphatic *blutig*, means rare (Germans once thought that the English tended to grill* their meat, leaving it red in the middle); medium-rare is *rosa*; medium is *medium*; well-done is *durchgebraten* or *durch*. If not sufficiently well-done for contemporary English taste, say *dieses Steak ist noch nicht durch* or *dieses Steak ist ja nur halbgar* (only half-cooked). See also ENGLISCH in II and V.

ETIKETT n.n. *die Etikette* dictates that one should arrive punctually in Germany, but *das Etikett* is a price tag or label (except in Austria and Switzerland, where *die Etikette* is used in both senses). *Ein gutes Etikett* thus promises a good wine, whose quality is attested by the label. In Munich's *Badischer Weinkeller* (famous for its traditional *ambience* as much as its extensive selection of wines from Baden and elsewhere), the wine buff can brush up on such *Etikett* definitions as *rassig** (= *herzhafter, lebendiger Wein mit angenehmer Säure*, 'young and lively', pleasantly acidic) or *voll* (= *mit höherem Glycerin-Extrakt und Alkoholgehalt*). It is, of course, illegal to increase the sweetness content by simply adding glycerine (*panschen*, to adulterate), and Austrian wines have still not fully recovered from the 1980s scandal. *Der Etikettenschwindel* – the fraud involved in putting a prestigious label on a bottle of plonk – is virtually unknown in Germany except as a politician's jibe meaning 'mere juggling with words': *das ist reinster Etikettenschwindel.* See also EISWEIN, KABINETT, LESE and PRÄDIKAT in this section.

EXTRA adv. either **1.** extra meaning additional (though this is not the main sense in German): *die Getränke sind extra*, drinks are extra. Figuratively, someone who always wants *eine Extrawurst* (and not just, like Oliver Twist, *eine Extraportion*), wants special treatment: *spiel nicht immer die Extrawurst!* (don't keep playing the prima donna). Similarly, *ein Extrablatt* is either a special edition of a newspaper, or figuratively something out of the ordinary (fittingly, the film maker Rainer Werner Fassbinder was often to be seen in Munich's *Café Extrablatt*).

or **2.** 'separately' – *wollen Sie das Hemd extra nehmen?* would you like the shirt wrapped separately (not 'as well').

or **3.** 'deliberately' (to annoy) – *das hast du extra gemacht*, you did that on purpose; or 'specially' (to please) – *ich habe eine Sachertorte* extra für dich gebacken*, I made a sachertorte just for you.

For the adjective, Germans use *noch* rather than *extra*: we need an extra chair, *wir brauchen noch einen Stuhl*, an extra bottle of champagne, *noch eine Flasche Champagner* (extra dry, *sehr trocken*).

FAUL adj. either **1.** especially when used of food (with the exception of *faule Fische*, which means hollow pretexts or a lame excuse), literally rotten. *Faule Eier* are bad eggs, and Schiller is remembered for putting *faule Äpfel*, rotten apples, in the drawer of his writing-desk (for inspiration, apparently), not on the stage. Putrid flesh, rotting foliage, stale air, offensive odours are all *faul*, but only 'foul' in the sense that we speak of foul water. Hence, *es schmeckt faul*, it tastes off, but *es schmeckt ekelhaft*, it tastes foul;

or **2.** used figuratively, though in the sense of 'suspect' rather than with the force of English 'foul' – *faule Ausrede*, flimsy excuse; *fauler Kunde*, shady customer; *fauler Witz*, crude joke; *fauler Scheck*, dud check. *Etwas ist faul im Staate Dänemark*, 'there's something rotten in the State of Denmark';

or **3.** lazy, idle. As a writer, Goethe was no slouch (*er war nicht schreibfaul*), and his Faust wins redemption by resisting the ultimate sin of sloth (*Werd' ich beruhigt je mich auf ein Faulbett legen. . .*, 'If ever I should recline on a bed of ease. . .', l. 1692). Karl Kraus was playing on meanings 2. and 3. when he wrote on a postcard from Elsinore to a fellow Shakespearean: *Bin etwas faul im Staate Dänemark*. For foul play, see ROBINSONADE and RÜDE in VII.

FEIN adj. *eine Feinbäckerei* (cake shop, patisserie) sells *Feingebäck*, and *ein Feinkostgeschäft* (delicatessen*) *Feinkost**. *Fein* is an invaluable, widely-used word, now less of a social minefield than when dictionaries defined *ein feines Essen* as a dainty or choice meal, but 'at a lower social level' a lavish, slap-up feast or blow-out. It has most of the nuances of 'fine' – *ein feiner Geschmack* is sensitivity in matters of taste, *ein feiner Kerl* is a good chap, while with a hint of irony *ein feiner Herr* (a real gentleman) becomes a well-dressed toff. *Die feinen Leute* also often has a negative slant: *Greif zu, wir sind hier nicht bei feinen Leuten* (Tuck in, we're not in fine company here). Similarly, *sie hat sich fein gemacht* (she's dressed to kill); *dazu ist sie sich zu fein* (that's beneath her); *nicht fein genug für ihren Sohn* (not good enough for her son); *ein piekfeines Internat* (a posh boarding school), and, inevitably (in line with *superklug, supermodern, superleicht*), *superfein*. By way of contrast, German aristocrats (according to *Die Zeit* on 25 August 1989) only use *ein v. mit Punkt, das ganze 'von' ist unfein* ('simply *v.* – it's vulgar to use the full *von*'), the point being that somebody by the name of von Berg would not be an aristocrat.

FEST n.n., adj. & adv. a religious festival (*frohes Weihnachtsfest!* Merry Christmas!), or else a party, reception, celebration, banquet, fête. Glasgow's 'Mayfest' has obvious affinities with Munich's *Oktoberfest* (confusingly held in September), and the word also suggests cultural activities of a more indigenous and popular kind than the official events offered by its Edinburgh rival (Germans come for *das Festival*, and go to Salzburg or Bayreuth or Donaueschingen for *die Festspiele*).

Freshly slaughtered pigs provide the excuse for a *Schlachtfest*, the sort of jolly village feast at trestle tables laid out end to end along the

main street which older Britons might remember from the Corona-
tion (albeit with tea and sandwiches rather than grilled* meat and
beer), while lovers of haggis and other *Delikatessen** might decide
on *Blutwurst* (black pudding) or what restaurants in the countryside
call *eine Schlachtplatte* ('slaughter platter'). Another popular traditional feature of German country life is the *Schützenfest*, reminiscent
of the shooting contests which Robin Hood invariably wins in disguise, and which Max, the hero of the first great Romantic opera,
Weber's *Der Freischütz* (1821), tries to win with the help of *Frei-
kugeln** (magic bullets). The fact that the villainous Caspar is killed
by his own bullet demonstrates that he is not *kugelfest* or *schußfest*
(bulletproof).

'Invulnerable', then, is one sense of the adjective *fest*, as applied for
example to Schiller's Wallenstein by his men in the (mistaken) belief
daß er fest ist (*Lager**, l. 355). It is more common in such combinations as *schnittfest* ('firm' tomatoes), *trinkfest* (able to hold one's
drink), *feuerfest* (fireproof), *stoßfest* (shock-proof), *seefest* (in possession of 'good sea legs'), *ein kußfester* (or *kußechter*) *Lippenstift* (kiss-
proof lipstick) or *einen Verbrecher dingfest machen* (to put a criminal
behind bars) – and is the equivalent of English 'fast' in *farbfest*
(colours not liable to fade or run), so you should check whether a
garment is labelled *kochfest* before you set your washing-machine on
Kochwäsche. It also lends itself to the same sort of punning as its
sometime synonym *sicher* (sure, safe – the *Luftwaffe*'s Starfighters, for
instance, after 250 crashes in the 1960s and 70s, acquired a reputation
for being *todsicher*, 'dead safe' but also 'death assured').

Though usually clear whether a compound derives from *Fest* (celebration) or *fest* (solid food, firm plan, steady girlfriend, permanent
job, tight grip, sound sleep), it is perhaps not always so at first sight:
das Festessen (banquet, Christmas dinner) but *die Festplatte* (computer hard disc); *das Festland* (mainland, dry land, Continent) but *die
Festwiese* (fairground, or in *Die Meistersinger von Nürnberg*, festival
meadow); *der Festpreis* (fixed price) but *die Festgabe* (presentation,
gift); even *die Festrede* (a speech on a special occasion) but *sich
festreden* (to get involved or stuck in a conversation).

FETT adj. used of fatty, rich, greasy food (low-fat is *fettarm*), or an
unhealthily fat person. In his own eyes Falstaff is at worst *dick* (see
PLUMP in VII), so that 'There live not three good men unhanged in
England, and one of them is fat and grows old' is probably not best
rendered as *und der eine von ihnen ist fett und wird alt* (Schlegel/
Tieck); on the other hand, *Fettsack**and *fettiger Talgklumpen* ('greasy
tallow-catch') are among the less forceful epithets which occur to Hal
and the others. Since people no longer keep a bowl of fat outside their

door to rub on their boots, *ins Fettnäpfchen treten* now means 'to put one's foot in it' only in a figurative sense. For dripping, see SCHMALZ below.

FLEISCHHAUER n.m. (alternatively, *der Fleischhacker*): there's no mistaking a 'hewer of flesh' in Austria (where the sign *Selcher* indicates a specialist pork butcher selling smoked meats, *Selchfleisch* or *Geselchtes*). German butchers are either *Metzger* or *Fleischer*, in the North *Schlachter*.

FLEISCHKÄSE n.m. meat loaf, which is not only cheese-shaped but also has the consistency of a soft cheese, such as ricotta.

FORM n.f. also a baking tin (*Backform*) or mould. Otherwise as in English, though the one thing *eine Form* is not is the form you have to fill in (*ein Formular**).

FRÜHSTÜCKSFLEISCH n.n. not bacon (*Frühstücksspeck** or *Schinkenspeck*), but luncheon meat – as spread on rolls for a mid-morning snack (*das zweite Frühstück*).

GANG n.m. also the course of a meal: *ein Festessen** mit sieben Gängen* is a seven-course banquet. See GANG in II for several other meanings.

GARNI adj. an *Hotel garni* offers no 'garnishings' other than bed and breakfast, whereas a meat dish which is *garniert* or *mit Garnierung* comes with vegetables. *Eine Garnitur* is a 'set' of things, such as crockery, a military outfit (*erste Garnitur*: dress uniform, hence 'first-rate'), or matching underwear.

GASTHAUS n.n. not a guest-house (*eine Pension**), but an inn. In both town and country, *ein Gasthaus* (or *eine Gaststätte*) provides *gutbürgerliche** Küche*, whereas *ein Restaurant* tends to be more specialized, and probably more expensive. It may be used simply as one's local pub (*eine Kneipe* or *eine Bar** do not serve meals), and it often provides quite adequate accommodation, too (indicated by the sign *Fremdenzimmer*, or simply *Zimmer* – and if there are vacancies, *Zimmer frei*). See also LOKAL below.

GERM n.m. or n.f. North German *Hefe* (baker's yeast) is *der Germ* in Bavaria and *die Germ* in Austria, where they eat *Germkrapfen* instead of *Berliner** (doughnuts), and *Germknödel* instead of *Hefeteigklöße* (yeast dumplings – an apple dumpling is known as *Apfel im Schlafrock**).

GLÜHWEIN n.m. mulled wine – best made with a full-bodied red wine, sweetened and spiced with cinnamon, cloves, lemon peel and sugar, and served piping hot, nowadays (like *Jägertee**) much appreciated by skiers. Since the word is derived from *glühen* (to glow), there is no connection between *Glühwein* and glue (*der Klebstoff*); nor, indeed, between mulled wine and *der Müll* (refuse/garbage), except that the spices and the contents of one's *Mülltonne** both undergo a process of grinding or 'mulling'.

GLUT n.f. embers, glow, flush, ardour. But a glut is *eine Schwemme* or *ein Überangebot* (the *Butterschwemme* caused by EC agricultural policy is, of course, better known as *der Butterberg*). Someone who gluts himself is *ein Schlemmer* (a slimmer barely exists as a noun, though *jemand, der abnehmen will* is sometimes called *ein Kalorienzähler*).

GRILL n.m. a barbecue, as well as the grill on a cooker or the grillroom in a restaurant. *Grillen* has replaced *auf dem Rost braten*: the occasion is now *ein Grillabend* or *Grillfest**. *Wollen wir heute abend grillen?*, – perhaps at one of the forest sites provided by the local authorities, usually complete with rough benches round a central barbecue.

Also a radiator grille (*Kühlergrill*), though not the grille on an old-fashioned lift (*ein Fahrstuhlgitter*). Nor has *eine Grille* anything to do with grilles: it's a cricket (and figuratively, like *ein Tick**, *eine Laune* or *eine Schrulle*, a silly notion: *das ist so eine Grille von ihm*).

GUSTO n.m. for Austrians, *Gusto* retains its Italian sense of taste (see DEGUSTATION above) rather than a more general enthusiasm or zest, so that *ich hätte Gusto auf einen Kaiserschmarrn* simply means: I feel like a *Kaiserschmarrn* (a sugared, cut-up pancake with raisins – see also PALATSCHINKEN below); *ein Gustostückerl*, a real delicacy; *er ist nicht nach meinem Gusto*, he's not my cup of tea. The Germans' sense of *Ordnung* sometimes inhibits them from doing things *nach eigenem Gusto* (ad lib, just as they like, or as the Austrian revellers in *Die Fledermaus* put it, *chacun à son goût*), though not from acting 'with gusto', *mit Genuß* or *mit Schwung*.

HAPPEN n.m. (or *das Häppchen*) – snack, mouthful. *Wollen wir woanders hingehen und einen Happen essen?* (Shall we go and have a bite to eat somewhere else?); if the proprietor is too greedy: *hier sind die Preise ganz schön happig* (the prices here are a bit steep). *Ein in maulgerechte Happen zerteiltes Osteuropa* (an eastern Europe broken up into tasty morsels) is Wilhelm Bittorf's description of the power vacuum left by the Habsburgs and the Tsar after the First World War – tempting Germany's expansive appetite (*Der Spiegel*, 14 August 1989).

HASCHEN v. now also to smoke hash (*das Hasch* – mince hash is *das Haschee*), but the main meaning is to catch or grab. *Die Kinder spielen Haschen* (play tag), *man hascht nach Beifall* (fishes for praise), but *das Glück läßt sich nicht haschen* (happiness is not there for the taking). Austrians call a poor wretch *ein Hascher* or *Hascherl.*

HAUSBACKEN adj. only used figuratively (of people or clothes) in the sense of homespun, homely, drab, unadventurous. A homemade dish is *hausgemacht*, if baked by oneself *selbstgebacken.*

HERB adj. has no connection with a herb (herbal tea, *Kräutertee**) or its aroma, but signifies a sharp smell or tangy taste. *Ein herber Weißwein* is simply a dry white wine (though the designation on *das Etikett** will be *trocken* or *sehr trocken*); if it is too dry: *dieser Wein ist mir zu herb*; if it is distinctly acidic: *dieser Wein ist mir zu sauer**. Figuratively: *eine herbe Enttäuschung*, a bitter disappointment, *ein herbes Gesicht*, a severe face, *herbe Worte*, harsh* words.

HERING n.m. especially in North Germany, herrings are prized as the most versatile of fish – eaten young and salted as *Matjes* (*mit Pellkartoffeln*, with potatoes boiled in their jackets); soaked in water, then milk, filleted, rolled around an onion or gherkin, skewered and pickled as *Rollmöpse*; marinaded fillets alternating with layers of onion, salt and pepper as *Bismarckheringe*; or baked with alternating layers of sliced boiled potatoes (*Salzkartoffeln*) and onions in a *Heringsauflauf*; dipped in flour, fried, and soused when cool in vinegar, onion, bayleaves, and mustard seed as *eingelegte Bratheringe*; with sour cream in a steaming *Heringstopf*; or after they have been smoked as *gedörrte Heringe*, *Räucherheringe* or *Bücklinge* (kippers*).

But they are false feathered friends – *eine Heringsmöwe* is not a herring-gull (*die Silbermöwe*) but a lesser black-backed gull. Ornithologists will also know that *die Kohlmeise* is not a coal tit (*die Tannenmeise*) but a great tit; nor is *die Schellente* a shelduck (*die Brandgans, die Brandente*) but a goldeneye; *ein Rabenschwarm* is not a swarm of ravens (*der Rabe*) but of carrion crows (*die Rabenkrähe*); and *ein Milan*, as in French, is a kite. Given its shape, *ein Hering* is also a tent peg. A herringbone suit: *ein Anzug mit Fischgrätmuster.*

KABINETT n.m. an off-dry 'quality wine' (the first *Prädikat** or category of *Qualitätswein*), originally intended for private use (see KABINETT in II). As an abbreviation of *Kabinettwein* it is masculine whereas a political *Kabinett** is neuter, though the implication of quality is common to both (and central to *ein Kabinettstückchen* – a clever move in politics or a brilliant piece of showmanship, for instance on the football field).

KAFFEE n.m. coffee. A café is *ein Café*, but the traditional Viennese *Kaffeehaus* such as Landtmann, or Sperl, or the Café Central with its refurbished *Jugendstil* decor and indestructible fur-hatted old ladies from much the same period, is unique. As Gustav Gugitz informs us (*Das Wiener Kaffeehaus*, 1940, p. 9), by the 1780s the seventy-odd public coffee-houses in a city of 215,000 served as a virtual substitute for parliament. Legend has it that Vienna's *Kaffeehauskultur** began with the coffee and coffee-making equipment left behind by the Turks after the siege of the city in 1683 (when, finally, *die Österreicher besiegten* die Türken*). From then until the 1880s, Yemen jealously guarded its monopoly in exporting coffee from the harbour at Mokka, a fact still remembered in Vienna where coffee ranges from mild and milky to black and strong: *weiß – licht – gold – Melange – braun – Kapuziner* (unlike *Cappuccino*, this has a single drop of milk) – *Mokka*. *Ein Einspänner* is black coffee in a glass with plenty of *Schlagobers**; *ein Mazagran* is cooled with ice cubes and has rum added. In his reminiscences of pre-war Vienna (*Die Tante Jolesch*, 1977, p. 239), Friedrich Torberg notes that even *eine Teeschale* is a cup of coffee (the size of a large tea-cup – *eine Schale* Tee* when filled with tea), *ein Piccolo* is a medium-sized cup (but see PIKKOLO below), and *eine Nußschale braun* the smallest, but strongest. The Viennese often add fig to their coffee, and it is always served with a glass of water. They also stress the last syllable of the word and think it comically 'Prussian' not to do so. See also SACHERTORTE below and WITZ in V.

What we call ersatz coffee, the Germans have traditionally called *Muckefuck* (which is derived from the Rhenish word for dusty soil, *mucken*, and *fuck* meaning *faul** – no connection, then, with *mucken*, to mutter: *keinen Mucks von sich geben*, not to make a sound, not to say a dickybird; *es wurde mucksmäuschenstill**, you could have heard a pin drop).

KANNE n.f. a teapot (*Teekanne*) or coffeepot (*Kaffeekanne*), though one usually orders an individual *Kännchen Tee* or *Kännchen Kaffee*, which comes with *ein Kännchen Milch oder Sahne*, a small jug of milk or cream. For cans of beer, see DOSE above.

KARNEVAL n.m. a more institutionalized activity than in English-speaking countries, especially in the Catholic Rhineland (Cologne, Düsseldorf, Mainz), where it is referred to as *die fünfte Jahreszeit*, and in Bavaria. *Karneval* begins promptly – and for the uninitiated British visitor, confusingly – at 11.11am on 11 November (German Remembrance Day, on the Sunday two weeks before Advent, is called *Volkstrauertag*). It then submerges until the planning stage begins on 6 January, culminating on *Rosenmontag* (Rose Monday – actually derived from the Bavarian pronunciation of *rasen*, to revel) and *Fastnacht* (Shrove Tuesday, before the Lenten fasting begins) with *Karnevalszüge* (parades) and *Karnevalsbälle* (balls), *Sitzungen* (conventions) and '*Büttenreden*' (speeches), all under the auspices of universal *Narrenfreiheit* (jester's licence) and accompanied, like the *Karnevalsprinz* and his princess, with roars of *Alaaf!* or *Helau!*

Fastnacht in turn provides an alternative name for carnival, especially in the west and south: *der Fasching*. The one day in the year when women traditionally run the show (*führen das Regiment**) is known as *Weiberfastnacht* – the Thursday before *die drei tollen Tage* begin and *Kravatten**/*Schlipse** are in danger of being snipped off. This symbolic severing of ties introduces an evening on which, famously, anything goes.

KARTON n.m. a carton containing liquids only in such combinations as *Milchkarton* (milk carton) or *Weinkarton* (wine box); otherwise either **1.** a large cardboard carton or cardboard box (such as a *Schuhkarton*, shoe-box); or else **2.** the material itself: *aus Karton* means made of stiff paper/board/cardboard. Books are either *gebunden* (hardback) or *kartoniert* ('in boards', though this is nowadays synonymous with *Paperback*).

KEKS n.m. & n.n. not a cake (from which it is derived: *der Kuchen*) but a biscuit*/US cookie. *Das Gebäck* covers not only all sorts of biscuits, but also buns, pastries, tarts.

KIPPER n.m. not a kipper (see HERING above), but a tipper truck – *kippen* also means to tipple (*wollen wir noch ein paar kippen?* shall we sink another glass or two?) and *eine Kippe* is a cigarette butt (Heinrich Böll, an inveterate smoker, invented '*Kippologie*' in his *Irisches Tagebuch*, 1957). For 'to kip' meaning 'to sleep', see *Penner* under TRAMPEN in VII.

KNACK- in cpds. not knack, but crack: the sound made by a *Nußknacker* (nutcracker) or *Knäckebrot* (crispbread). Figuratively, too, one's mind or one's marriage might receive a *Knacks*. On the other hand, *knacken* in the jargon of sexual pursuit means to pick up or 'pull' (*eine knackige Frau*, a real cracker) – at the risk of being put down as *ein alter Knacker* ('past it'). The knack here is also the German title of that archetypal 1960s film, *Der gewisse Kniff* (*The Knack*, 1965). One hopes there is no connection whatever between a *Knackwurst* (a kind of frankfurter which makes a cracking sound when you bite into it) and what comes from the knacker's yard (*die*

Abdeckerei, formerly *die Schinderei* or *der Schindanger**). 'I'm knack-ered', *ich bin kaputt, ich bin fix und fertig*.

KONSERVIEREN v. to preserve food. Most German bread (though not *Toastbrot**) is *ohne Konservierungsmittel** (without preservatives) – you will give a strange impression of British customs if you ask for *Brot ohne Präservative** (bread without contraceptives). Fruits preserved in a jar are *Eingewecktes* (*eingeweckte Pfirsiche*, preserved peaches; *Pfirsichmarmelade**, peach preserve), in Austria *Eingesottenes*; pickled vegetables such as *saure Gurken* are *Eingelegtes*, while *einmachen* and *einkochen* cover both processes. *Von Konserven* (or *aus der Dose**) *leben* is to live on tinned foods.

KOST n.f. not cost (*der Preis, die Kosten*), but food, fare, board. *Kost und Logis*, board and lodgings. Nor does *wie köstlich!* mean 'how costly' (*wie teuer!*), but 'that was exquisite' or else (if one is amused) 'that was priceless'. *Rohkost* is raw fruit and vegetables, *schwere Kost* something indigestible, and figuratively, 'heavy going'. *Hausmanns-kost* (derived from the *Hausmann* or lodger of old) is plain staple fare, figuratively 'run of the mill', unlike the genuine home-made quality of food prepared *nach Hausfrauenart*. But the verb *kosten* means either 'to taste/sample' (see PROBE in X) or 'to cost'.

KOTELETT n.n. a chop – usually pork if not specified, since lamb has only recently gained in popularity through Germany's large Turkish community, and *Lammkeule* (leg) or *Lammrücken* (saddle) seem more common than individual *Lammkoteletts* (not *Koteletten*: these are the mutton-chop whiskers sported impressively by Emperor Franz Joseph and others, though Austrians may call these, too, *Kote-letts*). No cook has yet managed to convince the Germans that *Pfefferminzsoße* goes quite well with lamb.

KRABBE n.f. in everyday usage a shrimp or prawn (strictly speak-ing, *eine Garnele*), as in a *Krabbencocktail*, whereas our small seashore crab is *ein Krebs*, and the larger edible crab *ein Taschenkrebs*. See also SCHELLFISCH and SCHALE below.

KRAUT n.n. cabbage; or a herb* (*Heilkraut*, medicinal herb; *Kräuterbutter*, herb butter); or the non-edible tops or leaves of plants and vegetables; or an abbreviation of *Sauerkraut**. When the newly-recognized though still somewhat morose East Germans set up their London embassy in 1974, they were inevitably known not just as *Krauts* but as *Sauerkrauts** to distinguish them from their West German neighbours a few doors away in Belgrave Square. Naturally, since the sauerkraut (or *choucroute*) centre of Europe is Alsace, the Germans see no reason to call themselves cabbages of any kind, nor to murmur the French equivalent of *mon petit chou* in their beloved's ear (see AMIS in I). But just as the English once looked down on the Irish squireen amidst his potatoes, so the Germans have traditionally disparaged the *Krautjunker* (lower gentry-cum-agrarian entrepreneur – see GUT in III) on his *Krautacker* * in remotest Prussia (if not Saxe-Coburg, as implied by the caption to a *Punch* cartoon in 1845: 'Happy among his native *kraut* my princely Albert wanders').

Another word for cabbage is *der Kohl*: red cabbage is *Rotkohl*, in the south *Blaukraut*, whereas *Rosenkohl* * or *Röschen* are everywhere Brussels sprouts; *Wirsingkohl*, or simply *Wirsing*, is savoy cabbage; *Weißkohl*, white cabbage. *Grünkohl*, curly kale, plays a prominent part in North German (Friesland) cuisine and custom: *Kohlfahrten* are office outings during the winter involving large amounts of braised kale and fatty meats, *Schnaps* and vigorous *Kegeln* (see BOWLING in VII).

Chancellor Kohl has no doubt learnt to live with this – on the satirical TV show *Lach- und Schießgesellschaft* Dieter Hildebrandt once memorably addressed a cabbage, like Yorick's skull, as '*faul* *, *faul*' – as also with the fact that, since the eighteenth century, *kohlen* has meant to tell lies or talk rubbish (*red' keinen Kohl!* stop talking nonsense) and *jemanden verkohlen* to pull somebody's leg. Consolation may come from the thought that though *das Unkraut* is a weed, *Unkraut vergeht nicht* means something like 'old soldiers never die', 'it will take more than that to finish me off'.

KÜCHE n.f. the kitchen, to which Swabian women are, or were, proverbially confined (the three 'Ks' are *Kinder, Küche, Kirche*, children, kitchen, church), but also its products. *Die deutsche Küche* is German cuisine, while *ein Kuchen* is a cake (US cookie, *ein Keks* *) and *ein Küchlein* a little cake, not a kitchenette (*eine kleine Küche*, or if part of the living room *eine Kochnische*).

LAKE n.f. brine (also *Salzlake*), the salt and water used to pickle (*einpökeln*) fish such as *Pickelheringe* *. Not to be confused with *die Lache*, meaning a puddle, whereas a lake is *der See* *. *Das Laken* is a sheet.

LESE n.f. not lees or dregs (*der Satz* or *der Bodensatz*), but harvest, vintage, picking. *Spätlese* (generally medium-sweet) and *Auslese* (luscious, concentrated) are signs of quality – the second and third *Prädikat* * or category of *Qualitätswein*. Those who, like Tennyson's Ulysses, wish to 'drink Life to the lees', *trinken bis auf den letzten Tropfen aus*.

LIEBFRAUENMILCH n.f. the most popular German wine abroad (alas). According to legend, the 'milk of Our Lady' in its plenitude moistened the ground. The names of German wines often have ribald associations around which a risqué story is sometimes woven, but an application to patent the name *Schlüpferstürmer* ('knicker-stormer') was rejected as *sittlich verwerflich* (morally reprehensible).

According to the *Mitteilungen der deutschen Patentanwälte* in 1985, an appeal to such well-known precedents as *Kröver Nacktarsch* (Bare Bum) and *Naumburger Engelgrube* (Angels' Hollow) was said to be inadmissible since they had become so well established (*sich derart eingebürgert**) that no one was offended by them any longer.

LIMONE n.f. not a lemon (*die Zitrone*), but a lime. *Heiße* or *kalte Zitrone* is fresh lemon juice, *Limonade* the fizzy soft drink. Goethe remembered a recent visit to Italy, 'the country where the lemon tree flowers', in his *Wilhelm Meister* (1795), when the mysterious girl Mignon sings *Kennst du das Land, wo die Zitronen blühn*. Besides Schubert, the song inspired Beethoven, Schumann, Liszt and Wolf, though naturally enough it is not the lemon but the lime or linden tree (unrelated to the citrus fruit), which in Schubert's incomparable setting of Wilhelm Müller's *Der Lindenbaum* captures the melancholy inwardness of the Germans' own *Heimat**.

LOKAL n.n. not one's local pub, but a traditional restaurant (a *Speiselokal*, known as a *Gasthaus** or *Gaststätte* or *Wirtshaus*), though one where one can simply have a drink; or else a *Weinlokal* (wine bar*). Nor is *ein Wahllokal* the 'local of one's choice', but a polling station. 'My local' is *mein Stammlokal** or *meine Stammkneipe*.

LUNGENBRATEN n.m. not 'roast lung', but loin roast or fillet – in Austria, the best cut of pork, beef or veal (German *Lendenbraten*). But *Lungenhaschee* is a hash made with calf's lights, known in Bavaria as *Lüngerl* and in Vienna as *Beuschl*.

MAHL n.n. a repast or banquet, but not the usual word for a meal, which it is sometimes quite tricky to translate. *Die Mahlzeit* ('mealtime') is also more of a formal term (*warme Mahlzeiten*, hot meals), though *Mahlzeit!* (an abbreviation of *gesegnete Mahlzeit!* – said as grace before and after meals) is the most common casual greeting at work between around 11am and 2pm (from mid-afternoon it becomes *schönen Feierabend!**, 'have a nice evening'). The food itself is *das Essen*, and some variation on *essengehen* is the usual way of talking about being invited for a meal, or having had a meal. As the day for most people begins earlier than in Britain, 'elevenses' is often a *zweites Frühstück* (a generous *Butterbrot*, sandwich, often brought to work in the ubiquitous *Aktentasche*, briefcase). The Swiss have their own unmistakable abbreviations for breakfast (*Zmorge*), elevenses (*Znüni*), lunch (*Zmittag*) and supper (*Znacht*).

Dinner or supper in German is *das Abendessen*, more formally *die Abendmahlzeit*, but *das Abendmahl* is now used only of Communion (*das Letzte Abendmahl*, the Last Supper). So when Kleist's Michael Kohlhaas demonstrates absolute trust in his man Herse's account of his maltreatment by saying: *und das Abendmahl, wenn es zur Sprache kommt, will ich selbst nun darauf nehmen*, he means that, if the issue is raised, he will 'take Communion', that is, swear a holy oath to that effect (and not, as the anonymous translator in the *Dublin Magazine* has it: 'After supper, when my wife and I talk over our affairs together, I will decide what is to be done' – 1853, volume 41, p. 562).

MARMELADE n.f. traditionally any jam made from (usually non-citrus) fruit, marmalade only if specified as *Orangenmarmelade* or *Zitronenmarmelade*. But the EC ruled in 1982 that henceforth only citrus fruit should go into *Marmelade*, while any other jam made of crushed fruit and sugar should be known as *Konfitüre* (formerly a more wholesome product made with whole fruit only). See also TOAST below.

MASS n.f. the preferred 'unit of measure' (*Maßeinheit* – see MASS in II) of the Bavarians, namely, a litre of beer (or shandy – *eine Radlermaß* is what a *Radler/Radfahrer*, cyclist, might safely drink) – though they tend to forget that it was imposed on them as part of the decimalization system by Napoleon. The north-German measure varies between 0.2 and 0.3 of a litre, but the alcoholic content is greater.

MAST n.f. pig feed (a ship's mast or an electricity pylon is *der Mast*). Only a *Mastschwein** like the Empress of Blandings should indulge in the sort of *Kur** known humorously as *eine Mastkur* (fattening diet).

MELANGE n.f. in Austria, white coffee (a blend* is *eine Mischung*). See KAFFEE above.

MENAGE n.f. in Germany, a cruet stand; in Austria, rations or provisions (*menagieren*, to draw rations). A *ménage* in the broader sense is *der Haushalt* (which, like *der Etat**, is also a budget), while a *ménage à trois* is germanized into a 'triangular relationship', *ein Dreiecksverhältnis*.

MENÜ n.n. a set meal (*das Tagesmenü*, meal of the day), as distinct from a meal *à la carte*. The menu is *die Speisekarte*.

MOORHUHN n.n. grouse (see MOOR in III). A moorhen is *ein Teichhuhn.*

MUSKELKATER n.m. what looks like a 'muscular tomcat' (*der gestiefelte Kater,* Puss-in-boots) in fact means aching muscles (*ich habe Muskelkater in den Armen,* my arms are stiff and aching). This derives from overexertion of a different kind, since *ein Kater* is also a hangover – if only because it sounds like *Katarrh**, or, alternatively, like *ein Katzenjammer* ('caterwauling'; 'the blues'). Another equally maligned animal in this context is the ape: *einen Affen (sitzen) haben* is to be drunk; *sich einen Affen kaufen,* to go and get tight. Besides such recognized pick-me-ups as Jeeves's prairie-oyster, a German *Katerfrühstück* also emphasizes the beneficial effects of *Matjes,* young pickled herring*.

NATUR adj. '*au naturel*', that is to say, fish or schnitzels not cooked in breadcrumbs (*paniert**), coffee or tea without milk and sugar (but see *schwarzer Tee**). Alternatively *nature* (Swiss usage), *Natur-,* or *naturell.* (A person's temperament or disposition is *sein Naturell*).

NIPPEN v. to nip only in the sense of to sip (*sie nippte an ihrem Kaffee,* not *sie nippte ihren Kaffee*); not to bite or pinch (*zwicken, kneifen*). He's just nipped out to the pub, *er ging auf einen Sprung in die Kneipe.* No connection with *Nippes* or *Nippsachen,* china ornaments, knick-knacks, bric-à-brac.

NOUGAT n.m. or n.n. invariably one of the soft-centres in a box of *Pralinen* – a brown, cocoa-flavoured filling made from powdered almonds or hazelnuts and sugar – whereas the hard, chewy, white *Konfekt** associated with Montélimar, or something like it, is sold in Germany as *türkischer Honig.*

OBERS n.n. in Austria, what goes 'on top' of coffee or pudding* – cream (*die Sahne*); if whipped, *Schlagobers* or simply *Schlag**.

PALATSCHINKEN n.n. not a form of ham (*der Schinken*), but stuffed pancakes, similar to French *crêpes* though the curd cheese, soured cream, lemon and raisin filling is generally more substantial. An Austrian speciality, often thought to have originated in Hungary (*palacsinták*) but in fact derived from Romanian *placinta* and, ultimately, Latin *placenta,* which is, perhaps surprisingly, a cake. See also *Kaiserschmarrn* under GUSTO above.

PANIEREN v. does not mean to fry in the pan (*in der Pfanne*), but in breadcrumbs (from French *pain*) – though both *ein paniertes Schnitzel* and *ein Schnitzel natur** (without breadcrumbs) are, of course, fried. If not specified (*Kalbsschnitzel* – veal, *Putenschnitzel* –

turkey) they are made of pork, though *Wiener Schnitzel* is invariably a veal escalope. *Schweineschnitzel* or *Wiener Schnitzel* are served without sauce (but often with apple *Kompott* on the side); a *Paprikaschnitzel** comes with a paprika/capsicum sauce, and *Jägerschnitzel* in a spicy mushroom sauce (the least obscure of Elgar's *Enigma Variations*, Nimrod, is based on his friend and publisher Jäger, 'the hunter'). As standards of cuisine are consistently high, *eine Schnitzeljagd* is clearly not a hunt for the best schnitzel, but rather a paperchase (since *Schnitzel* are also wood-shavings or scraps of paper).

PAPPE n.f. cardboard (*ein Pappband** is a hardback book, *ein Pappbecher* a paper cup) or roofing felt (*Dachpappe*), but also, in baby talk, 'pap' (like *der Brei*, a mush or goo), or, more pejoratively, a sticky mess, slops, muck (colloquially, *ich kann nicht mehr papp sagen* means 'I'm full to bursting'). Conversely, *nicht von Pappe sein* means to be pretty tough (exercise, teacher), quite something (blow), a real stinker (cold), a bit steep (price), strong stuff (speech, drink), etc.

PAPRIKA n.m. both the spice and also what we call (green, red, yellow) peppers. *Pfeffer** refers only to the spice, as in *Pfeffersteak*, steak *au poivre*.

PARADEISER n.m. in Austria (except for Tirol and Vorarlberg in the west), an alternative word for *die Tomate*. Other common Austrian variations are *der Erdapfel* for *die Kartoffel* (potato, also South German); *der Karfiol* for *der Blumenkohl* (cauliflower); *Fisolen* for *grüne Bohnen* (green beans); and *Ribisln* for *schwarze/rote Johannisbeeren* (blackcurrants/redcurrants).

PASTETE n.f. a pie or 'pasty', but also pâté (*Leberpastete*, liver paté).

PATRON n.m. the boss (also *der Chef**). The patrons are *die Gäste* or *die Kunden*.

PENETRANT adj. of smells and tastes: pungent, overpowering; but also used of people: *ein penetranter Bursche* is pushy and a pest.

PFEFFERKUCHEN n.m. 'pepper cake', in fact gingerbread. A popular variety of this, associated especially with Nürnberg, is *Lebkuchen*.

PICKEL n.m. no connection with pickled gherkins or herrings (see HERING, KONSERVIEREN, LAKE, SAUER in this section). *Ein Pickel* is a spot/pimple, or else a pickaxe (*Spitzhacke*), iceaxe (*Eispickel*), or the spike after which the Prussian *Pickelhaube* is named (see HELM in II).

PIKKOLO n.m. the musical instrument, but also a quarter-bottle of champagne, or a trainee waiter (see also KAFFEE above for its special Viennese meaning).

PRÄDIKAT n.n. rating or grade. *Qualitätsweine mit Prädikat* are quality wines with specific attributes or styles, the scale rising (in ascending order of ripeness, or sugar content before fermentation) through *Kabinett**, *Spätlese**, *Auslese* to *Beerenauslese*, *Trockenbeerenauslese* and *Eiswein**, though today's taste for drier wines means that a *Spätlese Trocken* would be bone-dry. The selection of grapes (*Auslese*) began in Germany, while the idea of late picking, imported from Yquem in Bordeaux, is particularly suited to the late-ripening *Riesling* grape (*Edelfäule** is 'noble rot'). See also PRÄDIKAT in IV.

PUDDING n.m. not a synonym for the sweet course or dessert (*der Nachtisch, die Nachspeise, das Dessert*), but a small blancmange such as *Schokoladenpudding* or *Vanillepudding*, eaten cold. *Pudding* is always *sturzfähig* ('set'/'turned out' of a *Puddingform**), whereas *Vanillesoße* or *Vanillecreme* is custard in its more runny form. This, too, is served cold when it accompanies other dishes, as are the *Milchreis* (rice pudding) and *Grießbrei* (semolina pudding) which German children also enjoy, and the favourite north-German pudding of *rote Grütze* (a compote of red fruit in a sauce of semolina, sago, cream, or simply milk). Since *Plumpudding* is known only by reputation, it makes an interesting present (and has been known to impress even when eaten unboiled). For black pudding (*Blutwurst*), see FEST above.

PUFFER n.m. (short for *Kartoffelpuffer*) potato cakes or fritters, so called because they go '*Puff*' in the pan. Also a railway buffer; or a buffer state (thus Britain thwarted French 'separatist' plans at Versailles to deprive Germany of its Western provinces, insisting it should remain undivided *als Puffer gegen den russischen Bolschewismus*). See also the strange derivation of PUFF in VI.

PUR adj. 'neat', as in *zwei Whisky pur*.

QUALM n.m. not the qualms of conscience (*Gewissensbisse*) or misgivings (*Bedenken*) a smoker now feels before lighting up in public, but the thick smoke or fug that causes them. *Er qualmt wie ein Schlot*, he smokes like a chimney.

QUELLEN v. of rice, peas, lentils: to swell after soaking. Otherwise, to pour or stream forth – the opposite of to quell (among the many ways of conveying repression in German are: *bezwingen, bändigen, zügeln, überwinden, unterdrücken, niederschlagen*, and in

Freud's sense, *verdrängen*). Natural spring water is *Quellwasser* – from *eine Quelle*.

RAR adj. rare (*er machte sich rar*, he kept himself to himself, made himself scarce), but rare meat is *roh*, and a rare steak *blutig* or *englisch**.

REFORMHAUS n.n. not a reformatory or house of correction (*eine Besserungsanstalt* or *Erziehungsanstalt*), except in as much as it sells the sort of health food which is good for you: *Reformwaren* or *Reformkost* (see KOST above, and for Dr Jäger's woollen *Reformkleidung*, KULTUR in II).

REIF adj. not rife (*weit verbreitet*), but ripe (fruit) or mature (cheese, wine, people). Hence *druckreif* (ready for printing), not to be confused with *der Reifendruck* (tyre pressure). For *Mittlere Reife*, the *Realschule** leaving examination, see ABSOLVIEREN in IV.

RESTAURATION n.f. still used in Austria of an inn or tavern (German *Gaststätte*); in the south generally, you can restore the tissues after a train journey in the *Bahnhofsrestauration* (often a first-class restaurant as well as a refreshment room). See also RESTAURATION in II.

REVANCHIEREN v. *ich werde mich revanchieren* can mean 'I will have my revenge', but is more likely to mean you want to reciprocate generosity or repay hospitality (the invitation may be left open but is seldom forgotten, whereas the Germans tend to view English invitations as insincere). *Eine Revanchepartie** is simply a return match, not a grudge game (*einen Groll hegen*, 'to harbour a grudge'), but *Revanchepolitik* is a less friendly way of getting one's own back.

RIECHEN v. whereas 'reek' suggests unpleasant smells, *riechen* is neutral: *riech mal!* just smell that (either *ein Gestank*, a stink, or *frische Brötchen*, fresh rolls). Exclusively pleasant smells *duften*. 'He reeks of alcohol': *er hat eine Fahne*, 'a flag'.

RIND n.n. not a rind (of cheese, *die Rinde*; of bacon, *die Schwarte*; of fruit, *die Schale**), but beef (*Rindfleisch*). *Rinder* or *Rindvieh* are cattle.

RÖMER n.m. what we sometimes call a 'rummer' – a wineglass with a clear glass bowl and cone-shaped, ringed stem of brown or green glass (corresponding to the brown bottles used for *Moselwein* and the green for *Rheinwein*). Also the name given to the town hall of Frankfurt am Main, though the 'Rome of the North' from which

Constantine the Great ruled the Empire was Trier. A further link with the Romans* (*die Römer*) is *ein Römertopf* (earthenware casserole or chicken brick).

ROSENKOHL n.m. 'rose cabbage', actually the (Brussels) sprouts or *Röschen* which it produces (a *Röschen* is also a little rose, and *Dornröschen*, 'little thorn rose', is Sleeping Beauty). See also KRAUT above.

ROSINE n.f. not resin (*das Harz*) or rosin (*Geigenharz*, better known as *Kolophonium*), but raisin. *Rosinenkuchen* is a sweet currant bread, like barm brack/barnbrack – the yeasted fruit bread traditionally served at Halloween in Ireland though now eaten all year round. Add almonds, lemon peel, spices and a lot more butter, and it becomes the traditional Christmas *Stollen*.

RÖSTI n.p. *rösten* means to roast (especially coffee beans), to toast (now also *toasten**), but also to fry in the pan, so *Röstkartoffeln*, like *Bratkartoffeln**, are fried or sauté potatoes (just as *Röstzwiebeln*, the crowning glory of *Wiener Rostbraten*, are fried onions). Also known in the south as *Geröstete*, and when made from grated potatoes as *Rösti* in Switzerland, where the *Röstilinie* is said to divide German-speaking (and German-eating) Switzerland from French or *welsch** Switzerland in the same way that the *Weißwurstlinie** separates Bavaria from the rest of Germany. *Auf dem Rost braten* is synonymous with *grillen** (to barbecue).

RUMPF n.m. Germans eat *Rumpsteak* (usually a thick sirloin without the fat), but *der Rumpf* is the whole torso or trunk of a person or animal, living or dead (also a ship's hull, or a plane's fuselage). 'Rump': *der Hintern, der Hinterteil, die Arschbacke** (a term which is *salonfähig*, fit for the drawing room, is sometimes said to be *weniger barsch als der Arsch*, less crude than 'arse').

SACHERTORTE n.f. not a tart (see TORTE below), but the classic Viennese chocolate cake – moist, heavy, delicious, with apricot jam under a coating (*Glasur*) of chocolate. The presence, or absence, of this *Aprikosenmarmelade** has long been the subject of a Swiftian struggle between the *Hotel* Sacher and the *Konditorei* Demel, to which the last Sacher in the male line sold the recipe in the 1930s (the Court of Appeal *in zweiter Instanz** noted the decline of the House of Sacher as a sad parallel to that of the House of Habsburg). However fraught the history of *Original-Sachertorte*, even an expert in decadence such as Leopold von Sacher-Masoch (masochism being the family's other claim to fame) would have baulked at the cream-filled simulation purporting to be *Sachertorte* in Germany.

SALAT n.m. salad, but also lettuce (*grüner Salat*; *Kopfsalat*; a head of lettuce is *ein Salatkopf*) or endive (*Endiviensalat*). Our summer meal of cold meats, sliced egg, tomato, cucumber, beetroot and lettuce is known only to those Germans who visit England, and who will also wonder why sliced tomato and listless lettuce soaked in malt vinegar should sometimes be known as a continental salad. A German *Salat* or side salad generally contains tomato, grated carrot, celeriac and coleslaw, and is always freshly dressed (*angemacht*), while *eine Salatplatte* as a main dish will satisfy the most confirmed and hungry vegetarian.

SALZKARTOFFELN n.p. 'salt potatoes' are boiled potatoes. Germans occasionally add salt to cooked food, though never before tasting it first.

SANDKUCHEN n.m. 'sandcake' – a dry, Madeira-type sponge cake made from *Kartoffelmehl* (potato flour), sometimes called *Sandtorte*. Both *Kuchen* and *Torte** usually mean gateau rather than the sort of sponge cake you can eat with your fingers (*Rührkuchen*; if fatless, *Biskuitkuchen**) – a manoeuvre which epitomizes the gulf between Tonio Kröger, Thomas Mann's sensitive *alter ego*, and his unproblematical schoolfriend, Hans Hansen, seen munching *ein großes Stück Sandtorte, wobei er die hohle Hand unters Kinn hielt, um die Krümel aufzufangen* ('catching the crumbs under his chin in the palm of his hand').

SARDELLE n.f. anchovy. Sardine: *die Sardine*.

SAUER adj. either **1.** sour (*Schweinefleisch süßsauer*, sweet and sour pork), off (*Sauermilch*), tart (*Sauerkirschen*, sour cherries), acidic (*ein sauerer Wein*);

or **2.** pickled – *Sauerkraut**is, of course, pickled cabbage, generally boiled with caraway seeds (*Kümmel*), and *Sauerbraten* braised beef marinated in vinegar. Austrians call soured boiled rump or pot-roast *der Tafelspitz* (it was what the Emperor Franz Joseph ate every day from the age of fifteen until his death, aged 86). However, *Sauerstoff** is not vinegar (*der Essig*) but oxygen.

Die Sauregurkenzeit – the summer months when gherkins are picked and pickled and little business is done – is a slack period, or the silly season in politics and journalism (see SOMMERTHEATER and SCHRECKEN in II).

Jemandem das Leben sauer machen means to make someone's life a misery. This echoes Luther's famous translation of the Apocryphal *Buch Jesus Sirach*, 11.11: *Mancher läßt es sich sauer werden und eilt zum Reichtum, und hindert sich nur selber damit*, lamenting the strenuous efforts made to acquire wealth as merely a further obstacle to salvation. But a person who is *sauer* is more than merely sour (*verdrießlich, griesgrämig, verbittert*), he's angry: *ich bin ganz schön sauer.* The even more forceful exclamation *das ist eine Sauerei!* (it's a bloody disgrace) derives from *die Sau* (sow; cf. *eine Schweinerei* under SCHWEIN below).

SCHALE n.f. the shell of an egg (*Eierschale*) or nut (*Nußschale*), but also the skin of fruit or vegetables, the rind* of cheese, or husk of grain. Hence, *Erbsen schälen* (or *enthülsen*) is to shell peas, *eine Tomate schälen* to skin a tomato, *einen Apfel schälen* to peel an apple. In addition, a bowl or serving dish, and in the south, a cup (see the additional meaning of *Nußschale* under KAFFEE above). A drink which has gone flat or which tastes stale is *schal* or *abgestanden.*

SCHANK n.f. not the shank of one's leg: the 'shrunk shank' which, according to the melancholy Jaques, characterizes the sixth age of man in *As You Like It* (Act II, Scene 7) becomes his *dünner Unterschenkel* in *Wie es euch gefällt.* A horse's shank, though, is known, rather curiously, as *der Unterarm* (on Shanks's pony, however, is *auf Schusters Rappen*); a shank of beef as *eine Hachse* (see *Schweinshaxe* under EISBEIN above); the shank of a spoon as *der Stiel,* and of a key as *der Schaft.*

In Austria, *die Schank* or *die Ausschank* is a bar (from *ausschenken,* to serve drinks), specifically the room or counter where the drinks are served (German: *der Schankraum, der Ausschank*), and *Schankbier* *is draught beer.

SCHARF adj. hot, highly seasoned, but not unpleasantly 'sharp' in the sense of very sour*. *Würstchen* *, when served on a plate, are traditionally accompanied by *Senf* (mustard; very hot mustard is *Löwensenf*) and either *Meerrettich* (horseradish, in Austria *Kren*), which is *scharf,* or *Sauerkraut* *, which is not. See also SCHARF in I and VI.

SCHELLFISCH n.m. haddock, not shellfish (these are technically *Schalfische,* but in a culinary context *Meeresfrüchte,* like French *fruits de mer*; see also KRABBE above). So called because its flesh flakes apart in shell-shaped pieces (see SCHALE above and SCHELLE in IX). Place alternate layers of salted haddock and sliced potatoes in a buttered casserole, add pepper and an onion browned in butter, and bake with an egg and cream topping to make *Schellfisch nach Hamburger Art*.*

SCHLAG n.m. in Austria, especially Vienna, short for *Schlagobers* * (which is also the title of a frothy concoction by Johann Strauss).

Kaffee mit Schlag is coffee with (low fat) whipped cream, known elsewhere in the south as *Schlagrahm*, and generally as *Schlagsahne*. However, *nimm Dir noch 'nen (einen) Schlag* means 'have a second helping'.

SCHLEIM n.m. gruel (*der Haferschleim*, oat gruel; *der Haferbrei*, porridge). *Schleimsuppe* is gruel soup for children or invalids – tastier than it sounds, though *Schleim* indeed *is* the word for slime, mucus or phlegm (*schleimlösende Mittel*, expectorants). Of people, *schleimig* is as unpleasant as 'slimy'.

SCHMALZ n.n. a sentimental, 'schmaltzy' film or piece of music is *der Schmalz*, whereas *das Schmalz* is dripping. Served in little grey stoneware jars in the best restaurants in northern Germany, *Gänseschmalz* (goose dripping, rather than *Schweineschmalz*, pork lard, or *der Talg*, suet) is a delicious appetizer, usually 'on the house'. In the south, however, *Schmalz* generally means *Butterschmalz*, clarified butter. *Schmalzgebäck* is pastry with the consistency of doughnuts.

SCHOLLE n.f. not sole (*die Seezunge*), but plaice, probably the Germans' favourite sea fish (but see HERING above), eaten off the bone with *Salzkartoffeln**, *Speck** and *Buttersoße*.

Also an ice floe or a clod of earth. The call of what Irishmen refer to as 'the oul' sod' is more regional in Germany: *die heimatliche* Scholle*. A turf or sod is also known as *eine Sode*, but *Sodbrennen* is not connected with burning turf: it's heartburn.

SCHOPPEN n.m. originally a half-litre measure, now in the south a quarter-litre (also *ein Viertel*) – a glass or small carafe of wine or half-pint of beer (and in Switzerland, a *Saugflasche* or baby's bottle). *Zum Frühschoppen gehen* is to go out for a morning/lunch-time drink, and perhaps a game of cards, usually on a Sunday. *Der Frühschoppen* was also the name of a long-running, serious, Sunday-morning discussion programme on TV.

SCHWARZBROT n.n. broadly used of brown breads such as *Roggenbrot* (rye bread) as well as black *Pumpernickel**.

SCHWEIN n.n. either a pig, or pork. Also, of course, a term of abuse (though the much-maligned *Schweinehund* is actually the dog used on a *Saujagd* to chase *Schwarzwild**, wild pigs); *eine Schweinerei* is a disgusting business, a scandal, a mean trick, a filthy joke. But *ein armes Schwein* is simply 'a poor sod'. There is more condescension than pity in one recent joke: *ein kluges Westhuhn und ein dummes Ostschwein machen Joint-venture: Ham-und-eggs* (a clever hen from the West and a stupid pig from the East set up a joint venture: ham and eggs). On the other hand, *das Glücksschwein(chen)* is a symbol of good luck – hence *Schwein gehabt!* which means 'that's a bit of luck', not 'what a pig of a business'. *Wer Schwein hat, ist keins*: roughly 'nothing succeeds like success'.

A propos pigs, readers of *Schwein oder Nichtschwein*, the inspired German rendering of P. G. Wodehouse's *If Pigs had Wings*, will have no difficulty recognizing the pun on Hamlet's dilemma, *Sein oder Nichtsein?* Nor will they be surprised that Lord Emsworth's favourite reading, Whiffle's 'homeric masterpiece' *On the Care of the Pig*, recommends rigorous adherence to the theories of one Wolff-Lehmann, undoubtedly a German *Wissenschaftler** (see MAST above and SPECK below).

SEKT n.m. not a a religious sect (*eine Sekte*), but German sparkling wine (*Schaumwein*) – the price will alert you to the fact that it is not *Champagner*. Originally a sweet wine ('*vin sec*' only in so far as it was made from dried-out *Trockenbeeren* – see PRÄDIKAT above), the story goes that in 1830 the actor Ludwig Devrient called for 'a cup of sack' in Lutter und Wegners Weinstube in Berlin to celebrate his success as Falstaff, and was taken to mean champagne.

SELLERIE n.f. usually means celeriac (*Knollensellerie*) rather than celery (*Stangensellerie*). See SALAT above.

SET n.m. or n.n. specifically, one of a set of tablemats or place mats (normally used in the plural, *Sets*).

SITZFLEISCH n.n. 'sitting flesh' – actually refers to endurance rather than excess weight. *Sitzfleisch haben* is an ability to sit still; figuratively, to stick at it. Helmut Kohl, for instance, is well endowed with *Sitzfleisch* (but see also SPECK below) and famous for 'solving' problems by 'sitting them out', *aussitzen* (humorously, this also means to overstay one's welcome). *Kein Sitzfleisch haben*: to get fidgety (*nervös**). The cognate *sitzenbleiben* means to be 'left sitting' at a dance, or 'on the shelf', or to have to repeat a year at school (see GYMNASIUM in IV).

SPECK n.m. bacon fat rather than lean (*durchwachsener Speck*, *Schinkenspeck*). Diced fried *Speck* is often added to other dishes such as *Speckknödel* (dumplings), or *Scholle* mit Speckkartoffeln* (plaice with boiled potatoes, parsley, *Speck*, and a butter sauce), or the typically bitter-sweet combination of *Blaukraut* mit Äpfeln und Zwiebeln* (red cabbage with apples and onions). But bacon and eggs, *Eier mit Speck* or *Ham and Eggs*, is not really a German dish – unlike *Strammer Max*, an open sandwich of *gekochter Schinken*, boiled ham, and *Spiegelei*, fried egg (a poached egg is *ein verlorenes Ei*: 'forlorn').

Speck is commonly used to mean 'flab'. Chancellor Kohl, for instance, lends weight to this usage since he regularly spends his summer holidays at a 'secret' retreat in St Gilgen on the Wolfgangsee *beim Abspecken*, on a rigorous diet. See also SCHWEIN above.

SPEKULATIUS n.m. a small, spiced biscuit (*Keks**) in human or animal shape – a pre-Christmas speciality (perhaps because St Nikolaus is also called the *Speculator*), delicious with coffee.

SPENDIEREN v. to spend money is *Geld ausgeben*, but *spendieren* refers to what you spend it on: *ich spendiere eine Runde* (this round's on me); *bei seiner Abschiedsfeier spendierte er Champagner für alle* (at his farewell party he stood them all/treated them all to champagne). *Spendabel* is generous, open-handed (mostly with drinks). See also the limited sense of SPENDEN in II.

SPRITZER n.m. a spritzer (white wine with soda water) is in fact *ein Gespritzter* or *eine Schorle* in German – *ein Spritzer* refers only to a splash or dash of water (or perfume; and in the south, a shower of rain). *Ein spritziger Wein* tastes slightly tangy*, *pikant*; or, as the wine merchants say, it has a slight prickle, an almost imperceptible touch of effervescence.

STAMMTISCH n.m. (not only) Germans once identified with their *Stamm* or tribe; now they sit in their local *Stammkneipe* round the (weekly, sometimes nightly) *Stammtisch* – the table reserved for regular *Stammkunden*. Strangers should join *eine Stammtischrunde* only when invited. It is the natural habitat of Mr Average (*Otto Normalverbraucher*), sometimes linked with the local *Schützenverein* (comparable to a branch of the National Rifle Association in the United States).

But the place of a *Stammvater* or *Stammutter* is at the head of a *Stammbaum* (family tree), or in Darwin's *Abstammungslehre* (theory of evolution – see ART in X). They are one's progenitor/progenitrix. Had the famous debate taken place in German, 'Soapy Sam' Wilberforce, Bishop of Oxford, would have asked T. H. Huxley *ob er väterlicherseits oder mütterlicherseits vom Affen abstamme?* – 'if he was descended from apes on his father's side, or his mother's?'

STAMPER n.m. (or *das Stamperl*), a small, stemless wine or schnapps glass in Bavaria and Austria.

STEIN n.m. stone; in this context a stone mug (*Steinkrug*) – more often called *ein Maßkrug* or simply *ein Krug*, containing half a litre of beer in northern Germany, and a full litre or *Maß** in Bavaria (sometimes *Bockbier**). *Steinhäger* is a juniper-flavoured Westphalian schnapps; *Steinpilz* (*boletus edulis*, also known as *Herrenpilz*) the most sought-after mushroom – fleshy and full-flavoured. For the various *Steine* (pieces) in chess, see SPRINGEN in VII.

STILL adj. neither an adverb (*noch*; more emphatically, *noch immer*; sometimes in exasperation, *immer noch*; as ever, *nach wie vor*; see TEE below), nor a conjunction (and still, *und dennoch*), but an adjective only. Thus, *stör ich eu'r Spiel, wenn staunend ich still hier steh'?* does not mean 'spoilt were your sport if 'stonished I stand here still?' (an early *Stabreim** rendering of Alberich's dalliance with the Rhinemaidens, recalled by Lord Berners in his autobiography), but properly: if I stand here motionless, silently, even secretly. A better known musical example is, of course, *Stille Nacht, heilige Nacht.*

Still water (if not *stille Wasser*, which, say the proverb, *gründen tief*) is *Wasser ohne Kohlensäure*, fizzy water *Wasser mit Kohlensäure*. The verb *stillen* means to still, allay, satisfy, quench, and specifically, to breast-feed: *eine stillende Mutter* is a nursing mother.

STÖVCHEN n.n. 'little stove', actually a samovar, made of glass or copper and with a candle in the middle, for keeping a teapot or coffeepot warm (or your feet in the north of Germany, where *eine Stove* is a drying room and *ein Stövchen* also a warming-pan using hot coals).

STRAUSSWIRTSCHAFT n.f. one of the three meanings of *der Strauß* is a broom: home-grown wine for sale, like French *vente directe* or Italian *vento diretto*, is advertised by the display of a fir bush or broom of twigs outside the *Straußwirtschaft* (or *Besenwirtschaft* in the Stuttgart area). *Strauß* here derives from the plumage worn on helmets, and is still the word for a bouquet of flowers (to avoid committing a breach of etiquette – *um nicht gegen die Etikette* zu verstoßen* – one always, for inscrutable reasons, gives an odd number, never forgetting to half-remove the wrapping paper). Consequently, *eine Straußwirtschaft* has no connection with Germany's erstwhile Finance Minister (and subsequent Prime Minister of Bavaria), Franz Josef Strauß. Nor does *Vogel-Strauß-Politik* refer to an unlikely political alliance between Strauß and the leader of the SPD after the 1982 *Wende**, Hans-Jochen Vogel – it is derived rather from the second sense of *Strauß*, an ostrich, and signifies an ostrich-like or head-in-the-sand policy. The third meaning of *Strauß* is now somewhat dated: a struggle or battle, as in *einen Strauß ausfechten.*

SUD n.m. not suds (*das Seifenwasser*; lather, *der Seifenschaum*), but the liquid left after cooking: *den Sud des Gemüses abgießen*, to pour off the vegetable water; *den Braten aus dem Sud herausnehmen*, to take the roast out of its juice; *den Sud des Fleisches zu einer Soße andicken*, to thicken the meat stock into a gravy.

SÜSSWASSER n.n. not 'sweet water'/sugar water (*Zucker-wasser*), but fresh water as distinct from *Salzwasser*.

TANG n.m. (as in Scotland) seaweed. Not a distinctive after-taste (*ein starker Nachgeschmack*) or pungent smell (*ein scharfer* Geruch*).

TEE n.m. tea. However, *schwarzer Tee* is not black tea (*Tee ohne Milch*; lemon tea, *Tee mit Zitrone*), but tea as distinct from an infusion such as *Pfefferminztee* (peppermint tea), *Hagebuttentee* (rose-hip tea), *Kamillentee* (camomile tea), and many, many more. Skiers drink *Jägertee*, hot tea with rum. 'And is there honey still* for tea?' is tricky, since Germans prefer their *Honig* with breakfast rolls and enjoy mid-afternoon *Kaffee* und Kuchen* (even if they take tea instead of coffee), while an early evening meal is already *das Abendbrot*.

TIP n.m. a tip (on the 3.30, or the stock exchange), but not what you tip in a restaurant (*das Trinkgeld*). The art of adding a tip to the bill calls for a quick calculation: ask for the bill – *Herr Ober!* (or *Fräulein!*, nowadays also *Frau Ober!* or, even more politically correct if some-what peremptory, *Bedienung!*) *Die Rechnung, bitte!* – and when you get it, tell the waiter or waitress directly what you want to pay. Even if a service charge of 10% or 15% is included (*Service/Bedienung ist im Preis einbegriffen*), it is customary to round up the figure by a mark or two. If told *Das macht DM37,80* you might say *Vierzig Mark*, or if you have the exact amount, *Stimmt so!* (no change required).

In a sporting context, *tippen* means to place a bet (*im Toto/Lotto*, to do the pools/lottery). *Ich tippe auf Boris Becker* can mean either that I back him/put my money on him to win, or else that he is my tip to win. Also to tap or touch something lightly, and hence to type, though *das Tippfräulein* (sometimes rudely known as *die Tippse*) is more properly called *die Stenotypistin*, now more widely and blandly known as *eine Schreibkraft*. Germans like to describe the perfect holiday, accommodation, cuisine, as being *tipptopp*.

TIPPELN v. neither to indulge in heavy drinking (*süffeln, saufen*), nor to go for the occasional tipple (*picheln, einen trinken gehen, einen heben, einen kippen**), but to 'foot it', usually a longish distance (unlike *trippeln*, which is associated with children and women wear-ing high heels; see also WANDERN in VII and KISSEN in VI).

TOAST n.m. the delicious coffee and fresh rolls of a German breakfast more than compensate for the plastic containers of *Erdbeer-konfitüre* or *Aprikosenkonfitüre* most hotels serve, while the long-life

Toastbrot* occasionally on offer deserves no better. But a German *Toast* such as *Camembert mit Preiselbeeren* (with toasted camembert and cranberries), *Toast Hawaii* (with ham, pineapple, and cheese *au gratin*), or *Herrentoast* (with steak and garnish*) makes a delicious evening snack.

You can still propose a toast on more formal occasions, *einen Toast* (*Trinkspruch*) *ausbringen*; East Germans in particular were often obliged to listen to a *Toast* rather than drink one – a far cry from the sort of gathering which dashing Hungarian officers established as an Austrian tradition – *ein Mullatschak* or *Mullatschag*, concluding with the smashing of glasses (*mullattieren*).

TORTE n.f. cake or gateau, rather than our fruit or jam tarts made with *Mürbeteig* (short-crust pastry) or the (flaky) pastries known as *Plundergebäck**. Puff-pastry, stretched until it is thin enough to read a newspaper through it and used in *mille-feuille* or real *Apfelstrudel*, is *Blätterteig*. *Schwarzwälder Kirschtorte*, or simply *Schwarzwälder Kirsch*, is only one of many multilayered *Obsttorten*, though an *Obsttorte* or *Obstkuchen* may also be a single layer of fruit in a flan base (*der Tortenboden*) made of *Biskuit** (sponge). *Törtchen/Biskuittörtchen* are sponge buns with sugar or chocolate icing, whereas *Torteletts* are tartlets with fruit or cheese filling, and *Schnitten* fruit or cream slices. Tart as a taste is *bitter, sauer**. See also SACHERTORTE, SANDKUCHEN, PASTETE above.

TRAFIK n.f. in Austria, a tobacconist's shop (short for *Tabaktrafik*) which also sells newspapers and whose proprietor is *ein Trafikant*. So when Friedrich Torberg identifies the typical reader of Vienna's tabloid *Kronen-Zeitung* as *eine Trafikantenwitwe* (*Die Tante Jolesch*, 1977, p. 127), he does not mean the widow of a drugs trafficker, *ein Rauschgifthändler* or *Drogenhändler* (see FIXER in VII).

ÜBERKOCHEN v. not to 'over-cook' (*verbraten, zu lange braten*), but to boil over. By contrast, *überbraten* means only to roast or fry lightly (see also ÜBERSEHEN in II and ÜBERHÖREN in X).

VESPER n.n. *die Vesper* is vespers, but in the south *die* or *das Vesper* is also a break for food (*das Vesperbrot*) at any time of the day, though *die Vesperzeit* is usually in the afternoon. *Er vespert gerade*, he's just having his break. The implication is sometimes: he's guzzling.

WÄSSERN v. to soak (herrings, peas), or to water the lawn, but to water flowers is *Blumen gießen*; horses, *Pferde tränken*; and (scandalously) wine, *den Wein verdünnen* or *panschen*.

WEINBRAND n.m. not a brand of wine (*eine Marke**), but German brandy (since the word *cognac* was protected by the Treaty of Versailles), not to be confused with the cheaper *Branntwein* (also the general word for 'spirits*'; rotgut or hooch is *der Fusel*). See BRAND in IX.

WEINGUT n.n. an estate (*ein Gut**) which grows wine – no connection with a beer belly (*der Bierbauch*).

WILD n.n. (also *Wildbret*) game – venison if not further specified (*Wildschwein**, wild boar), while *Wildente* (duck) and *Wildgans* (goose) will appear on the menu under *Geflügel*. Since *wild* is also something illegal (see WILD in VI), the word for a poacher is doubly appropriate: *ein Wilderer*.

WOLF n.m. short for *Fleischwolf*: a meat shredder, mincer, grinder.

WURST n.f. salami (sliced on an open *Wurstbrot*, or in a *Wurstaufschnitt* selection), as well as the ubiquitous *Bratwurst mit Senf* (with mustard) or *Currywurst* (with curry sauce). There are local specialities served in pairs and closer in shape at least to the British banger, such as *ein paar Nürnberger*, or in Vienna *ein paar Würstel* (which – as *Die Zeit* observed on 18 May 1990 – *im ganzen Land auf gar keinen Fall Wiener genannt werden dürfe*, which should under no circumstances be called *Wiener* anywhere in Austria). *Warme Würstchen* are hot dogs. *Es ist mir Wurst*, it's all the same to me, I couldn't care less (see also EGAL in II).

ZINN n.n. tin, but also pewter: traditional hostelries might serve sausages and sauerkraut on a *Zinnteller*, sometimes even beer in a *Zinnbecher*. Tins of food are *Büchsen* or *Dosen**.

CLOTHES
and
HOUSES

KLEIDER
und
HÄUSER

ADJUSTIEREN v. to adjust or set (a mechanism, for instance; more commonly: *justieren*), but not in Austria, where it means 'to issue with a uniform': *die Soldaten wurden adjustiert* (the soldiers were kitted out). Hence, *was für eine Adjustierung!* what a get-up (i.e. what ostentatious dress).

ADRETT adj. not adroit in the sense of dexterous (*geschickt*, *gewandt*) or shrewd (*scharf**, *scharfsinnig*), but well turned out, nicely dressed. In a job description: *es gilt der Grundsatz, nett und adrett* (our rule is: always be friendly, neat and tidy). See also AKKURAT below.

AKKURAT adj. formerly used of an 'accurate' dress sense: *sie ist immer äußerst akkurat gekleidet* (always most fastidiously dressed), now more commonly *korrekt* or *adrett. Die Akkuratesse* is thus painstaking exactitude, meticulousness (*akkurat arbeiten*, to work precisely; *eine akkurate Schrift*, neat handwriting), or punctiliousness of behaviour, as when Gretchen complains to Faust that her mother *ist in allen Stücken so akkurat!* (l. 3114). In Austria, *akkurat* is often used as an adverb: *akkurat wie ein Professor!* (just* like a professor!); *es ist akkurat so!* (that's exactly it!). But the usual word for accurate/accurately is *genau*.

ANTIKE n.f. the *Antiquitäten* which Germans hope to find in English or French antique shops (*Antiquitätenläden*) are seldom connected with *die Antike* which is (Greek and Roman) antiquity, or a work of art from that period. This, of course, does not prevent today's *Antikmärkte* from designating their wares *antik* rather than, more properly, *kram**. See also ANTIQUARIAT in X.

APARTMENT n.n. a flat or small apartment with no more than one or two rooms (*eine komfortable Kleinwohnung*, according to Duden). Also a suite of rooms in a hotel – French pronunciation is optional, but the spelling is usually then *Appartement*. The East German writer Christoph Hein noticed that the word was also slipping into real existing socialism: *ein Gebäude mit Einzimmerwohnungen. Man nennt sie jetzt Appartements* (*Der fremde Freund*, 1982, p. 24).

BLOCKHAUS n.n. nowadays more often a log cabin (*eine Blockhütte*) or log-built house or chalet (*ein Blockbau*) than a military blockhouse (*ein Beobachtungsbunker*). *Ein Häuserblock* is a block of houses, usually divided into flats, but young Germans often aspire to build their own British-scale *Reihenhaus* – a terraced house with its own small garden. See also DOPPELHAUS and TERRASSENHAUS below.

BRAND n.m. not a piece of burning wood (*ein Feuerbrand*; a torch is *eine Fackel*) but the fire or blaze itself. *Brandstifter* are arsonists (see under BIEDERMEIER in II) and *ein Hausbrand* a house fire (in the old days, though, *Hausbrand/Hausbrandkohle* signified only the coal used for domestic heating). Horses or cattle may carry *ein Brandzeichen*, but branded goods are *Markenartikel** or *mit einem Warenzeichen versehen*. Curiously, the verb *branden* is connected rather with water than with fire – waves which surge, beat or crash on the shore *branden*, and *die Brandung* (see MARKE in III) is the surf.

COTTAGE n.n. a select residential area ('*Villenviertel*') on the outskirts of Vienna.

DEMOLIEREN v. *ein demoliertes Haus* has merely been vandalized, *ein abgerissenes Haus* has been demolished. Only the Austrians use *demolieren* in both senses – Karl Kraus, for instance, begins *Die demolirte Literatur* (1897) by equating the demolition of Vienna's Café Griensteidl with the wrecking of the city's intimate *Kaffeehauskultur** (*Wien wird jetzt zur Großstadt demolirt*). Figurative use is mainly humorous: *er sah ganz schön demoliert aus* (he looked a complete wreck); to 'demolish' food is *verschlingen, vertilgen, verdrücken, verputzen*.

DOPPELHAUS n.n. a 'double house' (US duplex), in fact two semi-detached houses (*das europäische Doppelhaus* was a common metaphor in the late 1980s, envisaging the peaceful coexistence of two ideologies still divided by the Berlin Wall). But new, purpose-built 'semis' are not common, while a detached *Einfamilienhaus*, especially in a desirable suburb (*eine Villa im Vorort*), is beyond the reach of all but the very wealthy, so families sometimes buy jointly, often dividing horizontally between the upper and lower floors of what then becomes a *Zweifamilienhaus*. Or else, since there is no mortgage interest tax relief, they rent until they can buy a more expensive house when they are older, taking advantage of an eight-year depreciation allowance.

German buyers must in any case save for years with a *Bausparkasse** before being allowed a *Hypothek* (mortgage); even then, it will be a much lower percentage of the purchase price than the 85% borrowed by the average first-time British buyer in the more volatile, speculative UK market. Even before reunification, only two Germans in five owned their own home, compared with two Britons in three. See also BLOCKHAUS and TERRASSENHAUS in this section.

DRESS n.m. specifically a jockey's outfit, more generally sports kit or strip, though not a dress (*das Kleid*; casual dress, *Freizeitkleidung*). But see also DRESSMAN in VI.

DRESSIEREN v. not to dress oneself (*sich anziehen*), but to train an animal to do something (*der Rottweiler wurde auf Einbrecher dressiert*, trained to attack burglars; *ein halbdressiertes Tier* is semi-trained), and hence also to condition a person. The noun is *die Dressur* (cf. dressage). Before Faust discovers *des Pudels Kern* (l. 1323) – the black dog following him is Mephistopheles – he is disappointed that there seems to be nothing preternatural about it: *ich finde nicht die Spur / von einem Geist*, und alles ist Dressur* (ll. 1173–4).

Dressieren is also used of decorating a cake, preparing meat, or dressing poultry, but not of dressing a salad (*einen Salat anmachen*), though *Dressing* is now a naturalized 'German' word for salad dressing. To dress a wound, *eine Wunde verbinden*.

FADE adj. of colours: pale, dull, watery (though a pair of faded blue jeans is *eine verwaschene Jeanshose*); of food: tasteless, bland. Austrians call people they think prissy, squeamish, boring or 'wet', *fad*. The opposite (things English having once been fashionable) is *fesch*: good-looking, fun-loving, fast-living (German *flott*); add a Slav ending, and you have the typically Viennese male chauvinist *Feschak* – a good bloke to his friends and something of a dandy.

FEUDAL adj. the ultimate accolade when describing a house, hotel, restaurant, or its furnishings: magnificent, sumptuous, splendidly* plush (see also NOBEL below). Though irony is not precluded ('posh', 'fancy'), it was a different sense of the feudal spirit which East Germans had in mind when they berated* the West as *feudal*.

FIRST n.m. the ridge of a house, or a mountain ridge. What the Germans call *ein Richtfest* is in Austria *eine Firstfeier* – the topping-out ceremony when the roof is decked out with a small tree (*der Richtbaum*) or wreath (*der Richtkranz*) – in which context note that Ibsen's *The Master Builder* is known in Germany as *Baumeister* Sölness*. For first, see ERST in VI.

FLAIR n.n. the Swiss still use the word in our sense of having a natural aptitude for something (*einen Flair für etwas haben*; in German, *ein Talent, eine Begabung*), but elsewhere it is applied to the distinctive and pleasing atmosphere of a place – Hamburg, for instance, has more right than most German cities to call itself *eine*

Stadt mit Flair – or to the attractive aura surrounding a person, as in *sie hat ein Flair von Vornehmheit* (an aura of nobility; see also FLUIDUM in VI). 'She has a flair for clothes': *sie hat einen Sinn für Kleider, sie hat Stil.*

FLICKEN v. not to flick (*er schnippte die Krümel weg*, he flicked the crumbs away), but to mend by darning or patching. *Ein Flickschuster*, once a cobbler, is now anyone who botches a job, and *Flickwerk*, patchwork, is equally pejorative: *diese Reform ist elendes Flickwerk geblieben*, this reform is a miserable hotch-potch. *Die Flick-Affäre*, however, was neither a patched-up nor a botched love affair, but a political scandal named after Karl Friedrich Flick, chief Daimler-Benz shareholder and the richest man in Germany (see FALL and SPENDEN in II).

FLUR n.m. a corridor, or the hall or landing of a house/flat (the floor is *der Fußboden*; on the ground floor, *im Erdgeschoß*; on the first floor, *im ersten Stock**), as distinct from *die Flur*, which is open countryside, fields, meadows, much celebrated in German poetry and song. Figuratively, *er steht allein auf weiter Flur* means he is out on a limb.

FOPPEREI n.f. not foppery (*die Ziererei*; a fop is *ein Geck* or *Stutzer*), but a dated word for leg-pulling (see NECKEN in VI). The verb is *foppen*, to tease: *sie fühlte sich gefoppt*, she felt she had been made a fool of.

GALA n.f. not the event, but the dress worn to a *Galaempfang* (formal reception), *Galavorstellung* (gala performance), *Galakonzert*, etc.

GALANTERIEWAREN n.f.p. formerly fashion accessories (the shop-sign over the Kafka family's wholesale business in the Palais Kinsky in Prague advertised *Galanteriewaren en gros*), now fancy goods, novelties, cheap costume jewellery (the real thing is *der Schmuck**), reflecting a debased, ironic perception of 'gallant' behaviour (*ein galantes Abenteuer*, an amorous adventure). See also BRAV in II and VI, KAVALIER in VI.

GARDEROBE n.f. where you leave your overcoat in the theatre (*der Garderobier/die Garderobiere* is the attendant, but also an actor's dresser), or hang it up at home. Also the contents of one's wardrobe (*eine völlig neue Garderobe*, a completely new outfit), though not the wardrobe itself (*der Kleiderschrank*).

GÜRTEL n.m. not a girdle (*ein Hüfthalter*), but the normal word for a belt, also in the sense of the Oxford Green Belt, or the US Wheat Belt. *Ein Schlag unter die Gürtellinie*, hitting below the belt.

HAUSEN v. to be poorly housed (*die Armen mußten in einer Baracke* hausen*), or else to wreak havoc (*wie die Wandalen/Vandalen hausen* – to vandalize; *wer hat denn hier gehaust?*, who's made such a mess here?). Hence, *wir haben im letzten Winter schrecklich mit unseren Holzvorräten gehaust* (we were terribly heavy on our wood supply last winter), though the Swiss are true to character in using *hausen* to mean just the opposite: 'to be economical' (see HAUSHALT below).

HAUSHALT n.m. household or housekeeping, but also the normal word for the national budget (see ETAT and LAST in III). Distinguish also between *haushalten*, to husband one's resources (*du mußt mit deiner Zeit besser haushalten*, you must be more economical with your time; *ich muß mit meinen Kräften jetzt haushalten*, I must conserve my energy) and *Haus halten*, to live in the grand manner (*in München, wo die Manns Haus hielten*, in Munich where the Manns resided).

Die Haushälterin is the housekeeper, not the householder. This is *der Hausbewohner* (occupant) or *der Hausbesitzer/Hauseigentümer* (owner); one might address one's hosts as *der Hausherr* and *die Hausherrin* (see under HOSTESS in VII) and the head of the household, nowadays probably in jest, as *der Herr des Hauses*.

HAUSIEREN v. not to house (*unterbringen* or *beherbergen*: *die Stuttgarter Staatsgalerie beherbergt gleich am Eingang eine riesengroße Beuys-Plastik**), but to hawk goods from door to door. *Hausieren verboten!* no hawkers. Also to peddle rumours: *er geht mit dieser Geschichte hausieren*, he's at it again, telling the same old story, bandying it about.

HEIMLICH adj. not 'homely' (*eine gemütliche, behagliche Atmosphäre*; *eine häusliche Frau*; if plain and unsophisticated, *unscheinbar*, *hausbacken**). Instead, *heimlich* now means secret, also secretive, clandestine, furtive. Nor does *unheimlich* mean 'unhomely' (*nicht gemütlich* – lacking in geniality, comfort, good cheer), but eerie, sinister, spooky, uncanny (see SCHAUER in X for *das Unheimliche* of Gothic horror stories). As an adverb, it is now a mere intensifier: *unheimlich viel Geld*, a tremendous amount of money, *unheimlich schön*, incredibly beautiful.

HEIMSUCHEN n.f. a *Heim* is usually a hostel or a home for the elderly etc., but *ein Eigenheim* (like *eine eigene Wohnung*) is a home of one's own – every German's dream of a little detached house in the suburbs. Nevertheless, *heimsuchen* does not mean 'to search for a house' (*wir sind auf Haussuche*, house-hunting), but literally 'to seek someone out at home', though not necessarily what Scottish law means by 'hamesucken', namely the assaulting of a man in his own house. It is merely what a tiresome visitor does. East German *Kulturministerin**Margot Honecker, for instance, once visited the dissident song-writer Wolf Biermann in an attempt to silence his criticisms of her husband's regime: *sie schwebte im Nerz die zwei Treppen hoch und suchte mich heim in meiner Bruchbude* (*Die Zeit*, 24 August 1990): 'after sailing up the two flights of stairs in her mink, she sought me out ('descended on me') in my shabby digs'. Figuratively, then, *eine Heimsuchung* is invariably unwelcome. It is what plagues Hamlet (*wäre ich nicht von schlechten Träumen heimgesucht*, 'were it not that I have bad dreams', II,2), and what haunted Rilke about the First World War, which he thought it best to confront as a natural catastrophe: *als ein Heimgesuchter in der Natur, oder heimsuchend wider seinen Willen* (as one who suffers nature's afflictions, or unwillingly afflicts them – *Briefe II*, pp. 141,42; see also *Hammer oder Amboß* under MORAL in V).

Isolated exceptions are the biblical *Fest der Heimsuchung Mariä*, Visitation of Mary (on 31 May), and the 'accommodation sought' ads in newspapers in southern Germany, which may be listed under *Heimsuchung*.

HERD n.m. a cooker or range (usually, in Germany, an *Elektroherd* rather than a *Gasherd*), or else a hearth, but not a herd (*die Herde*). Any link between the *Herdeninstinkt* which Nietzsche deplored and a proverb such as *eigener Herd ist Goldes wert* ('one's own fireplace is worth gold', meaning 'there's no place like home') is merely fortuitous, not linguistic. When the writer and revolutionary Georg Forster visited England in 1790, he attributed the widespread wearing of glasses to a weakness of vision caused by staring into open fires; the open fire is still the exception rather than the rule in centrally-heated Germany, where it is named after the chimney rather than the hearth (*ein lustiges Feuer brannte im Kamin*, a fire was blazing away in the hearth). The real focus of the home is the kitchen stove (*den ganzen Tag am Herd stehen*, to slave all day over a hot stove) – see also OFEN below.

The meaning of *Herd* as the centre of the house is preserved in such figurative terms as *Unruheherd* (centre of civil strife, trouble spot) and *Infektionsherd* (focus of infection).

HOSE n.f. the normal word for trousers or pants. While the garment is usually singular (*ein paar braune Hosen*, say, is rather old-fashioned), the figurative use is in the plural (*bei Meiers hat die Frau die Hosen an*, she wears the trousers). *Eine Hose* is sometimes also an abbreviation for *Badehose* (swimming-trunks) or *Unterhose* (underpants – see SLIP below). A panty-hose/pair of tights is *eine Strumpf-hose* (a hosier sells *Strumpfwaren**), the smallest size being called *lilliput*. In the south, it is still common to see men wearing *eine Bundhose* or *Kniehose* (hose in the sense of knee breeches – in the north, though less frequently, *Knickerbocker* or *Kniebundhose*), or else the looser-fitting *Lederhose*. For watering the garden one uses *ein Schlauch*, not *eine Wasserhose* – this is a waterspout and *eine Windhose* a whirlwind or tornado.

HUT n.m. & n.f. if masculine, a hat; if feminine, protection in general, not just for the head. *In Gottes Hut stehen*, to be in God's keeping; *der Hüter meines Bruders*, my brother's keeper; *sei auf der Hut!/hüte dich!* be on your guard.

But *den Hut aufsetzen*, to put on one's hat. *Hut ab!* I take my hat off to you, her, etc. *Hut ab, meine Herren, ein Genie*!* ('Hats off, gentleman, a genius') – Schumann, the first German critic to recognize Chopin.

For the more specialized industrial sense of *eine Hütte* (hut), see HÜTTE in III.

IMMOBILIEN n.p. real estate, property – *ein Immobilienhändler* or *Immobilienmakler* (in Austria, *Realitätenhändler** or *Realitäten-vermittler*) is an estate agent/US realtor – someone who deals in 'immovables' as distinct from *Mobilien* (a dated term for furnishings, chattels: now *das Mobiliar* or *die Einrichtung*).

INSTALLATEUR n.m. specifically, a plumber (also *ein Klemp-ner*, someone who deals with *die Wasserinstallation*), or else a specialized fitter (*Elektroinstallateur, Gasinstallateur*).

ISOLATION n.f., **ISOLIERUNG** n.f. insulation (*das Isolier-band**, insulating tape) – not a common problem in German houses since windows are double-glazed and, like doors, shut on to, rather than into, the frame – but also isolation in a medical, political, or penal sense. Since *eine Insel* (island) is both isolated and insulated, it seemed doubly appropriate when the 1948/49 blockade led to West Berlin's *splendid* isolation* and to its citizens being dubbed *die Insulaner* (see also BERLINER in II).

JACKE n.f. not a sports jacket (*ein Sportjackett*, now more widely known as *ein Sakko**), but a heavy knitted cardigan (*Strickjacke*), windcheater (*Windjacke*), or leather jacket (*Lederjacke*). Also the jacket (properly, *das Jackett*) of a suit, of a woman's two-piece *Jacken-kleid*, or of the traditional grey or green *Lodentracht* worn in southern Germany and Austria.

KAFF n.n. a depressing little village (probably from gypsy language) – no connection with *ein Café*, or even with the authentic patina of shabbiness of a traditional Viennese *Kaffeehaus**. *In diesem gottverlassenen Kaff ist überhaupt nichts los*, there's absolutely nothing to do in this godforsaken dump. See also NEST below.

KALT adj. since blocks of flats generally have a communal central heating system, *die Wohnung kostet DM2000 kalt* does not mean that the rent is a cool DM2000 (*glatt zweitausend Mark*), but that it excludes the energy/heating costs (*warm**: inclusive). If you feel cold, say *mir ist kalt*, not *ich bin kalt* (I am emotionally frigid). By the same token, be absolutely sure you want to say *ich bin heiß*.

Ich mache ihn kalt: I'll bump him off, make cold meat of him; but, without lethal intent, *ich stelle ihn kalt*: I'll neutralize the threat he poses, render him harmless, 'marginalize' him.

KANAPEE n.n. a sofa, couch, settee (now more often called *das Sofa* or *die Couch*), not a canopy (*der Baldachin*) or a canapé (*der Cocktailhappen, der Appetithappen*).

KAUTION n.f. not caution (*die Vorsicht*; an official warning is *eine Verwarnung*), but either bail, a commercial security, or a deposit on a flat – up to three months' rent*. One avoids having to pay a similar, though non-returnable, amount as *Provision** to the *Immobilienmakler** by finding accommodation directly through the *Immobilien** column in a newspaper. *Also*, Vorsicht*!*

KITT n.m. not a soldier's kit (*die Ausrüstung*), or gym kit (*das Sportzeug*), or a kit for model-making (*der Modellbausatz, der Bastelsatz*), but putty/adhesive cement. Used figuratively, *wenn ein Kind als Kitt für eine kaputte Ehe herhalten muß* (when a child serves to keep a broken marriage together); and as a synonym for *das Zeug* or *der Kram* (stuff, things, junk) in the phrase *was kostet der ganze Kitt?* (what does it all cost?/how much for the whole caboodle?), but not as in 'he's putty in her hands', *er ist Wachs in ihren Händen*. See also STOFF and PLUNDER below and KITTCHEN in I.

KLOSETT n.n. the lavatory, nowadays abbreviated to *das Klo*, while *die Klobrille* is the lavatory seat, not a special pair of glasses for reading in the loo. A closet is *ein Wandschrank*.

KNICKER n.m. a scrooge or skinflint (more common as an adjective: *knickrig*, stingy, mean). For knickers, see SLIP below.

KNITTERN v. not to knit (*stricken*), but to crease. Some material is *knitterarm* (crease resistant), even *knitterfrei** (non-crushable);

those who wear linen jackets or trousers inevitably conform to the *edel zerknittert* ('nobly crumpled') look.

KOMMODE n.f. a chest of drawers or tallboy, not an invalid's commode (*ein Nachtstuhl**). The Austrians still use the adjective *kommod* to describe a comfortable chair (*bequem*), or a convenient time (*passend, günstig*).

KOMPLETT adj. complete, all-inclusive (*das Schlafzimmer kostet komplett DM5000*), but also full: *ein komplettes Mittagessen*, a full lunch; and in Austria, full up (*voll besetzt*): *das Hotel/die Straßenbahn ist komplett.* *Das Komplet* is a dress with matching three-quarter length coat. *Die Komplet* is complin(e)/evensong in the Catholic Church.

KONFEKTION n.f. not confectionery (*Konditorwaren, Süß-waren, Süßigkeiten, Zuckerwerk*; nowadays, *das Konfekt* usually refers to chocolates), but off-the-peg (*von der Stange*) clothing; hence, *ein Konfektionsanzug* is a ready-made suit as distinct from one which is *maßgeschneidert**, made-to-measure, tailor-made. *Die Konfektion* is also the clothing industry, and *ein Konfektionär/eine Konfektioneuse* a somewhat dated term for a clothing manufacturer or executive, or a designer of *Konfektionswaren** (clothing which is *fabrikmäßig her-gestellt* or *konfektioniert*, and produced in *Konfektionsgrößen*, standard sizes).

KONSOLE n.f. a (usually S-shaped) wall bracket or ornamental stone projection (used, for instance, to support *ein Konsoltischchen*, console table), but not the usual word for a control panel (*das Kontrollpult*), the key-desk of an organ (*der Spieltisch*), or a TV console (*die Fernsehtruhe*). To console, *trösten*.

KORSAGE n.f. the bodice of a woman's dress, or a *bustier*, but not the floral decoration pinned on to it, which is *eine Ansteckblume*.

KRAM n.m. junk, stuff. Hence *der Krimskrams* or *Schnickschnack*, knick-knacks (in German *ein Knicks* is a click as well as a curtsy, while *ein Knacks* is a crack – see KNACK- in VIII). German homes seldom have flying ducks on the wall, but the ever-popular *Nippes/Nipp-figuren* (porcelain *objets d'art*) are a reminder that *Kitsch* is a German word. *Kramen* is not to cram (*vollstopfen*; to cram for an exam, *büffeln, pauken*; to cram-feed, *kröpfen*) but to rummage about or fish out, *ein Krämer* is a small shopkeeper, and *der Krämergeist** (petty-mindedness) the sort of thing Napoleon presumably had in mind when he called England a nation of shopkeepers. See also ANTIKE above and PLUNDER below.

KRAWATTE n.f. not a cravat (*das Halstuch*), but a tie. This is also *der Schlips*. Before the Germans adopted the new English fashion in the latter half of the nineteenth century, *Schlipse* were the loose ends of a cravat or bow tie (*eine Fliege*), or else coat-tails – the origin of the phrase *jemandem auf den Schlips treten*, to offend someone.

KREDENZ n.f. in Austria, still the usual word for a sideboard (French *crédence*), usually with further shelves on top, like a Welsh dresser (*eine Anrichte mit Tellerbord*). The verb *kredenzen* is a literary word meaning to proffer (*er hat mir ein Glas Champagner kredenzt*) – originally the job of the king's taster after he had 'lent credence' to the food or wine.

LACK n.m. lacquer (*Lackschuhe* are patent-leather shoes), wood or nail varnish (*Holzlack, Nagellack*), or gloss paint (specifically, the paintwork of a car). Theo Sommer's description of East Germany as *ein Staat ohne Lack und Lüster* (*Die Zeit*, 25 September 1988) was an apt and literal allusion to its lack of paint and bright lights (*ein Lüster* is both lustre and a chandelier, but for *lüstern* see LUST in VI). The impression given was thus doubly 'lacklustre' (*trübe, farblos, glanzlos**). 'He lacks for nothing', *es fehlt ihm an nichts*; 'for lack of money', *aus Mangel an Geld*.

LEGER adj. (French pronunciation) used of comfortable, informal clothing (*eine legere Jacke**); sometimes also of a casual, unforced manner (*er grüßte leger*), or casually sloppy behaviour, though this is more often called *schlampig* (the Austrians, in particular, being associated with *gemütliche Schlamperei*).

MANGEL n.m. no connection with *die Mangel*, a mangle or rolling-press (*jemanden durch die Mangel drehen*, to put someone through the mill). *Der Mangel* means lack or deficiency (*eine Mangelware* is a commodity in short supply), and hence any fault or flaw (*zur Vollkommenheit fehlte** *ihr nur ein Mangel*, 'all she needed to make her perfect was a single flaw' – Karl Kraus). One should always make sure to draw up an agreed *Mängelliste* with the landlord before taking on a new flat, *um späteren Reklamationen** vorzubeugen* (to avoid later complaints).

For *Mangelhaft* as a bad mark for homework or on a school report, see NOTE in IV.

MANTEL n.m. the usual word for an overcoat (*Wintermantel, Regenmantel*), whereas a mantle or cloak is *ein Umhang*. Figuratively: *unter dem Mantel der Dunkelheit entkommen*, to escape under cover of darkness. See also SACK below.

MASSIV adj. solid*, that is to say, not hollow but made of the same material through and through. Advertisements for English garden furniture *aus massivem Teakholz* (made of solid teak), or for *Schränke aus massiver Eiche* (cupboards made of solid – preferably German – oak, i.e. not merely *Spanholz mit Eiche furniert*, chipboard with an oak veneer) seem to have changed little over the years. *Massives Gold* is pure, solid gold. Similarly, *ein massiver Mann* is solid (also one sense of *kompakt*) rather than 'massive' (*ungeheuer, gewaltig, riesig*). Nor is *ein Massivbau* a massive building, but simply one made of stone, brick, concrete, etc. Figuratively, however, *massiv* is used much as is English 'massive' (*ein massiver Angriff*, a massive attack; *massive Lohnforderungen*, massive wage demands; *massive Kritik*, massive criticism); in addition, *massiv werden* means to turn nasty or threatening. See also KONSISTENT in III.

MASSKLEIDUNG n.f. not 'mass clothing' (what you buy off-the-peg is *Konfektion**), but made-to-measure (see MASS in II). *Ein Maßanzug* is a tailor-made suit.

MELONE n.f. like French *melon*, a bowler hat/US derby as well as a melon. *Mit Schirm, Charme und Melone* ('with brolly, charm and a bowler') was the German title of the TV series *The Avengers*.

METER n.m. or n.n. a metre (39.37 inches), but not the metre of a line of verse (*das Metrum*), a light meter (*das Belichtungsmesser*), or a parking meter (*die Parkuhr*; for meter-maid, see POLITESSE in VII). The electricity meter (*der Stromzähler*), water meter (*die Wasseruhr*) and gas meter (*die Gasuhr*) are now generally accessible from outside German flats. 'I am the gasman, where is the meter?' is a question which might have caused anxiety to German emigrés of a certain generation, since the English word sounds the same as the German word *Mieter* (tenant, lodger).

MODE n.f. not the general word for a 'mode' of doing things, which is *die Art** or *die Art und Weise*, but specifically 'fashion' – the way the French did things having once determined what was fashionable (*modisch*, but see also *fesch* under FADE above), or even *le dernier cri* (*der letzte Schrei*).

Karl Lagerfeld is *ein Modeschöpfer*, but *eine Modistin* makes or sells only women's headgear (like the milliner who originally dealt in silks and ribbons from Milan). For other fashion accessories or *Modeartikel* (though these are also fashion articles in newspapers/magazines) one goes to a *Modegeschäft* or *Modehaus*. Note that *modern* is sometimes synonymous with fashionable: you might say *das ist nicht mehr modern* instead of *das ist nicht mehr Mode*.

An artist's model is *ein Modell**, a fashion model *ein Mannequin*, a model type or one who looks the part *eine Modepuppe* or *ein Modepüppchen*, and a male model *ein Dressman**.

MONDÄN adj. not mundane (worldly: *weltlich, irdisch*; humdrum: *profan*, banal, alltäglich*), but chic, elegant, sophisticated; sometimes flashy, showily-dressed.

MUFF n.m. a muff, but also a musty smell (and the mould/mildew, *der Schimmel, der Moder*, which might cause something to smell *muffig*). Figuratively, fustiness or stuffiness – the target of a famous student slogan in 1968: *Unter den Talaren der Muff von tausend Jahren* ('Under the gowns of academe the whiff of a thousand years' decay'). As well as 'to smell musty', *muffeln* (or *müffeln*) also means to speak indistinctly or to mutter (also *murmeln** or *nuscheln*, while the normal word for muffling a sound is *dämpfen*), and hence to be morose or grumpy (*muffig* or *mufflig*). Consequently, *ein Muffel* is grouch, a real misery, and in compounds signals disinclination – a *Morgenmuffel*, for example, is someone who is not at his best in the mornings, a *Fußballmuffel* someone who is left cold by football, while an *Arzneimuffel* has an aversion to taking medicine.

MUSTER n.n. a pattern (*nach dem Muster stricken*, to knit from a pattern; patterned cloth is *gemustert*); or (as formerly in English) a commercial sample (*die Musterpackung*, sample pack); or, figuratively, a model or ideal. The hard-working Swabians, for instance, think of Baden-Württemberg as *ein 'Musterländle**', while most of those drawn south to its belt of sunlight industries find it at least 'passes muster' – *es genügt ihren Anforderungen*. Indeed, 'passing muster' corresponds to *mustern* in the sense of scrutinize or inspect, also to subject to medical inspection prior to military service (*der Musterungsausschuß* is the recruiting board – see DIENEN in I).

NEST n.n. a bird's nest, figuratively a hideout or lair, and hence the sort of sleepy village, *ein kleines verschlafenes Nest*, which appeals to commuters, *Pendler*. On the other hand, *ein elendes Nest* may be no better than a *Kaff**, so that, for example, Goethe's remark *dieses Weimar ist ein Nest* is not complimentary (see LOS in VII).

NEUBAU n.m. officially, a 'new building' is one built after 1 December 1949 as distinct from one built before the war (*ein Altbau*), but in practice now any new building (*eine Neubauwohnung*, newly-built flat, *eine Neubausiedlung*, new housing estate), also one still under construction, or a modern extension to an existing building.

NOBEL adj. 'noble by birth' is *von edler* or *adliger Geburt*, but a fine person, selfless action, generous thought, etc., are all *nobel*, as too (though often with an ironical slant) are a luxury hotel (*ein Nobelhotel, eine Nobelherberge*), posh restaurant (*ein nobles Restaurant*), or classy car (*ein Nobelschlitten*). See FEUDAL above and DEZENT in V.

OBJEKT n.n. as in English 'object', but an additional meaning is a property (*der Objektschutz*, protection of property; *ein ideal gelegenes Objekt am Stadtrand*, an ideally situated property on the outskirts of the town), or a building project (the sign at a large *Baustelle* customarily describes the *Bauobjekt* and names the *Bauherr* who has commissioned it – see under BAUER in III). In Austria, *ein Objekt* is the official term for a building; in East Germany, it is, or was, a publicly-owned facility such as *ein Ferienobjekt* (holiday camp) or *ein Gastronomieobjekt* (restaurant: *die Gastronomie* is indeed the art of good eating, but also, as here, the catering trade in general).

Die Tücke des Objekts denotes the seeming perverseness of the inanimate, the perception that things have a will of their own.

OFEN n.m. a stove for heating, or a central-heating boiler, as well as an oven for cooking (*der Backofen*, die Backröhre*; in Austria *das Backrohr*). In traditional South German and Austrian homes, the *Kachelofen* or tiled stove provides a pleasantly warm backrest to the wooden bench around the living-room table, as well as central heating for the whole house.

PASSEN v. of clothes, when assessing the compatibility of one garment with another, or with a colour, or a particular occasion: to suit, to match, to go with, to be fitting. But used absolutely: to fit. Thus, *das Kleid paßt Ihnen nicht* (that dress doesn't fit you) – 'to suit' here is *stehen*: *das Kleid steht Ihnen nicht* – but *die Farbe der Kravatte* paßt nicht zum Anzug* (the colour of the tie does not go with the suit). Used adjectivally: *schlecht passende Schuhe* (ill-fitting shoes), but *sie trägt immer den passenden Hut* (she always wears a hat to match the occasion). Shop assistants are keen to recommend *eine passende Hose zum Sakko**, a pair of trousers thought to match the jacket you have just bought. *Hose und Jacke* zusammen* would be called *eine Kombination*.

PENDANT n.n. pendant ear-rings, once *Pendants* or *Ohrgehänge*, are now usually called *Anhänger*, but a matching picture or ornament, or someone's opposite number or counterpart, *bildet ein Pendant* or *dient als Pendant*.

PERLE n.f. a bead as well as a pearl. *Zuchtperlen* are cultured pearls, *Holzperlen* wooden beads, while in Hermann Hesse's utopian novel *Glasperlenspiel* (1943) the game is played with glass beads representing whole cultures. Also a droplet (*Schweißperlen*, beads of sweat; *das Wasser perlt im Quell**), or a bubble (*Perlwein*, sparkling wine; *perlendes Lachen*, rippling laughter). Used humorously of a good domestic help: *sie ist eine Perle*, she's a gem/treasure.

PLAID n.n. or n.m. commonly a tartan travelling rug. A plaid skirt is *ein karierter Rock** – *im Schottenkaro* or *im Schottenmuster* if specifically tartan (though the French predilection for tartan skirts has yet to cross the Rhine). A kilt is *ein Schottenrock*.

PLUNDER n.m. junk or rubbish (see also KRAM above) rather than plunder, though originally *Plunder* meant all the clothes and household goods that thieves might plunder (nowadays the act is *die Plünderung* or *der Raub*, the loot itself *die Beute*). Thus, *fort mit dem unnützen Plunder!* away with all that useless rubbish – the learned lumber of the Schools, for instance. Germans have long practised *das Recycling* of their old furniture and other bulky refuse, and few student flats have not benefited from the *Sperrmüll* left outside houses, traditionally on the first Thursday of the month. For *Plundergebäck* (flaky pastry), see TORTE in VIII.

POLOHEMD n.n. not a polo-necked sweater (*ein Rollkragenpulli*), but a short-sleeved sports shirt or tennis shirt.

POMPÖS adj. of things, especially buildings, but not of people (though a pompous style of writing, or a pompous remark, may be *pompös*). A pompous person is *aufgeblasen* or *wichtigtuerisch*, but *eine pompöse Villa* is a grandiose villa, *eine pompöse Fassade* an ostentatious façade, *eine pompöse Ausstattung* pretentious furnishings (the discovery of which in in Erich Honecker's *Diplomaten-Siedlung* came as something of a surprise to many East Germans). An exception to this pejorative nuance would be Rilke's line celebrating one of his beloved aristocratic parks as *huldvoll, prunkend, purpurn* und pompös*, 'gracious*, resplendent, crimson and magnificent' (*Die Parke*).

PONY n.m. *der Pony* is a fringe (*der Pferdeschwanz*, ponytail), *das Pony* is the animal. *Das Mädchen mit dem Pony* could have either, or both.

PROPER adj. does not refer to a person's morals, but to general neatness and cleanliness: *die Wirtin ist ganz schön proper* means that the landlady keeps her establishment spotless and the window-box geraniums immaculate. Prim and proper is *korrekt**; to act in a way that is right and proper, *handeln, wie es sich gehört*. Painstaking, meticulous work is also *proper*: *sie hat propere Arbeit geleistet*, she made a proper job of it.

PULLUNDER n.m. German logic has extrapolated from what is worn over a shirt to what is worn under a jacket – a sleeveless pullover (*ein ärmelloser Pullover*). In addition, a tank top.

REALITÄTEN n.p. the realities, the facts, but also the Austrian word for *Immobilien**(property, real estate). An Austrian estate agent is *ein Realitätenhändler** or *Realitätenvermittler*, his office *ein Realbüro* or *eine Realkanzlei**.

ROCK n.m. not a rock (*der Stein, der Fels*; for a girl's best friend, see SCHMUCK below), but either **1.** a woman's skirt; or **2.** a man's jacket, though now mainly in an historical or specialized sense: *der grüne Rock des Försters* (the forester's green coat); *der schwarze Rock des Geistlichen** (the priest's black coat); *den bunten Rock anziehen* (to take the King's shilling). *Ein Gehrock* (frock coat) and *ein Überrock* (greatcoat) have now evolved into *ein Mantel* (overcoat); *ein Schoßrock* (tail-coat) is today *ein Frack* (though also a particular style of skirt; in Austria, simply *die Schoß*); and *ein Morgenrock* is a dressing-gown, not a morning coat or morning dress (*ein Cut* – short for *Cutaway*; if dark with striped trousers, *ein Stresemann* – after the Weimar statesman). Formal weddings with groom (*Bräutigam*) and best man (*Trauzeuge*) in morning coats are virtually unknown in Germany.

SACK n.m. either **1.** sackcloth; or **2.** a sack or paper bag (for coal, potatoes, corn, etc., for which *eine Plastiktüte* is unsuitable); or **3.** (in Austria and southern Germany only) a pocket. A trouser pocket here is *ein Hosensack* (elsewhere *die Hosentasche*), a coat pocket *ein Mantelsack** (instead of *Manteltasche*; German *Mantelsack* once meant a portmanteau, which is now *ein Handkoffer*, or a valise, which is now *eine Reisetasche*), and a handkerchief *ein Sacktuch* (otherwise *Taschentuch*; German *Sacktuch*, like *Sackleinen*, is sacking).
  'I'll hit the sack': *ich hau mich / ich geh in die Falle/Klappe, ich verzieh mich in die Flohkiste*.

SAKKO n.m. or n.n. a sports jacket. See JACKE, PASSEN, SACK above.

SCHAL n.m. a scarf or muffler. A shawl is *ein Umhängetuch* or *Umschlagtuch*, if part of an evening dress *eine Stola*; a headscarf is a *ein Kopftuch*, a ceremonial sash *eine Schärpe*.

SCHELLEN v. not to shell nuts or peas (*schälen*, see SCHALE in VIII), or a military target (*beschießen*; see also BOMBARDEMENT in I), but, like *läuten* or *klingeln*, to ring at someone's door (*es hat geschellt*, that was the bell). *Eine Schelle*, unlike *eine Glocke*, is generally a small, round bell, though it is also the bell-shaped suit (the equivalent of diamonds) on traditional German playing-cards, and in addition a clamp (hence *Handschellen*, handcuffs).

SCHERE n.f. ordinary scissors as well as shears (*Gartenschere*, secateurs; *Heckenschere*, hedge-clippers; *Drahtschere*, wire-cutters). *Eine Hummerschere* is a lobster claw.

SCHICK adj. (or *chic*) chic, though the currency of the word has become debased by overuse and association with the trendy *Schickeria* or *Schickimickis* (in-crowd, smart set). Despite appearances, *schick* has nothing to do with *schicklich* (proper, fitting: *es schickt sich nicht*, it's not seemly). *Sie hat wirklich Chic*, she really has style.

SCHMAL adj. not small (*klein*), but slim: *schmale Hüften*, slim hips; *eine schmale Taille*, a slender waist; *schmalschultrig*, narrow-shouldered; *schmallippig*, thin-lipped.

SCHMUCK n.m. jewellery. *Schmuck* is unrelated to Jiddish 'schmuck' (in German, *ein Bekloppter* or *Beknackter*), nor does it suggest something obnoxious or 'schmucky' (*Klunker* is sometimes used of excessively ostentatious jewellery: *sie stellte ihre Klunker zur Schau*, she was dripping with rocks). On the contrary, its figurative sense is embellishment: *der Garten im Schmuck der Blumen*; *das Schmuckstück des Dorfes war die Kirche* (*Schmuckstück*, jewel, is also a term of endearment: sweetheart). The adjective means neat, tidy, smart – *ein schmuckes Dorf, Haus, Mädchen*.

SEKRETÄR n.m. a secretaire or writing bureau as well as a secretary (see also STAATSSEKRETÄR in I).

SLIP n.m. not a slip/petticoat (*der Unterrock**), but the unisex word for briefs or knickers* (*der Schlüpfer* is specifically a pair of women's panties – again from the verb 'to slip', as one might slip into a dress, *in ein Kleid hineinschlüpfen*). East Germans continued to call men's underpants *eine Unterhose**, as in the standard shopping joke: *Gibt's hier keine Unterhosen?* (Have you no underpants here?) . . . *Nein, hier gibt's keine Hemden, keine Unterhosen im dritten Stock* (No, it's no shirts here. No underpants on the third floor).

SMOKING n.m. a dinner jacket – from English 'smoking jacket', just as *der Rock** and *der Frack* (tail coat, tails) derive from English 'frock' and from *le froc* which French monks wear. An English smock, however, is *ein Bauernkittel* or *Russenkittel*. The verb *smoken* (short vowel) does not mean to smoke (*rauchen*), but is used in needlework for smocking (*Smokarbeit*).

STEPPEN v. to step (usually *treten*) only in the sense of to tap-dance, otherwise to machine-stitch or to quilt – *eine Steppjacke* * is a quilted jacket, *eine Steppdecke* a bed-quilt (*eine gefütterte Bettdecke*; the traditional *Federbett* or duvet is not divided into compartments – see BETT in VI).

STICKEN v. not to stick or glue (*kleben*), but to embroider. See also STICKSTOFF in IV.

STOFF n.m. 'stuff' as a general or derogatory term is *das Zeug* (*du könntest endlich dein Zeug aufräumen*, do clear up your stuff; *dummes Zeug*, stuff and nonsense), but *der Stoff* is either **1.** 'stuff' in the sense of material, fabric, cloth (*Stoffreste* *, remnants); or **2.** any material or chemical substance (*der Stickstoff* *, nitrogen; *der Stoffwechsel*, metabolism); often used these days of dope/drugs: *er braucht dringend Stoff*, he badly needs a fix *; or **3.** subject matter or topic (*Stoff zum Nachdenken*, food for thought).

STORE n.m. *Stores* (pronounced stors) are net curtains, except in Switzerland, where they are window-shutters (German *Fensterläden*). In a nautical context (under the influence of English terminology) *der Store* is where the provisions are kept, but things are normally stored in a *Lager* *, while a department store is a *Warenhaus* *.

STRAPS n.m. borrowed from the English to mean (*pars pro toto*) a suspender belt – the equivalent German word, *der Strumpfhaltergürtel* *, seems to have as little erotic appeal as *eine Strumpfhose* * (tights/US panty-hose). A shoulderstrap is *ein Träger* (though a strapless dress is known as *ein schulterfreies* * *Kleid*), a watchband is *ein Uhrband* *, a strap for holding on to in the bus *ein Gurt* or *eine Schlaufe*, and for securing luggage *ein Riemen*.

STUHL n.m. not a stool (*der Hocker*, *der Schemel*), but a chair. When Metternich brought *Tischlermeister* * (master carpenter) Michael Thonet, a fellow Rhinelander, to Vienna in 1841, the man who had discovered how to curve wood artificially – by glueing and heating thin layers in a lime solution – created that distinctive feature of the Viennese *Kaffeehaus* * and subsequent all-time best-seller, the *Thonet-Stuhl* (or *Bugholzstuhl*), bentwood chair. In Austria, any chair is *ein Sessel* (a chairlift, for instance, is a *Sessellift*), whereas a German *Sessel* is an easy chair or armchair (Austrian *Polstersessel* or *Fauteuil*).

TEPPICHBODEN n.m. the short-pile or felt wall-to-wall carpeting on which more ornate carpets/rugs (*Teppiche*) or runners (*Läufer*) are laid.

TERRASSENHAUS n.n. not a terraced house (*ein Reihenhaus*), but either a split-level house built on a terraced slope, or a block of flats, stepped in such a way that each has a roof terrace (*eine Dachterrasse*). See also BLOCKHAUS and DOPPELHAUS above.

TONNE n.f. a metric ton, a navigation buoy, or a barrel/drum such as a *Mülltonne* (dustbin) or *Regentonne* (water butt), or even a *Primatonne* (an overweight Wagnerian soprano).

TORF n.m. peat (to cut peat, *Torf stechen*), not turf (*der Rasen*; squares of turf, *Grassoden*).

TRAM n.m. *die Tram* (Swiss *das Tram*) is the southern word for a tram (otherwise *die Straßenbahn*; in Vienna *die Tramway* is either a tram or one of its two carriages), while *der Tram* is a wooden beam (German *der Holzbalken*). Hence *der Tramboden* (German *das vorstehende Dach*), overhanging roof, which is so picturesque yet essential a feature of Alpine farmhouses, and *die Tramdecke*, rustic wood ceiling with carved beams.

UNTERBETT n.n. the quilt (*Steppdecke**) which goes on top of the mattress but under the sheet for extra warmth. What goes 'under the bed' is a *Nachttopf.*

UNTERBRINGEN v. not to 'bring under', but to put up or house (*gut untergebracht sein*, to have good accommodation, also to be well looked after). See Index for other *unter-* and *über-* compounds.

WAND n.f. not a wand (*ein Zauberstab**), but a wall – the internal wall of a house as distinct from an external or free-standing wall (*die Mauer**).

WARENHAUS n.n. not where wares are housed (*das Lager**, *das Lagerhaus*, *die Lagerhalle*, in dockland *der Speicher* – Hamburg has its own duty-free *Speicherstadt*), but where they are sold, i.e. a department store (also *ein Kaufhaus*). Berlin's best-known *Warenhäuser* are still the *Kaufhaus des Westens* (*KaDeWe*) and *Wertheim*, which is situated in the square which Alfred Döblin made the focus of his novel *Berlin Alexanderplatz* (1929). Berliners had need of their black humour amid the rubble in 1945: *da waren Häuser, da Warenhäuser. . .* ('there used to be houses there, stores there. . .').

WARM adj. means 'heating included' in the rent (*kalt**: 'heating extra'). Water, however, is metered* and charged separately.

WÄSCHE n.f. bed linen (*die Bettwäsche*), table linen (*die Tischwäsche*), underwear (*die Unterwäsche*). *Trag ich Wäsche unterm Rock**

oder geh ich ohne Wäsche? asks Jenny in Scene 6 of Brecht's *Aufstieg und Fall* der Stadt Mahagonny* (1929) to Kurt Weill's suggestive music. Also the act of washing: *große Wäsche* is a 'big wash', and a laundry *eine Wäscherei*.

WESTE n.f. a waistcoat/US vest, not a vest/US undershirt (*das Unterhemd*).

WIMPEL n.m. nowadays used only of small flags, pennants, bunting – not a nun's wimple (*der Nonnenschleier / die Nonnenhaube*).

ZIMMERHERR n.m. once a gentleman lodger, whereas *ein Zimmermann* – the hero of Lortzing's comic opera *Zar und Zimmermann* (1837), for instance – is a carpenter. Nowadays, a lodger is *ein Untermieter*, and a landlady who lets out rooms *eine Zimmervermieterin* or *Wirtin* (though in Austria this is also *eine Zimmerfrau*).

ZYLINDER n.m. a top-hat. A generation ago, any gentleman (or anyone who considered himself a gentleman) would wear a top-hat on ceremonial occasions like weddings or burials (see ROCK above). More recently, President von Weizsäcker always carried his, and then only when occasion strictly demanded, but chimney-sweeps continue the tradition of wearing them to work (see GLÜCKLICH in V).

LITERATURE, THE ARTS, THE MEDIA

X

LITERATUR, KUNST, MEDIEN

AGGREGAT n.n. in photography, lighting equipment such as batteries and a transformer (see APPARAT in IV). An aggregate, meaning total amount, is *die Gesamtmenge* or *die Gesamtheit.*

AKADEMIE n.f. as in *Kunstakademie* or *Musikakademie*, but in Austria also a concert, such as the famous *Akademie* held on 22 December 1808 at the *Theater an der Wien*, when the Viennese first heard Beethoven's fourth piano concerto, fifth and sixth symphonies, Choral Fantasy*, and much else besides.

AKT n.m. a two-act play (*ein Zweiakter*) is divided into *Akte* (the actors are *Schauspieler* and the structured action or plot *die Handlung*, not *die Aktion**), but in painting, sculpture and photography, *der Akt* means 'the nude'. Hence: *der weibliche/männliche Akt, das Aktbild, die Aktzeichnung, die Aktstudie, das Aktfoto, die Aktaufnahme* – as produced in *die Aktklasse* (life class) from *das Aktmodell* (life model) – but for nudism, see FREI below.

Most acts/actions or deeds are called *eine Tat* or *eine Handlung*, and *ein Akt* only when official or ceremonial or otherwise out of the ordinary (*ein symbolischer Akt*, a symbolic act; *ein Akt der Gnade*, an act of mercy; *ein rechtswidriger Akt*, an illegal act; specifically, *der Akt* is the sexual act; but an act in the legal/constitutional sense is *ein Gesetz*). The Austrians also say *der Akt* where the Germans say *die Akte* (file, record): *etwas zu den Akten* (or *ad acta*) *legen* means to file something away, though also 'to let the matter drop'.

ALSO adv. & conj. not 'also' (*auch, ebenfalls*), but either **1.** synonymous with *so** (thus, like that, that way), though now somewhat archaic, as in the biblical phrase *also steht geschrieben* ('thus it is written'), or in a parody of biblical language such as Nietzsche's *Also sprach Zarathustra* (1883–85);

or **2.** so, therefore, accordingly, consequently: *ich denke, also bin ich* ('I think, therefore I am'); *ich wäre also dankbar, wenn Sie. . .* (so I would be grateful if you would. . .); *Sauce wird in Österreich französisch, also ohne Endungs-e ausgesprochen* ('sauce' is pronounced in the French way in Austria, that is to say, without the final 'e');

or **3.** so, well, then: in a wide range of contexts expressing agreement (*also gut; also schön; also, es bleibt dabei*, so that's settled; *also machen wir's*, well let's do it then), resolution (*also los!* well, here goes; get cracking; *also, meine Herren*. . . well then, gentlemen. . .), relief (*na also!* you see, it wasn't so bad after all) though also reproach (*na also!* you see, what did I tell you?), outrage (*also nein, das geht nicht!/also so was!/also hören Sie mal!* well, really!), and much else besides, including the idea of summary or finality (*also, tschüs!* well, cheerio then). As Mark Twain ('I would rather decline two German beers than one German adjective') was relieved to discover on *A Tramp Abroad* (1896), what made *also* an indispensable interjection was the fact that its meaning depended solely on intonation, not on grammar.

ANTIQUARIAT n.n. the normal word for a second-hand bookshop as well as an antiquarian bookshop. See also ANTIKE in IX.

APART adj. 'apart' only in the figurative sense in which Byron was, by all accounts, *etwas Apartes* or *eine ganz aparte Erscheinung*, 'a thing apart' (in current usage, 'something else'), and one who in addition wore strikingly distinctive clothes, *der etwas Apartes trug*. More prosaically, apart meaning separated is *getrennt* (they live apart, *sie leben getrennt*), which might also be used to render the lines (spoken by a woman) in Canto 1, Stanza 194 of *Don Juan*: 'Man's love is of man's life a thing apart, / 'Tis woman's whole existence': *Der Mann liebt anders als er lebt, getrennt, die Frau liebt aus der Mitte ihres Wesens*. To stand apart in the literal sense in which Childe Harold became the archetypal hero of European Romanticism ('apart he stalked in joyless reverie, / . . . with pleasure drugged, he almost longed for woe') is different again: *abseits stehen* (also 'to be offside' in football) – though the condition is more commonly called *Weltschmerz* (a word coined only after Byron's death, by Jean Paul, in *Selina oder die Unsterblichkeit der Seele*, 1827).

Ein Aparte (French, *à part*) is an aside or stage-whisper.

ART n.f. not art (*die Kunst*; *ein Künstler* is an artist, *ein Artist* an artiste), but

either **1.** kind, sort, type. The essays which Herder collected in *Von deutscher Art und Kunst* (1773), for instance, celebrate 'The German Way in Art'. Yet this rendering is doubly misleading, for by *deutsch****** he meant popular as distinct from learned, and nordic or germanic rather than narrowly 'German' – the Gothic of Erwin von Steinbach's (d.1318) Strasbourg Minster, but also Ossian and the *spezifisch nordische Artung* of Shakespeare – while the influential historical section of what is essentially a *Sturm und Drang* manifesto focuses not on German art but on the evolution of all things German, *die Art, wie sich Menschen, Rechte und Begriffe allmählich gebildet**.

Martern aller Arten are the torments or tortures of every kind (today one would say *aller Art*) which Constanze imagines the lustful Selim Pasha plans for her in Act II, Scene 3 of *Die Entführung aus dem Serail*, but which she defies with the same constancy that Mozart hoped for in his own wife-to-be, Constanze Weber (see also WANKEN in VI).

In a biological sense: variety, breed, species – Darwin's *Origin of Species* (1859) is known in German translation as *Die Entstehung der Arten*. Another controversial book, Max Nordau's *Entartung* (1892), appropriated the biological metaphor to argue that Western culture now epitomized 'degeneration', a view inherited by Hitler. When the German people was presented with a choice between *deutsche Kunst* and '*entartete*' *Kunst* at two parallel exhibitions held in Munich the year after the 1936 Olympics, it showed it had at least retained its aesthetic judgement: over three million people eventually saw 650 of the 16,000 works confiscated that year – by Beckmann, Chagall, Dix, Grosz, Kirchner, Kokoschka, Nolde, Picasso: 112 artists in all – in the '*Schreckenskammer*' ('chamber of horrors') designed to demonstrate the perversions to which the nation had been subjected by an international conspiracy of Bolsheviks and Jews – five times as many as admired the wasp-waisted athletes of Arno Breker and other 'realist' Aryan art. Some 1,600 of the 'degenerate' paintings and sculptures also fetched high prices when auctioned the following year in Lucerne to raise foreign currency.

or **2.** way, manner, nature, style: *auf diese Art und Weise* (in this way); *das ist eigentlich nicht seine Art* (it's not like him); *nach Art des Hauses* (*à la maison*). Thus, *die feine* englische* Art* does not refer to Turner and Constable, but to what were once perceived and admired as the sophisticated but understated manners (customs, clothes, etc.) of the English. Similarly, the *Hochschulring deutscher Art* which protested at a modernist interpretation of *Der fliegende Holländer* under Otto Klemperer in 1929 was a group of academics concerned not only with German art, but with the defence of 'all things German'. (One well-known instance of a German artist being prevented from exercising his profession – see BERUFSVERBOT in II – was that of Emil Nolde, memorably recreated by Siegfried Lenz in his novel *Deutschstunde** in 1968.);

or **3.** behaviour. *Ist das vielleicht eine Art!* or *Was ist das für eine Art?* means 'what sort of a way to behave is that?' (and not 'call that art?' – *und das soll Kunst sein!*). An 'arty' type is *ein Künstlertyp**, whereas *ein artiges Kind* is a polite, well-behaved child – an unlikely source, therefore, for the irreverent observation that a Swabian citing Horace's maxim *lex mihi ars* ('art is the law to me') sounds as if he is saying *leck mich am Arsch!*

AUDIENZ n.f. only used of a ceremonial interview granted by either royal or ecclesiastical dignitaries, not of the audience at a film or play (*die Zuschauer*).

AUTOGRAPH n.n. not an autograph/signature (*das Autogramm*), but an autograph/original manuscript.

BAND n.n. quite distinct from *der Band* (*die Hamburger Goethe-Ausgabe in 14 Bänden*, in 14 volumes), from *die Band* (a straightforward anglicism – *Bands* are dance bands, jazz bands, pop groups), and from *die Bande* (*Räuberbanden*, robber bands). The many meanings of *das Band* (plural *Bänder*), all derived from the basic sense 'ribbon' or 'tape', include *das Tonbandgerät* (tape recorder), *die Bandaufnahme* (recording), *die Bandbreite* (frequency range, waveband); *der Bänderriß* (torn ligament), *der Bandscheibenschaden* (slipped disc); *das Fließband* (conveyor belt); *Bandnudeln* (tagliatelle). *Der Bandwurm* is a tapeworm – the word the Germans themselves apply, disarmingly, to those interminable sentences (*Bandwurmsätze*) whose meaning hangs suspended until, or has evaporated before, the final verb. By contrast, a word or look can speak volumes: *sein Gesicht spricht Bände*.

Like English 'bond', *das Band* (plural *Bande*) can mean an actual fetter or shackle, or else a figurative bond or tie of affection – the unbreakable *Band der Liebe*, for instance, by virtue of which Leonore liberates Florestan from the dungeon, *wo er in Banden liegt* (see WANKEN and WEIB in VI).

BLACKOUT n.n. or n.m. used when someone has a mental block or temporary loss of memory (*er hat einen Blackout gehabt* was the phrase memorably used to exonerate Helmut Kohl from blame over irregular party funding in 1985 – see SPENDEN in II); when the lights go out in a play or cabaret in order to emphasize the final *Pointe**; and on the rare occasions when the government imposes news censorship. It is not immediately associated with the War (*die Verdunkelung Londons während des Blitzangriffes**).

BLÄTTERN v. not to blatter in the Scottish sense of rain blattering against a window (*der Regen schlug heftig gegen das Fenster*), but to leaf or flick through a book or newspaper – *das Blatt* is an individual sheet of paper (or hand of cards), as well as a whole newspaper such as the *Hamburger Abendblatt* (hence: *es rauscht im deutschen Blätterwald*, there are murmurings* in the German press, the media are buzzing). Also to put down or count out one by one: *er blätterte die 1000 Mark* auf den Tisch*.

BOX n.f. has quite specific meanings in German: a loudspeaker; a horse's stall (but not a mobile horse-box – *ein Pferdetransporter*); the pits in motor racing; a partitioned-off parking place in a garage*; or a stand at an exhibition. Compounds (often proprietary names) include *Musikbox* (jukebox), *Kühlbox* (portable ice-box), *Skibox* (attached to the car roof).

Mostly, however, a box is *eine Kiste* or *ein Karton**, and for smaller objects *eine Schachtel* or *eine Dose**; in the theatre it is *die Loge*, in court *der Zeugenstand** for the witnesses and *die Pressebank** for the press. 'What's on the box?' *was gibt's im Fernsehen?* (for the colloquial *glotzen*, see STARREN below).

Boxing is *der Boxkampf*, but figuratively, *er hat sich durch die Menge geboxt* means 'he elbowed his way through the crowd', *er hat sich durch's Leben geboxt*, 'he fought his way through life' – a metaphor Brecht took literally when he set his *Kleine Mahagonny* opera of 1929 in a *Boxring*.

COUPLET n.n. a satirical song, frequently political, rather than the rhyming couplets (*Paarreim*) Wilhelm Busch used to such memorable effect (*Enthaltsamkeit ist das Vergnügen / An Sachen, welche wir nicht kriegen*, 'how nice to feel abstemious and self-denying when we don't get what we want, though not for want of trying' – see MORAL in V).

DEKORATEUR n.m. a window dresser or interior designer. Accordingly, *die Dekoration* usually refers to window dressing; or the décor of a theatre or restaurant; or such decorations as *Wimpel** or *Sträuße**. Or else a theatrical set (also *die Ausstattung*, hence the *Ausstattungsrevüen* for which theatres like the Metropol-Theater in Berlin were famous in the 1930s); *ein Dekorationsmaler* is either a scene-painter (the designer is *der Bühnenbildner*) or an interior decorator.

When Hitler was rejected by the *Kunstakademie** in Vienna as a *Maler* (artist), he became an *Anstreicher* (house painter), a point which Brecht takes up in his *Schlechte Zeit für Lyrik* (1939): *In mir streiten sich / Die Begeisterung über den blühenden Apfelbaum / Und das Entsetzen über die Reden des Anstreichers. / Aber nur das zweite / Drängt mich zum Schreibtisch*. It is a 'bad time for poetry' when it must respond to the house painter's tirades rather than the apple blossom. See also ENGAGIERT below, SCHMUCK in IX, and for military *Dekorationen*, TRESSEN in I.

ENGAGIERT adj. committed to a cause – Brecht, for instance, was *ein engagierter Schriftsteller* whose *politisches Engagement* was to Marxism. Theatre people also use the word *engagieren* to mean 'to engage or hire'; thus, a young Thespian will be looking forward to his/her first *Engagement*. Established actors' *Engagement*, however, in the sense of their active, enthusiastic involvement, sometimes seems to be in inverse proportion to their secure status as *Beamte** and their regular *Gage**. Though the word often suggests some broadly political agenda, German politicians do not assume that *ein engagierter Lehrer* is engaged in subversive activities – it is simply a teacher who is dedicated to his or her job.

Someone who says *ich bin schon anderweitig engagiert* is referring to the fact that at present he or she is emotionally committed to someone else. To be engaged to be married, however, is *verlobt sein*; a telephone, or lavatory, is *besetzt*.

EPISCH adj. the adjective from *die Epik* (epic poetry) and *das Epos* (epic poem) is applied to narrative literature in general, but in everyday speech, with some exceptions (such as *epische Breite*, epic breadth), lacks the modern figurative sense of 'epic'. *Das Boot* might be described as *ein Filmepos*, an epic of the screen, but one has to find a different adjective for an epic football match (*ein gewaltiges Fußballspiel*), an epic journey (*eine lange, abenteuerliche Reise*), or an epic achievement (*eine monumentale Leistung*).

What Brecht meant by *episches Theater* – apart from the broad range of materials and devices deployed and the intermittent presence of a narrator – has confused generations of playgoers aware that its *Verfremdungseffekte* or alienation effects evidently do not preclude 'dramatic' situations. Nor were catchy melodies taboo until Kurt Weill's music threatened to upstage the text, at which point Hanns Eisler was enlisted instead to supply appropriately grim accompaniment – Brecht's word for this was '*Misuk*', Ernst Bloch called it 'radical monotony'. Lotte Lenya's alienation took the form of a question: 'What would Brecht be without my Kurt's music?'

FABEL n.f. as in *Äsops Fabeln*; but also a myth or legend, including the sort of fantastic tale no one believes (*erzähl mir keine Fabeln*; *das gehört in das Reich der Fabel*) – hence *fabulieren*, to invent a story, spin a yarn, tell fibs, such tales being *fabulös*. *Die Fabel* is also sometimes used of the story-line, synopsis or plot of a novel/play. See also TEXTBUCH below.

FAGOTT n.n. a bassoon – not a bundle of sticks (*ein Reisigbündel*); a rissole of innards, bread and herbs (*eine Frikadelle*); or slang for a homosexual (*ein Schwuler*; see also PARAGRAPH in I).

Clearly a *faux ami* to the musicians of the Paris Opera who successfully resisted Daniel Barenboim's attempt to replace the lighter-toned French *basson* with the modern German instrument.

FAMOS adj. not famous (*berühmt*), but used to express enthusiastic approval: *das ist ja famos!* (that's capital), *eine famose Idee* (a wonderful idea), *ein famoser Kerl* (a marvellous chap, splendid fellow), *wir haben uns famos unterhalten* (we really hit it off, got on like a house on fire).

FEUILLETON n.n. not, as in French, a serial or instalment, but the arts or literature section of a newspaper. Also a feature article in the *Kulturteil* (as it is also called) – often a light, whimsical piece or *Glosse**. This was the original meaning, and in Austria remains the almost exclusive meaning, though the Austrian Duden's definition of *feuilletonistisch* (chatty, *populärwissenschaftlich**) reflects cultural values subtly different from the standard German definition in Wahrig (facile, glib, *unwissenschaftlich**).

FOLKLORE n.f. folksongs/folkdances rather than folklore. *Ein Folkloreabend* may suggest an evening of story-telling around the *Kaminfeuer* – the *Märchen* of the Brothers Grimm add more than a dash of modern psychology to the basic folklore (*Volksgut** or *traditionelle Volksweisheit*) – but is in fact a ceilidh: *folkloristische Kleidung* ('ethnic' clothing), folk songs, dancing. Set off by the craze for Irish folk music in the seventies, the Germans soon rediscovered or reinvented their own *Volksmusik*, especially in the conservative, Catholic south, where a fusion of *Volksmusik* with the blandly predictable German *Schlager* (light pop music) still fills the airwaves with evocations of faith, family and fatherland (or at least *Heimat**) such as the 1989 hit dedicated to the Virgin Mary, 'Patrona Bavariae'.

FRAKTUR n.f. a bone fracture (more commonly *der Bruch*), but also the 'gothic' typeface used by printers since the sixteenth century. As late as the 1930s, around half of all German books were being printed in *Fraktur*, but the growing conflict between blackletter *Fraktur* as a typographical expression of the Nordic soul and the modernists' espousal of roman type came to a surprising head on 3 January 1941, when Martin Bormann revealed that 'in reality the so-called gothic script consists of Schwabacher-Jewish letters' – *in Wirklichkeit besteht die sogenannte gotische Schrift aus schwabacher* Judenlettern – and that on Hitler's instructions roman type was henceforth to be used in newspapers, official documents, street-name signs, etc. (just as the neo-classical style was favoured for public architecture – see Robin Kinross, *Modern Typography*, London, 1992). At the time Schwabacher type was invented, shortly before *Fraktur*, Jews were of course not allowed anywhere near print shops. Nowadays, *Fraktur* is most in evidence in the headlines of the *Frankfurter Allgemeine Zeitung* ('*die FAZ*'). Figuratively, *Fraktur mit jemandem* *reden* (like *deutsch* mit jemandem reden*) means to be blunt with someone.

Few Germans now use (and not all can decipher) the old gothic handwriting or *deutsche Schrift*. Austrians call it *Kurrentschrift* – the German word for cursive or flowing handwriting as distinct from the *Druckschrift* (block letters) you use to fill in a *Formular**. German schoolchildren rarely start with printed letters, so there is no opportunity for the taunt: 'he hasn't learnt joined-up writing yet'. *Kursivschrift* is italics.

FREI adj. 'free', with multiple nuances including:

1. unimpeded, unhindered: a condition restricted for most Germans in 1790 to the realm of thought alone, when it was stirringly, if pathetically*, celebrated in the song *Die Gedanken sind frei* (see also under SCHWARM in VI); *freie Fahrt* haben* (to have the go-ahead, the green light, a clear run – see TEMPO in VII); *freimachen* (to frank/put a stamp on a letter, or to take time off; at the doctor's: *den Oberkörper frei machen*, to strip to the waist); *eine sturmfreie* Bude* (a room where visitors may enter unobserved by parents or landladies; *frei nach Kafka* (freely adapted from/based on a Kafka story); *frei ab 16* (a film licensed for over-sixteens); *sonnig und niederschlagsfrei* (sunny and 'free of precipitation') – suitable weather for that perennial source of curiosity to the British, *Freikörperkultur* or *FKK* (nudism), to which some of their less prurient though still euphemistically-inclined compatriots in the 1950s and 60s used to apply the German word for a playground, *Spielplatz*.

2. independent, freelance: *ein freier Schriftsteller* (freelance writer); *freiberuflich* (self-employed; see also *Freischütz* under FEST in VIII); but also *das Freiwild** ('fair game'); and *der Freitod* (suicide).

3. extemporary, unaided: *sich freischwimmen* is literally a test of one's ability to swim for 15 minutes without touching the bottom; figuratively (however inappropriate a metaphor in this context) to learn to stand on one's own two feet. In the opening pages of *Katz und Maus* (1961) we are told that Mahlke, the *grand Meaulnes* figure around whom Günter Grass's novel about growing up in wartime Danzig revolves, belatedly *schwamm sich frei* to join Pilenz and the other boys on a sunken minesweeper. When, as a returning war hero but equally the 'mouse' or hunted victim of the title, he chooses the same spot to disappear, it is Pilenz who betrays his friend and by way of atonement takes the priest's advice to write the story: *schreiben Sie sich frei*. See also *freisprechen* under KONZEPT in II.

4. outdoors: *im Freien* (in the open air); *das Freibad* (open-air swimming pool; *die Freilichtbühne* (open-air theatre); *das Freideck* (the roof or uncovered level of a *Hochgarage**).

In the theatre: *die spielfreie Zeit* is the close season; *ein spielfreier Tag* a rest-day; *der Sonntag ist spielfrei,* no performance on Sundays; 'free entry' is *frei, kostenlos* or *gratis,* and *ein Freiplatz* or *eine Freikarte* a complimentary ticket (though *ein Freiplatz* is also an outdoor court/pitch/ground).

On a more sinister note: after the *Währungsunion* (currency union) of 1 July 1990 introduced East Germans to economic realities, including unemployment, one heard the occasional wry allusion to the infamous slogan – itself a perversion of Max Weber's 'Protestant work ethic' – above the gates of Hitler's concentration camps: *Arbeit macht frei* ('work makes free').

FUNK n.m. besides funk music (a straightforward americanism), *der Funk* is the radio – from *funken,* 'to spark', applied in 1914 to the wireless telegraph (*ein Funker* is still a wireless operator or 'sparks'), and since the Twenties to radio, also known as *Rundfunk* since it is beamed out from a central *Funkturm.* Today, *Funk und Fernsehen* means 'radio and TV'; *er arbeitet beim Funk,* more generally, 'he works in broadcasting'.

The existence, before reunification, of nine autonomous broadcasting companies is a direct result of the Allies' decentralizing programme after the War (broadcasting in the Third Reich, like much else besides, was *gleichgeschaltet,* centrally controlled, with the emphasis on control). *Norddeutscher Rundfunk* in Hamburg and *Westdeutscher Rundfunk* in Cologne (founded as *Nordwestdeutscher Rundfunk* on the lines of the BBC Third Programme – one reason why Cologne is still a centre for early music), *Bayerischer Rundfunk* in Munich and *Südwestfunk* in Baden-Baden, together with other smaller stations (*Sender**) and, since 1990, the former 'east' and 'middle' German stations *MDR* and *ODR,* constitute the *Arbeitsgemeinschaft der Rundfunkanstalten Deutschlands – ARD* for short – whose function is to coordinate TV programmes for nation-wide transmission. They also each produce a *Drittes Fernsehprogramm* for the more discriminating viewer, as well as their own regional programmes.

But it is *Zweites Deutsches Fernsehen (ZDF),* based in Mainz, which best illustrates the federal principle in action. When Bonn attempted to gain control of this second, nation-wide network in 1961, the *Bundesverfassungsgericht* ruled that such a step was unconstitutional* in a famous judgement against what was (un)popularly known as *Adenauer-Fernsehen.* Inevitably, when a company such as *NDR* has a catchment area covering several *Länder,* it can find its coverage of politically sensitive issues subject to accusations of political bias by its paymasters (as with *Schleswig-Holstein* over the *Barschel-Affäre**; *Niedersachsen* over the *Spielbank-Affäre*).

GAG n.m. not the sort of gag a stand-up comedian delivers (*ein Witz*), but a humorous visual gimmick, as when a butler instinctively avoids tripping over a tiger-skin rug while balancing on a tray the glasses of wine he himself has to drink in place of his mistress's absent friends. This is the single running *Gag* in what the *Süddeutsche Zeitung*, on 13 July 1990, called *den weltberühmten, an jedem Silvester-abend ausgestrahlten Fernseh-Sketch 'Dinner for One'* ('the world-famous TV sketch *Dinner for One*, shown every New Year's Eve') – a fame which nevertheless seems to have eluded its deviser and star, Freddie Frinton, in his own country.

Ein Gag is also a publicity stunt (*ein Werbegag*), a technical special effect in the cinema or theatre, or a technical refinement or gadget which is unexpected rather than funny (*mein Photoapparat* hat einige besondere Gags*).

GAGE n.f. (French pronunciation) an actor's or musician's salary or fee (from the French for a pledge or security, though the French equiv-alent is now *un cachet* – only servants are paid *des gages*). See the additional senses of *engagieren* and *Engagement* under ENGAGIERT above.

GLANZ n.m. not a glance (*ein flüchtiger Blick*), but a gleam, sparkle, sheen, glare; figuratively, glory or splendour. Writing in *Die Zeit* on 16 November 1990, Wolf Biermann reflected on how his expulsion from East Germany in 1976 had exposed him to *ein großer Glanz von außen*, meaning 'the lustre of a celebrity bestowed by the outside world'. He doubtless meant his readers to think of Rilke's much-mocked line from *Das Stundenbuch* (1903): *Denn Armut ist ein großer Glanz aus Innen* ('for poverty is a great radiance from within'), and how – though with an irony alien to Rilke – it encapsulated the East's impoverished self-righteousness.

An ironical expression appropriate to an earlier occasion, when Biermann was visited by Margot Honecker (see HEIMSUCHEN in IX), is *welch Glanz in dieser Hütte*!* (roughly 'to what do I owe the honour?'). In its original form – *Wie kommt mir solcher Glanz in meine Hütte?* ('How comes such glory into my humble abode?') – from the Prologue to Schiller's *Die Jungfrau von Orleans* (1801), the irony is of a dramatic kind: Thibaut d'Arc has dreamt three times of his daughter sitting on the throne of France, but wrongly interprets it as a sign of her vanity and pride.

In a theatrical context: *Mephisto war die Glanzrolle Gustav Gründ-gens'* (Mephisto was Gründgens' greatest role); *er hat sich glänzend bewährt* (he gave a first-rate account of himself); *das Glanzstück des Abends* (the *pièce de résistance*). Alternatively: *mit Glanz und Gloria durchfallen* (to fail resoundingly).

GLOSSE n.f. not gloss in the sense of brightness or lustre (*der Glanz**), but a gloss on a text, and by extension a radio, TV, or newspaper commentary, usually light though polemical or satirical in tone (see FEUILLETON above). You might also say to someone who is forever making snide or sneering comments: *du brauchst nicht über alles deine Glossen zu machen.* The verb *glossieren* is used in all three senses – each the reverse of 'to gloss over' (to try to conceal: *vertuschen*; to make light of: *beschönigen*).

HARM n.m. *harmlos* has come to mean the same as harmless (innocuous, unsuspecting, innocent), but is derived from the now obsolete word *der Harm* meaning grief or 'sore affliction' rather than harm (*der Schaden, die Verletzung*). One can still use *abgehärmt* (careworn) or *verhärmt* (*ein verhärmter Ausdruck*, a worried expression), but encounters *gehärmt* only in such rarified regions as Rilke's tenth and final *Duineser Elegie* (1922) – *O wie werdet ihr dann, Nächte, mir lieb sein, / gehärmte* – celebrating the poet's Byronic acceptance of life's *Geheul, Gehärm* (*S.Werke* 2.207). And when Siegfried tells the Rhinemaidens *Nun lacht nur lustig* zu! In Harm lass ich euch doch* (*Götterdämmerung*, Act III, Scene 1), he proposes only to leave them grieving (*sich grämen*) that they had failed to seduce him into relinquishing the Ring.

HEFTIG adj. not 'hefty' in the sense of large and physically powerful. *Ein maßlos* heftiger Mensch* is rather a fiercely passionate person who flares up quickly and loses self-control. Drawing on his own experience in Weimar, Goethe created in *Torquato Tasso* (1790) the classic confrontation between the poetic temperament* as an *allzu heftig Wesen* and the sense of proportion and moderation (*Mäßigung**) of a conventional man of affairs – an incompatibility unlikely to be resolved by 'taking the waters' (*dein Blut durch eine Kur* verbessern*), the Duke's despairing advice to Tasso in Act V, Scene 2.

Nowadays, *Heftigkeit* may be even stronger – irascibility, vehemence, a violent temper. It is also used of severe headaches (*heftige Kopfschmerzen*), uproarious laughter (*heftiges Lachen*), fierce competition (*heftige Konkurrenz**), or making a big mistake (*er hat sich heftig geirrt*). But a hefty person/child/woman is *ein kräftiger Mensch, ein strammes Kind, eine dralle Frau*, a hefty book *ein dickes* Buch*, a hefty knock or blow *ein schwerer Schlag*, a hefty fine *eine hohe Geldstrafe*, a hefty bill *eine ganz schön hohe/fette* Rechnung*.

HISSEN v. to hoist a flag (*eine Flagge hissen*), or hitch up one's skirt (*die Frau hisste ihren Rock**), but not to hiss. German theatre and opera audiences *zischen* mainly when they dislike a director's* or producer's *Konzept** – notably at the *Bayreuther Festspiele*, where singers who fall short of expectations may also expect to be subjected to *Buhrufe* or even whistled off the stage (*ausgepfiffen werden*). When the audience applauds (though never before the act ends): *die Zuschauer klatschen Beifall.*

INTERPRET n.m. not an interpreter from one language into another (*ein Dolmetscher*), but of a dramatic part, piece of music, etc.– that is, a performer; or someone who interprets a literary or legal text.

KALENDER n.m. calendar, but also diary or appointment book (*ein Terminkalender**). *Ich schaue in meinem Kalender nach*, I'll check my diary. *Kalendergeschichten*, once common in almanacs, are anecdotes or short stories with a moral* purpose, though Brecht's *Kalendergeschichten* (1949), unlike Johann Peter Hebel's stories in the *Schatzkästlein* (*The Treasure Chest*), originally published in the Baden *Landkalender*, are not *erbaulich* (edifying) in any traditional sense. Any literary anthology of topical pieces might be published as a *Kalender*, for instance: *Kalender für/auf das Jahr 1996.*

KAPELLE n.f. a chapel, but also a band* of dance musicians, or a small orchestra (no longer so small in the case of the *Dresdner Staatskapelle*). *Ein Kapellmeister** is an old-fashioned bandleader, or an orchestra's director of music (the leader of the orchestra is *der Konzertmeister*).

KASSETTE n.f. has additional meanings besides an audio or video cassette: a small jewel-case or money-box; a slipcase for books (especially complete editions in paperback*, such as *eine neunbändige* Musil-Ausgabe, als Kassette DM149,–*) or boxed set of records, CDs or tapes; and in architecture, a vaulted panel in *eine Kassettendecke*, coffered ceiling.

KLAMMERN v. to staple or clamp, not to clamour (*etwas lautstark fordern, gegen etwas wettern**). However, since *eine Umklammerung* is a tight embrace/clinch/hug, the distinction may be somewhat blurred – *der Filmstar wurde umklammert* (mobbed). *Die Klammer* is also a bracket (*runde Klammern*, round brackets; *eckige Klammern*, square brackets), so *ausklammern* means to put outside the brackets, figuratively to ignore (*ein Problem ausklammern*).

KLANG n.m. the general word for sound or tone, not specifically a 'clang': *zu den Klängen eines Wiener Walzers tanzen* is to dance to the melodious strains of a Viennese waltz. Metallic sounds range from *das Klingen eines Glockenspiels* (glockenspiel) and *das Klirren von Schwertern* (swords) to *der Schall* or *das Dröhnen der Domglocken* (cathedral bells). Or, to put it onomatopoeically, from *klingling* (ting-a-ling) to *klingklang* (ding-dong).

'Clanging' dissonance was not what the audience in 1912 heard in Franz Schreker's progressive, though still lush and hyper-romantic opera, *Der ferne Klang* (literally, 'the distant sound' though it is tempting to think of it as 'The lost chord'). In 1913, to great popular acclaim, Schreker also conducted the first performance of Schoenberg's *Gurrelieder* of 1900 (*gurren* means 'to coo'). But Schoenberg's more radical experiments with *die Klangfarbe* (the tone colour of a sound) were as incomprehensible to the Viennese public as they were in tune with Kandinsky's experiments on *der Farbklang* (the resonance of a colour) in *Der blaue Reiter*, the journal in which he also reproduced colour sketches by Schoenberg in 1911. See also TON below (and for 'dropping a clanger', *ins Fettnäpfchen treten*, BLAM-IEREN in V).

KLAPPEN v. not to clap/applaud (*Beifall klatschen*), though it is used of clicking or snapping noises (*klappende Geräusche*), as when a door clicks shut/claps to (*die Tür klappt zu*), shutters knock against a wall (*die Fensterläden klappen an die Wand*), or when German soldiers used to click their heels together (*mit den Hacken klappen* – see DIENEN in I). Add an '*r*' to turn this into the noise made by a clattering typewriter (*die Schreibmaschine klappert*), a rattletrap (*eine Klapperkiste*), a rattlesnake (*eine Klapperschlange*), or the *Klapperstorch* which bites mummy's leg (*der Klapperstorch hat die Mutter ins Bein gebissen*) or goes to the Müllers (*zu Müllers ist der Klapperstorch gekommen*) after stopping off at the gooseberry bush.

Since *eine Klappe* is a flap, trapdoor, hinged lid, or clapperboard in filming, *klappen* also means to fold (*ein Klappstuhl**, *ein Bett zusammenklappen*); to raise or lower (*den Deckel nach oben/unten klappen*), and to tip backwards or forwards (*den Autositz nach vorn/hinten klappen*), while *halt die Klappe!* is a rather rude way of asking someone to be quiet.

A widespread figurative meaning of *klappen*, however, is to work out, to go smoothly: *es hat geklappt* (all went well/we managed it/I got the job, etc.).

KLISCHEE n.n. a cliché (see PHRASE in II), but also still used in its original sense of a plate or block in printing.

KOMIK n.f. not a comic/comedian (*der Komiker*) but a comic effect, as in *eine Szene von unwiderstehlicher Komik* (an irresistibly funny scene) or *die Komik der Situation* (the funny side of it). The comics children read are *Comic-Heft(chen)* or *Comics*.

KOMMENTAR n.m. a comment as well as a commentary. *Kein Kommentar!* (no comment).

KOMPRIMIEREN v. not to compromise (*einen Kompromiß schließen, sich auf einen Kompromiß einigen*; to compromise oneself is *sich kompromittieren*), but to condense (a book or article) or to compress (air, gas, or one's thoughts; consequently, *einen komprimierten Stil schreiben* is to write succinctly, concisely).

KONTERFEI n.n. not counterfeit (*das Falschgeld*, counterfeit money), but a slightly old-fashioned, hence sometimes humorous, word for a portrait or likeness.

KONZERT n.n. a concert or recital, but also a concerto. *Der Konzertmeister* is the leader of an orchestra/US concertmaster. See also AKADEMIE and KAPELLE above.

KRITIK n.f. a journalistic review, notice, 'crit'; or else a philosophical critique. Also 'the critics' in general, as well as the critical faculty, whereas an individual critic is *ein Kritiker* – someone the Germans like to think of as being solidly *wissenschaftlich**and whose review is thus ideally *eine wissenschaftliche Kritik* or *Rezension* rather than outspoken or opinionated.

KUNST- pref. either **1.** artificial (*künstlich*) – *Kunstleder* (imitation leather) and *Kunstseide* (artificial silk) are both *Kunststoffe* (man-made or synthetic materials); or else **2.** artistic (*künstlerisch*) – as in *das Kunstwerk* (work of art), *der Kunstflieger* (stunt pilot) or *der Kunstreiter* (circus/trick rider). Drawing on both meanings, *ein Kunststück* is a trick, but also an ironic exclamation: *Kunststück!* hardly surprising!, no wonder!

The Romantic genre of *das Kunstmärchen* (literary fairytale), exemplified in Ludwig Tieck's *Der blonde Eckbert* (1797) though perhaps better known in this country through the works of Oscar Wilde or Angela Carter, equally draws on both senses, for while it is crafted with psychological sophistication (see SENTIMENTALISCH in V) it is also, of course, imitative of the traditional *Volksmärchen* which the Brothers Grimm collected and published in 1812/14 (but to which they, too, it is now clear, made their own subtle alterations).

LITERAT n.m. a now generally derogatory term for a literary figure or man of letters (see POET below). Hence, *die Literaten* are 'the literati', whereas literacy extends from the rudimentary *Fähigkeit, lesen und schreiben zu können* to the uniquely German connotations of *Bildung**, lack of which marks out *der Analphabet*.

LYRIK n.f. the genre of lyric poetry or verse. A lyric poem is *ein lyrisches Gedicht*, the lyric of a pop song *der Text*.

MAGAZIN n.n. a radio or TV 'magazine programme'. In journalism, the *Süddeutsche Zeitung* on 29 June 1989 differentiated between *Der Spiegel, jenes bekannte Magazin* (that well-known magazine) and *Stern, jene Illustrierte, die so gerne Magazin genannt würde* (that illustrated which would so love to be called a magazine). The *Süddeutsche* has clearly no such problem; like *Die Zeit*, it simply calls its weekend colour supplement a *Magazin*.

Ein Magazin is also a storeroom – for weapons, or library stock, for instance – or the magazine of a gun. Austrians sometimes call a shop *ein Magazin*.

MASKE n.f. a mask (the *Maskenkleid* worn to a *Maskenball* is full fancy-dress), but in a theatrical context, or in film credits, 'make-up'.

MEINEN v. 'to mean', but also (more tentatively) 'to think', 'to reckon', 'to be of the opinion'.

MIME n.m. a 'Thespian'. The humorous note was not yet uppermost in Schiller's day when, in the *Prolog* to *Wallensteins Lager* with which the Weimar theatre reopened in 1798, he celebrated the ephemeral glories of the actor's art: *Dem Mimen flicht die Nachwelt keine Kränze* ('Posterity weaves no garlands for the actor'), concluding that to satisfy the best of one's contemporaries is nevertheless to achieve immortality: *Denn wer den Besten seiner Zeit genug / Getan, der hat gelebt für alle Zeiten.*

A mime such as Marcel Marceau, however, is *ein Pantomime*, whose art is *die Pantomime**, though the silent expression of emotions is simply *mimisch* (*der Pantomime drückt verschiedene Gefühle durch Mimik aus*). The verb *mimen* is also used in this context, but has the additional sense of pretending or play-acting (*er mimt den Unschuldigen*, he's playing the innocent). To mimic is otherwise *nachahmen* or *imitieren*.

MODERATION n.f. in broadcasting, 'presentation': *die Moderation hat . . . presented by. . . . Der Moderator* is thus the presenter of a TV or radio programme, not a religious dignitary such as *der Oberhaupt der Church of Scotland*. In other contexts the verb *moderieren* sometimes retains the older sense of moderation (see MASS in II) or mediation, as when former SPD chairman Hans-Jochen Vogel was said to have mediated successfully between Willy Brandt and Oskar Lafontaine on their attitudes towards German reunification: *Vogel moderierte zwischen Brandt und Lafontaine, und zwar erfolgreich.*

Somewhat less ubiquitous than *der Moderator*, if more fatuous to English ears, are *der Showmaster* (compère) and *der Talkmaster* (the presenter of a *Talk-Show*) – the latter unconnected to the German word *der Talk* (talc) or *Talkpuder* (talcum powder).

NOVELLE n.f. *Ein Romanschriftsteller* or *Romancier* writes *Romane* (novels); *ein Novellist* writes *Novellen* (novellas). These are something of a German speciality. In Kleist's famous novella *Das Erdbeben in Chili*, for instance, a large earthquake in Chile (many dead) leads to the even more monstrous slaughter of those held responsible. Written in 1807 in part as a clandestine call to arms against Napoleon, it is also a *Novelle* in the sense explained in Section I: a mooted amendment or change to the existing decree (namely, submission to French domination). The story nicely complies with a succinct definition of the genre given by Goethe in a conversation with Eckermann in 1827: *eine sich ereignete, unerhörte Begebenheit* (an unheard-of event which actually happened).

PAMPHLET n.n. a lampoon, invariably hostile. An informative brochure is *eine Broschüre*, a literary pamphlet *eine Druckschrift*, a political pamphlet or one for distribution in the streets *ein Flugblatt* or *eine Flugschrift*.

PANTOMIME n.m. mime* or a mime artist. The traditional British children's pantomime has no German equivalent (leaving aside the double entendres aimed at accompanying adults, it might be described as *ein Weihnachtsmärchen*).

PAPERBACK n.n. nowadays generally as in English, though until quite recently *ein Paperback* was a paper-backed version of a larger-format book, unlike the *Taschenbuch* which you can slip in your pocket.

PATHETISCH adj. 'if I may speak pathetically' is not at all what the East German should have said when interviewed by the BBC after the Berlin Wall was opened: *wenn ich pathetisch reden darf* actually means 'if I may be permitted an emotional reaction', though other nuances are solemn, fervent, passionate, dramatic. Sometimes, as with *das Pathos* (strong emotion), the sense is one of inappropriate solemnity or feeling; thus, *pathetische Phrasen** are high-sounding, bombastic, or else unduly sentimental.

As a musical expression, 'with great emotion' – embodied, for instance, in the a-b-c-b phrase with which both Beethoven and Tchaikovsky begin the works known as *Pathétique* (and which Purcell, too, had used for Dido's Lament 'When I am laid in earth'). So when in Ken Russell's *The Music Lovers* Tchaikovsky's brother is made to suggest the subtitle for the symphony after reflecting on the composer's piteous life, it only reveals the improper use of the word in English.

Pathetic meaning piteous is *mitleiderregend, kläglich*; woefully inadequate, *jämmerlich, erbärmlich, kläglich, miserabel*; ridiculous, *lächerlich*. 'It was pathetically obvious she was ignoring him: *es war peinlich* zu sehen, wie sie ihn ignorierte*.

PHOTOGRAPH n.m. a photographer, not a photograph (*eine Photographie, ein Photo, ein Foto*).

PLAKATIV adj. not 'placatory' but, on the contrary, 'strident' – the language of *das Plakat* (placard or poster). The desired effect is bold and striking (*eine plakative Wirkung*) – indeed, it might be said that only someone wishing to make such an effect would actually use the word. 'Placatory', on the other hand, is either *besänftigend* (*jemanden besänftigen*, to soothe someone, calm them down), *versöhnlich* (*versöhnliche Gebärden*, conciliatory gestures), or *beschwichtigend* (Chamberlain's policy of appeasement is known as *Beschwichtigungspolitik* – see WISCH in V).

PLASTIK n.f. sculpture as a plastic art (*eine plastische Kunst*), or an individual piece of sculpture (also *eine Skulptur*). *Ein Plastiker* is another word for *ein Bildhauer* (sculptor). Figuratively, *Plastik* suggests vividness – *den Vorgang plastisch schildern*, to give a graphic account of the event; *die plastische Wirkung eines Bildes*, the three-dimensional effect of a painting; *eine plastische Sprache*, vivid language; *plastische Gebärden*, graphic gestures. Finally, *die Plastik* is also plastic surgery.

The synthetic material (*Kunststoff**), however, which is *plastisch* in the sense of malleable or workable, is known as *das Plastik*, and in East Germany as *der Plast*, colloquially *die Plaste*. According to *Die Zeit* on 5 April 1991, Western chemists have finally discovered how to dispose of the two million '*Plasteschüssel*' ('plastic bowls' – one of the less complimentary terms for the *Trabant** car): bacteria, which will convert *die 650-Kilogramm Plaste innerhalb von nur drei Wochen in zehn Kilogramm Biomasse**.

PLAY-BACK n.n. a TV recording, but also double-tracking or miming* to a previous recording. To play back a tape recording is simply *abspielen*.

POET n.m. a poet or bard – until the authentic *Originalgenie** came to be known as *ein Dichter* or 'true poet' in the Romantic era, since when the word *Poet* tends to be used humorously or ironically, and *das Poem* to designate the work of a mere versifier or poetaster. The sixteenth-century poet and cobbler Hans Sachs, for instance, wrote over 6,000 works in rhyming couplets*, but when Wagner in Act I of *Die Meistersinger von Nürnberg* borrowed one such *Knittelvers* *for his Hans Sachs to describe his twin trades – *ich bin ein Schuh-/macher und Poet dazu* – it is a rhyme calculated to make us smile. *Poetisch* and *Poetik*, however, do not have pejorative undertones, nor, though archaic, does *die Poesie* (*ein Poesiealbum* is an autograph* album in which young girls used to get their friends to inscribe verses or bons mots).

In what is sometimes called *die Goethezeit* or Age of Goethe (1749–1832), Germany acquired the reputation of being *das Volk der Dichter und Denker* (a nation of poets and thinkers). Goethe himself, who preferred Sachs's earthy humour and vitality to the philosophers' abstractions, is the supreme *Dichter* – at once *Lyriker* * (lyric poet), *Dramatiker* (dramatist), *Romancier* * (novelist) and *Novellist* * (writer of novellas). Nevertheless, the title he gave to a selective reconstruction of his early life and works, *Dichtung und Wahrheit* ('poetry and truth'), is used in our more sceptical times to suggest a gap between fact and fiction.

The word *Dichter* (accorded to all creative writers, not merely lyrical poets) evokes dimensions of inwardness, of the special nature of German *Kultur* *, indeed of the divine spark which 'dictates' works. Lessing had modestly disclaimed the title of *Dichter* (and was taken at his word, to the detriment of his reputation), while Thomas Mann, a pre-eminently self-conscious artist (see SELBSTBEWUSST and SENTIMENTALISCH in V), much resented early criticism which labelled him a mere *Literat* * rather than a *Dichter*. Rilke, on the other hand, the archetypal *Dichter* (and inspired '*poète*' of Jean Cocteau's films), went so far as to compare what he experienced in 1922 as the *Diktat* * of poetic inspiration with the allegedly authoritative voice of the Italian 'dictator' (a naivety which illustrates Karl Kraus's warning that the otherworldly *Volk* * *der Dichter und Denker* acclaimed by Mme de Staël would offer little resistance to the coming generation of *Richter und Henker*, 'judges and executioners').

POINTE n.f. the punch-line of a joke.

POSSE n.f. not a sheriff's posse (*das Aufgebot*) but a theatrical farce, associated above all with Vienna and Johann Nepomuk Nestroy (1802–1862), for example his *Einen Jux will er sich machen* and *Lumpazivagabundus*. See also SCHWANK below and SKURRIL in V.

PRÄMIERUNG n.f. the giving of awards or bonuses, as well as the presentation ceremony itself (*die Prämie* means bonus or prize as well as premium). The 'world première' of a play or film is *die*

Uraufführung or *Erstaufführung*, though Germans also use the word *die Premiere*.

PROBE n.f. not something which explores by penetration, such as a dentist's probe or a space probe (both *eine Sonde*) or a police probe (*eine Untersuchung*). The basic sense is rather of testing: *die Probe* is a rehearsal, *proben* to rehearse, *probieren* to try out or have a go. Thus, *bei den Proben haben wir verschiedene Möglichkeiten probiert, aber dann die endgültige Fassung gründlich geprobt* (during rehearsals we tried out various possibilities, but then rehearsed the final version thoroughly). An operatic *Sitzprobe* is a run-through with the singers not yet acting, while the *Generalprobe* is the dress-rehearsal. Further examples are *die Probezeit* (probation), *die Probefahrt* (test run), *die Stichprobe* (spot check), and *das Probestück* (sample or specimen) – for instance, *Gesteinsproben vom Mond*, samples of moon rock.

Or else a tasting, such as a *Weinprobe*. Here the verb is *probieren* (*probier mal*, try some). See also DEGUSTATION and KOST in VIII.

PURPURN adj. crimson, whereas purple is *violett* or *lila*.

PUZZLE n.n. an abbreviated anglicism, for it refers only to a jigsaw puzzle, as does the verb *puzzeln* (which is also used figuratively: *er puzzelte stundenlang an der Lösung des Problems*). Any other puzzle is *ein Rätsel*.

REALIEN n.p. formerly the 'real facts' of science, or science and modern languages as school subjects (see REALSCHULE in IV), now familiar in such reference works as the *Sammlung Metzler* series '*Realien zur Literatur*'.

REALISIEREN v. in a financial context, to realize, to make or conclude a sale. Otherwise, to carry out – a programme, plan, idea or project, that is, to produce. Consequently, *eine Realisation* is a production for TV, radio or the theatre.

REQUISITEN n.p. theatrical props, under the charge of the *Requisiteur*.

ROBINSONADE n.f. one of the numerous imitations spawned by Defoe's novel after 1719; or else an adventure holiday such as those organized by the *Club Robinson*, or some other enterprise undertaken in the same spirit. Kafka, a self-styled Robinson Crusoe, seems to have been more concerned with the journey back to civilization: *Dieses ganze Schreiben ist nichts als die Fahne des Robinson auf dem höchsten Punkt der Insel* (All my writing is no more than Robinson's flag on the highest point of the island – to Max Brod, 12 July 1922).

But it was another Englishman, the goalkeeper J. Robinson (1878–1949), after whom a *Robinsonade* in football is named: a flying save at the feet of an attacker. A prophet without honour in his own country, Robinson's tactic was put to memorable, if bone-shatteringly inaccurate, use by the German goalkeeper Toni Schumacher during the 1982 World Cup (see also KICKER and RÜDE in VII).

ROMAN n.m. neither an inhabitant of Rome (*ein Römer**), nor a Roman Catholic (*ein Katholik* or *ein Römisch-Katholischer*), but a novel – the work of a *Romanschriftsteller* or *Romancier*, not a *Novellist* (someone who writes *Novellen**).

Apart from the *Bildungsroman**, the German novel has travelled less well than its more metropolitan English, French and Russian cousins. Thomas Mann's standard explanation for this was caricatured by his brother Heinrich in Chapter 5 of *Der Untertan* (1911), when 'loyal subject*' Diederich Hessling, intoxicated by a performance of *Lohengrin*, declares that *the* German art is music, next comes drama which can be set to music and which you do not have to read, then of course portrait painting because of the pictures of the Kaiser. '*Und der Roman?*' his fiancée enquires. '*Der ist keine Kunst. Wenigstens Gott sei Dank keine deutsche: das sagt schon der Name* ('That's not art. At least, thank God, not German art: you can tell by the name'). Thomas, in turn, caricatured his brother in the *Betrachtungen eines Unpolitischen* of 1918 (*Reflections of an Unpolitical Man*, in fact the intransigent though probably cathartic apologia of a Romantic aesthete) as a francophile '*Zivilisationsliterat*' for whom literature is the twin sister of politics, and more affectionately in *Der Zauberberg* (1924) as Settembrini, to whom the Germans' love of *Bier**, *Tabak und Musik* are all, as Nietzsche too had come to believe, *politisch suspekt* (see also KULTUR in II, FATAL and IDEELL in V).

What one can indeed tell from the name *Roman* is that the novel goes back to the vernacular French, Italian or Spanish 'romance', as distinct from learned Latin. (The Arthurian romances of the Middle Ages are known in German as *Artusromane*, whereas *Romanze* refers to a specific lyric form popular with the Romantics.) Similarly, *ein Romane* is someone who speaks a Romance language – *eine romanische Sprache*, including *Rumänisch* (Romanian) and the *Romantsch* spoken in several remote Swiss valleys – while *ein Romanist* is a student or teacher of such languages (see WELSCH in II). *Romanisch* also designates the style of architecture we call Romanesque or Norman.

SCHAUER n.m. a shower of rain (*vereinzelte Schauer, zeitweise sonnig*, scattered showers with sunny intervals), but also a shudder (*ein Schauer lief ihm den Rücken hinunter*, a shiver ran up and down his spine; *mich schauert/schaudert bei dem bloßen Gedanken*, the very thought of it makes me shudder). It is this latter sense which gives us *die Schauergeschichte* and *der Schauerroman**, dubbed 'gothic' when they came into vogue in the 1790s and 1800s since they were often set in Germany and attributed to German sources. Typifying the dark but popular side of Romanticism, their pleasurably spine-chilling plots and effects were in turn bloodcurdling, eerie, uncanny, morbid, macabre, creepy – all aspects of *das Unheimliche* (literally 'un-homely'; see HEIMLICH in IX, IDEELL in V).

Due to the familiar process of linguistic devaluation, however, *schauerliche Menschen* are now merely awful or dreadful people, while *ein Schauermann* is quite unconnected – a docker/stevedore/US long-shoreman ('the bogey man' is *Schwarzer Mann* or *der Butzemann*).

SCHMIEREN v. from the root meaning 'to smear' (or spread – also *streichen** – cheese on one's *Butterbrot*, for instance) are derived **1.** theatrical expressions from the application of grease-paint, such as *eine Schmiere* (a flea-pit of a theatre), *eine Schmierenkomödie* (slapstick or pantomime*), *ein Schmierenkomödiant* (ham actor), *ein schmieriges Lächeln* (a slimy/oily smile); **2.** a pejorative term for writing, especially journalism: *ein Schmierer* is a scribbler or hack (also a slogan-dauber or a graffiti-writer) and in Austria someone who cribs in school (from the *Schmierer* which contains both a text and its translation). *Ein Schmierfink* is if anything stronger, perhaps a scandal-monger or muckraker (though also a child who scrawls or is generally messy). There were accordingly several unpleasant echoes when Karl Kraus said of the sentiments expressed in Franz Werfel's poetry: *die Gefühle gehen wie geschmiert* (literally, 'as though greased' – glib, smooth); **3.** to give bribes – *Schmiergeld*; and **4.** to clout someone – *jemandem eine schmieren*.

Schmiere stehen means to keep guard or be the look-out.

SCHMÖKER n.m. an old book or thick tome, usually of little merit, though of a kind which encourages *schmökern*, (to browse or bury oneself). No connection, then, with a smoker/stag night, *ein Herrenabend*.

SCHNEIDIG adj. not snide (*eine abfällige Bemerkung*, a snide remark) but, usually in a military context, dashing. It also evokes the clipped speech of the military – not for the faint-hearted, *die keinen Schneid haben* (who have no guts), *die den Schneid verloren haben* (who have lost their nerve). 'The dashing white sergeant' would doubtless have been *ein schneidiger Bursche*, a fine fellow who cut a dash – what the Austrians call *ein fescher Bursche* (see FADE in IX) or *ein verfluchter Kerl.* As a musical tempo (like *flott*): rousing, *allegro spirituoso* or *vivace.*

SCHWANEN v. as in *mir schwant nichts Gutes* (I've a feeling something nasty is going to happen). Any link with *der Schwan* is merely fortuitous, though *ein Schwanengesang* (swan-song) may well convey a sense of foreboding – the Heine settings in the collection known as *Schwanengesang*, for instance, though it was given that name only after Schubert's death by his publisher. A rather more literal swan-song is that of Wagner's '*Schwanenritter*', Lohengrin, when he addresses his means of transport: *Mein lieber Schwan!* (one tenor who missed the boat memorably extemporized: *Wann fährt der nächste Schwan?* 'When does the next swan go?'). Nowadays, the phrase *mein lieber Schwan!* (a favourite of Brecht's) signifies surprise, or else a friendly warning: 'Watch it, my lad'.

For 'swanning around', see WANDERN in VII.

SCHWANK n.m. not a swank (*ein Angeber*; it's just a lot of swank, *es ist nur Schau*), but a theatrical farce, often in dialect and especially popular in Bavaria (see SKURRIL in V, also POSSE above), or a comic tale or escapade (see *Streich* under STREICHINSTRUMENT below). The verb *schwanken* is synonymous with *wanken** (to sway, stagger, totter; vacillate, waver, dither), so that *seelische Schwankungen* are fluctuations in one's mental or emotional state.

SCHWUNG n.m. 'swing', especially its many figurative senses: momentum, zest, verve. Something in full swing is *in Schwung*, music played *mit Schwung* is decidedly *andante con moto* (though Glenn Miller's music is known in Germany, too, as *Swing*). There is a splendidly defiant gesture in Rilke's poem *Ode an Bellmann*: *Ist nicht der Husten beinah schön, im Schwunge? / Was kümmert uns die Lunge!* – more prosaically 'Is not the resonance of a cough almost beautiful? Why worry about the lungs'.

This echoes a more specific sense of the verb *schwingen*, namely 'to vibrate' – its poetic cognate *die Schwinge* (*auf den Schwingen der Begeisterung*, on wings of passion) replete with erotic possibilities. Thus Goethe's Suleika, Marianne von Willemer (1784–1860), in his *West-Östlicher Divan* (the word means 'collection'): *Ach, um deine feuchten Schwingen, / West, wie sehr ich dich beneide: / Denn du kannst ihm Kunde bringen, / Was ich in der Trennung leide* ('Ah, how I envy you, West Wind, your moist pinions, for you can bring him word of how I suffer while we are apart').

SENDER n.m. the sender of a (personal) letter is *der Absender*, who generally writes his or her name and address on the back of the

envelope, whereas *der Sender* is a radio or television transmitter/
channel/station, and *die Sendung* a transmission (see FUNK above).
Eine Sendepause is a gap in transmission when the station is off the air,
but also, figuratively, a deathly silence.

SENTENZ n.f. not a grammatical sentence (*der Satz*), or a judicial
sentence (*das Urteil, die Strafe*), but an aphorism or maxim, as in *eine
gnomische Sentenz* (a gnomic utterance). In German, *sentenziös* can
mean either aphoristic (*sentenzhaft* is perhaps less ambiguous) or
'sententious' in its more recent English sense of affectedly or
pompously formal. When Nietzsche writes of Laurence Sterne: *seine
Sentenzen enthalten zugleich eine Ironie auf alles Sentenziöse*, he seems
to mean that Sterne's aphorisms are at the same time ironical of all
that is weighty or moralizing (*Werke* I.781) – though perhaps the
irony here also lies in the theological sense of *Sentenzen* as the
pronouncements of the Church Fathers.

SIGNATUR n.f. not a full signature (*eine Unterschrift*), but the
abbreviated form with which German business letters are frequently,
and indecipherably, signed or initialled (*signiert*) without an accompanying printed name. Also a symbol on a map, or a library shelf
mark. *Das Signet* is a publisher's mark, colophon, logo.

SO adv. **1.** sometimes corresponds to English 'so': *ich hab' mich so
gefreut* (I was so pleased); *es ist aber gar nicht so einfach* (but it is really
not so easy);

2. thus, in this way, like that: *sei doch nicht so* (don't be like that);
SO ist das! (I see!/so *that's* the way things are); *so IST das!* (that's just
how it is) – here it means much the same as *also**, and as Mark Twain
noted of *also*, the meaning of *so* may similarly depend on intonation.
So oder so conveys a stark choice, even a threat, an impossible alternative, 'one way or the other'; it is a phrase both Hitler and Goebbels
used repeatedly and emphatically of the choice between total victory
or annihilation allegedly facing the German people in 1944/45;

3. such: *so ein netter Mann* (such a nice man), *so ein Idiot!* (such an
idiot!). *So ein Tag* (what a day) – the beginning of a favourite
Karneval* song which must have seemed particularly apt on 9 November 1989: *So ein Tag, so wunderschön wie heute, so ein Tag, der
dürfte nie vergehn* ('A day like today should never fade away' – see
MAUER and POWER in II);

4. (as an interjection): *so* (oh, really); *ach so!* (I see!, aha!, of
course!); *so, gehen wir!* (right then, let's go); *na, SO was!* ('well I
never') – not to be confused with 'so what?' (*na, also* / na, wenn schon
/ na, und?*)

Ein Soundso is not a (real, proper) so-and-so (*ein gemeiner Kerl;*

you old so-and-so, *du bist vielleicht einer*), but merely an unspecified person (*Herr Soundso*, Mr What's-his-name).

SONG n.m. since Brecht and Weill, generally used of a satirical/ political song, unlike the traditional German *Lied*. What we call the Song of Solomon is *Das Hohe Lied*.

SONNYBOY n.m. not a familiar, sometimes threatening, form of address ('now listen to me, sonny boy', *nun hör mal gut zu, mein Junge*), but rather, as in the Al Jolson song, someone of a sunny disposition – at times applied ironically ('sunny Jim') to a smooth charmer, though not, one suspects, when Germany's most popular chat show host or '*Talkmaster*' (see MODERATION above) is invariably introduced as *unser Sonnyboy*.

SPIEL n.n. not long-winded waffle (*langweiliges Geschwafel, Bla-bla*) or glib talk (*das Geschwätz*; a sales 'spiel' is *eine Story**), but the product of man's *Spieltrieb* (play instinct – see BILDUNG in IV): either **1.** a game or match; or **2.** (short for *Schauspiel*) a play in the theatre (*ein Spielfilm* is a feature film); or **3.** acting, or the act of playing (a game, a musical instrument); or **4.** gambling (*Pech im Spiel haben*, to be unlucky at cards); or **5.** a deck of cards (*das Kartenspiel*) or chess-set (*das Schachspiel*).

SPOT n.m. not a spotlight (*das Spotlight, der Scheinwerfer*; to be in the spotlight, *im Rampenlicht stehen*), but a commercial, advertisement, ad (short for *Werbespot*). A two-minute spot in a TV programme, however, is *zwei Minuten Sendezeit* im Fernsehen*, and a spot/turn/act/number in a show *eine Nummer**.

STARREN v. while *ein Star* is a star (*der Starspieler*, star player; *der Filmstar* – but see STAR in VII for quite different meanings), *starren* does not mean to play a starring role (*die Hauptrolle spielen*), but to stare. Also to be frozen stiff (*Hamburg starrt vor Kälte*), or bristling with weapons (*die Soldaten starrten von Waffen*). Someone who is *starrsinnig* (mulishly stubborn, obstinate) is *ein Starrkopf*, while *ein starrer Blick* is a glassy stare (for the difference between German and English attitudes to eye contact, see GAFFER in VI).

STATIST n.m. not a statistician (*ein Statistiker*), but a film extra or a supernumerary in the theatre (also known as *ein Komparse/eine Komparsin*: *die ganze Komparserie*, all those with walk-on/bit parts). Hamburg's *Thalia* theatre recently advertised for *Statisten zwischen 30 und 50 Jahren. Die Bewerber sollten ein gepflegtes Äußeres haben, da sie für die Darstellung von Kurgästen* vorgesehen sind* (Extras aged between 30 and 50. Applicants should have a well-groomed appearance since they are to play visitors to a spa). Acting skills were clearly supernumerary, even though the play was Ibsen's *Wenn wir Toten erwachen* (*When we dead awake*).

The opposite of *eine Statistenrolle* is *eine tragende Rolle*, a major role, one which 'carries' the main weight or responsibility (a term applied, jocularly, also to *Statisten* required to carry, say, a spear or a suitcase).

STREICHINSTRUMENT n.n. from *streichen* in its more recent, gentler sense of *streicheln* (to stroke) rather than to strike (*schlagen*). *Die Streicher* are thus the strings in an orchestra, who play *Streichinstrumente*, whereas the percussionists, *die Schlagzeuger*, play *Schlaginstrumente*. The woodwinds are *die Holzbläser*.

Ein Streich is nowadays a prank or escapade, such as those of Wilhelm Busch's beloved *Max und Moritz* (1865; see MORAL in V, PRANKE in VI, and COUPLET above), and in its grown-up version a 'sudden stroke' such as a *Schildbürgerstreich* (see BÜRGER in II) or *Staatsstreich* (coup d'état) – not forgetting *der Streik*, taken from English 'strike' despite the available German phrase: *die Arbeit streichen*, to eliminate work. But *ein Streichholz* (match) is so called because it is lit by a stroking action, while *streichen* means to smooth (*die Haare aus der Stirn streichen*, to push one's hair back), to spread (*Streichwurst, Streichkäse, ein Brot mit Butter streichen*), or to paint (*frisch gestrichen!* wet paint!), though also on occasion, as we have seen, to 'strike through', *durchstreichen*, in the sense of cancel or delete.

SYNCHRONISIEREN v. to synchronize (watches, or voices with lip movements), but also to dub. Clearly, *Bild und Ton* waren schlecht synchronisiert* means that the film was badly synchronized/out of synch (also *asynchron*), while *der Film war schlecht synchronisiert* generally means that the film was badly dubbed. Though dubbing rather than subtitles (*Untertitel*) is the norm for foreign films, the voices used seem to have changed little over the years. *Alle berühmten englische/amerikanische Schauspieler haben feste* deutsche Synchronstimmen*, all famous English and American actors are dubbed with steady/firm/sonorous voices in German.

TAKT n.m. either **1.** a bar of music; or **2.** rhythm, beat; also the phase or stroke of an engine (the *Trabant** was *ein Zweitakter*, two-stroke); or **3.** tact. In this latter sense: *Taktgefühl* (tactfulness, only rarely 'rhythmic sense'), *taktvoll* (tactful). In the former: *Taktwechsel* (change of beat), *Taktstock* (baton), *taktfest** (able to keep time).

TALKMASTER n.m. see MODERATOR above.

TAPPEN v. not to tap (*klopfen*) or tap-dance (*steppen**), but to walk with faltering steps (*tappende Schritte*) or grope (in the dark, *im* *finstern/dunkeln tappen*; of more erotic fumblings, *fummeln*).

TEXTBUCH n.n. not an educational textbook (*ein Lehrbuch*), but the script of a film or play, an opera libretto, or a book of (pop) lyrics. Accordingly, *ein Texter* writes the words (*der Text*) for pop songs, or advertising text. Note also *im Klartext*, 'in clear', that is, not codified – the equivalent of 'in plain English'.

TON n.m. a sound, or sound in general (see also KLANG above). Hence, on the technical side: *der Tonfilm* (sound film, talkie), *das Tonbandgerät** (tape recorder), *der Tonmeister** (sound mixer), *der Toningenieur* (sound engineer), *der Tonassistent* (sound operator). In music: *der Ton* (a musical tone), *die Tonleiter* (scale), *die Tonhöhe* (pitch), *der Tonfall** (intonation, tone of voice), *die Tonart** (key). Some differences in designation are worth noting: B flat is *B* (thus, *B-dur* is the key of B flat major, *B-Moll* is B flat minor), B is *H*, E sharp is *Eis*, and E flat is *Es* (the key of Mozart's masonic music, and thus, for him, of intellectual enlightenment, albeit of the Catholic variety – see under UNMENSCH in II). Accordingly, BACH in German musical notation is B flat, A, C, B natural. Note also *der Ton macht die Musik*, meaning that it depends on the way you say something whether it is offensive or not.

To set a text to music is *vertonen*, *eine Tondichtung* is a tone poem, *ein Tondichter* or *Tonsetzer* a composer. Both these terms are now somewhat old-fashioned, but just as Brecht called himself a *Stücke-schreiber* ('play writer') rather than a *Dramatiker* to underline his rejection of the past, so Thomas Mann made Adrian Leverkühn, the pioneering hero of *Dr Faustus* (1949), a *Tonsetzer* (someone who 'sets down notes') rather than a *Komponist*, basing his musical development on that of Arnold Schoenberg, the inventor of the *Zwölfton-technik* or *Reihentechnik* who was thus a 'tone-setter' in more ways than one, *jemand, der den Ton angibt*. (Schoenberg was less pleased at being identified with the syphilitic hero of the novel.)

Note that *der Ton* also means clay, so that *das Tongeschirr* is earthenware and *eine Tonpfeife* a clay pipe. *Das Tontaubenschießen* should not be transliterated as the shooting of those who are tone-deaf ('*tontaub*' does not exist – such people are described as having *kein Gehör für Tonhöhen*) but refers to the popular Continental sport of clay pigeon shooting (the equally misleading French *ball-trap*).

A ton weight, finally, is one of the meanings of *eine Tonne**.

TRAKT n.m. the wing or section of a building, or a stretch of motorway, but not a biblical tract or philosophical treatise. This is *ein Traktat*, such as Wittgenstein's *Tractatus*, while the verb *traktieren* has come to mean to maltreat, to torment.

TRICKFILM n.m. a cartoon film, but also a 'trick film' with sequences in slow-motion (*mit Zeitlupe*) or in reverse (*rückwärts-laufend*).

TÜRKE n.m. a Turk, but also media jargon for a fabricated or simulated documentary; *türken* means to diddle someone or fiddle something, as in *ein Interview türken* (to make up an interview) or *getürkte Papiere* (forged papers).

More broadly, *einen Türken bauen* ('to build a Turk') means to cook the books or construct a pretence, something which is not what it seems, a 'scam' (also, more innocently, to blunder). This probably derives from the long threat of Turkish invasion, and certainly pre-dates the influx of Turkish *Gastarbeiter* in the 1960s and 70s (some two million of Germany's six and a half million *Ausländer* are Turks). It has nothing to do with inferior building standards, just as 'jerry-building' has nothing to do with allegedly inferior German work-manship.

ÜBERHÖREN v. not to overhear something, but to miss hearing it, to fail to catch it; or to ignore it deliberately, as in *das möchte ich überhört haben!* (I'll pretend I didn't hear that, I'll let that pass) – for 'turning a blind eye', see ÜBERSEHEN in II. To overhear something accidentally is *zufällig hören* or *zufällig mitbekommen**, if deliberate *belauschen*, but to render John Stuart Mill's critical insight that the artist is 'not heard but overheard' one would have to say something like: *man hörte, wie er dachte* (rather as Wittgenstein's pupils tell of having 'watched him thinking').

VERS n.m. a single line of poetry, or a verse in the Bible. *Etwas in Verse setzen* is to put something into verse, but the verses or stanzas of a poem* are *Strophen*.

VEXIERBILD n.n. a puzzle* picture, such as the profile of a girl which can also be seen as a witch. The slightly dated verb *vexieren*, much favoured by Thomas Mann, means to puzzle rather than to vex/irritate (*irritieren** can mean one or the other).

VORWORT n.n. foreword, but in Austria also a preposition: *verbinde das Vorwort* (German *Fürwort*) *mit dem richtigen Fall**, the preposition should be followed by the correct case.

WASCHZETTEL n.m. not the 'washing label' or instructions how to wash a garment, but the blurb on the inside cover of a book.

WENN conj. 'when' (whenever), but also 'if'. Ex-GI Elvis Presley was clearly promising he would look up each of the girls he had left behind *when* he returned to Germany: *Wenn i' komm', wenn i' komm', wenn* *i' wieder wiederkomm', kehr' i' ein, mein Schatz, bei dir* (in the words of the soldier's song *Muß i' denn*). But the soprano who exclaimed 'when she is a singer, then am I none' had simply transliterated the insult from her native language: *wenn sie eine Sängerin ist* (and it's a big 'if'), *dann bin ich keine.* Unambiguously, in a 1930 film with the prophetic title *Das Lied ist aus* (the song is at an end), Robert Stolz's song *Wenn das Wörtchen 'wenn' nicht wär* can only mean 'If only the little word "if" didn't exist'.

WURM n.m. a worm, but also a poetical term for a snake (*die Schlange*), or even a dragon (*der Lindwurm, der Drache**). Fafner, in Wagner's *Ring*, turns himself into a *Wurm*, but a production which makes him a worm does so at its peril. *Ein Ohrwurm*, besides being an earwig, is a snatch of music (*ein paar Takte**) or catchy tune (*eine eingängige Melodie*) which worms its way into your ear (cf. *wurmen*, to rankle – see MORAL in V).

Das Wurm, however, is a child: *ein armes/elendes Wurm*, poor little mite; *ein liebes/niedliches Wurm*, sweet little creature.

ZENSUR n.f. not censure (*der Tadel*), but either an examination mark or essay grade (*wenn es auf die Zensuren zugeht*, when report time approaches), or else censorship. Similarly, the verb *zensieren* can mean either to censor (Austrian *zensurieren*) or to mark (see NOTE in IV).

In Germany, the constitution could not be clearer: *eine Zensur findet nicht statt* (there is no censorship). However, freedom from prudery and freedom of speech are comparatively recent acquisitions. In his day, as Heine sardonically observed, the *Zollverein* (tariff union) bestowed outward 'material' unity on the Germans, while the 'truly spiritual' unity of ideas was the gift of the censor: *Er gibt die äußere Einheit uns, / Die sogenannt* materielle; / Die geistige* gibt uns die Zensur, / Die wahrhaft ideelle** (*Deutschland – Ein Wintermärchen / Germany – A Winter's Tale*, 1844).

ZITAT n.n. not a citation for some praiseworthy action (*die Belobigung, die lobende Erwähnung*), or a summons to attend court (*eine Vorladung vor Gericht*), but a quotation such as Goethe's famous last words, however apocryphal: *Mehr Licht* ('more light'). Whether these words were spoken in the Saxon accent he heard daily in Weimar and which many Germans find mildly risible (Ulbricht, for instance, *sächselte*), or in his native Frankfurt/Hesse accent (in which, 57 years earlier, he had rhymed *Ach neige, / du Schmerzenreiche – Urfaust*, ll. 3587–8), it has been suggested that he *might* have been about to say: *Mir liegt das Kissen schief* (my pillow needs straightening).

Index of Head-Words

abort, nm VI
absolvieren, v IV
acker, nm III
adäquat, adj VI
adept, nm IV
adjustieren, v IX
adressaten, np III
adrett, adj IX
advokat, nm I
affekt, nm V
afrikaner, nm VII
after-, in cpds V
aggregat, nn X
akademiker, nm IV
akademie, nf X
akkord, nm III
akkurat, adj IX
akquisition, nf III
akt, nm X
aktion, nf II
aktivist, nm II
aktuell, adj I
allee, nf VII
allüren, nfp VI
alp, nf III
also, adv and conj X
alternativen, np II
ambulanz, nf VII
amis, np I
ampelkoalition, nf II
anger, nm III
angina, nf VII
ängstlich, adj VI
animierdame, nf VI
antibabypille, nf VI
antike, nf IX
antiquariat, nn X
apart, adj X
apartment, nn IX

apotheke, nf VII
apparat, nm IV
appell, nm I
appendix, nm VII
argument, nn V
aroma, nn VIII
arrest, nm I
arriviert, adj V
art, nf X
as, nn VII
asozial, adj II
assessor, nm I
asylant, nm II
audienz, nf X
ausholen, v VII
ausländisch, adj II
autocar, nm VII
autograph, nn X
autonome, nm II

backbord, nn VII
backe, nf VII
backen, v VIII
bad, nn VII
bagage, nf VII
bagger, nm III
baiser, nn VIII
bald, adv VII
ballaststoffe, np VIII
band, nn X
bandage, nf VII
bangen, v VI
bank, nf III
bann, nm II
bar, nf VIII
baracke, nf I
base, nf VI
basis, nf II
bastard, nm VI

bauer, nm III
beamte, nm I
bedecken, v VIII
beefsteak, nn VIII
bekommen, v VIII
beraten, v III
berg-, in cpds III
berliner, nm II
berufsverbot, nm II
besiegen, v I
betbank, nf V
bett, nn VI
biedermeier, nn II
bier, nn VIII
bilanz, nf III
bildung, nf IV
billion, nf III
biskuit, nn or nm VIII
blackout, nn or nm X
blamieren, v V
blank, adj III
blättern, v X
blau, adj VIII
blenden, v VIII
blessieren, v VII
blind, adj I
blinker, nm, blinken, v VII
blitz, nm II
blockhaus, nn IX
blond, adj VIII
blutig, adj VIII
bockbier, nn VIII
bombardement, nn I
bombe, nf I
bowling, nn VII
box, nf X
branche, nf III
brand, nm IX

fern-, in cpds VII
fest, nn, adj & adv VIII
fete, nf VI
fett, adj VIII
feudal adj IX
feuilleton, nn X
fidel, adj VI
fieber, nn VII
filiale, nf III
finanzer, nm I
fir tree, III
first, nm IX
fixer, nm III
flair, nn IX
flanken, v VII
flasche, nf VI
flattern, v VI
fleet, nn VII
fleischhauer, nm VIII
fleischkäse, nm VIII
flicken, v IX
flinte, nf I
flipper, nm VII
flirt, nn VI
fluidum, nn VI
flur, nm IX
flut, nf VII
folie, nf III
folklore, nf X
fopperei, nf IX
forcieren, v III
form, nf VIII
format, nn II
formular, nn I
fraktion, nf II
fraktur, nf X
franc, nm, franken, nm
III
französisch, adj VI
frauenzimmer, nn VI
frei, adj X
freier, nm VI
fremdgehen, v VI
frequenz, nf IV
freund, nm VI

frivol, adj VI
frühstücksfleisch, nn
VIII
frust, nm VI
führer, nm VII
führer, nm II
fund, nm III
funk, nm, X
funktionär, nm I

gaffer, nm VI
gag, nm X
gage, nf X
gala, nf IX
galanteriewaren, nfp IX
galerie, nf I
gang, nm II
gang, nm VIII
garage, nf VII
garderobe, nf IX
garni, adj VIII
gasthaus, nn VIII
gau, nm or nn II
geist, nm V
gelernt, adj IV
gemeinschaft, nf II
gemeinsinn, nm II
genial, adj V
genie, nn V
germ, nm or nf VIII
gift, nn II
glanz, nm X
glosse, nf X
glücklich, adj V
glühwein, nm VIII
glut, nf VIII
golf, nn VII
gotha, nm II
grab, nn III
grad, nm IV
grant, nm IV
gratifikation, nf III
graziös, adj V
gretchenfrage, nf II
grill, nm VIII

gross, adj III
gully, nm or nn VII
gültig, adj I
gummi, nm VI
gürtel, nm IX
gusto, nm VIII
gut, nn III
gymnasium, nn IV

habilitation, nf, IV
hafen, nm VII
hai, nm VII
hallo, interj VII
halt, adv VII
halten, v VII
handeln, v III
handwerk, nn III
hang, nm IV
happen, nm VIII
harm, nm X
harsch, nm and adj VII
haschen, v VIII
haus, nn III
hausarbeit, nf IV
hausbacken, adj VIII
hausen, v IX
haushalt, nm IX
hausieren, v IX
hearing, nn I
heftig, adj X
heil, nn, adj and interj
VII
heimat, nf II
heimlich, adj IX
heimsuchen, v IX
helm, nm II
hemmen, v V
herb, adj VIII
herd, nm IX
hering, nm VIII
hissen, v X
hochschule, nf IV
honorar, nn III
hose, nf IX
hospiz, nn VII

INDEX OF HEAD-WORDS